*We Have Heard That God Is with You*

# *We Have Heard That God Is with You*

PREACHING THE OLD TESTAMENT

Rein Bos

WILLIAM B. EERDMANS PUBLISHING COMPANY
GRAND RAPIDS, MICHIGAN / CAMBRIDGE, U.K.

Published 2008 by Wm. B. Eerdmans Publishing Co.

2140 Oak Industrial Drive N.E., Grand Rapids, Michigan 49505 /
P.O. Box 163, Cambridge CB3 9PU U.K.

Printed in the United States of America

14 13 12 11 10 09 08      7 6 5 4 3 2 1


**Library of Congress Cataloging-in-Publication Data**

Bos, Rein, 1955-
    We have heard that God is with you: preaching the old testament / Rein Bos.
        p.      cm.
    Adapted and translated from the Dutch by the author:
    Wij hebben gehoord dat God met u is. Zoetermeer: Boekencentrum, c2004.
    Includes bibliographical references and index.
    ISBN 978-0-8028-0770-0 (pbk.: alk. paper)
    1. Bible. O.T. — Homiletical use.   2. Bible. O.T. — Hermeneutics.
    I. Bos, Rein, 1955- Wij hebben gehoord dat God met u is.   II. Title.


BS1191.5.B67    2008
251 — dc22

                                                        2008013160

www.eerdmans.com

# Contents

# *Preface*

## Our Psalms

It happened in an average Christian congregation. They had invited a Jewish rabbi to tell something about the role and place of the Psalms in the liturgy of the synagogue. One of the participants was impressed by his lecture. During the break she approached the rabbi to tell him so and said: "It is moving to hear how well you know our psalms." Undoubtedly, the expression "our psalms" was meant in a positive way. Nevertheless, one is overwhelmed by the misunderstandings wrapped up in that expression, not to mention the possible implications and consequences.

This little story brings up the theme of this book. It deals with questions concerning the relation between Old and New Testaments. How does one read the Jewish Scripture in a Christian context? The Christian Bible contains two parts: the Old and the New Testaments. That is not obvious. Because when Jews talk about the Bible — they call it Tanak — they mean the collection of books that Christians call Old Testament. Apparently, one can also read the books of Tanak/Old Testament without the New Testament. That's what Jews do, till the present day. Christians read the books of Tanak/Old Testament in combination with the writings of apostles and evangelists. That means that Christians face a serious problem, because what is the relation between the collections of books of Tanak/Old Testament on the one hand and those from the New Testament on the other hand?

## What the Reader Can Expect

The practice of sermon preparation confronts every preacher time and again with the hermeneutical problems and questions related to this issue. We can even say that it is exactly the act of preaching that questions the relation between Old and New Testaments. When we open both Old and New Testaments in the pulpit, the hermeneutical questions arise automatically.[1] How do we connect in a responsible way an Old Testament text with the situation of the congregation? What are the place and the role of Jesus Christ in that connection? Does a sermon on the Old Testament have to mention Jesus Christ to be a genuine biblical and Christian sermon? What are the role and place of Israel in the preaching of the Christian church?

This book tackles these and related questions and offers both a practical and a scholarly based guide for this important theological issue. It offers a creative "hermeneutical grammar" to preach the Old Testament in a Christian context. The main characteristics of this "grammar" are:

- It belongs in the weekly process of sermon preparation;
- It meets the vital interest of listeners in the pew, i.e., it makes the Bible come alive as a relevant message for their lives;
- It offers creative keys for opening the various dimensions of the books of Moses and the prophets;
- It enables contemporary preaching to testify that Jesus of Nazareth is the Christ in accordance with the Scripture, without implying that the New Testament church has replaced or superseded Israel as the people of God;
- It gives account to the post-Holocaust context;
- It enables the preacher to connect the concrete multicolored experiences of life and faith of contemporary believers with the testimony of Scripture;
- It makes the different elements of the testimony about "the world to come" of the Old Testament operable for relevant preaching today.

This book is devoted to the practice of preaching and sermon preparation. It constructs and elaborates a contemporary hermeneutical grammar. Multiple sermon examples are offered to illustrate the way this model

1. Zimmerli 1984, p. 5.

can be used in the process of sermon preparation and how it can serve the practice of preaching. Each chapter is a rich meal for the busy preacher looking for creative options for preaching that will be faithful to Scripture. Some readers may wish to begin with chapters 12-15, which elaborate the new model, and then return to a consideration of classical hermeneutical models (chapters 1-7) or read about the biblical theological and hermeneutical background and ingredients of the presented model (chapters 8-11). Chapter 16 elaborates the model by means of three texts: Exodus 3, the songs of the servant of the LORD in Deutero-Isaiah, and Psalm 22.

## Prospective Readers

Clergy, professors, seminarians, and theology students will take a keen interest in this important new presentation of Old Testament hermeneutics and homiletics. This book is in fact meant for everyone, both professional and non-professional, who is interested in questions and issues concerning the relationship between the Old and the New Testaments. *We Have Heard That God Is with You* will provide a fascinating, unique, and fundamental text for courses in different areas of the theological discipline. First of all it is a fundamental textbook for preaching the Old Testament, both for the practice of preaching and for homiletical and hermeneutical theory. It is a challenging resource for every preacher who wants to preach the Old Testament. This book can also serve as an introduction in the field of biblical studies. And it offers, last but not least, a contribution to the dialogue between Jews and Christians. This book makes the "harvest" of post-Holocaust theology operational for the practice of preaching.

This book can be read at different levels. It can be used in the first place as a "how to" book for preachers: how to preach the Old Testament in a Christian context. It gives a usable route for the practice of sermon preparation. It is my hope that this book will serve preachers in their interpretation and proclamation of the Scriptures. I hope that their sermons on texts in the Old Testament will nurture a living relationship with the God of Israel as we know him through the Jew Jesus of Nazareth.

## Title and Cover

The title of the book is taken from Zechariah 8:23: "Thus says the LORD of hosts: In those days ten men from nations of every language shall take hold of a Jew, grasping his garment and saying, 'Let us go with you, for we have heard that God is with you.'" The prophet depicts a Jewish person in exile who is preparing to go back to Jerusalem. Till recently, the exiles were despised and rejected. But now they are surrounded by a procession of people from the nations who want to go with them. They have to show the procession the way to the God of Israel and the Israel of the LORD.

The person in the red robe on the cover of the book is the main image of the altarpiece *The Adoration of the Lamb,* painted by Jan and Hubert van Eyck (1426-1432). This altarpiece is in the St. Baafs Cathedral in Ghent (Belgium). Art historians still disagree with each other about the identity of this image. The question is: Is it God or Jesus?[2] There are arguments for both options. Some characteristics of the painting point to God. We can see a tiara on the head of this person. In classic iconography, that symbol of honor and dignity belongs to God. The hands show no *stigmata*. And both the Hebrew *sabaoth* (hosts) and the Latin *Hic est Deus potentissimus propter divinam majestatem* (This is God Almighty in his divine majesty) point to God. There is also an argument based on the composition of the altarpiece. Below the panel with the person in the red robe, we can see a dove and the Lamb. That could imply that we see vertically the images of the Trinity.

On the other hand, there is also some evidence that points to Jesus. On the tapestry behind the figure, we can see clearly three classical symbols that belong iconographically to Christ: the pelican feeding her young, the branch of the vine, and a banderole on which is written *Jesus Christ.* There is also an argument in the composition that points to Christ. The figure in the red robe has Mary and John the Baptist on his left and right sides, respectively. The composition of these three persons goes back to the Deësis-motif of prayer. That belongs iconographically to the motif of the Last Judgment where Christ — and not God — is depicted between Mary and the Baptist.

---

2. A huge bibliography exists about this piece of art. Schmidt (1996) gives the arguments for the different positions on the identity of the person in the red robe (see also Panofsky 1964, pp. 212ff.; Dhanens 1973).

The painting's ambiguity of God and Jesus intrigued me from the first moment I saw this altarpiece. There is even evidence for the possibility that the Van Eycks deliberately mixed the iconographical particularities of the two images. And that points to the kernel of my hermeneutical proposal. On the one hand we have to say that whoever has seen Jesus has seen the God of Israel (John 14:9). And on the other hand, the gentiles have no access to this God apart from the Jew, Jesus of Nazareth.

There is an extra particularity to mention about this altarpiece in St. Baafs Cathedral that has to do with the theme of this book. The far lower left panel of the altarpiece is called *The Just Judges*, portraying the witnesses from the Old Testament. This panel was stolen in April 1934. The Bishop of Ghent received a blackmail letter that led to investigations, by both the police and officials of the church. But they never retrieved the panel. And even many years later, people were still guessing and searching for possible suspects. The original panel has therefore been replaced by a copy made in 1945 by Jef Vanderveken. It means that the Christian church doesn't possess the "original" Old Testament judges but has to satisfy itself with a copy!

## Redaction

In the notes I refer to the name of an author, the year of a particular publication, and the page number(s). More detailed information about the books, articles, and sermons can be found in the extended bibliography at the end of the book.

When illustrative examples of sermons are quoted, "( )" refers to a small omission from a single word to a sentence at the maximum; "(. . .)" refers to the omission of a larger portion, for instance, a paragraph.

The appropriate notation of the Hebrew Holy Name of God is still in debate. I use the notation "invented" by the translators of the English King James Version, "LORD,"[3] written in capitals. In my judgment, this notation does justice to both the notation of this name in Hebrew and the way Jews pronounce the name while reading aloud.

3. The Dutch *States Translation* (The *Statenvertaling*) was published in 1637 and translated the Holy Name in a comparable way: HEER. See also Seitz 2001, pp. 131-44; Brueggemann 2002, pp. 238-40.

I tried to use inclusive, gender-neutral language as much as possible, also in the use of pronouns referring to God and the LORD. I did not change the male references to God in quotations from Scripture. And I also did not feel free to edit the wording in the sermon illustrations. As far as they occur in these illustrations, they are quoted from the original.

## Acknowledgments

Every preface of a book is in a certain sense a fulfillment of Jesus' words, "many who are the last will be first" (Mark 10:31). And that is because words in a preface are usually an author's last written words. A preface is therefore a specimen of "realized eschatology" because authors look back (for themselves) on that which is to come (for the readers).

In this last and first word, I would like to express my gratitude to those who supported me in completing this book. Without help and support this book might not have appeared, at least not in its present shape. First of all, my thanks to my editor, Roger VanHarn of Wm. B. Eerdmans Publishing Company, who believed in this project from the start. The initial encouragement of James F. Kay and Bruce L. McCormack meant a lot to me. I express a special word of thanks to colleagues and friends who read and commented on one or more chapters: (alphabetically) Clifford Blake Anderson, Dale P. Andrews, Charles L. Bartow, Sallie Ann Brown, Richard A. Lischer, Kendall R. Soulen, James A. Wallace, Don S. Wardlaw, Dawn Ottoni Wilhelm, and Paul S. Wilson. Flaws and inconsistencies in the result are of course my responsibility. I also cherish the friendship and collegiality of the members of the *Dutch Homiletical Society,* the *American Academy of Homiletics,* and the international *Societas Homiletica.* I am indebted more than I can express to my friend Robert Rustenburg. Because of his dyslexia he hasn't read a word of this book, but our friendship is present in every chapter. And last but not least, I want to express my gratitude and love to my wife, our daughter, and our son, with whom I share daily life. It is because of them that I experience life as a gracious gift of the LORD.

# I. THE OLD TESTAMENT IN THE THEORY AND PRACTICE OF PREACHING

# 1. One Bible — Two Testaments

## 1.1. The Old Testament and the Christian Church

An aged Scottish woman attended her church regularly. She was a loyal servant of God and she read her Bible every day. She used to talk about how difficult it was to understand the *King James Version*. The *Living Bible* was fairly new at that time and her children bought her a copy. She started reading in Genesis. A few weeks later she talked to her children and her face got red. "Do you know the kinds of things the Old Testament is talking about?" she said. She went back to her *King James*. Some of the things the Old Testament talked about she was much happier not understanding.[1]

Those who try to understand the kinds of things the Old Testament is talking about face serious questions indeed. We hear about violence, concubines and polygamy, mistreatment of women, palace revolutions, political intrigues, archaic social practices and behavior, and endless genealogies. Commenting on Genesis 38, the story of Judah and Tamar, Paul Long expresses the astonishment and estrangement that these kinds of passages can call forth.

> I've been a Christian for 20 years now and I want to say that I have never heard the story of Judah and Tamar preached or taught. Every story and major character of the first book of the Bible is taught — from the stories surrounding Adam and Eve, Noah, Abraham, Isaac and Jacob to Joseph, but not this one. ( ) I believe that the story of Judah and Tamar is one of many stories and teachings in the Bible that is

1. See Goettsche 1999a.

3

THE OLD TESTAMENT IN THE THEORY AND PRACTICE OF PREACHING

avoided by many people because it disturbs us. Frankly, if you take a hard look at the passage, it can be considered by some as bordering on pornographic material. It's about sex, and more sex, about prostitution, incest, and illegitimate children.[2]

Those stories not only caused severe difficulties in interpretation in the past, but still do. What to think of those passages in Scripture where God orders a war and even the destruction of cities and the inhabitants (see, e.g., Josh. 10 and 11)? The tough words of judgment in the books of the prophets also cause problems for current readers. What do we do, for example, with the opening verses of Zephaniah (1:2-6)?

> I will utterly sweep away everything from the face of the earth,
> says the LORD.
> I will sweep away humans and animals;
> I will sweep away the birds of the air and the fish of the sea.
> I will make the wicked stumble.
> I will cut off humanity from the face of the earth, says the LORD.
> I will stretch out my hand against Judah,
> and against all the inhabitants of Jerusalem;
> and I will cut off from this place every remnant of Baal
> and the name of the idolatrous priests;
> those who bow down on the roofs to the host of the heavens;
> those who bow down and swear to the LORD, but also swear
>     by Milcom;
> those who have turned back from following the LORD,
> who have not sought the LORD or inquired of him.

Have these words anything to do with the gospel of Jesus Christ? Must we not say that the New Testament is a better, richer, and deeper book with more "gospel" in it than the Old Testament? Does the church need an *old* Testament when we also have a *new* Testament? In a sermon series on the Minor Prophets, James R. Van Tholen included a sermon on the first verses from Zephaniah. He makes the feelings and thoughts of estrangement explicit.

> Zephaniah sees not only the end of Assyria; he sees the end of everything. He sees creation thrown into reverse by a God who can do it.

2. Paul Long 2002.

And then, just in case his audience somehow gets the idea that God's own people are excused from this catastrophe, he goes on:

> I will stretch out my hand against Judah,
> and against all the inhabitants of Jerusalem. (v. 4)

This is the word of the Lord, but it's hard to respond this time, "Thanks be to God." When we read about the end Zephaniah prophesies, about his "de-creation," it's hard to imagine that there is a gospel to be found here, that Zephaniah can offer us any hope whatsoever. And we certainly wouldn't be the first ones to hear these words and feel that way.[3]

No wonder, then, that we ask whether the Old Testament is still relevant for contemporary Christians.

## 1.2. The First Apostolic Council

The penetrating questions about the authority and interpretation of the books of Moses and the prophets arose almost immediately in the Christian church.[4] We can read in the book of Acts how this issue is implicit and explicit in discussion from Pentecost and forward.

> Then certain individuals came down from Judea and were teaching the brothers, "Unless you are circumcised according to the custom of Moses, you cannot be saved." And after Paul and Barnabas had no small dissension and debate with them, Paul and Barnabas and some of the others were appointed to go up to Jerusalem to discuss this question with the apostles and the elders. (Acts 15:1, 2)

In the next verses of Acts 15, Luke offers as it were the "minutes" of that meeting of apostles and elders.[5] This meeting in Jerusalem is called "the first Apostolic Council." The main issue at that meeting was the question about whether it was necessary for non-Jews to be circumcised and to keep the instructions and commandments in the Law of Moses in every detail.

3. Van Tholen 2003, p. 224.
4. Childs 1992, pp. 55-57.
5. For the first apostolic council see Marshall 1980, pp. 242-56; Schneider 1982, pp. 168-89 and pp. 189-92; Pesch 1986, pp. 68-90.

Behind that question was and is a matter of huge theological importance, i.e., the authority of the books of Moses and the prophets for non-Jewish disciples of Jesus of Nazareth. The young church had both Jewish and non-Jewish members. The Jews called the books of Moses and the prophets "the Scriptures." The mixed community faced the important question regarding what the Jewish Scriptures had to say to both Jewish and non-Jewish members in the post-Easter and post-Pentecostal era.

The discussion at the council resulted in a deep disagreement. The wording of Luke in his record of this meeting makes clear that the attendees had a hot discussion. The issue "caused trouble" and a "commotion took place." They "argued forcefully and at length" and had a "sharp dispute" and "no small dissension and debate."[6] Expressions like these in proceedings of a meeting in our days point to huge struggles and crackling conflicts!

## 1.3. Marcion

The first Apostolic Council made an important hermeneutical decision, but the dissension wasn't brought to an end. The crackling conflict emerged quite soon in the history of the church. The theologian Marcion (85-160 CE) lit the fire in the second century. He was puzzled by the ambivalent experiences in everyday life. What kind of God first creates life with pleasure and destroys the same life next by a stupid accident or a wasting disease? Are we who live amidst "herbs and grass, rain and drought, fruitful and barren years, meat and drink, health and sickness, riches and poverty"[7] safe and secure in the hands of God, our heavenly Refuge? Or do we have to reckon with the possibility that there is not only a "good" God, who acts on behalf of our salvation, but also a God who continuously causes

---

6. The quoted expressions are taken from Acts 15 in the translations of the American Standard Version, the English Standard Version, the King James Version, the New International Version, the Amplified Bible, the New Standard Revised Version, the New Living Translation, and the Contemporary English Version.

7. Exactly these existential questions are the background of the heavily discussed Question and Answer 27 of the Lord's Day 10 of the Catechism of Heidelberg. One can raise important hesitations and even objections against the formulation of this answer. But even then, we have to do justice to the existential struggle with the issue of monotheism of the authors.

trouble for humans, a God who punishes, sweeps out, rages, and tears down? This concept of two opposing and competing Gods is called dualism. In that concept the "good" God is connected with the One called *Abba* by Jesus Christ, the source of salvation, forgiveness, hope, comfort, and healing. His opponent is the God of the Old Testament, the One who is responsible for the painful experiences in life.

Marcion gave a simple and misguided but far-reaching solution to the existential and theological dilemma. He saw an unbridgeable antithesis between the stern, rigorous, and cruel Creator-God of the Old Testament (the so-called *Demiurge*) and the God whom we meet in and through Jesus Christ. Marcion was appalled by the vengeance of a God who orders the awful slaughters of human beings, the rowdy God who opposes, thwarts, and frustrates lives. Marcion refused to spiritualize or allegorize the Old Testament text to solve this kind of interpretative difficulty.

From that perspective, Paul was the preeminent apostle for Marcion. He expanded Paul's distinction of law and gospel into an antithesis between the God of the Old Testament and the God of Jesus Christ, a God of love and mercy. According to Marcion, the God of the Old Testament is identical with the "God of this world" (2 Cor. 4:4). Jesus came to rescue and release us from the reign of this God of law, revenge, violence, and war. Jesus brought us under the reign of the "good" God, the Savior. For that reason, Marcion denied the Old Testament and accepted as authoritative only the letters of Paul and a heavily revised, even "expurgated" version of the Gospel of Luke. That gospel of Marcion opens as follows:

> In the fifteenth year of the reign of Tiberius Caesar, and Pontius Pilate being the Governor of Judea, Jesus came down to Capernaum, a city in Galilee, and was teaching on the Sabbath days; and they were astonished at his doctrine for his word was in authority.

Marcion connects Luke 3:1 and 4:31 in the opening of his own gospel. He leaves out every reference or allusion to the Old Testament. Nevertheless the evangelists rooted their message firmly in the soil of Israel and the books of Moses and the prophets. We just have to think of the songs of Mary and Zechariah in the first chapters of Luke's Gospel (1:47-55, 68-79). Those songs can be seen as creative compositions of strings of Old Testament quotations. Because of the impact of his proposal, Marcion got the nickname "the theologian with the hammer."

The church rejected Marcion and affirmed its belief in the one and only God, the LORD of Israel. This did not mean, however, that the church did not have difficulty with the Old Testament or its interpretation. The following chapters will make clear that there has always been a feeling of unease with the Old Testament, for both its literary style and its content. But despite all those difficulties, the church affirmed that the God who had revealed himself in the Old Testament to Abraham, Moses, and the prophets was the same God who revealed himself in Jesus Christ. The church thus affirmed that there was no dichotomy between God as Creator and God as Redeemer. The church also made the bold statement that the books of Moses and the prophets were indeed the Word of God and would never cease to be that. Successive synods and councils affirmed that statement in the first centuries. The church was convinced of the fact that it would be a fatal mistake to preach the gospel of Jesus Christ independent of the Old Testament and disconnected from its Jewish roots.

## 1.4. The Birth of the Hermeneutical Issue

Thus, the church accepted the books of Moses and the prophets as "Holy Scripture." Those books were in fact the Scriptures of the church for at least the first hundred years of its history.[8] The young church also accepted certain writings of apostles and evangelists as authoritative. The collection of those books was called "New Testament."[9] As a result, the writings of Moses and the prophets were called "Old Testament." But by doing so, important interpretative questions began to appear. What is the relation between the books of the already-existing "old" Scripture to the "new" writings? The question remained, how to proclaim the good news about Jesus Christ "starting with Moses and the prophets" (Luke 24:27). For the Old Testament does not speak directly about Christ. At first sight, this statement seems obvious. But once stated, a lot of questions arise. When the Old Testament does not speak directly about Christ, how do Christians read the Jewish Scriptures in such a way that they testify of him?[10] The

8. Kelly 1978, pp. 52-56; Barrera 1998, p. 514.
9. Grant 1980; Gamble 2003.
10. "We must recognize that, from a Christian point of view, most of this 'book' (or collection of 'books') is not 'about' Jesus Christ, even though we want to recognize him as the supreme Word of God" (Motyer 2000, p. 143). Smend says, "daß jede Generation unter

question about how to connect the Old Testament with the testimony about Jesus Christ presented itself with full force.

In a long and sharp dispute over almost two thousand years, biblical scholars have struggled with that question. The reflected answers are called *hermeneutical theories*. These theories try to provide keys that can open Old Testament texts in a Christian context. They offer formula-like ways to characterize its content: promise and fulfillment, law and gospel, salvation history, shadow and reality, typology, prophecy and fulfillment, structural analogy, antitheses, and history of tradition — to mention a few examples.[11]

It appears that classical homiletical textbooks from all over the world avoid wrestling with the homiletical implications of this hermeneutical problem.[12] Also, more recent homiletical textbooks either don't deal at all[13] or only marginally[14] with this issue. Consequently, when confronted with the hermeneutical issues, the preacher is actually left empty-handed in both the study and the pulpit.[15] Every preacher by default has to construct his or her own hermeneutical key.

The issue of the relation between Old and New Testaments touches almost every aspect of congregational life: Christian education, pastoral counseling, and spirituality. Every theologian and preacher discovers

sich einen alten Streit wieterficht, der unweigerlich damit vorgegeben ist, daß ( ) das Alte Testament nicht, wenigstens nicht unmittelbar, von Jesus Christus spricht und doch Christuszeugnis ist" (Smend 1995, p. 6). Oeming opens his inquiry to the relation between Old and New Testaments with the question "Auf welchen hermeneutische Prämissen beruht ein legitimes christliches Verständnis einer Heiligen Schrift, in der von Jesus Christus keine Rede ist?" (Oeming 1987, p. 11; see also Marquardt 1990, p. 297; Brueggemann 1997, pp. 729ff.).

11. There is a huge list of literature for each of these hermeneutical models. A good introduction is offered by B. W. Anderson 1963, Baker 1976/1991, Hasel 1979, Goldingay 1981, and Preuß 1984.

12. Davis 1958.

13. Craddock 1985; Buttrick 1987; Long 1989; Theissen 1995; Killinger 1996; Allen 1998.

14. Schütz 1981, pp. 81-87; Bohren 1986, pp. 119-21; Hirschler 1988, pp. 198-212; Dingemans 1991, pp. 97-100; K. Müller 1994, pp. 69-73; H. M. Müller 1996, pp. 222-27; Engemann 2002, pp. 282-87. Vos devoted a section to this issue, but it was written by the Old Testament scholar Prinsloo (Vos 1995, pp. 374-92). Vos edited this chapter himself in a revised version of this book. There were only some minor (mainly redactional) changes compared with the first edition by Prinsloo (Vos 1996b, pp. 106-19).

15. Exceptions are the books of Allen/Holbert 1995; Greidanus 1999; Davis 2005.

sooner or later that the relation between Old and New Testaments is not just one of the problems of interpretation, but a problem that touches the kernel of the enterprise of theology and proclamation.[16] The relation between Old and New Testaments is closely connected with important issues — for instance, the authority of Scripture, the extent of the canon, the order of Old Testament books, the unity of God, the person and work of Christ, and the relation between Jews and Christians. Every Christian theologian who enters the field of the Old Testament has to plow through a vast landscape of theology! Surely that is one of the reasons for the "strange silence of the Old Testament in the Church."[17]

## 1.5. "Old" Testament?

This book uses the traditional expressions Old and New Testaments to describe the two parts of the Christian Holy Scripture. In some cases I use the expression "the Scriptures" (Matt. 21:42; Luke 4:21; John 5:39; Rom. 1:2), and I have a certain preference for the expression "Moses and the prophets" (Luke 16:29, 31; John 1:46; Acts 26:22; 28:23). Apostles and evangelists used these expressions themselves to point to Israel's Holy Scripture, what we eventually came to call Old Testament. Of course the names we give these ancient Jewish documents carry their own presuppositions, intended as well as unintended presuppositions.[18] Consider other names and ex-

16. "No problem more urgently needs to be brought to a focus than ( ) the relation of the Old Testament to the New. ( ) It is a question which confronts every Christian in the Church, whether he be a professional theologian, a pastor of a congregation, or a layman. It is no exaggeration to say that on this question hangs the meaning of the Christian faith" (B. W. Anderson 1963a, p. 1). "What is the exact relationship between ( ) the revelation of Jesus in the New Testament and the revelation of God in the Old Testament? Though it may seem hard to believe, the fact is that this basic and important question has scarcely been given a clear answer over the past twenty centuries of Christian living. And that fact has conditioned the whole of theology" (Segundo 1983, pp. 487-88). "Indeed, it would be no exaggeration to understand the hermeneutical problem of the Old Testament as *the* problem of Christian theology, and not just as one problem amongst others, seeing that all the other questions of theology are affected in one way or another by its resolution" (Gunneweg 1978, p. 2). "The touchstone of Christian hermeneutics is the relationship between 'Old' and 'New' Testament'" (Barrera 1998, p. 560). See Kelly 1978, pp. 64-69.

17. Allen/Holbert 1995, p. 9.

18. See also Seitz 1998, pp. 61-74.

pressions besides the expressions used by apostles and evangelists for the Old Testament, for example, *the books of Moses and the prophets* (Luke 16:29, 31; 24:27; Acts 26:22), the *Law and the prophets* (Matt. 7:12; 11:13; 22:40; Rom. 3:21), *the Scriptures* (Matt. 21:42; John 5:39; 1 Cor. 15:3-4), *Tanak,*[19] *ancient Israelitic writings,*[20] *Israel's Scripture,*[21] *literature of ancient Israel,*[22] *first Testament,*[23] *ancient Testament,*[24] *Jewish Bible,*[25] *Israel's book of faith,*[26] *Hebrew Testament,*[27] *books of the old order,*[28] *the original Testament,*[29] and *Hebrew Bible.*[30] It is my conviction that relations between Jews and Christians and between synagogue and church are not served at all with a discussion just on terms or expressions. Christians can more effectively show their respect for Jews and the synagogue by how they use the terms *Old* and *New Testaments*.

The field of hermeneutics expanded enormously during the last decades of the twentieth and the beginning of the twenty-first centuries. In order not to lose the way in the fields of all those models, concepts, and visions, I had to make restricting choices. First of all, this book has mainly Protestant theologians and preachers as partners for discussion and reflection. I don't want to imply that there are no important and interesting developments and concepts outside that tradition. But it is a simple fact that as a Protestant theologian I am more familiar with that tradition. The second restriction has to do with the fields of philosophical hermeneutics. In view of the enormous amount of literature in this area, one needs a high level of expertise to be a serious partner in discussion. I therefore restrict myself to the area where I can make well-founded statements. I invite colleagues in related disciplines to discuss the results of this study based on their own expertise.

19. Bouhuijs/Deurloo 1981, pp. 57-58.

20. Vriezen 1948.

21. Juel 2003, p. 285; Soulen 1996 (the New Testament is called "Apostolic Witness").

22. Vriezen/Van der Woude 1976.

23. Allen/Holbert 1995.

24. Barnard 1992 (Dutch original: Aloude Testament).

25. Dohmen/Stemberger 1996.

26. Ter Linden 1999.

27. Barnard 1979, p. 264. He calls the New Testament "The Greek Testament."

28. De Jonge 2003, p. 3. He calls the New Testament "the book of the new order of the gospel."

29. Bloom 1987. He calls the New Testament "the belated Testament."

30. Knight/Tucker 1983; Brooks/Collins 1990; Holbert 1991; Marquardt 1988/1990. The last one calls the New Testament the "Jesus-writings" ("Jesus-Schriften").

## 1.6. Outline of This Book

Those readers who want to jump right into the deep can start with chapter 10, which offers the contours of my own proposal for a hermeneutical model. Chapters 11-14 elaborate the four dimensions of that model.

For those who start from the beginning, I offer a "guide" or "floor plan" of the book. The first part outlines the hermeneutical and theological problems and questions that preachers face when they prepare a sermon on an Old Testament text. Hermeneutical keys can be seen as answers to, or guidelines for, the questions related to the relation between Old and New Testaments. Chapters 2-6 portray the homiletical profile of five prominent and often-used hermeneutical keys: allegory, typology, salvation-historical approach, promise and fulfillment, and the model of Karl Barth. Those concepts were chosen because they are widely used in the practice of preaching. Each chapter deals with the next issues:

- A general description of the particular hermeneutical key (§§1 and 2);
- In what way does this key connect the Old Testament with Jesus Christ (§§3)?
- In what way does this key connect the text with the situation of the congregation (§§4)?
- What is the role and the place of both the Israel in Old Testament times and the present-day Israel (§§5)?
- An evaluation of the strong and weak elements (§§6).

Each of the paragraphs 2-5 is to be illustrated by one or more sermon examples so that the reader can see how these keys function in the practice of preaching. Chapter 7 collects the insights and results of the previous evaluations.

The second part of the book is devoted to the construction of a new hermeneutical strategy, a contemporary model of the fourfold sense of Scripture. The second part also gives an account of what led to the construction of this model, to the ingredients that form the new concept. That material has been derived from recent fresh approaches to the Old Testament quotations in the New Testament (chapter 8). The history of interpretation provides us with useful and crucial elements for a contemporary hermeneutical key (chapter 9). Those elements are woven together in a proposal for a new hermeneutical model of the fourfold sense of Scripture:

*sensus israelicus, Christological sense, ecclesiological sense,* and *eschatological sense* (chapter 11). As strange as it may sound, there are nevertheless few more awkward questions in the history of biblical interpretation than the issue of defining what is meant by the "literal sense" of a text. This question is to be discussed in chapter 10.

The third part of this book speaks to the practice of preaching and sermon preparation by offering a homiletical elaboration of the four dimensions of my hermeneutical grammar (chapters 12-15). I offer multiple sermon examples to illustrate the way this model can be used in the process of sermon preparation and how it can serve the practice of preaching. Chapter 16 offers a perspective on the challenges and possibilities of this concept in the practice of preaching the Old Testament in the Christian church. This chapter is also illuminated with several sermon illustrations. Some readers may wish to begin with this third part, and then return either to the classical hermeneutical models portrayed in the first part, or to the elements used for the construction of my own model (second part).

# 2. Allegory

## 2.1. Saying Something Else

Literature and storytelling have used allegory from ancient times on. We can find it in Dante's *Comedia Divina,* in Kafka's *The Trial,* and in Orwell's *Animal Farm.* Popular movies like *Star Wars* and *The Lord of the Rings* also make use of allegory. What the author of a book or the director of a movie actually wants to say — or at least wants to suggest — is hidden behind or wrapped up in another story. The term "allegory" is derived from the Greek *alle-goria,* literally meaning "saying something other than what one seems to say."[1] There is a deeper story hidden behind the story that can be read in a book or seen on a screen. In *Animal Farm,* for instance, George Orwell is telling more than a simple story about a farmer and his cattle; he is actually criticizing Russian society after the revolution of 1917. It may even be said that if we don't look further than the adventures on the farm, we misunderstand what Orwell actually wants to tell.

The underlying theme of every allegorical story is a message about the ongoing battle between "Good" and "Evil." The entities in the story are symbols or vehicles for something or someone other than their original or literal meaning. It may be that this other something or someone is deliberately intended by the original author, as, for example, in John Bunyan's *Pilgrim's Progress.* It may also be that the "other meaning" is provided by the interpreter; but even then the interpreter thinks he is bringing out the intended meaning of the original author.

---

1. *Oxford English Dictionary* (Volume 1) 1989, p. 333. For this reason, some argue that allegory is "unethical." "If you interpret a text by allegorizing it, you seem to be saying that it means something which it patently does not" (Louth 1983).

Allegorical interpretation as a means of opening biblical texts has a long history.[2] The interpreter informs his audience not only about grammar or history of the text but gives his audience a view into the "inner side" and the spiritual meaning. He does so, because he is convinced that the text itself wants to say more than the literal or historical meaning. Usually, the interpreter sees the text as a symbol of a truth of the Christian faith. A sermon by Adrian Dieleman on 1 Kings 17:1 can illustrate the use of allegory in the practice of preaching. The sermon concentrates on the confession of Elijah: "My God is Yahweh."

> Our text marks the start of the struggle between Jezebel and Elijah. In actual fact, though, the struggle was between God and Satan, the church and the world, the Spirit from above and the beast from below. It was a spiritual struggle involving all the powers of the universe. Our text, then, shows the antithesis, the struggle, between good and evil, light and darkness, the kingdom of God and Christ and the dominion of Satan.
>
> We see the universal dimensions to the struggle just by looking at the names of the two human protagonists. Throughout Scripture the name "Jezebel" is a symbol for what is evil, wicked, and opposed to God. The name "Jezebel" is reserved for those who try to destroy the church and the people of God through idolatry and godless living. The name "Elijah," by contrast, is a symbol for those who wholeheartedly serve and worship the Lord.[3]

A lot of features and expressions typical of allegorical interpretation are present in this illustration. The struggle between Jezebel and Elijah is "in actual fact" a portrayal of a struggle on a deeper and spiritual level, i.e., the struggle between good and evil, light and darkness, the kingdom of God and Christ and the dominion of Satan. Every witness about physical struggle is in fact a vehicle for the witness about "a spiritual struggle involving all the powers of the universe." The names "Jezebel" and "Elijah" are symbols and point to something greater than their historical meaning. These names are therefore put in quotes.

And that is exactly why allegory can count on skepticism among theologians. This mistrust is as old as the use of allegory. From the begin-

2. De Lubac 1998a and 1998b.
3. Dieleman 2003.

ning, the criticism was that allegory disconnects a text from its historical and literary context. Critics say that as a result, allegory is open to almost any added meaning and can lead to absurd and obscure interpretations.

Hence, Scripture is no longer a book that can be read and interpreted by every member of the congregation but a book with hidden secrets that can only be interpreted by a spiritual elite of insiders. Because of that, a lot of theologians have a kind of intuitive reflex and natural defense mechanism against allegory and allegorical interpretation. The expression "it is allegorical" is not just a neutral descriptive utterance, it is above all a negative judgment.[4] Allegory is almost the worst of all sins in interpretation of Scripture for those who are trained in contemporary exegetical methods. Luther fumed, for instance: "Allegorizings are awkward, absurd, invented, obsolete rags."[5] Because of this attitude, a (serious) discussion of allegory can only be found on the periphery of some deserted areas of the theological landscape.[6]

But allegorical interpretation shows up time and again despite the natural defenses, the reflexes, and even the fuming. Paul Wilson observes in striking imagery: "Weed it out of the flowerbed and it appears in the vegetable garden; dissuade a student of using it in exegesis and it appears in a sermon."[7] And indeed, allegory appears both in the flowerbed of sermons of great theologians like John Calvin and Karl Barth and in the vegetable garden of pietistic writings, not to mention the widespread use of allegory in the hymns of every denomination. That means that every congregation is confronted by allegorical interpretation, if not in sermons then at least in hymns and songs. And that has happened as recently as yesterday! That means that we had better take a serious look at this hermeneutical key.

## 2.2. A Deeper Sense

The word "allegory" itself is not found in the Old Testament. But there are passages that are (very probably) meant to be interpreted in an allegorical way. We can think of Ezekiel 23 where the story is told of two adulterous sisters, Oholah and Oholibah.

4. Young calls allegory "an embarrassment" (Young 1993, p. 104).
5. Quoted by Farrar 1961, p. 338.
6. Pietron 1979.
7. Wilson 2001, p. 112.

> The word of the LORD came to me: Mortal, there were two women, the daughters of one mother; they played the whore in Egypt; they played the whore in their youth; their breasts were caressed there, and their virgin bosoms were fondled. Oholah was the name of the elder and Oholibah the name of her sister. They became mine, and they bore sons and daughters. As for their names, Oholah is Samaria, and Oholibah is Jerusalem. (Ezek. 23:1-4)

It is clear that the prophet is not just telling an "innocent" story about two sisters. At a deeper lever this story criticizes Israel and Judah, two sister-nations, who are unfaithful to the LORD. Adultery is a commonly used image for superstition. The related names of the sisters point to the relation between Israel and Judah.

Both the word "allegory" and the allegorical method can be found more than once in the New Testament.[8] One of the places is 1 Corinthians 9:9, where Paul quotes Deuteronomy 25:4 (cf. 1 Tim. 5:18).

> For it is written in the Law of Moses, "You shall not muzzle an ox while it is treading out the grain."

Usually, an ox was muzzled to prevent it from eating the grain or grass of another farmer's pasture. But a threshing ox was allowed to satisfy its hunger by taking mouthfuls of the material it was working on. Violation of this commandment was punished with cudgeling.[9] The commandment expresses concern for animals. Paul applies it to the needs of humans, especially those who are responsible for the ministry of the proclamation of the gospel of Jesus Christ.

> Is it for oxen that God is concerned? Or does he not speak entirely for our sake? It was indeed written for our sake, for whoever plows should plow in hope and whoever threshes should thresh in hope of a share in the crop.

Paul argues that if God ordained ample provision for a threshing ox, it is obvious that this God is even more concerned about adequately rewarding those who devote time and energy to the ministry of the Word. Paul spiri-

---

8. See also Wilson 2001, pp. 117-22.
9. Barrett 1980, pp. 205-6; Barth *CD* III/3, p. 174.

tualizes the original, literal, and material meaning of the commandment of Moses and applies it to the relationship between congregation and minister and the minister's service to the LORD.

Paul offers another clear allegorical interpretation when he quotes the Genesis story of Hagar and Sarah in Galatians 4:21-23. The apostle focuses on the two sons of Abraham: Isaac and Ishmael. Paul argues that Genesis is not dealing with sons born according to the flesh. There is meaning at a deeper level.

> For it is written that Abraham had two sons, one by a slave woman and the other by a free woman. One, the child of the slave, was born according to the flesh; the other, the child of the free woman, was born through the promise. Now this is an allegory: these women are two covenants. One woman, in fact, is Hagar, from Mount Sinai, bearing children for slavery. Now Hagar is Mount Sinai in Arabia and corresponds to the present Jerusalem, for she is in slavery with her children. But the other woman corresponds to the Jerusalem above; she is free, and she is our mother.

Paul sees a deeper sense in the story of the two sons of Abraham. He interprets this story in the light of the gospel of free grace that he was commissioned to proclaim.[10] Paul himself says that "this is an allegory" (4:21).

This type of interpretation is no exception in the early church. The writings of the church fathers in the first centuries are swarming with allegorical interpretation of Moses and the prophets.[11] Allegory was for them not a novelty. Greek interpreters had employed this hermeneutical key to explicate the poems of Homer and Hesiod.[12] Jewish biblical scholars also used this mode of interpretation. Allegory was widely used as a common hermeneutical strategy in Christian interpretation up until the Middle Ages. Thomas Aquinas (1225-1274), one of the most significant and honored of Christian scholars, skillfully uses the allegorical key in connecting the Old Testament with Jesus Christ. Aquinas opens a sermon on Malachi 3:1 ("The Lord Whom ye seek shall suddenly come to His Temple") with the next sentence:

---

10. Bruce 1982, pp. 214-15.
11. Frör 1961, pp. 116-18, 163; Longenecker 1975; Froehlich 1984, pp. 8-10; Young 2003, pp. 335-38.
12. Kelly 1978, p. 8.

These words can be explained — firstly, of the advent of the Lord to the material temple; secondly, allegorically, of His advent in the womb of the Virgin.[13]

## 2.3. Christ's Community with Us

When we look at the background of allegorical interpretation from its beginning in the early church, we see at least two issues that have to do with the relation between Old and New Testaments.[14] First of all, this hermeneutical key made it possible to connect the (pre-Christian) witness of Moses and the prophets with the salvation in and through Jesus Christ. Christ was seen not only as the ultimate meaning, but as the only possible meaning of the Old Testament. This Christological meaning of the text was seen not only as the contribution of the interpreter but as the intended meaning of God, the original Author. The conviction that Christ was the true meaning of Moses and the prophets was in fact the reason for the preservation of the Old Testament as part of the Holy Book of the church of the gentiles. This hermeneutical key made it possible to see the image of the Son in and through the image of the Father, as in the Van Eyck altarpiece on the cover of this book.

Allegory offered in the second place an instrument to give meaning to passages and words that sounded hard, "tough," or even "too Jewish" in the ears of gentiles. One could think of texts on the cultic institutions in tent and temple, hard sayings on war and violence, and stories with archaic social relations.

The imagery of the Old Testament love poetry of the Song of Songs becomes a vehicle for a greater and deeper truth, as allegorical interpretation looks beyond the description of two loved ones. It looks even further than the language of love and intimacy between the LORD and Israel, as is heard when Israel reads this book on the feast of Pasha. Christian allegory interprets this love poetry as a description of the intimate and gracious relation between Christ and his bride, i.e., the Christian church. That can be heard in a sermon by Charles Holt on Song of Songs 2:14. The text reads: "O my dove, in the clefts of the rock, in the covert of the cliff, let me see

13. Thomas Aquinas, in: Fant Vol. 1, p. 196.
14. Childs 1992, p. 14.

your face, let me hear your voice; for your voice is sweet, and your face is lovely."

> The Song of Solomon is rich in descriptive language, picturing Christ the heavenly Bridegroom and His Bride, the Church. The entire book flows with a love that all but defies description. ( )
>
> In chapter five, verse two, the bride is likened to a dove by her beloved. She hears him knocking, saying, "Open to me . . . my dove." ( )
>
> These references to the bride as being a dove are of particular interest. They become very significant when viewed in the light of their application to the Church, the Bride of Christ. ( )
>
> In Bible times one of the chief uses of the dove was for sacrifice. Doves often were used when a lamb was too expensive for the offerer. Alluding then to this use of the dove in sacrifice we recall Paul's words in Romans 12:1, "I beseech you therefore, brethren, by the mercies of God, that you present your bodies a living sacrifice, holy, acceptable unto God, which is your reasonable service."
>
> Living for Christ demands our sacrifice. The entire history of the Church has been one of sacrifice. Men and women in all walks of life have sacrificed fame, fortune, popularity, prestige, friends, and many their very lives in sacrificial service to their beloved Lord. The call to the Church today is still to sacrifice. May we see that as Christ's dove, we may be called upon at any time to sacrifice for Him, even to the laying down of our lives.[15]

This sermon portrays Christ as the heavenly bridegroom and the church as his bride.

The Song of Solomon is a love song, abounding in metaphors and oriental imagery. It depicts the wooing and wedding of a shepherdess by King Solomon, and the joys and heartaches of man and wife. Spiritual life finds its highest fulfillment in the love of God for covenant-partner Israel and the love of Christ for the church.

When preaching uses this interpretative key, it sees a detailed testimony to Christ not only in the Song of Solomon but in every part of the Old Testament. The little foxes that ruin the vineyard (Song of Sol. 2:15) point to everything that keeps the congregation away from the Groom. The crimson cord in the window of the house of Rahab in Jericho (Josh.

15. Holt 2003.

2:18/1 Clement 12) refers to the saving blood of Christ. And the wooden stick that made the iron ax head float (2 Kings 6:6) means in fact the cross of Christ.

Bernard of Clairvaux wrote no less than eighty-six sermons on the Song of Songs. The focus of all these sermons was the glorious love between Jesus and the individual believer. Throughout the Catholic liturgy, especially in the Little Office, there is a consistent application of the Song of Songs to the mother of Jesus, the "Blessed Virgin Mary."

## 2.4. Enemies of Israel and Haters of the Church

One of the distinctive features of allegory is that the Israelitic, Jewish character of the text is replaced by a Christian content.

Charles Haddon Spurgeon (1834-1892) wrote a famous commentary on the Psalms titled *Treasury of David*. In his exposition of Psalm 48, Zion and Jerusalem are replaced by the church. Expressions used by David to describe Mount Zion, the city of Jerusalem, or the temple, are used by Spurgeon to portray the life and call of the church. As an illustration of his approach, I present his commentary on two phrases of this poem. First his comment on words from the second verse: "Beautiful for situation."

> Jerusalem was so naturally, she was styled the Queen of the East; the church is so spiritually, being placed near God's heart, within the mountain of his power, upon the hills of his faithfulness, in the center of providential operations. The elevation of the church is her beauty. The more she is above the world the fairer she is.

And next the expression, "The kings were assembled, they passed by together" from verse 4.

> They came and they went. No sooner together than scattered. They came one way and fled twenty ways. Boastful the gathering hosts with their royal leaders, despairing the fugitive bands with their astonished captains. They came like foam on the angry sea, like foam they melted away. This was so remarkable that the psalmist puts in a note of exclamation, Lo! What! Have they so suddenly fled! Even thus shall the haters of the church vanish from the field. Papists, Ritualists, Arians,

21

Skeptics, they shall each have their day, and shall pass on to the limbo of forgetfulness.[16]

Zion and Jerusalem don't slip out of the picture but are replaced by the Christian church. The text has primarily meaning for "us," members of the Christian church. One could call this a "churchalizing" of Zion and Israel. The Christian church absorbs and replaces Israel. "Churchalizing" preserves the material and tangible character of the text but replaces the concrete Israel with the visible church.

Spiritualizing goes even a step further than "churchalizing." Spiritualization evaporates the material character and sees the text as referring to spiritual and transcendent realities from the Christian tradition.

The second verse of Psalm 87 says: "The LORD loveth the Gates of Zion more than the dwellings of Jacob." Hedley Palmer focuses on this imagery.

> The Gates give access to the city. The Gates give power over the city — control the gates and you control the city. The Gates are the place where the elders meet — the place of Justice. When we consider all the spiritual implications, it is a joy to realize that God delights to give us access to His Mighty Presence. He also loves to have access into our lives. The Gates must be open. We first gained access into the presence of God when we allowed Him to have access into our lives. When we accepted His Word, believed in our hearts, we opened the gates that He might enter. When we did that, we surrendered ourselves to Him. In ancient days if a city was at war and the enemy pressed to the very gates, the moment those gates were opened the citizens surrendered. But God is not our enemy. He comes to the gates and we open our hearts and surrender our lives to Him. How wonderful it is to realize that we have freely given God power over our lives. This is the Joy of Mount Zion — God reigns.[17]

The blessing with children becomes the blessing of spiritual offspring. Seeing souls being born into the family of grace is even the ultimate goal and greatest blessing of preaching.

16. Spurgeon (no date), pp. 360, 361.
17. Palmer 1996.

## 2.5. Defeating Giants in Our Lives

Allegorical interpretation offers the preacher the possibility to preach rec-
ognizably and relevantly to contemporary listeners. The questions, fears,
and uncertainties of the members of the congregation are from the start
focused on by the preacher and the sermon. That can be illustrated by
means of a sermon from Marjory Zoet Bankson on Numbers 21:4-9, Moses and the serpent-staff as a sign of God's presence.

> Watching the news of war in Iraq this week, it is not hard to imagine
> the scene in our Old Testament scripture for today . . . sandstorms, sun
> glare and thirst, danger and despair. They remembered Egypt, with its
> cool shadows and plentiful water, and they wanted to go back, even if it
> meant slavery again.
>
> In response to their complaining, God sent them a plague of poi-
> sonous snakes! When the Hebrews cried out for mercy, Moses was told
> to shape a bronze serpent and elevate it on a pole and the mere sight of
> it would cure their ills. His staff was a sign of God's nearness and heal-
> ing . . . a way thru the wilderness. It is important to remember that
> God did not kill the snakes nor did God snatch them out of harm's
> way. Moses' staff was a sign of God's presence with them in the wilder-
> ness. (. . .)
>
> Now, as Christians in America, we find ourselves in the wilderness
> . . . surprised . . . disoriented by our dependence on God. It is not so
> much that we left Egypt on purpose, but it is that religious faith and
> church membership have become increasingly marginalized in our
> culture, as money became the measure of all things. ( )
>
> The world has changed and we are stranded in the desert with the
> strange image of Moses' staff to guide us during Lent. What hope is
> that in this troubled time?[18]

Allegory makes the Old Testament stories transparent for present-day
troubles and joys, questions and issues. There is no distance between the
text and the present situation, or between the there-and-then of the text
and the here-and-now of the congregation. Therefore, it isn't necessary to
bridge the historical and literal gap between text and situation. The world
of the text and the world of the hearers become close neighbors. This char-

18. Bankson 2003.

THE OLD TESTAMENT IN THE THEORY AND PRACTICE OF PREACHING

acteristic of the allegorical key makes it attractive for use in weekly sermons, especially in popular meditative material.

Sermons written along these hermeneutical lines can be transparent for the congregation, and allow an intertwining of text and pastoral care in the practice of preaching.

This key enables the preacher to come close to the actual experiences in the life and faith of the congregation. But there is a price to be paid, one that has to do with the material and historical character of the text. In the case of sermons about the Song of Songs, the actual love between a particular man and wife disappears. The "true" meaning has to with spiritual realities. The timely, the material, and the particular of the text become symbols for the timeless, the spiritual, and the general in the sermon.

As a result, allegory makes it possible to give meaning to difficult passages and hard sayings in the Old Testament. The difficulties that arose, for instance, by passages on war and violence can "easily" be gotten around by allegorizing.[19] Allegory also makes it possible for these passages to speak directly to the present-day congregation. For example, consider this sermon from Kevin Weeks on the well-known story of David and Goliath (1 Sam. 17).

> Do you remember the times when you've struggled with something or you've been fighting a battle and it's left you feeling like you've been run over by a Mack truck? We feel like we're always spending our time trying to defeat a giant? If we're fortunate enough, we don't make it there often, but the reality is, we all make it there at some time. In some cases, we're up against a problem or distraction. In other cases, we're fighting sin that has got a hold of us, and as much as we want to defeat that giant in our lives, it rears its ugly head again and again.
>
> We've all been to the place where we've had to deal with giants; giants like worry, doubt, fear, anxiety, depression, or insecurity. Whatever it has been, we've wandered through those dry valleys looking for answers, and sometimes we come up empty. We feel a lot like David standing in the intimidating shadow of Goliath.[20]

The bodily, physical struggle between David and Goliath is in this sermon translated into the inner struggle in the soul of the individual hearer. The

19. Holladay 1995, pp. 136-56.
20. Weeks 2001.

giant Goliath is transformed into "giants" like worry, doubt, fear, anxiety, depression, or insecurity. "David" is not so much a person but an attitude to face those gigantic enemies in the soul. The sling and the stones, David's advanced weapons, are translated into "trust and inner power." This interpretation is in fact completely dependent on the preacher. Thus, the interpretation and application cannot be controlled anymore by the hearers. There is no reference to, or accountability for, the "original meaning" of the author.[21] There is thus a timeless kind of interpretation. We can hear the same mood in a sermon by Bernard of Clairvaux (1090-1153), who used the same hermeneutical strategy to preach on the same passage.

> Now if we remember that, according to the Apostle's testimony "the law is spiritual" (Rom. 7:14) and has been "written for our learning" (Rom. 15:4), not only to delight us with a history of external events as with the contemplation of a beautiful exterior surface, but also and more particularly to nourish our minds with the sweetness of its mystical signification as with the marrow of the corn: if we bear this in mind, we ought to consider who is typified by the mighty Goliath that, elated and inflated with the wind of his own vanity, presumes alone to defy the people of God, even after they have already entered the promised land and triumphed over innumerable enemies. It is my own opinion that this proud man may be viewed not unreasonably as a type of pride.[22]

One page further in the sermon:

> It seems to me, therefore, that by the five stones taken from the torrent we may not unreasonably understand the fivefold work of the word of God, that is to say, the word of warning, the word of promise, the word of charity, the word of example, and the word which relates to prayer.

## 2.6. Evaluation

The interpretation of the Old Testament confronts the reader with some difficult problems. We not only face contradictions between texts, but also

21. Young 1993, p. 108.
22. Bernard of Clairvaux 1971, pp. 150-51.

the impossibility and incomprehensibility of a substantial number of texts. And there are of course the notorious texts on war and terror that caused and still cause problems and difficulties for the faithful.[23] Those difficulties stimulated a search for meaning behind the words of the text and not in the words themselves. The interpretation gets around the material toughness of the text by spiritualizing and even "churchalizing" the meaning. Allegorical exegeses helped the Christian church to tackle interpretative difficulties with Old Testament texts.

A strength of this hermeneutical key is undoubtedly the possibility of connecting the exposition of a biblical text with contemporary issues and questions. In using allegory, a sermon can be transparent, relevant, and recognizable for present-day hearers. That's because allegory doesn't stick to the exterior of the text's literal or historical dimensions. Allegory offers the text a chance to do more than just share grammatical or historical information; it becomes the source of the depth and richness of the Christian tradition as a whole.

The critical questions raised against allegory in the course of history are still valid regarding sermons that use this hermeneutical key. This kind of interpretation is almost completely dependent on the person of the interpreter, i.e., the person of the preacher. The preacher can't hang *every* meaning on a text, but still quite a lot. And the hearers of a sermon have hardly any possibility of controlling the assigned meaning. The texts of Moses and the prophets are seen as cryptograms to be deciphered by specialists, because the "real" meaning is located at a level the average reader cannot understand without guidance. The real "mystery" of the text is to be found "beneath" the literal or plain sense.[24] Exposition and application of Scripture are thus restricted to a spiritual elite: the higher and spiritual sense can only be properly understood by a (presumably) spiritual person. A person who still is too much impressed by the "flesh" will surely be tempted to be satisfied with the literal meaning of the book and thereby errs. Finding and determining the literal or plain meaning is not enough for interpretation. That effort serves a greater and deeper goal, i.e., to "see" the spiritual sense, hidden within the letters of a text.

In the practice of preaching the Old Testament, we should note two other problems with sermons that give a "churchalized" or Christological

23. Holladay 1995.
24. Juel 2003, p. 290; R. P. C. Hanson 1980, p. 420.

coloring to the text. First, allegory turns the material character of God's goodness and salvation into a spiritual affair. Allegorical sermons on, for instance, the Song of Songs, pass by the book's groundedness in earthly love between two people. Instead, such sermons focus on the mystical love between Christ and the congregation,[25] thus offering a dimension of spirituality. Allegorical interpretation and mysticism have always been brother and sister. That's why allegory has always proven to be vulnerable to Gnostic influences,[26] with a denial of the earthly, material character of creation. All through history the allegorical interpretation has been in one way or another a handmaid to asceticism. For example, as it was developed by Origen and his followers, allegorical interpretation "became the Trojan horse of a type of Christian spirituality which was markedly ascetic."[27]

There is a second, related drawback. Allegory runs the risk of disconnecting the Old Testament from Israel and the Jewish context. The witness to Jesus Christ is seen as the most appropriate sense of both Old and New Testaments.[28] As a result, this hermeneutical key is not only vulnerable to Marcionistic influences but is also defenseless against a-Semitic and even anti-Semitic tendencies.

25. The allegorical interpretation of the Song of Songs isn't specific for the Christian interpretation. There is a also a long Jewish allegorical tradition. Rabbi Akiba (ca. 50-132) interpreted, for instance, the Song of Solomon allegorically to refer to the love between Israel and God.

26. Greer 1989.

27. Old 1998a, p. 338.

28. The true meaning of the Old Testament "must be raised to the level of the normative literal sense, which the New Testament provides" (Preus 1969, p. 15).

# 3. Typology

## 3.1. The Next Babe Ruth

The Rookie of the Year Award is given to the individual player from each league who has the best rookie season. This award became known as the Jackie Robinson Award in 1987 and is given for the best pitching, hitting, and fielding during the first year of the rookie's eligibility. Usually this award calls forth comparisons. Has this rookie the potential to become the next Bob Gibson, Babe Ruth, or Mark McGuire? Similarly, in basketball one can hear the hopeful question, "Is this the next Michael Jordan, Scottie Pippen, or Earvin 'Magic' Johnson?" And then the reader gets a list of similarities that remind us of these great ballplayers.

In a sense, the reverse happens in sermons using typology as a hermeneutical strategy. The preacher points to Old Testament persons, events, offices, and institutions and lists the qualities, gifts, or features that are in the end all come together in Jesus. There are, for instance, some elements in the life of an Old Testament person that remind us of a miracle or the suffering of Christ. Sermons can use that particular element as a bridge between the Old Testament text and the witness of Jesus Christ.

Typology, as a hermeneutical key to open up the meaning of Old Testament texts in the context of Christian preaching, sees in Old Testament places, persons, events, institutions, offices, or objects prefigurations of the person and ministry of Jesus Christ.[1] Typology links the connection between Old and New Testaments in terms of structural similarity between type and antitype. Old Testament persons and events already show a

1. Von Rad 2001a, p. 365.

fragment of the salvation that will be fully revealed in Jesus Christ. Seen from that perspective, Old Testament types look forward to the coming of Jesus and carry a promise in themselves.[2]

The new words and acts of the LORD in Jesus Christ, as recorded in the New Testament, are described with well-known words and familiar images from the books of Moses and the prophets. Vice versa, the well-known words and familiar images of the Old Testament world look forward to and long for a "new" world with greater acts and words of God. The analogy between earlier and later words or events is not based on the conviction that history is cyclic, but rather on a confidence that God's acts and words in past, present, and future have a kind of parallel structure. With Grant R. Osborne, we can describe typology as a

> hermeneutical concept in which a biblical place (Jerusalem, Zion), person (Adam, Melchizedek), event (flood, brazen serpent), institution (feasts, covenant) office (prophet, priest, king), or object (tabernacle, altar, incense) becomes a pattern by which later persons or places are interpreted due to the unity of events within salvation-history. ( ) The "type" is the original person or event and the "antitype" ( ) the later "copy" that fulfills the former.[3]

We can recognize this key already within the Old Testament. When the prophets promise a return from exile, it is depicted as a new exodus (Hos. 2:14; Isa. 52:11f.; Jer. 16:14f.). Amos points to this new beginning when he speaks about the raising up of the fallen booth of David. God will raise the ruins of Jerusalem and rebuild it as in the days of old (Amos 9:11). This new Jerusalem will be a restored old Jerusalem (Isa. 1:21-26). The new beginning has even the character of a new creation (Isa. 11). Isaiah uses the Garden of Eden as a type for the new paradise (Isa. 9:1; 11:6-9). Second Isaiah expects a new exodus from Babylon analogous to the exodus from Egypt (43:16-21; 48:20-21; 51:9-11). And several prophets see David as typical of the king who is to come (Isa. 11:1; Jer. 23:5; Ezek. 34:23-24; Amos 9:11).

This pattern is not only visible and valid within the Old Testament but also between the two Testaments. There is continuity in God's involvement in the history of Israel and the presence of this God in Jesus Christ.

---

2. The concept of typology can be connected with the concept of promise and fulfillment (Von Rad 1963; 2001a, pp. 328-35); see Wilson 2001, p. 125.

3. Osborne 1988, p. 930.

The unity of the God of Israel and the One called *Abba* by Jesus Christ is closely connected to the unity of Old and New Testaments. The presence of this God in Jesus Christ is an expression of loyalty and faithfulness to the "structure" of the actions on behalf of Israel.[4]

Earlier events and persons show a theological pattern and structure that draw the contours of later events. Of all these words and events it can be said: that's typical of the LORD.

The God who acts in world history may be expected to be consistent in future words and deeds. So, for typology, particular situations can become a key to interpreting similar situations: the external can explain the internal, the known can explain the unknown, the public explains the hidden, and the lesser looks forward to the greater. The concrete and material promise of land, for example, points typologically forward to the all-embracing realm of God or the re-creation at the end of times.

A difference, perhaps the key difference, between New Testament typological readings of the Hebrew Scriptures and later Christian typology is the existence of the New Testament itself. Whereas New Testament writers retroactively read forward-looking patterns within the Tanak in relation to their understanding of the Christ, later Christian typologists compared texts between the two Testaments in an exclusively Christological way.

## 3.2. Prefiguration of Christ

What is said about typology thus far in this chapter sounds almost the same as what was said about allegory in the previous chapter. What is the difference between those two hermeneutical keys? Basically, allegory is ahistorical. This hermeneutical key empties as it were the Old Testament words of their literal meaning and historical background and fills those words with the gospel of Jesus Christ. Old Testament words mean in fact something other than the words' exterior seems to say. Ultimately, the historical and literary meaning of words, images, and metaphors of Moses and the prophets evaporate and become vehicles for the New Testament kerygma.

Unlike allegory, typology wants to do justice to history and the literal

---

4. Wolff does not speak of typology but of "analogy in structure" (Wolff 1963; see also Gunneweg 1978, pp. 178-80, 195-98; Preuß 1984, pp. 120-39).

meaning.[5] In typology the "relationship between type and antitype is real and historical, based on an analogous correspondence that exists between them."[6] Particular Old Testament persons, institutions, and events give a foretaste of the ultimate salvation that God already had in mind at that moment but will be revealed in full glory at a later moment. That means that there is an eschatological yearning in the Old Testament types; they look forward to and long for the definitive breakthrough of God's decisive redemption.[7]

The difference between allegory and typology can be illustrated by means of the interpretation of the Song of Songs. In §2.3 I gave an illustration of the allegorical application of this Old Testament love-poetry. A sermon by David Legge illustrates the typological interpretation. The sermon is based on Song of Songs 5:6, which praises the relation between Solomon, the great king, and a common Shulamite girl.

> We believe that it was literally a love song between probably Solomon and a Shulamite girl. But there is a deeper spiritual meaning within this book. The holiest rabbis of Old Testament literature have seen within this book the relationship of Israel, who is the wife of the LORD, and of course Jehovah who is the Bridegroom. Of course we have to see that [in] the Old Testament, you see it in the book of Hosea where God is estranged from his Old Testament wife.
>
> But as we go into the New Testament we see here a typology of the mystical relationship and union between the Lord Jesus Christ and His

---

5. There is a vast disagreement whether typology is related or opposed to allegory. Wilson is aware of the differences between these two hermeneutical keys, but calls them nevertheless "close cousins," "members of the same family," and "close relatives" (Wilson 2001, pp. 116, 118, 122). Childs treats allegory and typology for that reason in one and the same paragraph (Childs 1992, pp. 13-14; see also Barr 1966, pp. 103-49). Froehlich states similarly that a sharp antithesis between Alexandrian allegory and Antiochene typology is a mere contemporary construction (Froehlich 1984, p. 20; see also Young 2003, p. 337). On the other side of the spectrum, Lampe and Woollcombe see an unbridgeable gap between allegory and typology (Lampe/Woollcombe 1957). And Bailey stresses that "typology is a controlled form of analogy not to be confused with allegory" (Bailey 1992a, p. 15). See also Kelly 1978, pp. 69-75.

6. Osborne 1988, p. 931. "Only *historical facts* — persons, actions, events, and institutions — are material for typological interpretation. ( ) These things are to be interpreted typologically only if they are considered to be *divinely ordained* representations of types of future realities that will be *even greater or more complete*" (Goppelt 1982, pp. 17-18; emphasis mine).

7. Schrage 1995, pp. 405-7.

church. Although Israel is the wife of the LORD in the Old Testament, the church of Jesus Christ is the bride of Jesus Christ being prepared for that day — the marriage supper of the Lamb, when we will enjoy in heaven that union, that marriage between us, His church, and the Lord Jesus Christ, the Bridegroom.[8]

Typological interpretation stresses in the first place that the Song of Songs presents a love song between two persons. And this love-poetry is not just an unimportant vehicle for a testimony about the divine love between the LORD and Israel as covenant partner. For that reason, those who want to do justice to the historical and physical context of the words of Scripture have more affinity with typology than with allegory.[9]

The starting point and frame of reference for typology is a specific historical context of persons and events, which have their own material and historical value. In a second step of interpretation, typology looks for parallels between a particular event or person and a later fact in the course of history, especially those in relation to Jesus Christ. The theological basis and kernel of typology is therefore that the LORD is and will be consistently active in the redemptive history of Israel.[10] Because the LORD is a reliable God, we may expect analogous words and acts in comparable circumstances. God's reliability and faithfulness thus fuel the hope for similar words and acts in the future.

## 3.3. The Larger Story of Jesus Christ

In typology, both type and antitype are historically concrete entities, each with their own meaning and validity. However, both entities also form part of a pattern of prefiguration, recapitulation, and fulfillment by reason of God's reign in history. Typology sees thus in Old Testament events, personages, ceremonies, and objects foreshadowings of Christ and his ministry. A sermon by Gregory Fisher on Isaiah 52:13–53:12 illustrates how this hermeneutical key gets its place in the practice of preaching.

8. Legge 2002 (the use of the Name of God slightly edited).
9. Goppelt, for example, tries very hard to bring all the Old Testament quotations in the New Testament under the heading of typology, even where Paul explicitly uses allegory (Goppelt 1978 and 1982); see also Silva 1987, p. 48; Wilson 2001, pp. 122-26.
10. Baker 1996, p. 195.

Isaiah 52:13–53:12 form for us a wonderful picture of the Lord Jesus Christ. The Old Testament is full of "Types and Shadows" of what is to come in the New Testament. These "Types and Shadows" were meant to prepare us for the reality that would come in the Lord Jesus Christ.[11]

All Old Testament types have their end and goal in full glory in Jesus Christ, the ultimate antitype. Sermons using the typological hermeneutical strategy portray Jesus as the one who surpasses the Old Testament type in meaning and importance. Jesus is not only a "look-alike" of Moses, Solomon, and Jonah. He is expressively more, larger, and more important than these Old Testament persons (Matt. 6:29f; 12:41, 42; Heb. 3:3). Typological interpretation uses explicitly increasing and amplifying expressions for the New Testament in relation to the Old Testament.[12] That can be illustrated by way of a sermon from Eric Hollingsworth on Genesis 18:1-8, in which three visitors promise a son to Abraham and Sarah.

> Isaiah 41:8, we read this earlier, God called Abraham "my friend"! James 2:23: "And the Scripture was fulfilled which says, 'Abraham believed God, and it was accounted to him for righteousness.' And he was called the friend of God." So on what basis was Abraham called the friend of God? On what basis could a *holy God* walk up to the tent of this *sinful man* on a hot summer day for a friendly visit? Only on the basis of the righteousness of Jesus Christ, credited to his account. Only because Jesus died for Abraham's sins, John 15:13; "Greater love has no one than this, than to lay down one's life for his friends."
>
> But remember, this visit by God, as astounding as it is, is still just a type, a pattern, a shadow, of a better and far greater reality to be enjoyed by God's New Covenant people. In the Old Covenant shadow, God merely *visited* Abraham, but, in the new covenant reality, God's spirit dwells within us.[13]

---

11. Fisher 2004.

12. Goppelt formulates this programmatically: "The concept of typology ( ) may be defined ( ) as follows: only historical facts — persons, actions, events, and institutions — are material for typological interpretation. These things are to be interpreted typologically only if they are considered to be divinely ordained representations or types of future realities that will be even greater and more complete" (Goppelt 1982, pp. 17-18). "Zum kirchlichen und theologischen Gebrauch der typologischen Methode gehört das Element der Ungleichheit, der Überbietung des Alten durch das Neue" (Marquardt 1990, p. 223).

13. Hollingsworth 2004.

In typology, the physical reality of the text does not "evaporate." The story is indeed understood in its own historical and literary context. But the Old Testament stories point to the "larger" story of, e.g., the fulfillment in Jesus Christ as it can be found in the New Testament. Abraham is "just" a type; the New Testament reveals a "better and far greater reality." The Old Testament gives witness about God's salvation but points "only" typologically to the ultimate salvation in Jesus Christ. For typology, the Old Testament persons and events are referential, and in the most literal sense provisional in character; they look forward to the accomplishment in Jesus Christ, especially in his atoning ministry. A sermon by Tom Walker titled "Some Things You'll Never Find Apart from Jesus" illustrates this line of thought.

> The offerings of the Old Testament had to be repeated year after year. There was no permanent efficacy in the blood of bulls, goats, birds or other animals. The shedding of the imperfect animal blood merely pointed ahead to the perfect, atoning blood of the Son of God, the Lord Jesus Christ. Christ is the anti-type or the fulfillment of the fore-shadowing, of the blood sacrifices in the Old Testament.[14]

As a result, we can discern two parts in the construction of a sermon. The sermon starts usually with an explanation or exposition of a certain passage of Scripture. The second part "expands" and "enlarges" the wording and imagery of the first part so that they can serve as "stepping stones" for the proclamation of Jesus Christ. The actual salvation for the present hearers is presented in the second part of the sermon. As a result, the meaning of the Old Testament type disappears behind Jesus Christ. In a sermon on Joshua 1:1-9 and Hebrews 4:1-11; 11:1-16, Stephen Sizer traces the idea of the Promised Land from the Old Testament into the New Testament.

> How we view the land of Israel/Palestine is a complex issue and one on which Christians hold passionate and sometimes contradictory views. This was the place where people could receive all of God's blessings and commune in fellowship with Him. This is where the image of land begins in the Bible. This land of paradise was lost in the Fall but a fore-taste of heaven is reflected in the imagery of the promise made to Abraham.

14. Walker 1998.

The LORD repeated — and even amplified — this promise several times.

> These promises were restated to Moses. "So I have come down to rescue them from the hand of the Egyptians and to bring them up out of that land into a good and spacious land, a land flowing with milk and honey — the home of the Canaanites, Hittites, Amorites, Perizzites, Hivites and Jebusites" (Exodus 3:8). As we have already seen in previous sermons, these images are paradigms. The land of the Bible is not and never ever did flow with literal milk and honey. It is indeed a beautiful land but the biblical imagery points to a restored paradise in the future. From the very beginning this Old Covenant shadow would have to wait for the New Covenant for the actual fulfillment of the promise. The land in the Old Covenant was not an end in itself. That is why ( ) the tabernacle, the place of worship in the Old Covenant, was never intended to have a settled location in God's plan of redemption. It pointed to Jesus Christ who would "tabernacle" among His people in the incarnation and since Pentecost through the abiding presence of the Holy Spirit. The sacrificial system could never atone for sins but only foreshadow the ultimate sacrifice of the sinless, perfect Son of God.[15]

The Old Testament is from the beginning (only) image, paradigm, and (fore)shadow. They all await the actual fulfillment and ultimate foundation for the proclamation of salvation, i.e., Jesus Christ.

## 3.4. Biblical Characters as Moral Examples

For typology, the ultimate meaning of the Old Testament is referential: a particular type points to Jesus Christ. Persons, events, and institutions of the Old Testament have the same function as John the Baptist on the central panel of the famous *Isenheim Altarpiece* of Matthias Grünewald (1475-1528): pointing to the Savior as the Lamb who takes away the sin of the world.[16] That means that the actual salvation for the hearers — i.e., the reconciliation between God and man through the suffering, death, and resur-

---

15. Sizer 2000.

16. The altarpiece is dated 1512-1515. For an image of this altarpiece see for instance wga.hu/frames-e.html?/html/g/grunewal/2isenhei/1view/1view1c.html.

rection of Jesus Christ — must be proclaimed from the New Testament. That can be illustrated by means of a sermon by Paul E. Penno on the promise of land to Abraham.

> God gave Canaan as just a down payment to Abraham. It was just a type pointing forward to the greater fulfillment of God's promise. "For the promise, that he should be the heir of the world, was not to Abraham, or to his seed, through the law, but through the righteousness of faith" (Rom. 4:13).[17]

The expression "just a type" runs the risk of making the Old Testament promise irrelevant for the present-day reader and listener. That means that the actual and ultimate salvation can only be proclaimed from the New Testament. The most the Old Testament text can do is to give moral guidance. The Old Testament types become thus persons with an exemplary behavior or faith.[18] Naomi H. Rosenblatt uses that hermeneutical strategy in her book *Wrestling with Angels* when she portrays Abraham.

> Abraham's advanced age is what makes his leap of faith so impressive. His midlife crisis is a familiar phenomenon, but his response to it is not. Most of us gripe about our lives and fantasize about making a radical change. But how many among us actually heed our soul's call to "go forth"? Most of us conclude we are better off bearing whatever disappointments we may harbor in our lives. By the time we reach middle age we have too much at stake to make bold course corrections. We have our reputations to worry about, assets to protect, bills to pay, children to feed and educate. Rather than take a blind leap of faith into the unknown, we usually settle for buying a new car or taking up a new hobby. Abraham remains an inspirational role model because he demonstrates the power of faith to overcome cynicism, despair, and defeatism at any age.[19]

Stories about other people are always attractive. News and even (or especially?) gossip about other people rarely fail to attract attention. It is like honey to flies. For that reason *People* magazine is one of the most popular

---

17. Penno 2002. The lesson from Scripture was taken from Galatians 3:15-18.
18. Overstreet 2001.
19. Rosenblatt 1995, p. 105.

on the newsstand. Historical fiction and biographical books are consistently among the books most often purchased in bookstores and borrowed from libraries. For that reason, Elmer L. Towns recommends the use of biographical preaching and biographical Bible study as an important strategy.

> When God created people, He intended for them to be social creatures (Gen. 2:18). As a result, people are drawn toward other people. People like people. As a result, biographical lessons are more interesting than other approaches to Bible study. The Psalmist affirmed, "I have rejoiced in the way of Your testimonies (that is, biblical biographies), as much as in all riches" (Ps. 119:14). This social tendency that God gave us means that people not only like people, they identify with people. Your students who struggle to apply a biblical principle to their lives will find it easier when they follow the example of someone else who models that principle. The old adage "monkey see, monkey do" is somewhat derogatory. I like it better this way: "People see, people do." The Psalmist wrote, "I cling to Your testimonies" (Ps. 119:31) and considered them his counselors (Ps. 119:24). Understanding this principle, Paul repeatedly called upon those he reached for Christ to follow the example of the Christian life he modeled for them in his own life (2 Thess. 3:7, 9; 1 Cor. 11:1; Phil. 4:9).[20]

This kind of exemplary use of Old Testament types was already common practice in the intertestamental period, in the New Testament, and in the apostolic writings.[21] The book of Wisdom of Jesus Sirach (ca. 170 BCE) offers in chapters 44–50 a long list of names, their benefactions, faith, and courage. The persons on this list are presented to the reader as examples. After general praises in the introduction, the list of names begins with Enoch.

> Enoch pleased the LORD and was taken up, an example of repentance to all generations. (Jesus Sirach 44:16; see also 49:14)

We can find a similar list of examples of faith in the New Testament (Hebrews 11 and 12). In the apostolic period we can read a list with shining examples, the heroes of faith named in the first letter of Clement to Cor-

20. Towns 1998, p. 20.
21. Greer 1989, pp. 137-40.

inth (1 Clement 17–18). The author offers the reader a list of biblical characters noted for their humility. Along typological lines, sermons admonish listeners to be servants of the LORD, to be a light for the world.

In a sermon on Genesis 14:17-24, Bruce Goettsche draws several lessons from this passage. One of the lessons is that

> we learn that the best way to face a formidable foe is through faith. Abraham took his 318 men (trained though they were) and went against an army that was much larger. Remember, this is an army that subdued almost the entire area of Canaan. Abraham knew that he could not prevail by his own strength . . . so he trusted the Lord.
>
> The foe you face may be something other than an invading army but just as formidable. Cancer or some other devastating illness, mental deterioration, relationship problems, constant anxiety, legal problems, the plague of emotional distress, the effects of suffocating loneliness.
>
> Friend, the mountain may be different, but the solution is the same. Those times when we know we are most helpless are the times when we need to be most trusting. God can see us through. He can lead us to victory over the most overwhelming odds. When you doubt that, remember Abraham, or David with Goliath, or Elijah with the Prophets of Baal, or Moses facing Pharaoh. God has a proven track record of success in "hopeless" situations.[22]

There is a certain paradigm, strategy, or "floor plan" for God's actions in history. Because of God's "proven track record of success in 'hopeless' situations" we can count on comparable actions in comparable situations. Therefore listeners are admonished to imitate the positive examples portrayed in Scripture.

Besides the lists with positive examples, there are also lists with deterrent examples: persons who did not behave well. Paul, for instance, draws some lessons from the bad behavior of Israel (1 Cor. 10:6). Despite the fact that Israel was liberated out of Egypt and experienced God's grace in the desert, they nevertheless went their own way. And as a consequence they had to accept the effects of their disobedience: most of them didn't enter the Promised Land.

22. Goettsche 1999a.

> Now these things occurred as examples (literally: *tupoi*) for us, so that
> we might not desire evil as they did.

Events and persons from the Old Testament get the function of deterrent
examples for the listeners and readers. This line of the negative examples is
loud and clear in so-called "fire and brimstone" sermons.[23]

## 3.5. Made Ready for Christ

What is the role and place of Israel in the hermeneutical strategy of
typology? That can be illustrated by way of a sermon by William Klock on
Isaiah 1:10-20 and Hebrews 9:11-15. The title of the sermon is "Our Great
High Priest."

> I think it's very appropriate that our lessons take us back to the Old
> Testament sacrificial system on what we could call the Christian Day
> of Atonement in the Church Year. Our New Testament lesson builds
> on the Old Testament. It contrasts the type in the Old Testament with
> the fulfillment of the type in the New Testament. We see how the ful-
> fillment surpasses the type in every way.[24]

The consequence of the surpassing of the Old Testament type is that the
Old Testament itself is also surpassed by the New Testament. And therefore, the church surpasses Israel and takes over the role of Israel in God's
ongoing history of redemption. A sermon by Hedley Palmer on Psalm 48:1
can serve as illustration.

> Of this Psalm, Luther once said, "David is celebrating the truth of
> God." What a wonderful theme — the truth of God! That truth has its
> fulfillment from generation to generation. There are two reasons here
> for praising God. One is for the boundless excellence of His nature —
> Great is the Lord. The other is for the excellence of His acts. The city —
> the Mountain of His Holiness — is Jerusalem and a type of the Church.
> Notice the Panorama of the Church in this Psalm. Praises flow be-
> cause of the prospect which meets every eye. Beautiful for situation —

23. Bos 1992; Claußen 1999.
24. Klock 2005.

> beautiful for extension. Jerusalem was a joy to the beholder — the joy
> of the land. So also is the Church. We must ever remember that a great
> part of human happiness has, in one way or another, resulted from the
> existence of the Church. Without the Church of Jesus Christ in history,
> the human scene would be very desolate indeed.[25]

The role and place of Israel are restricted to a "mere type." The Jews' longing for Jerusalem, and the longing of contemporary Jews for peace in the tangible Jerusalem, disappear behind the curtains of the church and the Christian longing for the "new Jerusalem" in heaven.

When Israel is silently replaced by the church, Jews are swallowed up by Christians. That does not always happen explicitly in sermons that use typology as the hermeneutical key, but the theological ingredients for an implicit annexation are present. Historically speaking, the use of typology in the practice of preaching has almost always turned out negatively for Jews, Israel, and Judaism.

This hermeneutical key considers the covenant between God and Israel as preparatory and provisional, both in the sense of temporary and the sense of preview. The covenant has no intrinsic value for Israel anymore. It has only meaning in relation to the coming of Christ. Typology paved the way to read the books of Moses and the prophets with exclusive Christian and Christological eyes. And because the Jews did not (do not) have this sight, they saw (see) only the literal meaning of the texts and were seen as blind persons who miss the deeper — and thus ultimate — meaning of the text.

## 3.6. Evaluation

Generally speaking, Old Testament types have the following characteristics:

a. They are thoroughly rooted in history. Jonah's experience (Jon. 1:17) is just as real as the New Testament antitype, i.e., the death and resurrection of Christ (Matt. 12:40).
b. Types point in one way or another forward to the life and ministry of

25. Palmer, no date.

Jesus Christ. Melchizedek (Gen. 14) becomes, for instance, the pre-figuration of Christ's eternal priesthood (Heb. 7).

c. Types are definitely designed as an integral part of a progressive re-demptive history. Jesus is "larger" than Moses, Solomon, and Jonah (Matt. 6:29v; 12:41, 42; Heb. 3:3).

d. Types are edificatory, having exemplary meaning for God's people.

Typology and typological interpretation of the books of Moses and the prophets was and has been a widely used hermeneutical key from the earliest days of the church up to the present, in both the Reformed and the Catholic traditions.[26] Undoubtedly, that has to do with its evident strengths and dimensions. Typology wants to do justice to the concrete history, keeping God's loyalty and faithfulness in the center of its consider-ations. That is true both within the Old Testament and between Old and New Testaments.[27]

The other side of this coin is that in typology, the Old Testament be-comes a temporary truth that would ultimately be replaced with the com-ing of Christ, as a shadow is replaced by light, as the old is replaced by the new. This way of presenting the coming of Christ makes the history that preceded him in fact empty and senseless in itself. It tends to oppose Old and New Testaments as two opposing images of God (justice opposed to love), of cult (ritualistic opposed to spiritual), of salvation history (an-nouncement opposed to realization), of morality (imperfect opposed to perfect), and of life (under fear as opposed to love). It is like the images of *synagogia* and *ekklesia* that oppose each other above the entrances of sev-eral European cathedrals (cf. the introduction to chapter 11).

A major presupposition of typology is the concept of progress in the movement from type to antitype. This concept sees a progressive develop-ment in history (from the perspective either of the history of religion or of salvation history). An almost unavoidable element of this concept is there-fore an asymmetric relation between Old and New Testaments: the latter is more developed and offers a richer gospel. The Old Testament is the "starter" for the actual "main course" of the New Testament. Typological

26. "In der söntaglichen katholischen Predigtpraxis, dem 'Predigt-Alltag' also, ist die typologische Sicht des Alten Testamentes immer noch sehr beliebt und dürfte zum durchschnittlichen und gängigen Verständnis gehören" (Schöttler 2001, p. 297).

27. "The use of typology rests on the belief that God's ways of acting are consistent throughout history" (W. W. Klein 1993, p. 130).

interpretation understands the Old Testament as the preliminary stage of that which is to be fulfilled — greater and more enclosing in Jesus Christ.[28] That also has a consequence for the way this key finds its application for the congregation in sermons. The Old Testament types get the role of moral example. A sermon by Richard Jordan on Exodus 15:1-11 can serve as an illustration.

> The Exodus was the foremost of God's saving acts for the people of Israel. No other event in the history of Old Testament Israel was so dramatic. The people were to commemorate this event every year at the Feast of Passover and the Feast of Unleavened Bread. The Jews to this day remember Passover.
>
> The Exodus, being the foremost of God's saving acts in the Old Testament, was a type of God's ultimate saving act. A type is an event that more than foreshadows a greater event; it is almost that event in miniature. We are more familiar with this word in prototype. A prototype is the first type. The final reality is called the antitype.[29]

This kind of Christian proclamation is vulnerable to Marcionistic tendencies.

The Old Testament types have a provisional and exemplary character.[30] Types become role models with the risk and danger of becoming moralistic examples. But Moses and the prophets don't inform us primarily on the life and morals of Abraham, Isaac, and Jacob. Scripture's first and main interest is to reveal God's redemptive purposes for humankind and creation.

And last but not least, we have to mention the issue of Israel. God's firstborn son (Exod. 4:22) disappears completely from sight in sermons that are woven on the pattern of typology. For the physical Israel, the only remaining role is in supplying a Christian Jesus. There is a real danger and risk of annexation and absorption of the Old Testament by the Christian church and her preaching. History has proven that this is not only a possible but a real danger. This danger may even be an inner necessity of typology. A sermon by Paul Mizzi on Genesis 28 — the story of Jacob dreaming about a ladder — can serve as an illustration.

28. Gunneweg 1978, p. 174.
29. Jordan 1998.
30. H. Berkhof 1986, p. 269.

"And he said to him, Verily verily I say unto you, Hereafter thou shalt see heaven open, and the angels of God ascending and descending upon the Son of Man" (John 1:51). This statement of Jesus alludes to Jacob's vision of a ladder or stairway stretching from earth to heaven (Genesis 28:12). Jesus presents himself as the reality to which the stairway pointed. The patriarch saw in a dream the reunion of heaven and earth through the One Mediator, Jesus Christ, which is now brought to reality both for Jacob and for all believers.[31]

What was "only" a dream for Jacob is brought to reality in Jesus Christ. That means that the old covenant is seen as only a prefiguration and precursor of the new covenant, and has been fulfilled in the new covenant to the extent that it can no longer claim any significance for Israel or the gentiles.

31. Mizzi, no date.

# 4. Promise and Fulfillment

## 4.1. Be True to Your Word

Some time ago there was a UPS commercial on television that showed a harassed mother on her way to send a package. She promises her children that if they are good the whole time they are in the UPS store, she will buy them a special present. One of them pipes up, "A puppy?" Judging that it will take some time in the store, the mother says, "If you are good the whole time, I will buy you each a puppy." The UPS transaction doesn't take as long as she thought or feared it would take; it takes only a few minutes. The mother keeps saying, "Is that all?" The final scene of the commercial shows the mother walking away with two children and two puppies. Besides praising the quality of the service of UPS, the commercial also warns parents: Be very careful what you promise your children, because they will remember and they will expect you to be true to your word.[1]

The LORD speaks, and the words of this God have the character of promises. He asks Israel to read his lips and trust the words spoken. The LORD continually brings into being with deeds what this God has promised with words. The relationship develops in the course of time and is shaped along a chain of promises and fulfillments. This chain ends in "the fullness of time" in the paramount fulfillment in Christ (Gal. 4:4). The promises to Abraham about land and descendants, the promise of a good and broad land flowing with milk and honey, the promise to David and his house about his kingdom, swells and rises in the course of history. In the end, those promises are embodied in the One that comes in the name of

1. Kirk, no date.

44

the LORD. In Christ, the promise is replaced by fulfillment, shadow by reality, just as an engagement is replaced by a marriage.

Scripture itself provides the pair of expressions "promise and fulfillment." The Gospels proclaim that Jesus fulfilled the words and promises of Moses and the prophets. The Gospel of Matthew contains over sixty explicit or substantial quotations from the books of Moses and the prophets. The evangelist takes every opportunity to testify that the Scriptures were fulfilled in the words and acts of Jesus. The Old Testament references are introduced by a more or less fixed formula: "This happened to fulfill what was spoken by the prophet. . . ."[2] From the start, in the first chapter, the evangelist uses this formula to interpret the character of Mary's pregnancy (1:21-23).

> She will bear a son, and you are to name him Jesus, for he will save his people from their sins. All this took place to fulfill what had been spoken by the Lord through the prophet: "Look, the virgin shall conceive and bear a son, and they shall name him Emmanuel," which means, "God with us."

We can say that Matthew coined the pair of words "prophecy and fulfillment." From there it found its way to the hermeneutical literature.[3] Quite soon, the word "prophecy" got the meaning of foretelling. In the context of the relation between Old and New Testaments that foretelling became a "prediction about future events concerning Jesus." That meaning can be heard in both the practice of preaching and theological reflection. Kim Riddlebarger opens a sermon on Acts 1 and Ezekiel 36 and 37 as follows.

> In approximately 570 BC, the prophet Ezekiel spoke forth the word of the Lord as recorded in Ezekiel 36 and 37.

He proceeds a little further:

> And as we have heard in our Old Testament lesson this morning, Ezekiel foresaw a glorious age in which the Spirit of the Lord would bring life to a multitude of dead bones. (. . .)
> In this amazing vision Ezekiel saw a glorious Messianic age, some

---

2. See the excursus "The Formula Quotations" in Luz 1989, pp. 156-64.
3. See Zimmerli 1963; Bultmann 1963; Gunneweg 1978, pp. 21-31.

> six hundred years yet in the future, which would dawn in the person and work of Jesus Christ. We see this unfolded in our gospels, and which continues to unfold before our eyes in the Book of Acts.[4]

"Speaking forth" becomes "foreseeing," and this in its turn becomes "foretelling." Those changes of meaning take place in just a few sentences. The sermon says that Ezekiel predicted the future. As a result, the meaning of the words for the particular time of Ezekiel gets lost from view. And that means that the words of Moses and the prophets have no meaning for Israel itself, neither the Israel in Old Testament times nor the present-day Israel.

This hermeneutical concept can be discerned through the course of church history. We can hear the same paradigm, for instance, in a sermon by Augustine (354-430) on Joel 2:32: "Then everyone who calls on the name of the LORD shall be saved."

> Wishing to show that the prophets had foretold the time when all nations were to believe in God, the holy Apostle appealed to the testimony of the written word: "And it shall come to pass that everyone that shall call upon the name of the Lord shall be saved." For prior to this the Israelites alone called upon the name of the Lord, Maker of heaven and earth. Other nations used to invoke their deaf and dumb idols, by whom they were not heard, or the demons, from whom they heard to their detriment. But when the fullness of time came, then was fulfilled what had been predicted, "And it shall come to pass that everyone that shall call upon the name of the Lord shall be saved."[5]

Augustine understands the prophet's testimony as a "foretelling" of the time when all nations were to believe in God.


## 4.2. Promise, Prophecy, and Prediction

This concept implies that the Old Testament prophets spoke above the reality of their own time and context. Sermons in this mode portray the promises of the prophets as explicit predictions about the words and min-

---

4. Riddlebarger 1998.
5. Augustine, in: Fant Vol. 1, pp. 125-26.

istry of Jesus Christ, even about minor details. As a result, "promise" became gradually understood as prediction. The words "promise," "prophecy," and "prediction" became interchangeable.[6] One can thus compile as it were "checklists" or "encyclopedias" of Old Testament predictions that come to fulfillment in the New Testament,[7] especially in the life, crucifixion, and resurrection of Jesus Christ.[8]

| *Predictions about the Messiah* | *OT source* | *NT fulfillment* |
| --- | --- | --- |
| born of woman | Genesis 3:15 | Matthew 4:1 Colossians 2:15 Revelation 12:9, 17 |
| descended from Abraham | Genesis 22:18 | Galatians 3:8 Acts 3:25 |
| descended from David | Isaiah 11:1 | Acts 13:22, 23 Romans 15:12 Revelation 5:5; 22:16 |
| born in Bethlehem | Micah 5:1 | Matthew 2:1 Luke 2:4-7 |
| admired by important people | Psalm 72:10-11 | Matthew 2:1-11 |
| came as fugitive from Egypt | Hosea 11:1 | Matthew 2:15 |
| not wrangle or cry aloud | Isaiah 42:1-4 | Matthew 12:18-21 |
| entered Jerusalem on a donkey | Zechariah 9:9 | Mark 11:1-10 Matthew 21:1-11 Luke 19:28-40 John 12:12-19 |
| sold for thirty pieces of silver | Zechariah 11:12 | Matthew 26:15 |
| crucified and forsaken by God | Psalm 22 | Matthew 27:35, 39, 43, 46 |
| abandoned by friends and family | Psalm 38:12; 69:9 | Mark 14:50 |
| buried in the grave of a rich person | Isaiah 53:9 | Mark 15:42-47 |

6. Barrera 1998, p. 520.

7. See the several sites on the Internet (e.g., aboutbibleprophecy.com, prophecywatch .com).

8. About the so-called *testimonia lists* in the New Testament see Greer 1989, pp. 138-40.

One could easily get the impression that all a first-century Jew had to do was follow Jesus around, ticking off prophecy fulfillments on his Old Testament Messianic Prophecy Checklist in order to have known everything that Jesus was going to do before he ever did it.

Alan J. Meenan preached in Advent 1999 a series of sermons on Old Testament Messianic prophecies. The overarching title was "Can This Be the Christ?" On subsequent Sundays the lections were taken from Genesis 3:1-15, 1 Chronicles 17:1-5, Isaiah 7:14, 9:6, 40:3, 11:2-5, 42:1, and Zechariah 3:8-9, 9:9, 12:10, 14:4. The fourth sermon looks back on the route thus far.

> We've been asking the question, "Can this be the Christ?" It was asked long ago by the young woman who met Jesus by Jacob's well in the region of Samaria. She ran back to her village of Sychar, grabbing hold of anyone who would listen and invariably shouting in their ear, "Come meet a man. . . . Can this be the Christ of God? Can this be the Messiah?" To help us in the decision whether or not we believe Jesus' claims, we have looked together at a variety of ancient messianic promises written hundreds, and some even thousands, of years before Jesus was ever born. Throughout the Old Testament, we've discovered that the ancient bards forecasted the coming of a Redeemer who would conquer evil and set humankind free. They were very specific, almost to a fault. Through them, God sent us a number of signposts to tell us how we might recognize the Messiah when He came. The prophets tell us not only that He was going to come; but how He would come. They told us when we might expect Him. They told us a variety of the things that He would do. They told us what He would be like so that we might clearly perceive the Messiah when, in fact, He appeared.
>
> We have gone back to the most ancient of documents as we looked at the books of Genesis, Chronicles and Isaiah. Immediately after the fall, God made a promise that the Messiah would come from the seed of Abraham and that He would be related to a woman in a special way. He would come from the tribe of Judah. He would come from the house of David. He would work tremendous miracles. The Spirit of God would rest upon Him. And we've seen again and again how in every detail Jesus Christ satisfies the deepest scrutiny that one can bring to the texts. Now I want to go even one level deeper as we study together the prophecy of Zechariah.[9]

9. Meenan 1999.

The preacher makes clear that "the ancient bards forecasted the coming of a Redeemer" in detail. Sermons based on prophetic texts use this hermeneutical strategy with particular zeal. And within the prophetic corpus we can trace this hermeneutical key especially in sermons on texts from Isaiah. But we can also discover this hermeneutical strategy in sermons on texts from another genre, albeit less frequently.

## 4.3. History Prewritten

The hermeneutical key of promise and fulfillment centers on Jesus Christ. The Old Testament looks forward to him and the New Testament gives witness to the reality of his coming. The preaching and proclamation based on this hermeneutical paradigm is primarily interested in this prospective and prophetic Christological character of the Old Testament and has less interest in the actual meaning of the promises for Israel as a nation. At the deepest and ultimate level, every Old Testament text has a Christological content.

The use of this hermeneutical key in the practice of preaching can be illustrated by way of a sermon from Rex Marre, delivered on Good Friday 2004. The lections were taken from Isaiah 52:13–53:12, Psalm 22, 1 Corinthians 1:18-31, and John 18:1–19:42.

> The message of Good Friday is that God provided the answer to the world's problems when in His great love He died on Calvary's cross 2,000 years ago.
>
> Isaiah prophesied this 700 years before it happened; He was despised and rejected by men — a man of sorrows and acquainted with grief — and we hid as it were our faces from Him.
>
> All we like sheep have gone astray — we have turned — every one — to his own way — and the Lord has laid on him the iniquity of us all. Surely He has borne our griefs and carried our sorrows — yet we esteemed Him stricken, smitten by God and afflicted.
>
> But He was wounded for our transgressions — He was bruised for our iniquities — the chastisement for our peace was laid upon Him — and by His stripes we are healed.[10]

10. Marre 2004.

In this model, Jesus Christ is not only the "fitting last paragraph" of Moses and the prophets, but everything and everyone in the Old Testament is a preparation for and reference to him. The Old Testament is directed to and centers on the expectation of the coming Messiah. The Old Testament is, so to speak, already the history of Jesus prewritten several centuries earlier. That can be heard in a sermon by Damian Phillips on Isaiah 53.

> Isaiah 53 was written as an eyewitness account of the trial and crucifix-ion of our Lord Jesus Christ. This account was written 750 years before Jesus' death on the cross. The accuracy of the Isaiah 53 account should be enough to say, "Wow, God knew all along what he was going to do!"[11]

The fourth song of the suffering servant is read and interpreted as if it has an exclusively Christological meaning and as if Jesus is the actual object. The prophets are seen as divinely inspired "future-tellers." The prophets told many centuries ahead about the birth, life, suffering, and resurrection of Jesus Christ. The New Testament tells us in what way the Old Testament predictions came through in Jesus Christ. And even when the words of a particular prophet refer to an event in his own time, the deeper and ulti-mate meaning of his words refers to the ministry of Jesus. There is a real risk that Christ absorbs the Old Testament words completely.

The ears of the listeners are almost immediately directed from the Old Testament text and its historical and literary context to the person and ministry of Jesus Christ. A sermon by Wil Pounds on 2 Samuel 7:1-17 and Luke 1:31-33 illustrates how this model gets a place in the practice of preaching. The title of the sermon is "Messiah ben David."

> The prophet Isaiah saw the coming of a child with four names who would rule as Prince of Peace (Isaiah 9:7). He said,
>
>> There will be no end to the increase of His government
>>> or of peace,
>> on the throne of David and over his kingdom,
>> to establish it and to uphold it with justice and righteousness
>> from then on and forevermore.
>> The zeal of the Lord of hosts will accomplish this.
>
> Other Hebrew prophets at various times prophesied of the coming

11. Phillips 2001.

of this same person (cf. Daniel 2:44; 4:3, 34; 6:26; 7:13-14). Ezekiel wrote, "My servant David will be king over them, and they will all have one shepherd; and they will walk in My ordinances and keep My statutes and observe them. They will live on the land that I gave to Jacob My servant, in which your fathers lived; and they will live on it, they, and their sons and their sons' sons, forever; and David My servant will be their prince forever" (Ezekiel 37:24-25; cf. 34:23-24).

It is obvious that no earthly kingdom has eternal duration. Earthly kingdoms perish, one by one, and other kingdoms take their place. This was true in Israel. After 350 years, the kingdom of David came to a physical end. Once the dynasty had fallen in 586 BC, devout Jews continued to treasure the divine promises made to David. They were confident that Yahweh would again fulfill them in a very special son of David they called the Messiah (translated "Christ"). So how then could it last for eternity?[12]

The promise to Solomon and his descendants is not fully exhausted in them. The promise that the "seed" of David should endure forever is attained only in the ultimate fulfillment in Christ.

The homiletical elaboration of this hermeneutical concept shows great continuity in the history of preaching. We can hear the same paradigm, for example, in a sermon by John Chrysostom (about 347-407) on Epiphany Sunday. Chrysostom was a gifted and eloquent preacher. His name means, literally translated, "Golden Mouth." He was designated by a future pope as the patron saint of Christian preachers.[13]

When Jesus therefore was born in Bethlehem of Judah, there came wise men from the east to Jerusalem, saying: Where is he that is born king of the Jews? For we have seen his star in the east, and are come to adore him.

Isaiah had foretold that this would come to pass, saying: The multitude of camels shall cover thee, the dromedaries of Median and Apha: all they from Saba shall come, bringing gold and frankincense: and showing forth praise to the Lord. [Isa. 60: 6] This is He, Christ the Lord, Whom the Magi, having seen the sign of the star, announce as the King of the Jews. (. . .)

12. Pounds 1999.
13. See Edwards 2004, pp. 72-84; Old 1998a, pp. 171-222.

But perhaps someone will wonder how it was that the Magi knew of the Lord's Nativity from the sign of a star? In the first place we say that this was a gift of the divine goodness. Then we read in the books of Moses that there was a certain prophet of the Gentiles, Balaam, who foretold in definite words the coming of Christ and His incarnation from a virgin. For among other things he said: A star shall rise out of Jacob, and a scepter shall spring up from Israel. The Wise men, who saw the new star in the East, are said to be descendants of this Balaam, a prophet from the Gentiles. And seeing the sign of the new star they accordingly believed, knowing that the prophecy of their ancestor was fulfilled: in this showing themselves to be not alone his descendants in the flesh, but the heirs also to his faith. Balaam their prophet beheld the Star in spirit; with their eyes they saw it, and believed. He by prophecy foretold that Christ would come; they with the vision of faith knew that He had come.[14]

Every bit and piece of the Old Testament is set in a Christological perspective. Every detail of the life and ministry of Jesus Christ is thus already foretold in the books of Moses and the prophets.

## 4.4. The Listener as Spectator in the Theater of God's Glory

The previous paragraph made the role of the listeners implicitly clear. The actual and ultimate foundation for salvation is not to be found in the Old Testament text but in the One that is predicted in that text. The meaning of the Old Testament witnesses for the listeners is that they testify about a reliable God who made his ancient promises come through in the coming of Jesus Christ.

Because of this Christological absorption, there is little or no room left for the contemporary listener in the text. Sermons based on this hermeneutical concept bounce back and forth between the BCE time of a particular prophet and the life of Jesus in 30 CE. Something happened between the Old Testament and Jesus, but the congregation has no active role in that event. The contemporary listeners are spectators of a play in the arena of history, the theater of God's glory.

14. John Chrysostom, Epiphany.

The homiletical practice of this hermeneutical key can be illustrated by way of a sermon from John Hamby on Isaiah 7:14. The title discloses the hermeneutical key clearly: "Prophecies of Christmas."

> The Christmas story in the Bible begins earlier than you might expect, several hundred years earlier, in the Old Testament. One Old Testament prophecy after another promised the coming Messiah who would redeem the people of God. Whether you know it or not, the first promise of the coming Christ was given in the very first book of the Old Testament, in Genesis 3:15.
>
> The Prophet Isaiah writing nearly 600 years before the birth of Christ was able to see across the centuries and gave us an amazingly accurate picture of the birth of the Savior. He said (7:14), "Therefore the Lord Himself will give you a sign: Behold, a virgin shall conceive and bear a Son, and shall call His name Immanuel."[15]

The preacher proceeds in discussing more prophecies about the coming of the Messiah. The sermon goes several times back and forth from the Old to the New Testament. The listener is indeed spectator in the theater of history between Old Testament times and Jesus Christ. Listeners are invited to strengthen their faith and trust in the God who is the actual director of that history.

The value and meaning of the text for present-day listeners is that the (Old Testament) God proved to be faithful because the predictions came through in Christ. This God is still faithful and promises salvation to those who believe.

The consequence of this model from a theological point of view is that the Old Testament is in fact insufficient in itself to proclaim the good news to present-day listeners. The message of the prophets is waiting for the "finishing touch" from the New Testament.


## 4.5. Preview and Provisional

Salvation in Old Testament times has a provisional character; it is temporary in character and a preview of the real and ultimate salvation revealed in Jesus Christ. Israel is the forerunner of God's ultimate salvation. Ser-

15. Hamby 2003.

mons built on the hermeneutical foundation of "promise and fulfillment" leave only one role for Israel: supplier of the Messiah, a role in the margin.

Israel is as it were an "intermezzo" on God's trail through history. God's way with Israel can be seen as the engagement, a preliminary phase in a relation that is not only fulfilled in marriage (i.e., the coming of Jesus Christ) but also caught up by this coming. There is in fact no theological role left for Israel in the post-Easter and post-Pentecost era. The promises to Israel are taken over by the church. The church replaces Israel.

A sermon from Steven P. Vitrano on Genesis 15 can illustrate the way this hermeneutical key treats the role of Israel. The title of the sermon is "God's Promises Are for Believing."

> A most interesting story! But what does it say to us? Stories are good, I suppose, especially Bible stories. The pious would read and tell them just because they are in the Bible. But there is more to this story than that, at least for the apostle Paul. Many centuries later he wrote in Galatians 3:29:
>
> > And if you are Christ's, then you are Abraham's offspring, heirs according to the promise.
>
> Really? Christians are the offspring of Abraham, and heirs according to the promise God made to him? That's what Paul said! You mean God promised Abraham's offspring a son? Yes. That's what the offspring of Abraham have believed for centuries. (. . .)
>
> But have the promises been fulfilled? Has the promise of the son been fulfilled?
>
> Of course! That's what Christianity is all about. From the day of Jesus' baptism, when God called him his beloved Son, his disciples have proclaimed him to be the fulfillment of that promise.[16]

The promise of a son to Abraham is ultimately fulfilled in Jesus Christ. Christianity centers on that fulfilled promise. The covenant of the LORD with Israel (the engagement) has its ultimate goal and consummation in the covenant of God with the church (marriage). The meaning and relevance of this promise for Israel disappeared completely.

---

16. Vitrano 1988, pp. 97-98.

## 4.6. Evaluation

The "promise and fulfillment" model has a long history and still has wide-spread use in the practice of preaching on every continent.[17] For an evaluation of this model we have to take our point of departure in the Old Testament's way of speaking about promise and fulfillment.[18] God is for sure a promising God. The very heart and kernel of all those promises is given with the Name of God: I am who I am (Exod. 3:14). This name is the "Mystery-at-the Heart-of-All-Things."[19] This Name is ineffable and promises intimacy at the same time. The concrete history is under the tension of this promise. The kernel of this promise is the Name of God, and this name has, so to speak, so much power in itself that it is not exhausted when it fulfills itself at a particular moment in history. There is always a surplus in the promise left over, awaiting and longing for future fulfillments, i.e., actualizations of this wondrous name. The tangibility of Canaan belongs for sure to the Promised Land, but the promise of land has more in mind than the tangible Canaan. The surplus has to do with the intimacy of the covenantal relation between the LORD and Israel that can be practiced in the land.[20]

From that point of view we can make some evaluative observations. One of the attractive features of this model is that it offers preachers the possibility of emphasizing the strength of God's words. Sermons woven on this hermeneutical model make clear that God's promises don't return empty to the LORD, but accomplish their intended purposes (Isa. 55:10-11). This hermeneutical key reads the lips of God and takes seriously what can be read on those lips. It stresses the abiding and steadfast loyalty of the LORD's Word and words.

However, we also have to make some critical observations.

- First of all, we have to state that the richness of the witnesses of Moses and the prophets cannot be summarized under the heading of "promise." This is even truer when "promise" is understood as a pre-

17. Oeming states "daß der 'Weissagungsbeweis' immer noch der in der Praxis am meisten verbreitete hermeneutische Schlüssel zum Alten Testament ist." This is true for both the practice of preaching and scholarly commentaries (Oeming 1985, p. 84).

18. For this line of thought see Zimmerli 1963, pp. 89-122.

19. The expression is from Soulen 2000, p. 167.

20. Zimmerli 1963, pp. 92-93.

diction. We can also find laws, poems, prayers, and stories that are not promises.

- Second, we have to take notice of the fact that many Old Testament promises find their fulfillment already within the books of Moses and the prophets.
- Third, a lot of Old Testament texts quoted in the New Testament are in fact not prophecies at all, let alone predictions. They are statements or even prayers, but not promises.
- Fourth, the New Testament as a whole cannot be classified under the heading of "fulfillment." There is also "promise" in the proclamation of the New Testament. The book of Revelation, for example, ends explicitly with the dream of a new heaven and a new earth.

The pair of words "promise and fulfillment" is certainly part of God's covenantal relation with Israel and the nations. But this pair of words is not sufficient to describe fully and adequately the relation between Old and New Testaments. We also have to say that it is not possible to sum up everything in the relationship between the Old Testament and Christ under the single idea of this pair of words.[21] As fundamental and fruitful as this hermeneutical model is, it cannot by itself describe the multiplex nature of the relationship between the two Testaments. It doesn't catch the richness and multicolored character of either of the Testaments.

We also have to take account of the fact that not all the Old Testament promises have to do with the coming of the Messiah. The Old Testament does not present a single or elaborated "messianology."[22] In quoting the Old Testament, apostles and evangelists use allusions, more or less vague echoes, not elaborated and well-thought-out systems of predictions referring to "the" or "a" coming Messiah.[23] We hear (among others) about the coming of God (Ps. 98), about a pilgrimage of the nations to Jerusalem (Isa. 2:1-5), and about the consummation of creation (Isa. 65:17-25).

The expression "promise" is, in general ecclesial practice, usually understood as "prediction" despite the careful formulations of the adherents of this hermeneutical model in scholarly publications. This meaning can

21. Westermann 1970, p. 78.

22. Marquardt 1990, p. 66.

23. "Um etwas anderes als christologische *Assoziationen* kann es sich in der Hebräische Bibel und in anderen Texten der jüdischen Überlieferungen nicht handeln" (Marquardt 1990, pp. 65-66).

be found already in early pietistic breviaries. The pair of words "promise and fulfillment" has thus the notion of "a confirmation of the Book of Books"[24] from the time of classical apologetic treatments and onwards. This model has also found, in that tone and mood, a widespread use in children's Bibles (the influence of Bibles for children on the-implicit-theology in congregations can hardly be overestimated). When sermons use this hermeneutical key they give the impression "that the Hebrew writers had preview videotapes of Jesus Christ playing on the screens of their minds as they penned their foretelling."[25] The expressions "promise and fulfillment" are, however, not to be understood as a prediction coming through but as vows of loyalty held up. When a man and a woman promise each other to be there for each other for better and worse, in sickness and in health, they don't predict the future. They make a promise to be loyal and faithful to their vow of loyalty.

And it is either the consequence or the presupposition of this hermeneutical key that Moses and the prophets must have had a poor or insufficient understanding of their own words. But prophets were honest and passionate preachers, called by God to proclaim justice and righteousness and to call for faith and repentance in their own particular situation and context. In the model of "promise and fulfillment," however, their role is restricted to being predictors of Jesus. This hermeneutical model leads in fact to a depreciation of God's actual way with Israel in the course of history. Fredrick C. Holmgren shares this comment.

> Traditionally the church has viewed the relationship of the Old Testament to the New Testament to be one of promise and fulfillment. Recently, however, evangelical and mainline scholars have cautioned against a rigid application of this formula because it undercuts the integrity of the earlier scripture. Further, they point out that early Christians did not discover Jesus as a result of an initial study of the Old Testament. Rather the movement was in the opposite direction; that is,

24. That is the subtitle of a famous and notorious book by Werner Keller (1956). The title of a later version of this translation is *The Bible as History: Archaeologists Show the Truth of the Old Testament*. The original German edition was called *Die Bible hat doch recht* (trans.: The Bible is still correct) and was released in 1964. There are quite a few websites inspired by his thoughts. See, e.g., the site of the *Christian Apologetics and Research Ministry* (carm.org) with links to a lot of related sites.

25. Allen/Holbert 1995, p. 27.

from their "meeting" with Jesus Christians looked back to the Old Testament, their scripture, in order to gain understanding of what took place. . . . Christians "knew" by experience who Jesus was, but they needed the words and imagery of the scripture . . . to articulate this "knowing."[26]

Holmgren calls this a "believer's exegesis" or a "look-back exegesis" of a kind often practiced by rabbis using *midrash* and by the Qumran community.

In the hermeneutical model under discussion, fulfillment is, however, not the confirmation but in fact the end of the promise. The consequence for the practice of preaching is that the Old Testament has only preliminary value. There is a difference in specific gravity of Old and New Testaments: the New Testament is "heavier" or "thicker" in authority. The gravity of the value and authority of the Old Testament for both Israel and the church is so "light" that it actually evaporates.

In the practice of preaching, the words of the Old Testament keep bouncing between the Old Testament context and Jesus Christ;[27] the listener is just a spectator at the sideline.[28] The Old Testament offers us information that we know far better since the time of Jesus. Reading the Old Testament in a Christian context can be compared with reading a detective story while knowing in advance the answer to the question, "Who done it?" When the preacher tells the congregation only what they know already, the response will be a disinterested "So, what?"[29] Preaching is, however, called to answer precisely that question.[30]

---

26. Holmgren 1999, p. 13.
27. Engemann 2002, p. 284.
28. Baumgärtel 1952, p. 138.
29. Gunneweg 1978, p. 216; see Preuß 1984, p. 128.
30. Long 2004, pp. 152-53.

# 5. Salvation History

## 5.1. D-Day and V-Day

Movies like *The Longest Day* and *Saving Private Ryan* portray the events on and right after June 6th, 1944, the day of the invasion of Normandy by the allied forces. When we look back, we can say that this day was a decisive day and the battles on that day were key battles. It was *Decision-Day*, shortened to *D-Day*. Indeed, the war wasn't yet won; the invasion wasn't *Victory-Day*. But the invasion was clearly "the beginning of the end." And even though there were severe battles and deprivations ahead, the Allies had hit the German army and the German morale decisively. It would be therefore only a matter of time before the Nazi regime would be dismantled definitively.

From the other side we have to say that this day did not appear out of the blue. A lot of preparations were made in advance. The movies mentioned above give us an impression of the efforts of the Allied forces before D-Day. The German New Testament scholar Oscar Cullmann used this image to portray the essence of the salvation-historical approach and the meaning of Jesus Christ in God's way through history with humankind.[1] A sermon by Dale Rosenberg shows that this image found its way into the practice of preaching. The sermon was delivered on Easter 2003.

> In every war — including God's war against evil and death — there is a decisive battle that determines the outcome of the war. After this battle, there is no question as to what the future holds. That key battle establishes the victory. In the Civil War, it was Gettysburg. In the Napo-

1. Cullmann introduced this illustration (1964 and 1967).

leonic Wars, it was Waterloo. In WW II, it was Normandy. After Normandy, we knew what the outcome of the war would be. That beachhead allowed troops and arms to stream into the continent, and the fate of the Nazi army was then sealed.

It should be noted, however, that more Americans perished in battles following Normandy than died prior to it. Decisive victories do not always spell a quick end to the suffering and dying. D-Day and V-Day are almost never the same day. But through Good Friday and Easter, God wipes away all doubts about where history is headed and how it will end. Yes, suffering, pain, and death persist. Yes, the struggle continues. But the final overthrow of evil is inevitable. Life is stronger than death. Love is stronger than hatred. This is our hope. Christ is risen! Jesus is risen indeed! Alleluia! Like the women, we discover this truth together. Joy has risen where it vanished. Death is swallowed up in victory. Today we celebrate Easter victory against the day when its dimensions will be fully established.[2]

After a lot of preparations in Old Testament times, Jesus Christ invaded our world decisively being God's beachhead. Easter is God's *D-Day*. After this invasion, after the battle on the cross, and after the victory on Easter morning, there is no question as to what the future holds.

The origins of the salvation-historical approach go as far back in history as church-father Irenaeus (died about 200). The influence of the redemptive-historical approach on the development of theology has been and still is considerable, though with great variation and in ever-new forms. The concept developed itself into a seminal source for the disciplines of systematic theology, Old, and New Testament.[3]

## 5.2. God's Economy of Salvation

Moses and the prophets witness that the God of Israel travels a path with a particular nation in the concreteness of history. God's words and deeds on

2. Rosenberger 2003.

3. G. E. Wright 1952, Von Rad 2001a/b (Old Testament), Ladd 1974, Dodd 1928, Cullmann 1964/1967 (New Testament), and Pannenberg 1959 (systematic theology) were (among others) advocates of this paradigm. There are substantial differences between these concepts so that we cannot speak of "the" salvation-historical movement (see Baker 1991, pp. 145-78).

this path are connected with each other by a "golden thread." This coherence of God's words and deeds is called "economy (or history) of salvation."[4] God unfolds step by step the plan that existed even before the foundation of the world (Matt. 13:35; 25:34). Every next step of God in the path of history is a decisive step further on the way to the ultimate goal: the redemption and consummation of creation. We can also say that God is spinning a thread of salvation and redemption through the jungle of history. "In spite of switchbacks, stops, and starts, it progresses steadily to its ultimate goal."[5] The German Old Testament scholar Walther Zimmerli uses the image of a brook.

> When we survey the entire Old Testament, we find ourselves involved in a great history of movement from promise to fulfillment. It flows like a large brook — here rushing swiftly, there apparently coming to rest in a quiet backwater, and yet moving forwards as a whole toward a distant goal which lies beyond itself.[6]

Scripture is not to be regarded primarily as a collection of proof-texts or as a container filled with doctrines but as a witness to the LORD's redemptive steps in history. The Bible offers us the record of a linear saving history. It is the goal of the triune God to redeem humanity. Each event, person, and institution has its place in the scheme of this redemptive history.

The history of salvation between creation and consummation is marked by some decisive moments, the so-called *kairoi*. These special moments are characterized by "progressive reduction,"[7] which means a progressive process of representation with a decreasing number of persons. God starts with humanity as a whole (Gen. 1–11). When it became clear that they have failed to effectuate God's purposes, God chose one nation, i.e., Israel, as his covenant partner (Gen. 12:1-3). This nation is called to be a light for all the nations.

The blessing given to Abraham is meant to be stretched out to all the families of the earth (Gen. 12:1-3). God had chosen Israel to be an exclusive society, uncorrupted by heathen influences. This election was not

---

4. Greidanus 1970, pp. 122-25.

5. Greidanus 1999, p. 236.

6. Zimmerli 1963, p. 111.

7. Greidanus speaks of "redemptive-historical progression" (Greidanus 1999, pp. 203, 237-38).

grounded upon any merit of the chosen people but founded solely in the sovereign and gracious will of God. Israel was called to spread and share this calling with every nation.

When it became clear that Israel failed, it went in exile to Babylon in the sixth century BCE. But that disaster was not the last word. God went on, be it with even a smaller group, a "remnant" (Isa. 10:20-22; Jer. 23:3) or "righteous branch" (Jer. 23:5; 33:15; Zech. 3:8; 6:12). This remnant or branch is meant to be the representative of Israel and has to fulfill its calling. When this remnant also failed, there was only one option left: the coming of the suffering servant of the LORD (Isa. 42:1-7; 49:1-7; 50:4-11; 52:13–53:12). Hence, God sent the beloved Son (Mark 12:6). He will save the world and bring salvation in a way that God had always had in mind.

A sermon by Andrew Clark on Matthew 12:1-28 and Isaiah 42:1-4 can serve as illustration of the homiletical elaboration of this theological paradigm. The preacher points first to the meaning of these words in the context of Israel. In a following step, these words are "ultimately perfected in the person of Jesus." The title of the sermon is "Servants of God: Pattern for Living."

> The wonderful book of Isaiah was written some 600 or more years before the time of Jesus, yet in chapters 40–55, we have what are called the servant songs: songs about the Servant of God. Who is the servant? Well, it refers to three people.
>
> Firstly, the people of Israel, who, of course, didn't match up to all God had expected. The songs are a picture of what Israel should have been.
>
> Because Israel failed to be the servant of God, secondly and ultimately, the words are perfected in the person of Jesus. You can read the chapters 40–55 through and it is as if you are reading one of the gospel accounts of Jesus' life even though it was written so long before he walked on earth as the Servant and Son of God.[8]

The various lines of the witnesses of the Old Testament converge toward Jesus Christ, the Word made flesh. The various lines of the witnesses of apostles and evangelists radiate from him.[9] From this One, the lines widen again in history, starting with a small group of disciples and supporters but

8. Clark 2001.
9. L. Berkhof 1950, p. 142.

gradually growing to a movement that stretches itself out to the end of the earth and the end of the age (Matt. 28:19f.; Luke 24:47). To Christ there is a way of gradual reduction, from him a way of ongoing expansion.[10] God's original plan to save the world comes finally through.

Thus, Scripture doesn't offer us a set of metaphysical or ethical principles, no eternal truths in the image of earthly stories. The salvation-historical approach reads the Scriptures as witnesses of a living relation between a specific God (= the LORD), and a particular people (= Israel) with the purpose being the salvation of the whole world. The revealing acts of God cut a trail of redemption through history from creation to consummation.[11] Christ is the core and center of God's acts on behalf of salvation for humans and the world. That means that Christ is the center of God's redemptive economy. He is the center and frame of reference of this redemptive history. The period of the Old Testament gets meaning in retrospect and in relation to this center.[12]

## 5.3. Jesus Christ, the Midst of History

Our ordinary life is not too banal for God. It is exactly ordinary life that God wants to save. This salvific intention is the dynamic source of all God's words and acts in the process of history. This speaking and acting has its culmination in Jesus Christ (John 1:14; Heb. 1:1, 2). We can discern redemptive marks of the LORD in the history of Israel. When we look back from Christ to the previous history, we can discern footprints of the LORD that led to the coming of Christ. The history of salvation centers on him as the kernel of history. Therefore we can say that Christ is salvation history in person, and salvation history has Christ as its content.

The interpretation of every particular story, poem, or text must be done within this theological and hermeneutical paradigm, i.e., the ongoing process of redemption in history. Every moment in this history is correlated to and gets its meaning from the dynamics of this history. Every

10. See Greidanus 1999, pp. 191-95.
11. H. Berkhof 1986, p. 69.
12. Irenaeus stated that the Old Testament texts themselves speak of hidden truth that must be unlocked. Jews are reading them but do not have the explanation. The coming of Christ is supposed to be the hermeneutical key that unlocks all the mysteries of God's *oikonomia* from beginning to end (Froehlich 1984, pp. 13-14).

text must be interpreted in the light of its center, i.e., Jesus Christ. "(T)he way of redemptive-historical progression sees every Old Testament text and its addressees in the context of God's dynamic history, which progresses steadily and reaches its climax in the life, death, and resurrection of Jesus Christ and ultimately in the new creation."[13]

We can see in the Old Testament the book that records the preparation for God's *D-Day*. The way this works out in the practice of preaching can be illustrated by means of a sermon by Tammy Garrison on Exodus 2.

> Moses was saved and was a part of God's mighty plan of deliverance. One day, he would lead the Hebrew people up out of slavery in Egypt to freedom and prosperity in the land of God's promises.
>
> One day, from those people, another child would be born. He would live and teach love, forgiveness, sacrifice, and service. He would die on the cross for our sins, our decree of death, to pay our price. He would rise from the dead to live again, to make us his adopted brothers and sisters in the family of God, to give us a home in heaven with him.[14]

The idea of progress in revelation has as consequence for preaching that the Old Testament can only get a role as introduction or preparation for the ultimate salvation in Christ. Every sermon must lead to the proclamation of Christ. He is and must be the object and content of every sermon. That is the main idea of the hermeneutical concept of the so-called "Christocentric salvation-historical preaching." Christ reveals God's ultimate salvation. The Old Testament is the preparation for or prelude to this salvation. The mighty acts of God, the *magnalia Dei,* are in fact *magnalia Christi,* mighty acts of Christ. A sermon by Jason Cole on the fourth song of the Servant of the LORD (Isa. 52:13–53:13) makes this paradigm explicit.

> God had worked in His perfect plan to slowly show people what was to come through Jesus. The sacrificial system of the Old Testament previewed what was to come through Jesus. God worked it out so that he taught the people that the shedding of blood was needed for the forgiveness of sins. God instituted the sacrificial lamb, which would become a foreshadowing of Jesus the Lamb of God. God required that

13. Greidanus 1999, p. 237.
14. Garrison 2001.

the people offer a spotless lamb as a sacrifice so their sins could be forgiven. This all was to foreshadow that there was one day going to come a sacrifice once and for all. The Old Testament law and the sacrifices that were offered in the Temple were still powerless to save man.[15]

## 5.4. Salvation Is Nearer to Us Now

A sermon built on the foundation of the salvation-historical paradigm makes clear in what way a particular story fits into and is part of the overarching redemptive plan and purpose of God. This plan looks forward and runs to Jesus Christ. "Since Old Testament redemptive history progresses to its center of God's climactic acts in Christ, Christian preachers need only locate their preaching-text in the sweep of redemptive history to sense its movement to Christ."[16]

The way salvation-historical sermons treat the Old Testament looks like a visit to a museum. The preacher has the role of guide who tells the visitors the former function of the exhibited artifacts. The Old Testament is seen as a passed station. The ultimate salvation is proclaimed by apostles and evangelists. That can be illustrated by way of a sermon by Bruce McDowell on Genesis 21:1-27.

> Abraham and Sarah learned much about God from the birth of Isaac. They rejoiced in that. But we have reason to rejoice even more, for we see in the birth of Isaac a foreshadowing of the birth of Jesus, the Savior of the world. Isaac was a type of Christ. Abraham's whole life was in preparation for the line in which the Messiah would come. If we look at the details of Isaac's birth at first glance it is only of passing curiosity. But when we see them in light of their relation to the birth of Christ, we see their surpassing importance. In Isaac's birth we have the first stage of the fulfillment of promised blessing that would come to all nations through Abraham's seed, which is Christ.[17]

A sermon confronts the listeners with a history that is caught up by Jesus Christ. Sermons using the salvation-historical paradigm tend to be more

15. Cole 2004.
16. Greidanus 1999, pp. 237-38.
17. McDowell, no date.

objective and less existential. They are absorbed by sometimes lengthy explanations of biblical events. For the listener is only left a role as spectator. The redemptive-historical model has some difficulty in making clear in what way the listeners take part in the event of the text. Usually the characters in the text become examples for individual piety or behavior. The moral lesson of sermons is usually: try to be a David, Moses, Esther, etc. That can be illustrated by way of a sermon on Ruth 1:18–2:12 by Robin Langdon.

> When we are in a dark time is exactly when we need to come take refuge under God's wings because God is truly the one who will be a refuge for us during the tough times. And guess what? He also wants to use each one of us to be His lifeline of refuge for another person.
>
> Have you ever had a time when someone else's problem or pain just came to your mind? That was God encouraging you to be a Boaz. Have you ever noticed a person on our church lanai who was really hurting, despite what they said outwardly? That was God encouraging you to be a Ruth. God wants us to experience His love not only in the dark times, but also in partnering with Him to be the lifeline for someone else. Many of you are already doing that for each other and it has been life changing for many of us — not the least of all for me. (. . .)
>
> Keep grabbing those people and say to them, "Where you go, I will go. I will love on you, even when you feel like God has left you. And we will both see that God is holding onto us together."[18]

The listener is admonished "to be a Ruth."

## 5.5. The Church in the Place of Israel

The basic theological presupposition is that God's salvific plan culminating in Christ (see Eph. 1:3-14) is a unity, but that it is realized progressively over the course of time. Salvation history is built on the assumption of an irreversible progress of God's words and acts in history. The structure of God's acts and words contains a pattern of advancing salvation, also called "progressive recurrence." In a Bible Study Course Lesson on the theme "What Is the Church?" Mike Bennett and Peter Eddington make the following observation.

18. Langdon 2002.

The Israelites didn't have the heart needed to fully accomplish God's will (Deuteronomy 5:29). They resisted the Holy Spirit, as does all of mankind without the special calling of God. But God has a plan to make a *new heart* available to us all and to write His laws in our minds. With the coming of the promised Messiah, Jesus of Nazareth, the stage was set for a new phase in God's plan of salvation. This phase involves God working through a group of people — the Church — who are spiritually transformed by the Holy Spirit. God chooses them not only to receive salvation for themselves, but to carry out His work for the ultimate benefit of all humanity.[19]

God makes progressive steps forward in history. The ultimate goal of these steps is the definitive realization of redemption. That history started with humanity as a whole (Gen. 1–11), runs along the station of Israel and the "rest." None of these can meet God's expectations. It is the only begotten Son who fulfills the call. From Christ, the lines widen "to the end of the age" (Matt. 28:20). Because Israel failed in her calling,[20] the church takes over the role of Israel in the post-Pentecostal era. From that moment on, the church is called to be "a light for the nations." Israel is a people and a nation "like other nations" (1 Sam. 8:5) and has no special role anymore in God's history of redemption. A sermon by Mark Stephenson makes this explicit.

> Jesus picked the sign of baptism to replace circumcision. Jesus invented a new feast to replace an extremely important part of observing the law for the Jews. Jesus created what we call the Lord's Supper to replace the Old Testament Passover. The Passover was a symbol of God's deliverance of his people from the oppression of slavery. The Lord's Supper is a symbol of God's deliverance of his people from the oppression of sin.[21]

19. Bennett/Eddington 2000.
20. "(W)hat faith means as the way of salvation is wholly understood only by those who know the false way of salvation which we find in the law. . . . In the same way faith requires the backward glance into Old Testament history as a history of failure, and so of promise, in order to know that the situation of the justified man arises only on the basis of this miscarriage" (Bultmann 1963, pp. 74-75). Those words were first written in 1949, and they sound as if nothing had happened in the previous years!
21. Stephenson 2001.

The three-times repeated "replace" doesn't leave any room for doubt about the place and role of the Old Testament in the Christian church: it is old indeed. Preachers who use this hermeneutical model portray the Old Testament characters, institutions, and events as steps in the way to the ultimate goal or as symbols that are replaced by the new order of Jesus Christ. God's way with Israel and the redemptive acts along that way are in fact bracketed out as irrelevant for the contemporary congregation. There is no theological room left for God's way with Israel because this people has been replaced by the church. Sermons jump directly from creation and the fall to redemption in Christ. An example is the structure of the Apostles' Creed. This confession leaps immediately from the creation to Jesus Christ. There is no room in this confession for God's way with Israel. Textbooks on systematic theology often proceed from the doctrine of sin to Christology and soteriology. There is hardly any room and interest for the meaning of the covenant between the LORD and the firstborn son of this God (Exod. 4:22). This fuels the impression that after a long period of divine inactivity, Jesus drops down out of heaven (so to speak, as a "bat out of hell"!). The LORD's centuries-long way with Israel has no theological significance.[22]

It is clear that there is no abiding role for Israel in this concept. Its role in (salvation) history is restricted to be the "supplier" of the Messiah. Once the Messiah is born, the role of Israel and the Jews is over. From that moment on, the church takes over the torch, and the Old Testament "we" and "us" no longer refer to Israel but to the church.[23]

God chose the Jewish people after the fall of Adam in order to prepare the world for the coming of Jesus Christ, the Savior. After Christ came, however, the special role of the Jewish people came to an end and its place was taken by the church, the new Israel.[24]

In this concept Jesus is brought as it were "beyond the gates of Jerusalem" (Jer. 22:19) and is in fact no longer a Jew and a member of the people of Israel; he becomes the first Christian. There is no confessing room for Israel and God's acts on behalf of his first covenant partner.[25] The ultimate salvation is founded not in the Old Testament text but in the New Testament witness of Jesus Christ. We could say that after creation God

22. H. Berkhof 1986, pp. 225-26.
23. Schöttler 2001, pp. 373-78.
24. Soulen 1996, pp. 1-2.
25. Marquardt 2003, pp. 278-79.

disappeared for a while behind the curtains to appear again in Jesus of Nazareth.[26]

## 5.6. Evaluation

The salvation-historical hermeneutical strategy adopts a kind of "standard canonical framework"[27] with four stages of history. We can also say that the paradigm sees a drama or meta-narrative in Scripture consisting of four successive acts.[28]

- God creates the world and humanity.
- Humanity disobeys and falls, through the sin of Adam and Eve.
- Christ redeems lost humanity.
- God brings the final redemption and consummation of the world at the end of time.

When this meta-narrative or framework determines the theology of a sermon, we can discern both strengths and weaknesses in the homiletical dimensions.

a. Salvation history stresses the progress of God's salvific acts on behalf of humankind and creation in the course of history. That is certainly a strong element in this hermeneutical model. The LORD remains faithful to spoken words and promises given. Not a single word of these promises will remain empty or in vain. The foundation of this concept is the promising God: humankind is not heading for an empty future but for the consummation of creation and history. The promises of the LORD are the overarching principle of all the different texts, be it poems, stories, laws, or visions. Scripture is not a loose sum of independent texts but a coherent whole with Christ as its center. Scripture is the story of the LORD, the God who started the "rescue-plan" right after the fall and will accomplish this plan for salvation. This theological strength has, however, at least four homiletical Achilles' heels.

---

26. H. Berkhof 1986, pp. 221-22. Berkhof portrays the history of Israel before Jesus as an unproductive and unfruitful "experimental garden" (1986, pp. 248-53).

27. See Soulen 2000.

28. N. T. Wright 1992.

- The precondition that human history shows an ongoing progression is in the first place not free from evolutionistic tendencies, influenced by either historicism or romanticism. The experiences in the concreteness of history make clear that an ongoing progression is not evident.
- The second weakness has to do with the "one-way traffic" between Old and New Testaments. Generally speaking, most sermons make a hermeneutical movement forward in history, either a movement within the Old Testament or a movement in the relation between Old and New Testaments. The treatment of the subsequent links in the chain of light not only gets a certain order in the construction of the sermon but because of that order also an order of merit: the last step discussed is the most important step. The result of this model in the practice of preaching is often a sermon using an exclusive New Testament theology with some preliminary remarks from the Old Testament.[29]
- A third weak element is the strange position of Israel. This model stresses on the one hand the concrete steps of the LORD with Israel in history to give shape to his salvation. But actual sermons on the other hand don't pay attention to the theological significance of God's loyalty to Israel in Old Testament times and God's abiding faithfulness to the covenant with the firstborn son (Exod. 4:22). Both Old and New Testaments point to the historical Israel as the place where God's footsteps can be discerned. Sometimes it is even added explicitly that Israel forfeited this role as an elect nation because they didn't accept Jesus as the Messiah. The witness of Jesus Christ absorbs the Old Testament.
- Noticeably missing from this rehearsal of the Christian sacred story is any mention of the way of the LORD with Israel. "In this view, the Jews and their story are irrelevant to the story of the new true Israel, Christianity."[30]

b. Another strong element has to do with the sermon-structure. Sermons woven on the pattern of salvation-history have a clear structure. But this strength also has its Achilles' heels.

29. Childs 1992, p. 17.
30. Sandmel 2000, p. 165.

- The risk of schematism is surely present when this paradigm determines the construction of most of a preacher's sermons. The text runs the risk of disappearing behind the salvation-historical scheme, and the contents of the sermon will be highly predictable. Listeners who become acquainted with this hermeneutical model can foretell to a certain extent the line of thought and even the content of a particular sermon once they have heard the first lines.
- The application of salvation-historical sermons runs the risk of expressing itself in general terms, with a lack of relevance for the particular context of the listeners. Those sermons have themes like "God's faithfulness," "God's winning grace," or "the victory of God's kingdom."[31]

c. A third strong element of this hermeneutical paradigm is the attention for the "fact-ness" of the proclamation of the Old Testament. God's acts do not only exist as a "myth," but the stories, laws, and even the poems refer to God's concrete actions in the actuality of history. But we have to say again that there are risks involved.

- This attention for the "fact-ness" runs the risk of offering nothing more than (just) retelling the facts of the text.[32] Preaching runs the risk of becoming a visit to a museum exhibiting interesting but irrelevant ancient artifacts.
- The application for the listeners runs the risk of being stuck in a kind of recurrence of a fixed homiletical refrain about God's loyalty and faithfulness, celebrated on the major Christian feasts: the same God who acts in this text became human on Christmas, was crucified on Good Friday, was raised on Easter-morning, and ascended to heaven on Ascension Day. This God, in and through his Spirit, has been with us since Pentecost. This line of thought can be illustrated by means of a sermon by Alan Jackson on Genesis 11:1-9, the story of the Tower of Babel.

I'll tell you what it means. The Bible tells us that once, long ago, God intervened to confound the speech of arrogant empire-builders. But it

31. Fasol 1992, p. 225.
32. Childs 1992, p. 17.

also tells us that, at just the right time, God intervened once more. But this time it was to break down every language barrier. At Babel, God graciously intervened to put a stop to an enterprise that had become evil. At Pentecost, God graciously intervened again; but this time to give birth to a new enterprise that would one day draw all people together.

But we're not there yet, are we? You and I live in a world that is, at best, confused, bewildered, and divided. God has given us the image of the tower of Babel as a prodding reminder to all of us of our inclination to arrogance. But he has also given us his Son, Jesus who lived for us, who died for us, who rose again for us, and who prays for us. He has given us his Holy Spirit who can break through our confusion and self-will and draw us together in Christ. And he has given us this table as a blessed reminder that in him, and in him alone, shall true hearts everywhere their high communion find.[33]

Because of the continuity of God's words and acts, listeners can count on the same words and acts. Sermons woven on the pattern of salvation history therefore run the risk of churning out an enumeration of inner-biblical phenomena.[34] The listener becomes a spectator of an event from the past and is not invited to become a participant in the movement and dynamics of the text.

33. Jackson 2000.
34. The expression is from Preuß 1984.

# 6. Karl Barth

## 6.1. A Modern Church Father

The Swiss theologian Karl Barth (1886-1968) dominated theological discourse in the twentieth century. His heritage is still influential and important at the beginning of the twenty-first century. The huge volumes of his *Church Dogmatics* remain an impressive monument in the landscape of theology.

Barth was ordained as pastor in Safenwil, a small village in north-central Switzerland, on the 9th of July 1911. His first congregation was a community of farmers and laborers. Barth practiced intensively every dimension of working in the parish, but he considered preaching as his most important task. He preached almost every Sunday in Safenwil in the years between 1911 and 1921. That means that he wrote about 500 sermons in those years. That wasn't always an easy task. It happened more than once that he finished the preparation of the sermon only on Sunday morning.

He left Safenwil in 1921, after being appointed as professor for Reformed theology at the theological faculty of the Georg August University in Göttingen. After his appointment, he kept preaching, but substantially less than he had as a local pastor. He only preached once in a while. We can discern two periods in his preaching activities after 1921. The first period is between 1921 and 1948. After that, a "moratorium" or "break" followed.[1] When he started preaching again in 1954, the only congregation for whom Barth would preach was the inmates of the Basel prison. A friend observed

---

1. Hermelink 1987, p. 453; Denecke 1989.

that some people even toyed with the thought of committing a crime in Basel in order to have an opportunity to hear Barth preach!

Preaching lies at the heart of his whole personal and theological existence.[2] Barth himself says that even his *Church Dogmatics* can be read as a sermon.[3] Therefore we can say that Barth was not "also" a preacher; rather, he is primarily a homiletician.

## 6.2. Liberal Theology of the Nineteenth Century

*Progress in History*

As was very common in the German-speaking academic world at that time, Barth moved as a student from university to university to listen to lectures given by various eminent professors such as Adolf Harnack at Berlin (1906-1907) and Wilhelm Herrmann at Marburg (1908-1909). During his college and seminary years, he became deeply engaged with so-called "liberal theology." "Liberal" here has the meaning of "free": free from creedal, dogmatic, and ecclesial authorities. As a result, liberal theology did, for example, not speak in confessional or systematic theological terms about Jesus, who was portrayed as a human being, filled with the Spirit of God and as a teacher of the kingdom of God.[4]

Despite all wars, natural disasters, and other horrors that people experienced, there was a sense of optimism among the adherents of liberal theology. They believed that history was developing in an ongoing process of progress. They believed that man, with his "enlightened reason," would sooner or later be able to control the chaos of history more and more. This character of "liberal theology" was heavily influenced by the European Enlightenment. The key term of that movement is the notion of progress, the sense that all experience is future-directed, with the specific, calculated purpose of improving or bettering the world, society, and the individual. The congress of Vienna in 1814 marked the beginning of "a grand peace" in Europe. It was the beginning of a period of enormous cultural development

---

2. Busch 1994, p. 61; Genest 1995, p. 136.

3. *CD* I/1, pp. 47f., 80; II/2, p. 323; IV/3-2, pp. 802f., 876ff., 879ff.; see also Denecke 1989, p. 185.

4. *GA* I/8 (Predigten 1913), p. 147.

and fostered a climate of confidence that everything human was possible. Significant advances in technology, science, and medicine during the nineteenth century fueled this optimistic thinking. History became understood as the gradual but inevitable march of human achievement and civilization.

Within this cultural paradigm, the church expected the coming of the kingdom of God as a gradually increasing and developing process, along the way of ongoing evolution and human efforts. God was not so much a transcendent Being but more Someone (or Something) intertwined with the development of history and culture.[5] The increasing influence of God's Spirit would thus cause the ultimate victory over the animal nature of humankind.[6]

Echoes of this theology can be heard loud and clear in Barth's sermons from the first years in his parish.[7] That can be illustrated from a sermon on Isaiah 65:17-25, preached on the first Sunday of Advent 1913. Barth states that the congregation awaits today the coming of God's kingdom, just as the first Christians did.

> We don't have to grope or to guess about the future like the patriarchs of Israel. We know for sure where God's ways will lead us. Jesus has shown and opened that way. We don't need to doubt anymore or be insecure, as they did, whether such a future is possible. The life and death of Jesus gives us the assurance that God's Kingdom has its place already on this earth. These are our Christian Advent-thoughts: sure and well founded hope for the best that has begun in Jesus Christ and will be consummated through his Spirit.[8]

In 1913, when the European political scene is already nervous and full of unrest, Barth is still a dedicated and convinced liberal theologian. He is confident that the positive powers in history and culture can meet the evil powers of war and destruction. God's Spirit will continue to weave a golden thread of progress through the carpet of sin and deviation.[9] That golden thread is the gospel of love for God and the neighbor.[10]

---

5. For this *Kulturprotestantismus* see Graf 1990, pp. 230-43; Jacobs 1991, pp. 47-68.
6. *Predigten 1913*, pp. 57, 79, 115, 489.
7. *Predigten 1913*, pp. 57, 79, 115, 489.
8. *Predigten 1913*, pp. 614-29 (my translation). The quotation comes from p. 615.
9. *Predigten 1913*, p. 408.
10. *Predigten 1913*, p. 408.

## The Old Testament in Liberal Theology

Within liberal theological circles, the Old Testament was accorded a place within this optimistic, enlightened, and evolutionary paradigm. This theology saw a constantly and progressing perception of God within the Old Testament. Every step was caught up by the next move in the chain of increasing development. As a result, the Old Testament had no value of its own for preaching. It was the first, but outdated and superseded phase in the development of "God." In fact, the Christian church could say "good-bye" to the first part of the Bible.[11] That meant that the concept of Marcion was back again. From that point of view, it isn't surprising that the German New Testament scholar Adolf von Harnack made the following statement in his study *Marcion: The Gospel of the Alien God* in 1921.

> To reject the Old Testament in the second century was an error which the great Church rightly rejected; to retain it in the sixteenth century was a fate which the Reformation was still unable to escape; but to preserve it during the nineteenth century and beyond as a canonical document for Protestantism is the result of religious and churchly paralysis.[12]

The vision of the place and the role of the Old Testament as articulated in this illustration is widely present in Germany in the first half of the twentieth century. In close connection to this evolutionary vision of the course of history, German liberal theologians cherished the opinion that God had a special role for the German people. The outbreak of the First World War was also seen and interpreted in that perspective. This perspective caused a strange and absurd interpretation of Scripture in preaching. Emanuel Hirsch, a prominent liberal theologian, made the following statement in a sermon on Genesis 32, the story of Jacob wrestling at Peniel.

> We wrestle with God for ourselves and for our homeland. All the sacrifices of "good and blood" are nothing else than an attempt to force God to make a decision for the sake of us: we won't let you go unless you give us your blessing. Germany may not perish.[13]

11. For that reason, some liberal scholars proposed to replace the Old Testament with another Holy Book or at least expand the Christian Bible with some of those books.

12. The English translation is taken from Watson 1997, p. 43; see also Kraus 1970, p. 268.

13. Velema 1991, p. 27; see also Pressel 1967.

This sermon was preached just before the First World War burst out, giving that war an absurd theological justification.

## The Outbreak of World War I

Barth became more and more alienated from the liberal world of his teachers in the period prior to the outbreak of the First World War. An article in a journal just before the outbreak was the spark that ignited his serious doubts.[14]

> One day in early August 1914 stands in my personal memory as a black day. Ninety-three German intellectuals impressed public opinion by their proclamation in support of the war policy of Wilhelm II and his counselors. Among these intellectuals I discovered to my horror almost all of my theological teachers whom I had greatly venerated. In despair over what this indicated about the signs of the time I suddenly realized that I could not any longer follow either their ethics and dogmatics or their understanding of the Bible and of history. For me at least, 19th-century theology no longer held any future.[15]

Barth's crisis was not only the result of the common human experiences of fear, uncertainty, and threat that belong inevitably to every war. On a deeper level Barth started to reflect theologically on these momentous events. The scope of the devastation and human tragedy led him to the conclusion that nineteenth-century Protestant liberal theology was a mistake of immense proportions. It was a bitter experience of the "twilight of the gods" *(Gottesfinsternis),*[16] when Barth realized that his former teachers had sold their souls to the language of war, terror, and guns in the name of "human progress" and "the kingdom of God." It was clear for Barth that

14. Barth was misrecollecting the date on which he read the manifesto signed by the ninety-three German intellectuals. It was first published October 3rd, 1914. But there can be no question that the appearance of this document had a special significance for Barth in that he found Wilhelm Herrmann's signature on it (McCormack 1995, pp. 112f.).

15. Barth 1978a, p. 14. Kaiser Wilhelm I, at the beginning of World War I, delivered a speech from the balcony of the Schloss in Berlin, calling for national unity: "Political parties are a thing of the past, I recognize only Germans." The speech was written by Barth's former professor Adolf von Harnack.

16. Barth in a letter to Wilhelm Spoendlin (4 January 1915). Cited by Busch 1994, p. 81.

the "ethical failure" of his professors inevitably meant their theological failure. And thus "the whole world of exegesis, ethics, dogmatics, and proclamation that I held thus far as fundamentally trustworthy ( ) was undermined in its foundations."[17] Barth's whole theological stock-in-trade was turned upside down in the autumn of 1914.

To get new and solid ground under his feet, Barth started studying theology again. He was forced to rethink the nature, task, and contents of preaching.[18] The core question was: About what or whom are we talking when we say "God"? This question touches the very kernel of church and theology. Barth faced and experienced the difficulty and speechlessness of every preacher: What was he to preach on the coming Sunday? This struggle can be heard in more than one sermon from that period.

> For every sermon, I am forced to reflect on the use of the word "God." The small sentence "God is!" means nothing less than a revolution. For the sake of God, one may not confuse one's own concern with the concern of the church nor with any other good or necessary activities. And this is always about absolute primacy: *First* God's concern *(Sache),* and *afterwards* our concern. If humans were seriously in line with God, it would mean and cause the liberation of every social need.[19]

Barth's difficulty was not so much a technical or practical question, "*How* to say it?" or "*How* to preach?" The crisis penetrated more deeply. It was the fundamental question: *Can* I — being human — talk about and proclaim God? Barth spoke of his "increasing realization that our preaching is impossible from the start."[20] The question about God itself became problematic. Barth experienced the discovery of this problem, with all the related issues, as a deep and profound turn in his existence and his theologizing.

17. Barth 1968, p. 293.
18. Busch 1994, p. 87.
19. *Predigten 1914*, pp. 365f. Similar utterances can be found in other sermons of 1914 (see also pp. 23, 42, 47, 168, 193, 241). Translation from Busch 1994, p. 78.
20. Busch 1994, p. 90.

## God's Unique and Exclusive Word

For Barth the Bible is not a book about the inward religious consciousness
of the biblical writers and of Jesus himself, as was said by the liberal theologians. Scripture is a book about God, not about the history of people's feelings about God. Barth viewed the *subject matter (die Sache)* of Scripture
not as historical events or the interpretations of those events by the biblical
writers, but as the supra-historical Spirit of God who dwells outside the
bounds of history and human contingencies. This emphasis on the fundamental *discontinuity* between God and humanity (as opposed to liberal-
ism's view of humanity's basic harmony with God via inward religious feeling) became the basis for Barth's new way in theology.

The first major result of this new way was Barth's commentary on
Paul's letter to the Romans, first published in 1919 and substantially revised
in 1921. This second edition became a sensation in the German-speaking
theological world. It was a bombshell that landed on the playground of the
theologians. The work took the general form of a commentary, but it was
really more like a fiery sermon that continued on for more than 500 pages.
Barth criticized the tradition of nineteenth-century liberal theology at its
roots.

> The Gospel is not a religious message to inform mankind of their di-
> vinity or to tell them how they may become divine. The Gospel pro-
> claims a God utterly distinct from men. Salvation comes to them from
> Him, because they are, as men, incapable of knowing Him, and be-
> cause they have no right to claim anything from Him.[21]

For Barth, Scripture uses the word "God" exclusively for the One and
Unique God of Israel, Creator of all that exists and Redeemer who had no
other intention than goodness and salvation for all.[22] Because this God is no
construction or fabrication of man, this God can only be known in an act of
divine self-revelation. And that is what God did and has done in Jesus Christ.
In Christ God shows and proves to be the God-with-us. Therefore Christ is
the true Word and decisive revelation of God. All that we know and all the
church can say or preach about God is therefore completely dependent on
Christ, God's unique and exclusive Word, the very core of the "glad tidings."

21. Barth 1968, p. 28.
22. *CD* IV/1, p. 37.

Barth rejects and renounces every abstract or idealistic understanding of God — as if a human being could formulate beforehand what or who God must be. God is not a particular instance within a class — as if we could fill in the general generic name "god" with words and images from the Old and New Testaments to construct a Christian God. That is a false start for Barth. He wants to interpret the being of God strictly from his revelation in Christ. God's ultimate identity is revealed in Christ: the one who loves in freedom.[23]

## 6.3. Jesus Christ, the Name of God

*There Is Only One and Unique God*

Part of Barth's theological system was a new and fresh description of the relation between the Old and New Testaments.[24] Built on the above-stated theological foundation, one can draw two hermeneutical connections between Old and New Testaments. When we draw the line from Old to New Testament, we can say that God has always been God-with-us, even from before the foundation of the world. From that point of view we have to say that the New Testament brings no new or more important message than the Old Testament. The New Testament proclaims no higher or deeper knowledge. The God who speaks and acts in the Old Testament is the same God as the One who is revealed in Jesus Christ. Both Old and New Testaments give witness to the one and unique God, the LORD of Israel and the One called *Abba* by Jesus Christ. Following this line of thought, Barth could oppose the ideas of Marcion in classic and modern guise. This line of thought also offered Barth the opportunity to strongly oppose the liberal concept of a gradually developing God in the course of history and proclaimed by the teacher Jesus.

This theological foundation makes it possible to draw a second line as well, i.e., from New to Old Testament. Barth insists that the Old Testament proclaims no other God than the One that is present and acts in Jesus Christ. That means that the God of Israel was from eternity the God-with-us, i.e., God-in-the-mode-of-Christ. The way God acted in Christ is the

23. So the title of *CD* II/1, §28.
24. *CD* I/2, §14 (pp. 70-122).

way God acted on behalf of Israel and humanity from eternity. It is this second line that opens up surprising possibilities to preach the Old Testament in a Christian context. That can be illustrated by way of a sermon on Psalm 73:23 ("Nevertheless I am continually with you; you hold my right hand"). This "you" or "thou" is the LORD, God of Israel.

> What kind of a *"thou"* is this? Is it a *man?* Yes indeed, someone with a human face, a human body, human hands and a human language. One whose heart bears sorrows — not simply his own, but the sorrows of the whole world. One who takes our sin and our misery upon himself and away from us. One who is able to do this because he is not only man, but also *God,* the almighty Creator and Lord who knows me and you much better than we know ourselves. He is our neighbor, he is closer to us than we are to ourselves, and we may call him by his first name.
>
> Do you know who he is? The hymn already quoted gives us the answer:
>
>> *Christ Jesus is his name,*
>> *the Lord Sabaoth's Son;*
>> *He, and no other one,*
>> *shall conquer in the battle.*
>
> Brothers and sisters, we are now all invited to talk to him instead of talking to ourselves. We are at liberty to say to him: "Nevertheless I am continually with *thee*."[25]

The hermeneutics of this illustration is surprising and breathtaking. For Barth, the psalm does not portray a *type* of Christ, it does not look ahead to the coming Messiah, and it is not seen as a promise to be fulfilled in Christ. The text doesn't point to Jesus Christ, nor is he the hidden allegorical secret or mystery behind the text. For Barth, the "He" of the Old Testament *is* Jesus Christ. That is a fascinating hermeneutical concept for interpreting the Old Testament in a Christian context. For Barth, Christ is not only the speaking and acting Subject of the New Testament but also of the Old Testament![26]

25. *Deliverance to the Captives,* pp. 16/17.
26. God's "word in all words is His Word" (*CD* III/1, p. 24). "Understanding the text as everywhere and throughout witness to Jesus Christ is the single most important assumption undergirding Barth's reading of the plain sense of Scripture" (Greene-McCreight 1999, p. 174).

The first word of God is Christ. That word existed from eternity and became flesh in Jesus of Nazareth. The deepest essence and being of God is revealed in Christ: a God of humans, a God of reconciliation. The incarnation is not to be understood as God's humiliation (Luther) or hiding (Calvin) but, on the contrary, the incarnation is to be understood as the revelation of God's condescension,[27] the very and actual being of God. "(T)hroughout the Bible there is only a single theme, namely, God's own Word, his revelation, Jesus Christ himself."[28] Therefore Jesus Christ is the very core of Christian faith and thus of Christian theology and proclamation.

## A Broad Embedded Model

The sermon quoted in the paragraph above was delivered in 1954. But we can trace this hermeneutical concept back to the crisis in 1914. That means that there is continuity in the homiletical elaboration of the hermeneutical concept from the great crisis till the end of Barth's life.[29] That is remarkable when we take into consideration that a lot of Barth scholars see more than one diversion or new beginning, not only in his theologizing[30] but also in his preaching.[31] Because of those new beginnings, there are bendings in his thinking and theologizing that are sometimes so strong that they look like a buckle or twist. Barth himself gave reason for such thoughts and presumptions. At the end of his official academic career, he said about theological work:

> Anyone who sets out to do it can never proceed by building with complete confidence on questions which have already been settled, results which have been already achieved or conclusions which are already assured. He is directed every day, indeed every hour, to begin again at the beginning.[32]

27. *CD* II/1, p. 311.

28. Barth 1991, p. 103.

29. This supports the thesis of McCormack 1995.

30. So especially the major study of Von Balthasar 1992; see also Jüngel 1980; Schildmann 1983.

31. Hermelink 1987; Denecke 1989.

32. Busch 1994, p. 456.

His homiletical handling of the Old Testament, however, is marked by a notable continuity. There is one hermeneutical pattern dominant in his sermons after 1914. I give some illustration from subsequent periods in Barth's career to illustrate and substantiate this thesis.

In 1922, just after his appointment as professor in Göttingen, Barth preached on Proverbs 18:10 — "The name of Jehovah is a strong tower; the righteous runneth into it and are safe." Barth says this about the "name of Jehovah":

> If you will again ask me: what is the name of God and where and how shall we seek it? I can only reply that we usually do not seek Him, but only find Him; or far rather, only those, who already have found Him, can seek Him. He lets Himself be found — that's it. Where? (. . .) Jesus Christ, who is, in this man's land and for all its inhabitants, the spoken "I." Jesus Christ the name of God![33]

The expression "Jesus Christ the name of God" is clear and strong, especially because Barth stresses that expression with an exclamation mark.

We can discern the same hermeneutical pattern in a sermon preached on November 28, 1934. The text is taken from Jeremiah 17; the sermon concentrates on verse 7: "Blessed are those who trust in the LORD, whose trust is the LORD."

> We understand why it is said: "and the Lord is his trust." Not his own trust in God, not the depth of the knowledge of his sins, not his humility, not the zeal of his submission to the Lord! No: the Lord himself! Everything is dependent on those words "the Lord himself." We are not a blessed people because *we have* a trust; we are blessed because *He,* the Lord Jesus Christ, *is* our trust.[34]

The Subject of the text, "the Lord himself," is the foundation of trust and the trust itself. For Barth this Subject is Jesus Christ. And "we" — the attendees of this service — are blessed people because this Subject is our Lord and trust.

Twelve years later, in 1946, the landscape of Europe was dramatically

---

33. *Come Holy Spirit,* pp. 29-30.

34. My translation (German original: *Fürchte dich nicht,* pp. 40f. = *Predigten 1921-1935,* p. 364).

changed. The echoes of the atrocities of the Second World War can still be heard. In that situation, Barth preached on Psalm 55:22. The text reads "Cast your burden on the LORD, and he will sustain you; he will never permit the righteous to be moved." Barth asks from where or from whom can we get the courage to "cast our burden on the LORD" in the contemporary complex situation? In his answer, we can discover the same hermeneutical pattern: Christ is the very Subject of the Old Testament text.

> Therefore we have the Lord, i.e., our Lord Jesus Christ, and therein *is* He the Lord, that we let our burden be His burden. That we cast our burden on Him so that he carries our burden and brings it to its destination. Who is this Lord actually, who is Jesus Christ? I want to give a simple answer at this moment: He is the Lord of all those who have a burden.[35]

Barth makes "our Lord Jesus Christ" in a parenthesis to the actual Subject of the psalm. That means that Barth puts an equal sign between the Old Testament Name of God (LORD) and the New Testament *kurios*-title (Lord) of Jesus of Nazareth.

This hermeneutical pattern did not change when Barth started preaching again after the "preaching pause" (1948-1954). That can be illustrated from a sermon delivered on Ascension Day 1956. The sermon is on Psalm 34:5, "Look up to Him, your face will shine, and you shall never be ashamed."

> "Look up to Him!" This is what we commemorate on Ascension Day: the urgent invitation, the permission and the command, the freedom we enjoy as Christians and the obedience that is expected from us to look up to him, to Jesus Christ, who lived for us, died and rose again. He is our Savior who watches over us like an older brother watches over his younger brothers and sisters, yet in his protection is also their example and their master.[36]

When we take a look at the psalm, it is obvious that the Subject of the text refers to the LORD, the God of Israel. In this sermon, this God is without

---

35. My translation (German original: *Fürchte dich nicht*, pp. 308-9 = *Predigten 1935-1952*, p. 354).

36. *Deliverance to the Captives*, p. 44.

any explanation or justification — again in a parenthesis — identical with Jesus Christ.

In one of his last sermons, Barth preached on Psalm 31:15: "My time is secure in your hands."

> Yes, you may ask me, but does God have hands? Yes indeed, God has hands, quite different from these claws of ours, much better, much more skilful, much stronger hands. What does it mean to say "God's hands"? Let me put it this way first of all: God's hands are his deeds, his works, his words, which, whether we know it and want it or not, surround and embrace, bear and sustain us all on all sides. But after all, that could be said and understood figuratively, symbolically. There is a point where the figurative, symbolic ceases, where the question of God's hands become quite literally serious — that is, where all the deeds, works, and words of God have their beginning, middle, and end: "Your hands" — these are the hands of our Savior Jesus Christ. They are the hands which he held outstretched when he called: "Come unto me, all you that labor and are heavy laden, and I will give you rest."[37]

The hands of Psalm 31 are in fact the hands of the LORD. For Barth these hands are "the hands of our Savior Jesus Christ."

## Expectation and Recollection

Christ is for Barth Subject and content of both Old and New Testaments. The only difference between the Testaments is that the Word became flesh in the New Testament (John 1:14).[38] But that does not mean that the New Testament is a richer or deeper revelation. Both Testaments center around Christ as the ultimate revelation. The Old Testament looks forward in expectation and the New Testament looks back in recollection of the revelation of Christ in the flesh. The hermeneutical model of Barth can therefore

37. *Call for God*, p. 44. The sermon was delivered on December 31, 1960.
38. Kornelis Heiko Miskotte, Barth's personal and theological Dutch friend, said: "Wherein does the plus of the New Testament lie, what does it have that goes beyond the Old Testament? I hardly know how to state this, but what is new in the new covenant lies in the fact that the Word became flesh" (Miskotte 1967, pp. 163-64).

be indicated with those two words: expectation and recollection.[39] It should be clear that "expectation" does not mean that Christ is not yet there. Indeed, in Old Testament times Christ wasn't there in the flesh. But God acted and spoke already in the Old Testament in the mode of Christ. For Barth, "Christ was manifested as the Expected One even in the time of the Old Testament."[40]

In a similar way, after the first Ascension Day, God's acts and words will still be determined by the essence of God's being, i.e., the *philanthropia* (loving kindness, Acts 28:2; Titus 3:4) as revealed in Christ.[41] Recollection does not mean that God isn't present anymore or will act and speak in a different way than God did in Christ.

In this way, Old and New Testaments are typified: the Old Testament is the "witness of expectation" and the New Testament is the "witness of recollection." None of these witnesses is revelation in itself.[42] That qualification is only valid for Christ. That means that both witnesses have the same distance from Jesus Christ, the center of Revelation.

In accordance with the Christological creed and tradition of Chalcedon, Barth states that Christ is the unique and exclusive Word of God. And again, Barth marks his position in two directions. Against liberal theology Barth stresses that Christ is not only quantitatively greater but qualitatively someone other than a teacher of moral wisdom: Christ is the revelation of the God of Israel. But Barth opposes rigid orthodoxy at the same time, because in those circles the living Christ was lost and locked up in plain words of Scripture. Barth differentiates between God's revelation in Christ and the written witnesses of this revelation as found in the Old and New Testaments. That means that we cannot say that the Bible is or contains the Word of God itself. Instead, we have to say that the Bible contains the witnesses of the Word of God, the witnesses of God's revelation in Christ. Thus, Old and New Testaments are both in their own way witnesses of God-in-the-mode-of-Christ.

39. So the subtitle of *CD* I/2, §14.

40. *CD* I/2, p. 74. "This fact is confirmed in itself because it confirms itself" (*CD* I/2, p. 72). Because of its axiomatic character, Barth doesn't prove this statement but unfolds and elaborates it.

41. Miskotte 1967, pp. 115f.

42. "What is present in the biblical text and can be passed on ( ) is not revelation itself, but witness to God's revelation" (Barth 1991, p. 103).

## 6.4. Simple and Immediate

Barth sees a steadfast continuity in the essence of God's being, not only in the period of Old and New Testaments but also in the period afterwards. For that reason, words from Moses and the prophets can (almost) directly be connected with the present situation of the Christian church. A local congregation meets the same God who acted and spoke in Old Testament times, and that is the same God who acts and speaks in Jesus Christ. Barth connects Scripture in the most literal sense immediately — without hermeneutical intermediate stations or transitional stages — with the hearers of his sermons.

As a result, the (words of the) texts are loosened from their historical and literary background. The historical and cultural distance between the words of Scripture and the situation of the hearers of the sermon is of no hermeneutical and homiletical relevance.[43] A sermon on Deuteronomy 8:18 opens with a short introduction of only a few lines on the historical setting. Immediately after this introduction, Barth continues as follows:

But now, let us hear this word quite directly addressed to ourselves.[44]

The original historical and literary contexts of the words of Moses are of no relevance in what follows in this sermon.[45] The words of the text speak quite directly (*einfach ganz unmittelbar*) to the contemporary congregation.

A comparable construction can be found in a sermon on Isaiah 54:7-10 (1923). The first lines of text read: "For a small moment have I forsaken thee; but with great mercies will I gather thee. In overflowing wrath I hid my face from thee for a moment; but with everlasting loving kindness will I have mercy on thee, saith Jehovah thy Redeemer."

---

43. Therefore the "historical element cannot have an autonomous place in the sermon. Historical information will always be a burden in preaching" (Barth 1991, p. 105). Sermons on a biblical text turn out to be sermons on a certain theological theme or doctrinal topic. Preuß notes quite strikingly that the text has the character of an "only occasionally focused point of reference" ("nur ein gelegentlich angepeilter Bezugspunkt," Preuß 1984, p. 92; see also Denecke 1989, p. 210).

44. *Deliverance to the Captives*, p. 110 — German original: *Den Gefangenen befreiung*, p. 124 = *Predigten 1954-1967*, p. 105.

45. Bächli 1988, p. 69.

But can we indeed believe? Is not everything only an artificial human comfort with which we deceive ourselves? What shall I say? The Christian Church must learn again to proclaim the word of God's grace and to listen to it as to God's word. Otherwise it cannot be believed. Without this we hang and hover half way between as those who are apparently dead: not really condemned and not really pardoned, not really abandoned to the wrath of God and not really happy in hope, all by halves, all weak, all only "as if," all only figuratively and with reservation.

Perhaps this is the greatest calamity of our time that such preaching and hearing of the word of grace, as the word of God, has been taken from us and has not yet been restored to us. ( ) The Prophet says: "Thus saith the Lord, thy Redeemer, the Merciful One." This is the reality. Christ in his witness is the reality for which we hunger and thirst. We may doubt their witness and we do so continually; but we can also believe it, overcome our "no" through its "yes." God be praised, "who according to his great mercy, begat us again to a living hope by the resurrection of Jesus Christ from the dead!"[46]

Again, Barth pays hardly any attention to the historical and literary contexts of the words. The Old Testament prophet speaks immediately to the hearers of the sermon.[47]

## 6.5. The Natural-Historical Monument of God's Love and Faithfulness

Barth's various and even contrasting utterances on Israel cannot easily be outlined.[48] On the one hand, he can describe the Jews as "a living commentary on the Old Testament" and even as "a convincing evidence of God outside Scripture." On the other hand, Barth expresses himself in a sharp way about Israel and the Jews.

46. *Come Holy Spirit*, pp. 55-56.

47. I point also to the fact that Barth treats the Old Testament text in this sermon as a witness of Christ. The text gets the character of a stepping stone to reach the treatment of the Christian creed or doctrine. In this particular sermon, that theme is provided by the New Testament (1 Peter 1:3).

48. Despite the systematic structure of the *Church Dogmatics*, Barth develops his doctrine of Israel across a number of volumes. Relevant and important sources for this doctrine include *CD* II/1, p. 195; III/3, pp. 155-238; IV/1, pp. 3-78.

## *Israel: The Only Convincing Proof of God*

Barth quotes a well-known expression of Augustine who called the Jews "the librarians of the Church." The Old Testament is ultimately the book of their books, and originally their sacred canon without which even the church cannot ultimately live. The Word became Jewish flesh and the "I" of Jesus comes from Israel. The New Testament witness to Jesus the Christ stands on the soil of the Old Testament and cannot be separated from it.[49]

> The Gentile community of every age and land is a guest in the house of Israel. It assumes the election and calling of Israel. It lives in the fellowship of the King of Israel. (. . .)
>
> It is ( ) the Jew ( ), so miraculously preserved, as we must say, through the many calamities of his history, who as such is the natural historical monument to the love and faithfulness of God, who in concrete form is the epitome of the man freely chosen and blessed by God, who as a living commentary on the Old Testament is the only convincing proof of God outside the Bible.[50]

Barth accordingly calls for the abandonment of Jewish mission in the post-Holocaust era because mission among the Jews is theologically impossible.

> Mission is not the witness which [the church] owes to Israel. (. . .) What have we to teach him that he does not already know that we have not rather to learn from him?[51]

Christians have the promise of God insofar as they are branches engrafted into the Jewish tree. Jesus, his disciples, and Paul were part of Israel and directed their preaching first of all to their own people. Israel was not only the first addressee of God's message of merciful love from a historical point of view, but Israel is still the first addressee from a theological point of view.

> Yahweh is always the lover, the Bridegroom and Husband. And His lost people are always His Beloved, His Bride and His Wife. ( ) We have to reckon with the unfaithfulness of the Wife, but never with the un-

---

49. *CD* IV/1, p. 166; III/2, pp. 214f.; III/3, p. 212; IV/1, p. 171.
50. *CD* IV/3-2, p. 877; see also *CD* II/2, pp. 260f., 287.
51. *CD* IV/3-2, p. 877.

faithfulness of the Husband. We have to reckon with her rejection and abandonment, but not with a bill of divorce.[52]

Christians of all times and countries are the guests in the house of Israel. The "Church must live with the Synagogue, not ( ) merely as with another religion or denomination, but as with the root from which it has itself sprung." So it is, as Barth put it, that the church "still owes everything to those to whom it is indebted for everything."[53]

In 1966 Barth reemphasized in Rome the significance of Jewish-Christian relationship for the church. "There are today many good relations between the Roman Catholic Church and many Protestant churches. ( ) But we should not forget that there is finally only one actual great ecumenical question: our relation to Judaism."[54]

## Israel: Dreadfully Empty of Grace and Blessing

But there is another side of Barth's Israel-coin. When we continue to read in the just-quoted part of *Church Dogmatics* IV/3, we read sentences that seem to originate from quite a different world.

> Meantime the Synagogue became and was and still is the organization of a group of men which hastens toward a future that is empty now that He has come who should come, which is still without consolation, which clings to a Word of God that is still unfulfilled. Necessarily, therefore, the Jew who is uniquely blessed offers the picture of an existence which, characterized by the rejection of its Messiah and therefore of its salvation and mission, is dreadfully empty of grace and blessing. Necessarily he reflects the same existence without grace to which we poor heathen would be hopelessly abandoned apart from that which has taken place for us and has been manifested to us in the person of the one Jew.[55]

52. *CD* III/1, p. 316.

53. *CD* IV/3-2, p. 878.

54. Klappert 1980, p. 76. In the ecumenical movement "there is only one really important question: our relations with Israel." So Barth insists that ecumenism "suffers more seriously from the absence of Israel than of Rome or Moscow" (*CD* III/3, p. 225).

55. *CD* IV/3-2, p. 877.

The two contrasting visions on Israel are written on the same page! One meets this dialectical, even split vision on Israel on more than one occasion in Barth's writings.

Well known and notorious are the sentences in a letter to his pupil Friedrich-Wilhelm Marquardt of Berlin (dated September 5th, 1967). Barth wrote:

> I am decidedly not a philo-semite, in that in personal encounters with living Jews (even Jewish Christians) I have always, so long as I can remember, had to suppress a totally irrational aversion, naturally suppressing it at once on the basis of all my presuppositions, and concealing it totally in my statements, yet still having to suppress and conceal it. Pfui! is all I can say to this in some sense allergic reaction of mine. But this is how it was and is. A good thing is that this reprehensible instinct is totally alien to my sons and other better people than me (including you). But it could have had a retrogressive effect on my doctrine of Israel.[56]

One of the effects of this "irrational aversion" is surely that Barth paid no attention at all to post-biblical Judaism.[57] Barth gives the reason for that omission in the just-quoted letter to Marquardt.

> Biblical Israel as such gave me so much to think about and to cope with that I simply did not have the time or intellectual strength to look more closely at Baeck, Buber, Rosenzweig, etcetera.

That means for the practice of his preaching that the words of Moses and the prophets are understood as if they were exclusively meant for the church and have no relevance whatsoever for present-day Israel.

> The first Israel, constituted on the basis of physical descent from Abraham, has fulfilled its mission now that the Saviour of the world has sprung from it and its Messiah has appeared. Its members can only accept this fact with gratitude, and in confirmation of their own deepest election and calling attach themselves to the people of this

---

56. Barth 1981, p. 262.
57. Kornelis Heiko Miskotte urged Barth more than once to pay attention to post-biblical Judaism.

Saviour, their own King, whose members the Gentiles are now called to be as well.[58]

When Christ was born in the flesh, the role of Israel was over. Theologically speaking, the history of Israel came to an end.[59] The future of the synagogue lies in the church.[60] As a result, the history of Israel and the covenant between the LORD and Israel are covered behind the Christology of the church. We also engage this line of thought in Barth's sermons. A meditation on Leviticus 17:11 can serve as an illustration.

> The New Testament is therefore the fulfilled Old Testament. The Old Testament became past tense. But as such, it still speaks, as the necessary announcement and explanation of the New Testament, like the pointing finger of John the Baptist: Here is the Lamb of God who takes away the sin of the world.[61]

For Moses and the prophets, their role as "forefinger" to the actual revelation of God in Jesus Christ is all that remains. That means that there is almost no hermeneutical room for the distinctive and particular voice of the Old Testament.

## 6.6. Evaluation

For Barth, the Christian church preaches the God who from the very first beginning is the God who is revealed uniquely and exclusively in Jesus Christ. So, when we say that God is the Subject of Scripture, we say at the same time that Scripture in all her parts gives witness to Jesus Christ. And as a consequence, God-in-the-mode-of-Christ is the speaking and acting Subject of both the witnesses of expectation and recollection. Therefore Christ is the core, center, and foundation of Christian faith and theology.

58. *CD* III/2, p. 584.

59. Soulen 1996, p. 90.

60. *CD* II/2, p. 301; see also p. 201. Barth treats the doctrine of election in the same mood. Israel is witness to God's judgment while the church is witness to God's mercy (*CD* II/2, pp. 206, 210).

61. *Andachten* p. 73 (my translation). The meditation was meant for the Thursday after Easter.

This concept opens surprising possibilities for preaching the Old Testament in a Christian context. Barth can even say that the words from the Old Testament are spoken from the cross! A meditation meant for a second Easter day can illustrate that line of thought. I quote the first sentences from a meditation on Psalm 37:4 ("Take delight in the LORD, and he will give you the desires of your heart").

> The message from the cross reminds us again that with the Lord we have to undergo also our own unrest, our suppression, our judgment, our being sentenced, and our death. But in all those things and over all those things is the message of the cross also: take your delight in the Lord.[62]

From a strictly historical point of view, it would be nonsense to say that words from a psalm are a "message from the cross." But from a theological point of view, this expression goes for Barth to the very core of Christian faith. That is the important theological foundation for Barth's homiletical hermeneutics.

This theological paradigm solved a lot of hermeneutical problems and also had important homiletical implications. It opened up the possibility of preaching the Old Testament in a Christian context without getting caught up or entangled in hermeneutical models like typology, allegory, or salvation history.[63] The Old Testament is at once fully and completely a Christian book that has a rightful place in the pulpit of the Christian church.

The collapse of the historical distance between text and situation makes it possible for Barth to come quite close to experiences in the everyday life of the congregation, to their questions and burdens.

The reverse side of this construction is that Barth had radically to flatten out the diversity within Scripture. For the practice of preaching, it doesn't matter whether a text is pre- or post-exilic. For the practice of preaching, it isn't of any importance whether a text originates from Amos, David, Jeremiah, Jesus, or Paul. Barth opens up every text with the same

62. *Andachten* p. 66; see also p. 63 (my translation). In a similar way, Barth can state that Jesus Christ is the center of the Old and New Testaments (*Fürchte dich nicht*, pp. 308-9 = *Predigten 1935-1952*, p. 116).

63. That opened the possibility of reading and interpreting every part of Scripture in the light of the axiomatic unity, i.e., Jesus Christ.

hermeneutical key. *Magnalia Dei* were in fact *Magnalia Christi.*[64] Every text, every part of Scripture, whether it is in the Old or in the New Testament, has the same content, the same *"Gegenstand,"* i.e., Christ. That is in fact a higher kind of allegory.

The model of Barth is creative and ingenious. For the practice of preaching, however, it means that the Old Testament gets hidden behind the New Testament. The books of Moses and the prophets point as witnesses of expectation to God-in-the-mode-of-Jesus-Christ. That means that there is little or no hermeneutical room for the distinctive and particular voice of the Old Testament.

---

64. "Der Gottesknecht wird rein christologisch interpretiert; er ist nicht Präfiguration des Kommenden, sondern der Knecht Gottes ist/heißt Jesus Christus; Jes 53 handelt von seinem Kreuz" (Bächli 1987, p. 298).

# 7. Wanted: A Bunch of Keys

The hermeneutical models discussed in the previous chapters have roots that go back to the early days of the Christian church.[1] They were meant as keys to open up the meaning of the interior, the "God-sense"[2] of the Old Testament. Those keys were constructed to meet the theological questions and cultural challenges of their specific historical contexts. From that point of view these keys deserve to be handled and discussed with respect.

This attitude of respect and the recognition of their value in those specific contexts create at the same time not only the freedom but also the necessity of constructing a hermeneutical strategy that meets the theological questions and cultural challenges of our own context. For this enterprise we can use the strong and valuable elements of the keys discussed, try to avoid the risks mentioned, and add elements that are required in our own situation.

For that reason this chapter collects and integrates the results from the evaluations in the previous chapters under three perspectives: How do these models handle the issues concerning Jesus Christ (7.1), Israel (7.2.), and the listeners (7.3)? After this collective evaluation we can formulate preconditions for a sound theological and hermeneutical model that can serve the practice of contemporary preaching (7.4).

1. Longenecker 1975.
2. See for this expression Wilson 2001.

## 7.1. An Incomplete Painting

a. Sermons woven on the hermeneutical patterns of typology, salvation history, and promise and fulfillment proclaim *the actual and ultimate salvation* for the congregation from the New Testament. The Old Testament is for these keys not sufficient to proclaim God's redemption. That means that the New Testament is in fact seen as a better, richer, deeper, and especially more redemptive message.[3]

b. The Christological dimension in sermons woven on the hermeneutical patterns of typology, salvation history, and promise and fulfillment is usually focused on spiritual salvation. That means that there is a risk that the tangible and material character of the Old Testament is surpassed by a kind of "Christ-philosophy."[4]

c. Allegory and the model of Karl Barth succeed in opening a homiletical window on the Christological dimension of the Old Testament. The price for this success is that these models have to strip the Old Testament of its specific Jewish character. Both models make the Old Testament in retrospect a Christian and Christological book.

d. All of these models move on a hermeneutical one-way street. Passing the station of Christ in the practice of preaching is a hermeneutical point of no return. After this point the particular voice of the Old Testament is silenced, both in the structure of the sermon and in its contents.

e. Another feature of this hermeneutical one-way traffic is that earlier events, persons, and institutions are used to describe later events, persons, and institutions. This never happens in a vice versa way. The portrayal of Moses, for instance, provides apostles and evangelists with words and images to describe and interpret the Christ-event. But that never hap-

---

3. Gerhard von Rad says, for instance, that the exegesis of apostles and evangelists "often runs counter to our understanding of scripture: it nevertheless indicates that for Christians the Old Testament only has meaning in so far as it refers to Christ and was able to speak in the light of Christ" (1980b, p. 332).

4. "The Old Testament prevents the witness to Christ from being corrupted into philosophy about Christ" (Wolff 1963, p. 194). "Wherever the naïveté of the Old Testament is lacking, the exposition and application of the New Testament always runs into the danger of evaporating into 'Spirit,' 'light,' and love — the supreme expressions of a universality which is tenderly cherished by natural theologians as the most elegant form of flight from the reality of God" (Miskotte 1967, p. 178).

pens the other way around; i.e., the words and images of Jesus Christ are never used to interpret the calling and role of Israel.

f. The classical hermeneutical keys treat the Old Testament as a book that is caught up by Jesus Christ. Moses and the prophets are an incomplete painting or unfinished symphony. The revelation in and of Christ in the New Testament is seen as the completion of this painting. Consequently, every part of the Old Testament is interpreted from the perspective of its completion.[5]

The construction of the sermon, starting with the Old Testament text and ending with Jesus Christ, enforces the idea of a hierarchic relation between both Testaments. The "old" of "Old Testament" means indeed old-fashioned, antiquated, or out-of-date. The Old Testament is an unfinished symphony, waiting for a grand finale. That means that "insofar as the Church proclaims the Old Testament as Word of God, it is merely finding in it what it already knows from the fuller revelation in Christ."[6]

## 7.2. Dreadfully Empty of Grace and Blessing

a. The models discussed connect Old and New Testaments in an exclusively Christological way. There is no interpretative room left either for the theological meaning of God's way with Israel in Old Testament times or for God's way with contemporary Jews. The overarching theological paradigms of these hermeneutical models make all a "triple jump," from creation via the fall to Jesus Christ, as can be heard, for instance, in the first lines of the Apostles' Creed. These concepts thus dispossess Israel from the books of Moses and the prophets. Israel is in fact "dreadfully empty of grace and blessing" (Karl Barth).

b. Sermons sometimes underscore the previous statement in pointing to Israel's rejection of Jesus as the Messiah. Those sermons conclude

---

5. Greidanus 1999, p. 52. "All these writings of ancient Israel, both those which were concerned with her past relationship with God and those which dealt with her future one, were seen by Jesus Christ, and certainly by the Apostles and the early Church, as a collection of predictions which pointed to him, the saviour of Israel and of the world. ( ) The Old Testament can only be read as a book of ever increasing anticipation" (Von Rad 1981b, p. 319). N. T. Wright states similarly that the Old Testament period ended with "a story in search of a conclusion" (N. T. Wright 1992, p. 217).

6. Kraeling 1955, p. 236; see Bailey 1992a, p. 17.

that the church took over the role of Israel in God's history of redemption. Israel, the synagogue, and Judaism are treated under the sign of "however" or "yet."[7] The specific Hebrew I/we/us of the Old Testament texts are treated as a Christian I/we/us. The church thus absorbs Israel.

c. Another risk, connected with the previous issue, is that Jesus is loosened from and sometimes even opposed to his Jewish context.

d. A specific consequence of the classical hermeneutical strategies is that the Jews are considered blind to the deeper theological and spiritual meaning of their own Scriptures, whose only proper understanding is Christological.

e. All hermeneutical models treat Israel in one way or another as a symbol or cipher without a theological identity of its own. I discovered the following patterns describing and interpreting the relation between Israel and the church.

- The church has taken over the role of Israel (model of substitution);
- Israel became part of the church as the new people of God (model of integration);
- Israel in Old Testament times was the preliminary phase before the era of the church (model of development);
- Israel is the shadow of the reality of the church (typological model);
- Israel is the negative example as warning for the church (warning model);
- Israel is God's experimental garden (failure model);
- Israel is an illustration of the generally human (illustration model).[8]

What all these models have in common is an explicit order of merit between the church and Israel, the latter of course being inferior.

## 7.3. The Listener as Spectator

a. Sermons built on the foundation of typology, salvation history, and promise and fulfillment are often stuck in an enumeration of inner-biblical phenomena.[9] The meaning and relevance of an Old Testament text

7. Büttner 2002, p. 189.
8. Klappert 1980, p. 7.
9. Preuß 1984.

bounces between the two Testaments but does not reach to the contemporary situation of the actual listeners. The only role left to them is to be spectators of an event from the past, i.e., an event between the Old Testament and Jesus Christ.[10]

b. The models of allegory and of Karl Barth bridge the gap between the world of the text and the world of the contemporary listener quite directly *("ganz unmittelbar")*. The difference in time and place is considered to be irrelevant for the practice of preaching.

c. When sermons use a biblical character as moral example for the listeners, it is Christologically "retouched." That means that sermons remove elements from the portrayals of Old Testament persons that are considered, from a New Testament perspective, to be antiquated.

d. Old Testament sermons dominated by a Christological paradigm suffer from the risk that everyday life with all its fears and pleasures, all the questions and issues, disappears behind "the accomplished work of Christ."[11] The "Hallelujah" of Easter morning threatens to drown out the silence of Holy Saturday and the "Why?" of Good Friday.

## 7.4. Preconditions for a Hermeneutical Model

After this analysis, we can formulate the preconditions for a sound theological and hermeneutical model that serves the practice of contemporary preaching and meets the theological issues and cultural challenges of our own historical context.

a. A contemporary hermeneutical model has to reckon with the fact that Israel is the first addressee. In the post-Holocaust context we become aware of the fact that this refers not only to the Israel of Old Testament times but also to contemporary Jews.

b. A hermeneutical model must enable us to preach Christ from the Old Testament in such a way that the books of Moses and the prophets:

- are not absorbed by the proclamation of Christ;
- are not seen as a once-and-for-all-passed station on a one-way road;
- are not annexed by the Christian church and expropriated from Israel;

10. Gunneweg 1983a, p. 159.
11. Schöttler 2001, p. 305.

- are not flattened into a uniform prediction of Christ;
- are not removed from their material and tangible character.

c. A hermeneutical model has to prevent a sermon's listeners from being mere spectators of an event from the past, either in Old Testament times or between Old and New Testaments. A homiletical hermeneutical model should invite listeners to become participants of the "God-event" of the text.

d. And, *last but not least,* a hermeneutical model has to respect the unity of God without equalizing the diversity of Scripture. This element is an important instrument against Marcion in both ancient and contemporary guises.

It is clear that this list of preconditions cannot be amalgamated into a single key or simple strategy. There is no master key to open up simultaneously the different dimensions of meaning piled up in the books of Moses and the prophets. The only adequate way to come to grips with the multiplex nature of the Old Testament and the relationship between the two Testaments is to opt for a multiplex approach.[12] We need, so to speak, not a single master key but a bunch of keys. This is not meant in the sense that we can use the keys of allegory, typology, or promise and fulfillment next to each other. The hermeneutical key must in itself enable a multiplex approach.

The chapters in the next part of the book are devoted to the construction of such a multidimensional hermeneutical strategy. I give account of the way that led to the construction of this model, and I discuss the ingredients or construction material that is used for this concept. That material comes first of all from a new and fresh practical theological look at the Old Testament quotations in the New Testament (chapter 8). The history of interpretation provides not only useful but also important ingredients for a contemporary hermeneutical key (chapter 9). Chapter 11 integrates the different ingredients that were gathered in the course of time through reflection and meditation, analysis and intuition, scholarly research and the practice of preaching. The result is a layered or multidimensional hermeneutical concept, a contemporary model of "the fourfold sense of Scripture": *sensus Israeliticus, Christological sense, ecclesiological sense,* and *eschatological sense.*

12. Hasel 1979, pp. 117, 125-27.

The four dimensions of this model are elaborated in subsequent chapters (12-15) in the third part of this book. In these four senses or dimensions, the meaning of a text is on the one hand not restricted to the "boundaries" of the literal or lexical, syntactical, and grammatical meanings of the letters of the (individual) text but on the other hand does full justice to the "theological carrying capacity" or "theological elasticity" of the text as part of the whole of Scripture (the overarching Story of Scripture). This part therefore also pays attention to what is meant by the expression "literal sense" (chapter 10).

Chapter 16 offers the "eating of the pudding." I illustrate the four dimensions of meaning of three texts: Exodus 3, Psalm 22, and the poems on the servant of the LORD in Deutero-Isaiah.

## 7.5. Ingredients

My quest for a contemporary hermeneutical model started with a homiletical evaluation of the Old Testament quotations in the New Testament. I had the reasoned presumption that such an evaluation could yield new and seminal ingredients for a contemporary homiletical hermeneutics. A major presupposition of the classical hermeneutical models is that apostles and evangelists quote the Old Testament in a Christological context.[13] But my personal reading of Scripture tells me that not every Old Testament citation or allusion has that kind of Christological focus. That raised serious suspicion against the foundation and justification of the existing hermeneutical models. These models tried, so to speak, to open the colorful variety of the text with one and the same master key/picklock. Whatever hermeneutical model uses this key, it turns out that it gives entrance to one and the same Christological room.

My reasoned presumption and suspicion meant the beginning of a quest for a multidimensional hermeneutical model that would do justice to the theological and hermeneutical diversity of the Old Testament quotations in the New Testament. In other words: Can we construct or design a model with the character of a bunch of keys (instead of a single key) that allows us to unlock different windows on the Old Testament text?

The biblical-theological quest is not focused on a detailed inquiry

---

13. See Greidanus 1999, pp. 55-61.

about the specific way a particular apostle or evangelist quotes the Old Testament, nor about the question of whether apostles and evangelists used the Hebrew or Greek version of the Old Testament, nor which (Jewish or Greek) hermeneutical keys can be determined in the New Testament.[14] These are all important questions but belong to a different kind of project from the one presented here. This book is written for the practice of preaching, and arose from my interest in whether there were patterns discernible in the theological recontextualizations of Old Testament texts in the New Testament. The results of that quest are presented in chapter 9.

## 7.6. Marcion Again

The young church condemned the views of Marcion, and his views have been generally rejected ever since. But the shadow cast by this second-century theological giant still falls over today's Christian preaching.[15] In §6.2.3, for example, I mentioned Adolf von Harnack, a German liberal theologian of the nineteenth and early twentieth centuries. The question on the interpretation of the Old Testament was first posed and decided by Marcion but remains urgent today for all the members of the family of the Christian church. Marcion "remains the church's most regular occasion of apostasy."[16] We can hear the echo of his voice in every district of ecclesial practice up until our own time. No one will easily propose to get completely rid of the Old Testament. But we can hear voices in the congregation saying that they have serious troubles with the Old Testament. In a sermon on the first verses of Joshua, Alan Jackson makes those feelings and thoughts explicit.

> The book of Joshua, then, is a great piece of holy encouragement, a reminder that God promises to stand with us in the midst of adversity. Unhappily, however, there are some other elements in Joshua that cloud the picture. The book touches a raw nerve in modern readers because some read it as though God were condoning violence. Face it, more than once in this book God is depicted as authorizing a *jihad* — a

14. See, for instance, Gundry 1967; Vermes 1980; Longenecker 1975; Ellis 1985; Hays 1989; Juel 1988 and 2003; Marcus 1992; P. R. Davies 2003; Porton 2003.
15. Klein 1992, p. 7.
16. Jenson 1997, p. 42.

total holy war. In places we read of God expecting the Israelites to slaughter every man, woman, child, cow, horse, goat, cat, and dog in Canaan. *"Let nothing remain alive!"* God roars off the pages of Joshua. *"Woe to the Israelite who spares any person or who keeps back for himself anything from the land!" (. . .)*

But I confess that I'm not comfortable picturing God ordering *anyone* to plunge a sword into the heart of an infant nursing at its mother's breast. I agree with the judgment of church history that the teachings of Marcion were heretical. Marcion declared that the God of the Old Testament is a different God than the One in the New Testament. That's wrong, of course. But when you read certain passages in the book of Joshua, you can understand what jolted Marcion enough to make that claim.[17]

And there is a real risk and danger that the use of the classical hermeneutical models reduces the actual value and authority of the Old Testament exactly because of the understanding in this illustration.[18] "Though Marcion's teachings were branded heretical by the church in his own era and would be rejected out of hand by many contemporary Christian theologians, in practice, the church has often preached and taught as if Marcion had prevailed in the second century."[19] When that is true, there is a real risk that the authority of the Old Testament came to an end when Jesus cried "It is finished." From that point of view the Old Testament died on Good Friday and the New Testament rose on Easter morning. To counter this risk, Christian preaching needs a hermeneutical strategy that proclaims the same about the Old Testament as is accounted about the restored girl: "The child is not dead but sleeping" (Mark 5:39). Perhaps Paul too had in mind the books of Moses and the prophets when he wrote, "Sleeper, awake! Rise from the dead, and Christ will shine on you" (Eph. 5:14).

17. Jackson 2005.

18. "In almost all cases it is regarded as a preliminary stage to the Christ event and as a history which leads up to Christ; it is this goal which makes it a sacred history" (Gunneweg 1978, p. 183).

19. Duduit 1992, p. 10; see also Farris 1998, p. 149.

# II. INGREDIENTS OF A NEW MODEL

# 8. Hermeneutical Ingredients

## 8.1. The Hermeneutical Road

*Toiling and Moiling with a Dictionary*

The well-known Danish theologian and philosopher Søren Kierkegaard (1813-1855) tells a parable about a lover who has received a letter from his beloved. The love-letter is written in a language unknown to the lover and there is no one around who can translate it for him. Perhaps he counts this as a blessing in disguise, because the lover does not want anyone to be privy to the secrets between him and his beloved. What does he do? He takes a dictionary and a grammar and starts translating in order to obtain the translation.

> Now let us imagine that, as he sits there busy with his task, an acquaintance comes in. He knows that the letter has come, because he sees it lying there, and says, "So, you are reading a letter from your beloved." What do you think the other will say? He answers, "Have you gone mad? Do you think this is reading a letter from my beloved! No, my friend, I am sitting here toiling and moiling with a dictionary to get it translated. At times I am ready to explode with impatience; the blood rushes to my head, and I would just as soon hurl the dictionary on the floor — and you call that reading! You must be joking! No, thank God, as soon as I am finished with the translation I shall read my beloved's letter; that is something altogether different."
>
> So, then, with regard to the letter from his beloved, the lover distinguishes between reading with a dictionary and reading the letter from

his beloved. The blood rushes to his head in his impatience when he sits and grinds away at reading with the dictionary. He becomes furious when his friend dares to call this the reading of a letter from his beloved. But when he is finished with the translation, he reads the letter. All the scholarly preliminaries were regarded as nothing but a necessary evil so that he could come to the point — of reading the letter from his beloved.[1]

Preaching has the intention of letting Scripture resound for the congregation, to resound God's letter of love for humankind. For that effort, we need a dictionary and a grammar. But preaching has to do more than talk about the literary and historical dimensions of the biblical text — what I called earlier the "outer side" or "exterior" of the text. Preaching not only explains the exterior of the words, it interprets the kerygmatic interior in such a way that the listeners are invited and challenged to become participants of the God-event of the text or, as Paul Wilson calls it, the "God-sense" of Scripture.[2] It is the enterprise of connecting the world of Scripture with the world of the listeners.[3] This enterprise is risky, challenging, and promising at the same time. When preaching does not succeed in connecting those two worlds, the God of whom Moses and the prophets give witness remains, as David Buttrick puts it, "a past-tense God of past-tense God-events whose past-tense truth ('original meaning') may be applied to the world, while God remains hidden within a gilt-edged book. ( ) Failure to name God with the world can only certify God's absence!"[4]

Hence, it has nothing to do with preaching when a preacher gives only a skilled and scholarly exposition of the words of a text. When a sermon has nothing more or nothing else to offer than a kind of popularized scholarly exegesis, it fails completely the task and calling of preaching. The proclamation of the text has to be trans-ported, from one port of time and place to the port of our own context and culture. Interpreting biblical texts means ferrying the contents of Scripture across the river of time and place.[5] Preachers are bridge builders and lay the plank-work between cul-

1. Kierkegaard 2002, p. 80.
2. Wilson 2001.
3. See, for instance, Stott 1982, pp. 135-79 (preaching as bridge-building). For a critique of the image of bridge-building see Farley 2003, pp. 71-82.
4. Buttrick 1987, p. 18; see also Bos 1992, pp. 3-8.
5. The German *übersetzen* means both "to translate" and "to ferry across."

tures separated by thousands of years, between languages rooted in separate parts of the globe, and between audiences held apart by time and space. Bruce Shields says, "Our task is not to explain the gospel; it is not to describe the gospel; it is not even to contextualize the gospel. Our task is to actualize the gospel so that people can do more than just listen to it; our task is to help people to enter into it."[6] Members of the congregation don't attend church to hear how things were in past times. They come to hear how things are here and now, between them and the God of Israel.[7]

## Interior and Exterior of Scripture

Before the biblical texts got their final place in the present canon they were involved in a dynamic and complex process of reinterpretation. That process was intended to make the texts accessible and understandable to ever-new generations and audiences.[8] In every subsequent step of this process, the texts got a new place in a changed literary and kerygmatic context. As a result, new elements or dimensions of meaning were added to the reservoir of "old" meaning already piled up in the text.[9] Every time the congregation opens the Scriptures, this reservoir is waiting for a disclosure that will let the many-voiced meaning resound in the multidimensional sound-box of the canon of Old and New Testaments. Elaborating on this image, the wooden sound-box of a violin is the fixed exterior; when a musician pulls the bow across the strings, the air inside is full of movement. The tone and strength of this movement depend on the string that is touched, the stress of the bow, and the skill of the musician. The letters and words of a text are, so to speak, the walls of the sound-box of the Scriptures. While those walls are fixed, the kerygmatic contents of the box are dynamic, almost living, when the interpreter pulls the hermeneutical bow across the strings of the text. Augustine (354-430) already distinguished program-

6. Shields 2000, pp. 158-59; see also Long 1989, p. 79.

7. "It is true of course, that preaching cannot be reduced merely to telling of how things were, but it is certainly a telling of how things were in such a way that the hearers can understand how thing are, how things stand now between God and man in the 'ongoing history'" (Miskotte 1967, p. 201).

8. Childs 1985, p. 6.

9. Zimmerli 1969a, pp. 192-205; Childs 1978 and 1979; Von Rad 2001 a/b, p. 266; Kugel/Greer 1989; Menn 2003.

matically between the *signa* (signs or words) and the *res* (subject matter) of a text. The process of understanding Scripture means that we try to understand the *signa* not for their own sake but in order to come to an understanding of the *res* that the *signa* are referring to.[10] This distinction determines the process of interpretation for preaching. As Hugh Oliphant Old says, "In one way or the other, all the way through the history of the Church, it has been affirmed that there is an outward meaning of Scripture and an inward meaning of Scripture."[11]

In the process of sermon preparation preachers not only have to investigate the literary and historical exterior of a particular text (the wooden walls), but they must also listen to the multidimensional and dynamic reservoir of meaning that can be heard in the interior of a text.[12] Homiletical handbooks thus distinguish between (literary and historical) exegesis on the one hand and theological analysis of the subject matter of the text on the other hand. These two components are not independent and consecutive stations of a linear process of preparation. Exegesis and theological analysis can be seen as two juxtaposed elliptical focuses that enrich, stimulate, deepen, and correct each other. We need therefore instruments that enable us to open up both focuses in the process of sermon preparation.

In the slipstream of the Enlightenment, the disciplines of Old and New Testament have developed a sophisticated and advanced set of exegetical instruments to investigate the historical and literary exteriors of the text. The result of this kind of exegesis can be found in scholarly commentaries and theological dictionaries. The discipline of theological hermeneutics provides the keys to open up the doors of the interior of the texts so that the different voices of their subject matter can be heard and understood by contemporary readers and listeners. It is the task of homiletics to combine both sets of instruments for the benefit of preaching and sermon preparation.

Every search for a hermeneutical model is in fact an attempt to quantify (the "size") and to qualify (to whom or what the subject matter of the text relates) the kerygmatic interior of Old Testament texts. The history of

10. Augustine, *De Doctrina Christiana*, 1.2.2.

11. Old 1998b, p. 259.

12. Wilson distinguishes between "God-sense" and "literal sense" (Wilson 2001). "Die Predigt hat aus der Bibel und nicht über sie zu reden." Preaching is therefore something else as "einfache Schriftauslegung" (Barth, *KD* IV/3, p. 996). See also Long 1989, pp. 79ff.; H. M. Müller 1995, pp. 213-17; Shields 2000, p. 155.

the church shows a continuous and colorful reflection on these issues. The German systematic theologian Gerhard Ebeling (1912-2001) rightly states that we can discern three decisive moments in this dynamic history. During each of these three moments, theology came up with a new set of answers.[13] First, we have the hermeneutical approach of the early church. The concept of the fourfold sense of Scripture stayed essentially unchanged until the Middle Ages. Inspired by Humanism and the Renaissance, the Reformation caused a radical change in the hermeneutical paradigm; *ad fontes* (back to the sources) and *sola Scriptura* (only Scripture) became rallying expressions. The Enlightenment marks the third important turning point, i.e., the rise of historical-critical research. I restrict the following treatment to these three main stations, the moments where substantial and important shifts can be discerned on the hermeneutical road. I therefore make three big leaps through the history of interpretation.[14]

## 8.2. Apostolic Writings and Church Fathers

*The Beginnings of Hermeneutics*

Christian interpretation of the Old Testament in the first centuries of church history followed the tracks that were set by apostles and evangelists, who used strategies well known by the Jewish community.[15] The latter for its part went forth on the hermeneutical path set by the Tanak itself.[16] The early church thus inherited a body of traditional interpretation, which they followed in an unreflected way.[17] Their interpretation of Scripture was led mainly by a brief summary of the Christian faith, the so-called Rule of Faith *(regula fidei)*. This rule was flexible in wording but authoritative in content. It provided an "overarching story" in which the quest for meaning could take place.[18]

13. Ebeling 1954, p. 90; see also Frör 1961, p. 20.
14. For a more detailed treatment of the history of interpretation see Farrar 1961; Grant 1984; W. W. Klein 1993.
15. Kümmel, 1961; R. P. C. Hanson 1970; Longenecker 1975; Instone-Brewer 1992; Skarsaune 1996; Old 1998b, pp. 251-305; Trigg 2003, pp. 304-33.
16. Frör 1961, pp. 20-23; Fishbane 1996.
17. Young 2003, p. 334.
18. Greer 1989; Young 2003.

Theological reflection started in the third and fourth centuries in two important schools: Antioch and Alexandria. The school of Alexandria used instruments of Greek philosophy — especially from Platonism — to read and interpret Scripture.[19] The Alexandrians believed that Scripture had not only a literal, historical sense but also a spiritual meaning, referring to universal and eternal truths. This idea reflected Plato's philosophy. This spiritual or hidden truth of Scripture could be discovered through allegorical interpretation. A rival school arose in Antioch. The theologians of this school dismissed allegorical meanings and insisted on the historical and grammatical meaning. The school of Antioch insisted on the historical reality of revelation and was unwilling to lose it in a world of mere symbolism. The Alexandrian method of interpretation became in fact dominant in the following centuries. The heritage of Antioch was revived in the period of the Reformation.

## Origen

Origen (185-254) played a leading role in the Alexandrian school. He is considered to be one of the most seminal of Christian thinkers and one of the most creative Christian scholars,[20] one who left us both an impressive number of scholarly publications and a wealth of preaching material. Origen was the first theologian to reflect systematically on the questions and issues involved in the interpretation of Scripture.[21] His hermeneutical grammar can be found in the fourth book of his foundational four-volume work *Peri Archōn (On Principles)*.

Origen is not only the best-known theologian of the Alexandrian school but also the most debated member. That is true especially because of his view on the *apokatastasis pantōn,* the universal restoration, salvation, and restitution of all things (see Acts 3:21).[22] Origen included even Satan and the host of fallen angels in God's ultimate salvation. His ideas on this particular issue were officially condemned at the ecumenical council of Constantinople (553), but despite the condemnation, Origen remained

19. Procopé 1996.
20. Old 1998b, p. 252.
21. De Lubac 1998a, pp. 214ff.; H. M. Müller 1996, pp. 19-24.
22. Carleton Paget 1996.

an influential theologian. He enjoyed a great reputation in his own lifetime and in the century and a half that followed.

Origen was well trained in the literary methods of his day, especially a careful word-by-word reading and explanation of classic texts such as Homer. He applied the same method of interpretation to Scripture. A scholarly accountable way to read Scripture starts for him with determining the authentic text. We can therefore say that Origen became the first textual critic of the Old Testament. He prepared the so-called *Hexapla,* a book in which six versions of the Old Testament were written out in parallel columns (the original Hebrew and translations in Greek). After a determination of the text, Origen went on with a search for the literal sense. As he admonishes in the first book of *On Principles:*

> For let us inquire on what occasion these words were spoken by the Savior, before whom He uttered them, and what was the subject of investigation.[23]

To explain Scripture in this way, Origen drew on the best learning of his day, in history, geography, philosophy, medicine, grammar, even zoology. He learned Hebrew and asked rabbis about Jewish interpretation and traditions.[24]

## Rules of Interpretation

Finding the literal sense of the text was indeed a necessary first step, but only the first step in the process of interpretation. For Origen, "literal meaning" was not what we understand today under this expression. This expression referred for Origen to the materiality or "body" of the words, the exterior of the text. To open up the ultimate, i.e., the spiritual meaning — the meaning that testifies about God's redemption — of a text we have to dig deeper.

> The way, then, as it appears to us, in which we ought to deal with the Scriptures, and extract from them their meaning, is the following,

---

23. *On Principles* I, 4.

24. One of Origen's great accomplishments was thus the defense of Christianity against the attacks of Gnosticism without falling into the anti-intellectualism or fundamentalism that many Christians of his day had retreated to.

which has been ascertained from the Scriptures themselves. . . . For as man consists of body, and soul, and spirit, so in the same way does Scripture, which has been arranged to be given by God for the salvation of men.[25]

Origen justifies the threefold meaning on the basis of Proverbs 22:20-21, "Describe these things in a threefold way." This enabled Origen to "extract" a threefold meaning from Scripture. In that interpretative process every detail of the text has meaning because God is its ultimate author. The apostle Paul provided the underlying concept of his own exposition and application. The apostle states that the law is spiritual (Rom. 7:14). This spiritual meaning is in fact the decisive meaning of the Law of Moses. That meaning is not accessible for every reader. This deeper meaning is only understood by those who have received the Spirit of God (1 Cor. 12:8). Origen draws the conclusion from that passage that this rule applies not only to the interpretation of the Law (books of Moses). The meaning and focus of the whole of Scripture is centered around the spiritual core, the ultimate heart of its matter. The exterior of the words of the text is meant to serve the proclamation of this spiritual core of individual texts and the entire canon.[26] The outward form of Scripture is just a means to reveal spiritual meaning. The letters and words were, so to speak, vehicles for the true and ultimate spiritual meaning.

The three senses of Scripture refer also to the degree of people's faith, the depth of their relation with God. Preaching has to address the simple believer with the first dimension of the text, the "bodily" sense. The second dimension, the soul of Scripture, is meant for those who have made progress on the journey of faith. And the spiritual sense is meant for those whose soul is united with God. Origen uses different expressions to describe this deeper sense: mystical, typical, anagogical, metaphorical, and allegorical. Origen admonishes the listeners of his sermons to make progress on the path of faith and to strive hard in order to reach a next phase, from body to spirit, from spirit to soul.

---

25. *On Principles* IV, 11.

26. "Auch bei Origenes geht es in der Suche nach dem eigentlich Gemeinten meist allein um den geistlichen Sinn" (Kretschmar 1981, p. 31).

## The Practice of Preaching

From that perspective no detail of the text is insignificant for Origen. Every jot and tittle is therefore open for a whole range of interpretations. For example, names and numbers were understood to be symbols for spiritual truths. The mentioning of the number three thus refers to the Trinity, number four suggests the gospel, number five suggests the human senses, and number six suggests the days of creation. The Hebrew names of, for example, the Israelites' forty-two stopping places in the desert were in the same way interpreted as stages on the path of personal spiritual growth. Material things point to and mean actually spiritual truths: water points to baptism, wood refers to the cross, and manna means the Eucharist. This kind of interpretation offers a lot of possibilities for finding (or adding) spiritual meaning to a text.

Fundamental to this interpretation is the conviction that Christ is the principal key to understanding and opening the true meaning of the Old Testament. What is said in the Scriptures about Israel, Origen understands as referring to the individual soul and its ascent to God.[27] The sign by which Rahab makes her house known, the scarlet thread (Josh. 2:18), is understood as a reference to the gospel. Rahab mystically represents the church and the scarlet thread the blood of Christ. Origen states that there is no salvation outside the church, the house of redemption, just as only those in the house of Rahab were saved. In a sermon on this passage, Origen says:

> If anyone wishes to be saved, let him come to this house [the church], just as they once came to that of the prostitute. Let them come to this house where the blood of Christ is a sign of redemption. For that blood was for condemnation amongst those who said, "His blood be on us and on our children" (Matt. 27:25). Jesus was "for the fall and resurrection of many" (Luke 2:34); and therefore in respect of those who "speak against His sign" His blood is effective for punishment, but effective for salvation in the case of believers.
>
> Let no one therefore persuade himself or deceive himself: outside this house, that is, outside the Church, no one is saved. . . . The sign of salvation (the scarlet thread) was given through the window because Christ by His incarnation gave us the sight of the light of godhead as it

27. Old 1998a, p. 311.

were through a window; that all may attain salvation by that sign who shall be found in the house of her who once was a harlot, being made clean by water and the Holy Spirit, and by the blood of our Lord and Savior Jesus Christ, to whom is glory and power for ever and ever.

For Jesus was "set for the falling and rising of many" (Luke 2:34), and hence for those who deny His "sign" His blood works punishment, for those who believe, salvation. . . . Outside this house (i.e., the Church) none is saved: to leave it makes a man responsible for his own death.[28]

From that point of view, the Old Testament is interpreted as if it already contained the whole proclamation of the New Testament. So, Origen can find in the Old Testament every element and detail of the New Testament proclamation, for example, Christology, the ministries of the church, and the sacraments.

## The Relation between Exterior and Interior of a Text

Origen's concept of Israel parallels his vision on the meaning of the Old Testament text. Moses and the prophets gave witness that God had made a covenant with Israel. Origen starts by saying that Israel is a historic nation and Jerusalem is in the same way an earthly city. This first step in interpretation has to do with the exterior of the text. To make the next step, toward the interior of the text, Origen refers to Paul's distinction between inward and outward Jew. "For he is not a Jew who is one outwardly . . . but he is a Jew who is one inwardly" (Rom. 2:28f.). And when Paul speaks about "Israel after the flesh" (1 Cor. 10:18), Origen concludes that there is also an "Israel according to the Spirit." And God's promises that were not yet fulfilled in Old Testament times are fulfilled in the "Israel according to the Spirit." The Old Testament's promises concerning earthly goods are not to be understood in their literal and material character but in a spiritual sense. "Israel in the flesh" or "the outward Jews" deduce their roots and identity back from Abraham. The "Israel according to the Spirit" or the "inward Jews" connect their descent and identity with Jesus Christ. The "literal" Je-

28. This hermeneutical and homiletical practice is already to be found in the first letter of Clement.

rusalem is the capital of the earthly Israel. The heavenly Jerusalem is the ultimate destination for the "inward Jews." "Paul admonishes us to keep seeking Jerusalem that is above (Galatians 4:26; Colossians 3:1)." Origen uses this admonishment in retrospect as a hermeneutical key to interpret all the texts in the Old Testament that speak about "Jerusalem." The result is that the earthly Jerusalem and its meaning evaporate completely. The history of "Israel after the flesh" has to be understood metaphorically as a history of the "inward Jews."

### In Sum

Origen is in every aspect a child of his time and culture. He elaborates the tradition that was handed down to him by his predecessors. We can say that he codified the theological thinking of his own time. But his theology in fact detaches the Old Testament from Israel. "In fact, the tighter the grip of Christians on the Jewish Scriptures, the deeper the estrangement from the community of living Jews. For the patristic tradition after the triumph of Christianity, the Jews became the 'people of witness' for God's wrath on unbelievers."[29]

Origen made it certain that the church would retain the Old Testament as part of its Bible. He also provided the first real Christian interpretation of that Old Testament, both of the exterior and the interior of Scripture. And it is clear that for him the interior was the most important. The meaning given to the interior of Scripture even began to rule over the exterior of words and letters.

### 8.3. The Middle Ages

The development of the hermeneutical grammar after Origen underwent only marginal changes in the centuries that followed. Athanasius (ca. 295-373), Jerome (ca. 340-420), Augustine (354-430), Abelard (1079-1142), and Thomas Aquinas (1225-1274) mainly consolidated the hermeneutical track set in the first centuries.[30] The results of this track are elaborated in the

29. Froehlich 1984, p. 11.
30. De Lubac 1998a.

model of the fourfold sense of Scripture.[31] This model can be summarized in a well-known medieval Latin *dystich*:[32]

| | |
|---|---|
| *Littera gesta docet,* | The letter teaches what happened, |
| *quid credas allegoria,* | the allegory what you have to believe, |
| *moralis quid agas,* | the moral sense what you have to do, |
| *quo tendas anagogia.* | and the anagogy what to strive at. |

This *dystich* was not meant to be applied always or used as a key to disclose in every text a fourfold meaning. But the model could inspire and direct the thoughts of the interpreter of biblical texts. It had what we might call a heuristic function. It was a kind of direction indicator at a crossroad on the search for meaning for the interpreter's own situation. The model pointed to different possibilities of meaning in a particular text.

The first layer of meaning concentrates on the *literal sense,* the every-day and material meaning of the words and expressions. This historical, grammatical, or literal sense is the foundation of all other meanings and senses that can be discovered in the text. It was fundamental for an inter-preter to start with this first dimension. To neglect this first dimension may be compared with neglecting the alphabet while doing grammar.

The *allegorical sense,* the second layer of meaning, is concerned with the deeper sense of the words. That deeper sense was deduced from Chris-tian doctrine. The words and images of a text get the function of a hallstand for the whole set of clothing of Christian doctrine canonized by the church in creeds and dogmas. Words of Moses and the prophets were read as pre-dictions and foreshadowings of the secret that is completely revealed in the New Testament. Allegory in this context doesn't point to a more symbolic or metaphorical explanation. Allegory is meant in a more restricted way, i.e., in relation to the Christian system of belief. This dimension of meaning refers to the system of creeds and doctrines of the church, especially Christology.

The third layer of meaning, the *tropological sense,* has to do with the

---

31. The model of fourfold sense was also practiced in Judaism and Islam during the Middle Ages. The mutual relation and influence hasn't been researched (Dohmen/Stemberger 1996, pp. 128f.; Barrera 1998, pp. 468-90; H. F. Knight 2000, pp. 13-17).

32. The wording of the *dystich* goes back at least to Nicolas of Lyra (about 1330). The origins of the model of fourfold sense go of course back further in history (De Lubac 1998a, pp. 23ff.). We know the name of John Cassian from the first half of the fifth century (Cassian 2002, pp. 183-87; Barrera 1998, pp. 546ff.).

behavior and morals of the contemporary believer. In this dimension
Scripture is seen as a mirror for human behavior. While the allegorical
meaning has to do with the world of faith, the tropological dimension calls
for action. Scripture confronts us with our divine destination and calling
but also with our vulnerability and our sinful weaknesses. The *gesta Dei*
(footsteps of God) in the course of history are direction markers for the
footsteps of the congregation. The direction markers point the way for us
in social issues and the path of spirituality.

The fourth layer of meaning, the *anagogical sense,* looks with hope to
the future, the ultimate consummation of the text in God's heavenly kingdom. The anagogical sense looks ahead to the celestial glory, opening an
eschatological window on individual texts and Scripture as a whole.

Frequently referenced figures of the fourfold sense are: Jerusalem,
Babylon, Mount Zion, the manna in the desert, and the first word of God
in the creation of heaven and earth.[33]

| | historical/ literal | allegorical/ figurative | tropological/ moral | anagogical/ future |
|---|---|---|---|---|
| *Jerusalem/ Mount Zion* | a city in Judah | the church | Christian virtues | reward/heaven |
| *Babylon* | a city in Mesopotamia | the world | lack of virtues | punishment/ hell |
| *manna* | food for Israel in the desert | the Eucharist | daily spiritual strength for the faithful | the future unity of the soul with Christ |
| *"Let there be light"* | first act of creation | Christ as the light of the world | Christians as the light of the world | the light of God's eternal glory |

The letter of the text is in the first place the foundation for that which had
to be believed (the *regula fidei*). In a next step, the text offered guidelines
for the moral and spiritual life (the *regula vivendi*). And in the end, the text
pointed the way to God's eternity (the *via regia*).

This model was an ingenious and meticulously elaborated system to
disclose and give voice to the interior of a text in different contexts. We can
say that the model offered an extended and differentiated grammar for "de-
ciphering" the different dimensions of the inner-room (Matt. 6:6) of a text.

33. Dohmen/Stemberger 1996, pp. 161-66; Farrar 1961, p. 295.

At the same time, we have to add that in the course of time the meaning given to the interior of a text overgrew the exterior. The letter of the text could no longer bear the weight of meaning given to or found in the inner-room of the text. The reason for this derailment was not the text itself but the tradition and the ecclesial authority, which began to determine and even dominate the inner-room of Scripture, in both its extent and its contents.

## 8.4. The Reformation

### Shifts in the Hermeneutical Paradigm

The Reformation caused a radical change in the hermeneutical paradigm of the Middle Ages. At the core of this revolution was a shift in the relation between Scripture, tradition, and the ecclesial authorities. Martin Luther (1483-1546) was one of the two theologians who led this hermeneutical revolution. He affirmed Scripture to be the church's only and ultimate authority.[34] Luther thus broke with the hermeneutical rule of his day, which held that both Scripture and ecclesial hierarchy had equal authority. Luther responds with an explosion of "sheer disgust, anger, and contempt" to Erasmus's call for a balanced view of the authority of Scripture and of the church.[35] For the reformer, only Scripture is and can be the source and foundation of preaching and proclamation. This core presupposition is crisply formulated in the Reformation's motto *sola Scriptura,* i.e., only Scripture. This principle regarding the Word of God is at the heart of the Reformation movement. The *Formula of Concord,* a Lutheran confessional statement from 1577, stated it this way:

> We believe that the only rule and standard by which all dogmas and all doctors are to be weighed and judged, is nothing else but the prophetic and apostolic writings of the Old and New Testaments.

I will briefly discuss the elements of this principle that are of importance for our subject. Luther was in the first place convinced of the *perspicuitas,* the perspicuity, of Scripture. His rhetoric would allow nothing less than absolute certainty about Scripture's absolute clarity.

34. Luther's hermeneutic was embedded in the whole of his theology (see Ebeling 1959).
35. This outburst can be read in his book *Bondage of the Will* first published in 1525 (Luther 1969).

Let miserable men, therefore, stop imputing with blasphemous perversity the darkness and obscurity of their own hearts to the wholly clear Scriptures of God.[36]

Luther's conviction on this point fueled a decidedly polemical tone, and he refused to allow even the slightest hint that the message of Scripture might be obscure in any fashion. It was the matters essential to faith that were clear, if not in one place then in another.

Those who deny that the Scriptures are quite clear and plain leave us nothing but darkness. . . . In opposition to you [Erasmus] I say with respect to the whole Scripture, I will not have any part of it called obscure.[37]

The intrinsic clarity of Scripture made in the second place any official institution for mediating or determining its interpretation superfluous. Scripture is able to interpret itself *(Scriptura sacra sui ipsius interpres)*. Martin Luther expressed this viewpoint as follows:

No violence is to be done to the words of God, whether by man or angel; but they are to be retained in their simplest meaning wherever possible, and to be understood in their grammatical and literal sense unless the context forbids, lest we give our adversaries occasion to make a mockery of all the Scriptures. Thus Origen was repudiated, in old times, because he despised the grammatical sense and turned trees, and all else written concerning Paradise, into allegories; for it might therefrom be concluded that God did not create trees.[38]

The self-interpreting and living Word of God addresses believers directly, calling for faith, hope, and love. The appeal to Scripture as its own interpreter presupposes thirdly the coherence of Scripture as a whole. Despite the forty or more human authors, Scripture contains a profound unity and organic nature. Because of this unity Scripture is consistent with itself, allowing a canonical integrated reading of Old and New Testaments.[39]

36. Luther 1969, p. 111.
37. Luther 1958, p. 94; see also Barth, *CD* I/2, pp. 712, 719.
38. Luther 1982, pp. 189f.
39. "Newer exegesis, which does not presuppose the agreement of all biblical writings but rather investigates the individual statements, the writings, and the writers against the

The notions of the clear and self-interpreting Scripture led in the fourth place to the idea that the plain meaning of Scripture could be acknowledged by plain (lay) persons, at least its basic and essential message. The authority of the church and the authority of tradition were no longer decisive. Scripture became the book of the congregation and the individual believer.

> Nothing more pernicious could be said than this, for it has led ungodly men to set themselves above the Scriptures and to fabricate whatever they pleased, until the Scriptures have been completely trampled down and we have been believing and teaching nothing but the dreams of madmen.[40]

The right of interpretation was restored to every believer. Every faithful individual enlightened with "the inward testimony of the Spirit" was authorized and able to interpret Scripture appropriately.[41]

The common ground of these elements is the attention to the original, plain meaning of the words of Scripture. The system guarded by ecclesial authority, the fourfold sense of Scripture, thus lost its legitimacy. Luther, Melanchthon, Calvin, and all the other reformers were opposed in their own way to this medieval hermeneutical concept.[42] This is especially true for the polemics against allegorical exegesis. Luther, for example, fumed: "Allegorizings are awkward, absurd, invented, obsolete rags."[43]

## The Old Testament

We turn to John Calvin (1509-1564) to focus on the reformers' interpretation of the Old Testament. According to him the LORD's covenant with the patriarchs hardly differs, in reality and substance, from the covenant with us. The covenants with them and with us are one and the same. The differences between Old and New Testaments all belong to the mode of adminis-

---

background of their various thought structures and proclamation, has found within the canonical Scriptures many more gaps, leaps, and contradictions than someone like Luther could have suspected" (Weber 1981, p. 261).

40. Luther 1969, pp. 158-59.
41. Calvin, *Institutes* I, 7, 4.
42. Kraus 1982, p. 9.
43. Quoted by Farrar 1961, p. 338.

tration rather than to the substance.[44] So, there is in fact only one covenant and this covenant is spiritual in character and founded in Christ. That is true for both the Old and New Testament administration. Calvin gives three arguments for his thesis. The Jews were elected in the first place to hope for eternal life; God did not promise earthly, tangible riches. Second, the one covenant rests in the goodness and grace of God and not in the merits of human beings. And third, Christ is the core and center of this covenant. Calvin's concept of the relation between Old and New Testaments remains almost unchanged throughout the different editions of the *Institutes*.

Calvin pays extra consideration to the first element because of the controversy and conflicts raised on that particular issue. He states that not only the gospel of the New Testament but already the Old Testament has the intention of pointing further than the material and visible blessing of the earthly existence. The promises of the LORD are always richer than the tangible fulfillment; there is a "not yet" or "surplus" left in the earthly Old Testament promises. The gospel does not confine the hearts of men to the enjoyment of the present life or mere earthly delights but raises them to the hope of immortality, the treasure that is laid up in heaven.[45]

Calvin thus postulates the unity of Old and New Testaments. That means that both Testaments cannot contradict each other. This premise determines Calvin's exegesis and interpretation of Scripture. He points regularly and consequently to the unity — we may even have to say uniformity — of both Testaments. Calvin is convinced of the fact that Christ, speaking to and communicating with his people, has chosen Scripture as his garment. Christ is therefore the hermeneutical lens through which both Old and New Testaments are read.

## The Practice of Preaching

For Calvin it is clear and obvious that, for instance, Psalm 45 gives a description of the spiritual goods and blessings of the kingdom of Christ. Because Jews and other (sic!) pagan nations don't accept this truth, Calvin puts a considerable effort to explain this at length. The reformer states that Psalm 45 does not fit completely within the period of Solomon's reign.

44. Calvin, *Institutes* II, 10, 2; II, 11, 1.
45. Calvin, *Institutes* II, 10, 3.

There is a surplus of meaning in the words and contents of the psalm that surpasses Solomon. For that reason our hearts were lifted up to look for a kingdom that is more splendid than the kingdom of Solomon, a kingdom yet to come.[46] This is not only true for this psalm or a collection of texts, but for the Old Testament as a whole. According to Calvin, Moses and the prophets are especially focused on the salvation in Christ.[47] The earthly gift is not self-sufficient but points to, is a mirror and herald of, the glorious hope that is stored up in heaven.

The gospel of the New Testament is spiritual, because the Lord has engraved it on the heart.[48] The covenant in Old Testament times does not differ in reality and substance from this covenant in Christ. Both are one and the same. The faithful of the old covenant were also children of God and heirs of Christ; they too had Jerusalem as their mother.[49] Both Testaments point to the eternal kingdom of our Lord and Savior Jesus Christ.

The spiritual character of the covenant of the New Testament is the hermeneutical lens for reading and interpreting the Old Testament. There is only a gradual difference between both Testaments. Apostles and evangelists reveal God's grace more clearly and lucidly and lead our minds more directly to meditate upon it so that the inferior mode of exercise formerly employed in regard to the Jews can now be laid aside.[50] The most important part of the covenant is the promise that the LORD will be a gracious God to Abraham and his children. The gift of the earthly land is, so to speak, a mere "surplus" or "encore." This "surplus" points to a deeper level, to something that is far greater and more glorious than that which can be touched by human hands. Abraham never possessed the land that was promised to him. He was on a pilgrimage in the land, where he lived as an alien on his way to a better country, a heavenly one.[51]

The spiritual character was for Calvin related to the ultimate and deepest level of the "literal sense." This last expression was usually equated with the intended meaning of the original author. Calvin was a Humanist (see §8.5) and therefore a linguist. One of the important features of Humanist reading was to make the intention of the author explicit. For Cal-

---

46. See his commentary on Psalm 45.
47. Calvin, *Institutes* II, 6, 3; II, 7, 17; II, 10, 1; IV, 8, 5.
48. Calvin, *Institutes* II, 11, 8.
49. See his commentary on Galatians 4:7, 24.
50. Calvin, *Institutes* II, 11, 1.
51. See Calvin's commentary on Genesis 17:7f.; Hebrews 11:9f., 13b-16.

vin, God was the ultimate "Author" of Scripture. The authorial intention-
ality was for the reformer extended in such a way that it included the LORD
as the ultimate Author of Scripture as a whole. The doctrine of God generates and guards therefore a coherence and unity in the colorful landscape
of Scripture.[52]

## Israel

John Calvin's views on Israel appear to evidence a tension between rejection and acceptance. On the one hand, Calvin strongly insisted that God's
promise to and covenant with the people of Israel were unconditional, un-
breakable, and gracious. But we can also read contrary statements in the
writings of Calvin, in that he sees only a provisional meaning for Israel.[53]
Calvin says, for instance, that it looks at first sight as if Isaac's blessing of
Jacob is purely earthly in contents. But this blessing for Abraham and his
offspring is in the first place spiritual in character.[54] Genesis 27:28-29
speaks indeed about prosperity, peace, fertility, and an honored position
among the nations. The text is silent about the heavenly realm. Calvin
states that illiterate people, badly exercised in true piety, draw from those
verses the incorrect conclusion that the patriarchs were only interested in
earthly blessings. Those people don't see that the earthly, material blessing
is an external symbol that serves as garment for God's promise of spiritual
salvation.[55] Since Christ was not yet revealed, his kingdom was symbolized
in earthly images. When the fullness of time had come, God was revealed
to his people without veils. The earthly symbols served merely as pedagog-
ical means to point to the heavenly kingdom. Canaan is an image of the
non-visible glory that has been stored up in heaven.

For Calvin there is unity and continuity in the people of God from
the moment God created Adam and Eve. For that reason the reformer can
name the people of God in Old Testament times *ecclesia* (church). However, this name is not used for Israel as a whole but restricted to the small,
faithful remnant. In other words, Israel in Old Testament times referred to
the elect people. After the coming of Christ the elect are also to be found

52. Greene-McCreight 1999, pp. 107, 111, 118, 149, 158 (note 85).
53. Williamson 1993, p. 131; VanGemeren, 1983, p. 142.
54. See his commentary on Genesis 27:27ff.
55. See his commentary on Leviticus 26:3.

among the gentiles. And thus, the role of Israel in salvation history came to an end. Calvin has no special future expectations for Israel as a nation. The difference between old and new covenants is that before Christ the elect are to be found only in the people of Israel; after Christ the people of God include Jews (insofar as they believe in Jesus Christ) and gentiles.

### In Sum

Calvin turns to and insists on the literal sense of the text. But he was well aware that preaching cannot suffice with a mere treatment of the literal or historical exterior. Calvin "loads" the letter of the text with the proclamation of the "rule of faith" *(regula fidei)*, which centers around the proclamation of Jesus Christ. He is the ultimate and exclusive meaning of the interior of the text. The Old Testament thus becomes a Christian book because its content is "Christ-ened."[56]

All the reformers opposed in their own way the allegorical interpretation. The reformers wanted to balance the interior and the exterior of the text. In their hermeneutical and theological reflection, they gave preference to the literal sense, the exterior of the text, unlike most of the church fathers. But the practice of the exposition and preaching of the reformers was in fact governed by Christ as the alleged kerygmatic interior of Scripture as a whole. We can thus discern a tension between the hermeneutical theory and the practice of interpretation of the Old Testament. There are in fact some remarkable and surprising parallels between the practice of the reformers' preaching and that of Origen. Both see Christ as the ultimate content of the proclamation of Moses and the prophets.

### 8.5. Humanism, Renaissance, and Enlightenment

The Reformation can't be seen apart from the Renaissance and the rise of Humanism in the fifteenth and sixteenth centuries.[57] Those centuries were marked by a number of substantial cultural changes that upset the once

---

56. Calvin speaks of the New Testament as an "appendix," in Latin *accessio* (Commentary on 2 Timothy 3:17). He means the twofold sense of exposition and ratification *(Explicationem una com rerum exhibitione)*.

57. Barrera 1998, pp. 548ff.

relatively stable European political and ideological systems. Technical discoveries such as the compass and the printing press revolutionized navigation and communication. Geographical discoveries such as Columbus's voyage to the Americas in 1492 changed the worldview. Church and theology were of course also touched by these cultural shifts.

## Humanism

The guiding principle of Humanism is *ad fontes,* back to the sources. That meant mainly a turn to the original Latin and especially Greek writings from the classical period. Dictionaries and grammars of Greek and Latin were published at that time. As a result, universities in Western Europe were enlarged and new libraries were established. The libraries became centers of collections of important writings in the original languages. The universities became centers of research.

The Humanists' intention to read classical writings in the original languages was not restricted to profane texts. Research on the text of the New Testament was done with the same intention and instruments. Erasmus of Rotterdam (1467-1536) made an important contribution to the first edition of the Greek New Testament ever printed: *Novum Instrumentum omne, diligenter ad Erasmo Roterodamo recognitum et emendatum* (The entire New Testament, diligently researched and corrected by Erasmus of Rotterdam). The first edition was released in Basel (Switzerland) in 1516, just one year before the onset of the Reformation.[58]

Because original sources had become available, one was no longer dependent on the authoritative clerical interpretation of the tradition. Scholars used the same rational instruments in their research of religious sources.[59] There are thus explicit connections and parallels between the *ad fontes* of Humanism and the Renaissance on the one hand and the *sola Scriptura* of the Reformation on the other hand. As Robert McQueen Grant has said, historical exegesis "is even more a child of the Renaissance than of the Reformation."[60]

58. The second edition (released in 1519) of Erasmus's critical edition of the Greek New Testament was used by the translators of the King James Version. This Greek text later became known as the *textus receptus.*

59. Kraus 1982, p. 25.

60. Grant 1984, p. 128.

## The Enlightenment

The Enlightenment is both the logical continuation and the inescapable consequence of the Renaissance and Humanism. "Enlightenment" refers to an intellectual and cultural movement that dominates seventeenth- and eighteenth-century Europe. This "age of reason" movement wanted to set forth the emancipation and the liberalizing from every authority or institution in proclaiming the autonomy of every individual person. Trust in humanity and human reason replaced trust in divinity and clerical authority.

A new scientific method was developed to achieve true and certain knowledge based on empirical observation and systematic doubt. In intellectual circles, interest in non-empirical or spiritual realities began to fade quickly. The "enlightened" wanted something they could see and test and get their hands on. Isaac Newton's (1642-1725) laws of motion laid a foundation for a mechanistic worldview that came to dominate life and thought for centuries. The scientific revolution reduced the world to observable empirical phenomena and enthroned mathematics as "queen of the sciences," a position that theology had proudly occupied during the Middle Ages. This recalls a familiar story about the French mathematical physicist Pierre Simon de Laplace (1749-1827) and his work, *Mécanique céleste* (celestial mechanics). According to the story, Laplace made a personal presentation of a copy of his book to Napoleon Bonaparte (1769-1821). The French emperor glanced through the volume but did not find a reference to the Creator. He asked Laplace: "You say much about the Universe but you say nothing about its Creator?" Laplace is reported to have replied, "Sire, I have no need for that hypothesis."

Critical, "enlightened" research had no place for supernatural violation of the law of cause and effect, nor was special or divinely inspired revelation acknowledged. The truth of Scripture was seen as that which is accessible to and can be affirmed by reason. During the "age of reason" biblical scholars began to read Scripture with secular instruments. The meaning of biblical events, institutions, and persons was no longer interpreted from a confessional perspective but was studied using historical- and literary-critical means and methods. As with other ancient literature, Scripture had to be "explained in relation to the mundane causes, historical conditions, and cultural presuppositions of the times in which they were written."[61]

61. Harrisville/Sundberg 1995, p. 44.

## Hermeneutics Faces an "Ugly, Broad Ditch"

Up until the Reformation, the term "author" referred ultimately to God as the principal Author. The Renaissance and the Enlightenment sharpened the awareness that the words of Moses and the prophets did not come into being in a historical vacuum.[62] As a consequence, "author" became the word for the human writer or editor. The leading questions became questions of philology and history, questions that put the human authors and their historical and socio-political contexts in the center of the picture. Interpreters began to ask, "What did the original authors mean?" "When did they live?" "What did they know?" "What sources did they use?" "What was their intention?" As a result of these questions the meaning of the expression "literal sense" changed also. Critical scholarship understood "literal sense" primarily as the meaning that the human author directly intended. It was the task of the interpreter to come as close as possible to the original intention of the original author. The basic assumption and starting point of exegesis were strictly limited to a strong commitment to the letter and history of the text.

Attention for the one and only literal sense of the texts asked in a natural way for historical inquiry and research. This attention fueled the awareness of the historical, geographical, and cultural distance between the there-and-then of the text and the here-and-now of the contemporary congregation. That distance was felt as a great gap across which nothing could be transferred. The German philosopher Gotthold Ephraim Lessing (1729-1781) coined a famous expression when he wrote: "That, then, is the ugly, broad ditch which I cannot get across, however often and however earnestly I have tried to make the leap. If anyone can help me over it, let him do it, I beg him, I adjure him. He will deserve a divine reward from me."[63] That distance also contributed to experiencing Moses and the prophets as *Old* Testament.

## In Sum

The scholarly exegesis of the Enlightenment sought to interpret a text within its historical and literary context. That was a sign of esteem and re-

62. Dunn 2003, pp. 17-20.
63. Lessing 1967, pp. 53-55.

spect for the text and its original author. The text was allowed to say what it had to say without being interrupted by dogmas or used as a mere ventriloquist's dummy for the ecclesial tradition.

But the hermeneutic of the Enlightenment also had and still has some disadvantages. First, the relationship between and the unity of Old and New Testaments were expressed more in historical terms of development and less in theological terms. This caused in the end a devaluing of the theology and particular voice of the Old Testament.

Second, scholarly exegesis drew further back toward the linguistic and historical exterior of the text. Biblical scholars made well-reasoned statements about grammar, semantics, and syntax only. Exegesis became a kind of literary archaeology, and as a result the text fell more and more apart into sources, fragments, glosses, and editorial additions.[64] That gave rise to a varied and finely differentiated set of exegetical instruments, or as some say, "a heavy armor."[65] The research was directed principally at determining the authorship, place and date, structures, editorial additions, redactions, sources, and original meaning.

Third, it meant that the theological interior or "God-sense" of Moses and the prophets was increasingly lost. The reformers' effort to establish a (fragile) balance between interior and exterior of Scripture was distorted. The exterior began to rule over the kerygmatic interior. The hermeneutical questions became as a result more and more oppressive.

## 8.6. Evaluation

Throughout the history of interpretation we see a struggle to balance the meaning and importance of the (kerygmatic) interior and the (literary and historical) exterior of Scripture. Theologians of the patristic era and the Middle Ages paid great attention to the meaning of the interior of Scripture. In the course of time the ecclesial tradition and authority came to determine more and more the "size" and content of this interior. Biblical interpretation was not so much a case of philology and theology but was

64. See Marquardt 1988, p. 324.

65. Morgan/Barton 1988, chapter 6. The homiletical handbook of Fendt/Klaus calls the whole set of historical and literary critical instruments the "ganze schere Waffenrüstung der Wissenschaft" (Fendt/Klaus 1970, p. 61). And Hirschler uses the expression "historisch-kritischen Rüstzeug" (Hirschler 1988, p. 108). See also Carter Florence 2004, pp. 93-108.

determined by ecclesial authority and official institutions. The "inner room" of the words was so richly decorated with the furniture of fourfold meaning that it became in fact too loaded for the "carrying capacity" of the letter of the text.

The reformers tried to balance interior and exterior again. They wanted in fact to revitalize the interpretation of the school of Antioch. The *sola Scriptura* (= only Scripture) brought the interpretation under the discipline and regulation of the letter of the text. The text could no longer be used as a hallstand to hang all kinds of meaning on. Preaching had to give account of its interpretation in front of the self-interpreting Scripture *(Scriptura sui interpres).*

This new balance also wanted to do justice to Scripture as both a human product and a divine instrument. Calvin was on the one hand aware that the meaning of a text is not simply given with ink and paper, or with letters, words, and sentences. The reformer was on the other hand convinced that the letters and the ink refer to the "God-sense" of the words. This "God-sense" of Scripture as a whole is briefly summarized in the "Rule of Faith" *(regula fidei).* This rule provided the theological paradigm for its interpretation and as such the "fences" for the meaning of the interior of a given text.[66] Calvin stated that interpretation cannot exceed these fences without becoming wild and fanciful.

History shows the vulnerability of this Reformed balance. The Renaissance and Enlightenment focused more and more on the exterior of the biblical text. That was not only a radicalization but also a secular, non-metaphysical understanding of the literal meaning of the text.[67] Interpretation was entangled by the aim to get as close as possible to that which "really" happened and to separate (original) fact from (editorial) fiction. As a result, the distance between the there-and-then of the text and the here-and-now of the contemporary situation came to be felt as an "ugly, broad ditch."

The literary and historical research produced indeed a lot of information about the backgrounds of biblical texts. But one could not avoid the question about the relevance of this material for the practice of preaching and sermon preparation. The text fell apart in independent fragments. For sermon preparation, the results of this kind of exegesis did not suffice.

66. Grant 1984, chapter 8.
67. C. J. D. Green 2003, p. 136.

Preaching is more than just an enumeration of historical and literary details. One had to make an appeal to the discipline of hermeneutics in order to bridge the "ugly, broad ditch."

So, we can say that the meaning given to the interior of words overgrew the grammatical and historical exterior of the letters of Scripture in the period before the Reformation. But the meaning of the interior of Scripture became hidden behind the exterior of the text in the period from the Enlightenment onward. Exegesis became more a literary and less a theological discipline.

It may be obvious to say that we are not the first ones to open and read Scripture. Every generation is part of the ongoing process of interpretation. At this moment we are the last link in the chain, but former generations are also part of the communion of saints and the catholicity of the church. That means that church fathers, reformers, and present-day biblical scholars are equal conversation partners in the discourse about meaning and interpretation. "With a few notable exceptions, modern biblical scholars have paid little attention to pre-modern biblical interpretation. Such work was within the purview of historical theology. To the extent that biblical scholars addressed pre-modern interpretation at all, it was generally to treat it as a form of error, as a series of failed attempts to uncover the meaning of the biblical text."[68]

Keeping in view the ingredients provided by the history of interpretation, a contemporary hermeneutical model should integrate the gains of the different concepts used through the course of history.

a. A hermeneutical model has to balance the meaning of the interior and of the exterior of Scripture. The model has to be under the "discipline of the letter" and at the same time be open for the voice of God's Spirit that can be heard in the "inner room" of the text. We can't and won't go back behind the insights of either the Reformation or the Renaissance.[69]

68. Fowl 1997, p. xvii. Fowl mentions Brevard Childs as one of the "notable exceptions."

69. We can hear comparable voices in the Roman Catholic Church. See for instance the document of the Pontifical Biblical Commission, *The Jewish People and Their Sacred Scriptures in the Christian Bible* (English translation 2002). Recent developments "gave rise in contemporary theology, without as yet any consensus, to different ways of re-establishing a Christian interpretation of the Old Testament that would avoid arbitrariness and respect the original meaning" (II.A.4).

b.  Nor do we want to go back behind the results of literary and historical research. Dictionary, grammar, and syntax are indispensable tools for exegesis. But we have to keep in mind that these are only helpful instruments for the reading of the love-letter; they are not the love-letter itself. We can't reduce or restrict the interpretation of the love-letter of the LORD to a merely linguistic concern. This means that for the practice of preaching we have to construct a model that helps preacher and congregation to open the "God-sense" or kerygmatic interior of Scripture.

c.  A hermeneutical model that serves the practice of preaching has the character of a bunch of keys that can disclose the multidimensional character of the inner room of the biblical texts. We should therefore be inspired by the multidimensional patristic reading of Scripture. This hermeneutical key is at least a challenge in our search for a contemporary hermeneutical strategy.[70]

d.  A contemporary Christian theology should integrate in its hermeneutical strategy the abiding meaning for Israel of the books of Moses and the prophets.

e.  A scripturally founded hermeneutical model has to respect the unity of God.

---

70. Steinmetz 1980, pp. 27-38; Wilson 2001.

# 9. Biblical Theology

## 9.1. Quotation, Echo, and Allusion

In a popular TV show a few years back, participants were required to guess the title or the performers of a piece of music of which they were allowed to hear only a few bars. It was really surprising to see (and hear!) that they could recognize it after just a few seconds. It was also surprising how much just a few seconds could reveal: not only the title of the piece and the performers but even the recording medium (vinyl or CD).

The same can be true for an audience that is familiar with an existing text. Even the smallest hint from the text is enough to evoke the entire text. For ancient audiences, only a few words or bits of imagery from the books of Moses and the prophets would have caused the reverberation of a whole story, hymn, or prophecy. In addition to its many explicit quotations, the New Testament is filled with these kinds of implicit references to the Old Testament. You can't read Matthew, for instance, without having your ear tuned to the Old Testament, from which the evangelist quotes or to which he alludes four or five times per chapter. Richard Hays correctly states that "echoes linger in the air and lure the reader ( ) back into the symbolic world of Scripture. Paul's allusions gesture toward precursors whose words are already heavy with tacit implication."[1] Without mentioning their sources by name, apostles and evangelists offer a tapestry of Old Testament images, theology, story plots, expressions, and metaphors. The authors deliberately want to proceed within a certain tradition and embroider on existing patterns and with existing materials. This network of quotations, in-

1. Hays 1989, p. 155.

dications, (vague) allusions, terminological indebtedness, reminiscence, and echoes of words, images, and phrasings is called intertextuality.[2]

> The vocabulary and cadences of Scripture — particularly the LXX — are imprinted deeply on Paul's mind, and the great stories of Israel continue to serve for him as a fund of symbols and metaphors that condition his perception of the world, of God's promised deliverance of his people, and of his own identity and calling. His faith, in short, is one whose articulation is inevitably intertextual in character, and Israel's Scripture is the "determinate subtext that plays a constitutive role" in shaping his literary production.[3]

There is almost no single text in the New Testament without a reference, quote, echo, or allusion to the Old Testament.[4] Jesus' role in Matthew's account of the Sermon on the Mount is, for instance, an implicit but clear reference to Moses on Mount Sinai, yet the evangelist does not refer explicitly to that event. A similar "technique" can be found in Luke's version of the Transfiguration (Luke 9:28-36). These verses offer more of the Old Testament than the explicit words taken from Deutero-Isaiah (Luke 9:35/Isa. 42:1). Luke tells about the meeting of Jesus with Moses and Elijah (representing the prophets). These two speak with Jesus about his departure, literally: *exodus* (v. 31). Peter, one of the disciples, wants to make three dwellings. The Greek word used by the evangelist *(skēnē)* means tent or booth and refers to the Festival of Booths, as described in the books of Moses (Lev. 23:33-44; Deut. 16:13-17). Luke tells further that a cloud came and overshadowed the men on the mountain. This is a reference to the manifestation of the glory of the LORD in a cloud when Israel wandered in the desert. This cloud covered Sinai when Moses met the LORD on the mountain (Exod. 16:10; 24:15; 34:5; 40:34ff.). All these references are more implicit than explicit, yet deliberately present in the text. But clearly, the apostles and evangelists had the Scriptures constantly in mind while writing their Gospels and Letters. In fact, a quotation is sometimes intended to

---

2. Soulen/Soulen 2001, pp. 87-88; Vanhoozer 2005, pp. 332-34; for the specific relevance of intertextuality for preaching the Old Testament see Miles 2000, pp. 195-215.

3. Hays 1989, p. 16. The citation is from the literary critic Thomas M. Greene.

4. In Revelation, for instance, there is no formal quotation. But almost 70 percent of the texts of this book contain allusions to the Old Testament (Ellis 1977, p. 215; see Hays 1989; Marquardt 1990, pp. 52-237; Juel 2003, pp. 286ff.).

prompt the recall of an entire passage of Scripture. For example, Paul's quotation from the Old Testament in 1 Corinthians 10:7 is part of Exodus 32:6. This passage refers to the festivities of the Israelites after setting up the golden calf in the desert. In making this connection, the apostle isn't just quoting the words of a particular text, but intends to evoke the whole narrative of the golden calf and Israel's idolatry. A lot more can be mentioned to make clear that apostles and evangelists use the books of Moses, the prophets, and David as colorful stones to craft their own mosaics.[5] The Old Testament provides apostles and evangelists with imagery not only to describe the Christ-event but also to interpret this event in light of the LORD's way with Israel.

The examples given here make clear that the definition of "quotation" is diffuse. Depending on the extent of such a definition, the number of Old Testament references in the New Testament ranges from 250 to 4,000.[6] This chapter uses a narrower definition.[7] I am interested in (more or less) explicit and literal quotations and not in vague or implicit allusions or echoes. The phrase "more or less" makes clear that one cannot give sharp and conclusive contours. Every definition is open to discussion. But generally, an explicit quotation may be recognized by a change of style in the text. It may also be introduced with explicit quotation markers, i.e., words like "as it is written," "faithful is the word," or "that which had been spoken [by the LORD] through the prophet."

## 9.2. Recontextualization and Patterns of Communication

The change of style is not only a matter of grammar. In quoting the Old Testament, apostles and evangelists could also change the theological context of the words from Moses and the prophets. We can therefore speak of theological recontextualizations of Old Testament words, images, metaphors, and theology. In order to get those theological changes

5. Hollander uses the word "echo" to describe the "modes of allusion which are faint, subtle, and sometimes no more than a hum through a composition" (Hollander 1981).

6. Ellis 1985, pp. 150-87 (= Appendix I-IV); Greidanus 1999, pp. 50f., 185f.

7. See the list of Archer/Chirichigno (1983) and the list with Old Testament quotations in *Novum Testamenten Greace* (Aland 1979, *Appendix III: Loci citati vel allegati*, pp. 739-69). The editors of this last list emphasize that "opinions differ greatly in identifying quotations and allusions" (Nestlé-Aland 1979, p. 72*). See also Hays 1989, pp. 32f.

or recontextualizations into view, I made an analysis of the character of these recontextualizations. In the first step of research, I asked this question of the Old Testament originals: Who or what is the speaking or acting subject, and who or what is the object or addressee of the words or acts? In a second step I examined eventual changes of (one of) these elements in the New Testament quotations. I was interested in knowing if those changes or theological recontextualizations could be arranged in a pattern or structure.

Apostles and evangelists didn't make their hermeneutical rules explicit. It is even questionable whether they were aware of their own hermeneutical strategies.[8] But even if the writers of the New Testament didn't use a reflected hermeneutical system or set of rules, we can discern certain patterns of interpretation or contours in their implicit hermeneutics. And those patterns can help us to reconstruct their — explicit or implicit — hermeneutical strategy. It was a surprise to discover that there are indeed four clear distinguishable patterns of theological recontextualization of Old Testament quotations in the New Testament. We can therefore say that apostles and evangelists did not draw on the resources from Moses and the prophets in a purely ad hoc, disconnected manner but had a more or less integrated scriptural hermeneutic.

a. In the first place, there are texts with the same theological context in both Old and New Testaments. The Old Testament's original and the quotation in the New Testament both have their place in the communication between the LORD and Israel.

b. Second, there are quotations with a clear and explicitly Christological recontextualization.

c. Third, apostles and evangelists sometimes use the Old Testament to describe and interpret the situation of the young (both Jewish and gentile) church by means of Old Testament words, images, and metaphors — an ecclesiological recontextualization, as it were.

d. And finally, there are Old Testament quotations that are recontextualized in an eschatological sense.

---

8. Von Rad questions whether there can be found any structure or system in the "ad hoc associations," the "ad hoc allusions," or the "ad hoc actualization" of apostles and evangelists (Von Rad 1981a/b, pp. 330, 332). And Marquardt states that the "Jesus Writings" didn't develop a clear and "reproducible" system (Marquardt 1990, p. 218, my translation).

The following sections offer some examples of these four ways of reinterpretation or recontextualization; an extended treatment would go beyond the proportions of this chapter.

## 9.3. The Context of Israel

Analyzing the Old Testament quotations in the New Testament, I made some notable discoveries. The first was that apostles and evangelists quote words of Moses and the prophets in the context of Israel. The theological context was the same in both Old and New Testaments. As a result, the theological interior of the words of Moses and the prophets did not change in the New Testament context. The LORD (through one of the prophets or David) is the speaking or acting Subject in both Old and New Testaments. And, complementarily, Israel is the object of God's words or acts in both Testaments. Those quotations occur in historical surveys reviewing God's history with Israel or in quotations from the commandments in the books of Moses. Apostles and evangelists insist that the quoted commandments are still valid. We can think, for example, of references to the Ten Commandments (Matt. 5:21, 27; 15:4; Eph. 6:2f.; Heb. 4:4 with quotations from Exod. 20:12-14). Other instructions of Moses are quoted to indicate that every word may be confirmed by the evidence of two or three witnesses (Matt. 18:16 — Deut. 19:15), to portray the relation between man and wife (Gen. 1:27; 2:24; 5:2 — Matt. 19:4f.), or to discuss issues related to the so-called levirate duty, i.e., the marriage with a husband's brother (Matt. 22:24; Mark 12:19; Luke 20:28; Gen. 38:8; Deut. 25:5, 7; see also Tobit 4:12; 6:9-12; 7:12f.). From this perspective the experiences of the patriarchs and of the people of Israel get a place in the recital of the intervention and guidance of the LORD in the history of Israel (Acts 7; Rom. 9; Heb. 11).

Isaiah's question about the "spirit of the LORD" (Isa. 40:13 — 1 Cor. 2:16), Jeremiah's words about boasting in the LORD (Jer. 9:23 — 1 Cor. 1:31; 2 Cor. 10:17) and the fact that the thoughts of the wise are futile (Ps. 94:11 — 1 Cor. 3:20) are quoted by Paul without giving them a place in a new interpretative context.

From a hermeneutical point of view, we can say that for the apostles and evangelists Moses and the prophets not only *had* meaning for Israel in the past, but also *still have* meaning for Israel. The birth of Jesus Christ did not break the relation between the covenant-partners Israel and the LORD, between the Tanak and the community of the Temple or synagogue. There are texts that speak explicitly and extensively about God's remaining and abiding loyalty to his covenant with Israel (e.g., Luke 1:46-56, 67-80; 2:29-32; Rom. 9–11), extensive quotations from the Old Testament included. But apostles and evangelists also testify about this loyalty by using this key in their hermeneutical strategy. The discovery of this key meets an important omission in the classical hermeneutical models. In §7.1.2 I stated that the practice of preaching based on the classical models leads almost automatically to a neglect of the abiding meaning of the words of Moses and the prophets for Israel. The discovery of this element in inner-biblical hermeneutics leads to the conclusion that a contemporary hermeneutical model must have the key of Israel on its ring.

## 9.4. Written of Him

The books of Moses and the prophets have an abiding meaning for Israel. It is well known that the apostles and evangelists quoted Scripture in an explicitly Christological context without denying that first dimension of meaning. The writers of the New Testament use the Old Testament to describe and interpret the Jesus-event. Paul van Buren rightly says that the "Scriptures of Israel provided the vocabulary and imagery with which, and above all the story within the framework of which, the Apostolic Writings tell of the things concerning Jesus."[9]

Philip says to Nathaniel, "We have found him about whom Moses in the law and also the prophets wrote, Jesus son of Joseph from Nazareth" (John 1:46). Philip proclaims the good news about Jesus to the Ethiopian eunuch, starting with words taken from the Scriptures (Acts 8:35). Timothy gets the advice to continue studying the sacred writings that are able to instruct for salvation through faith in Christ Jesus (2 Tim. 3:15f.). Peter is convinced that the prophets testified in advance to the sufferings of Christ and the subsequent glory (1 Pet. 1:10f.).

Apostles and evangelists use the Old Testament in this way because they are convinced of the fact that the Scriptures "had been written of him" (John 12:16; 5:39). According to John, Isaiah saw the glory of Christ and

---

9. Van Buren, 1988, p. 31. Marquardt says that the Old Testament provided the "elementary particles" ("elementärteilchen") for Christology (Marquardt 1990).

spoke about him (John 12:41). Paul and Peter say that David spoke about the resurrection of Christ (Acts 2:25ff.; 13:32ff.). And Paul says that Christ died for us "according to the Scriptures" (1 Cor. 15:13). The Christ-event made such a deep impression on the apostles and evangelists that they sometimes give rise to the thought that Christ is the actual content of the Old Testament.[10]

The disciples of Jesus used words, images, and theology of Moses and the prophets to describe and interpret the life and ministry of Jesus Christ even in minor details.[11] One can think of the entrance into Jerusalem on a donkey (Matt. 21:5, 9 — Ps. 118:25f.; Isa. 62:11; Zech. 9:9), the division of Jesus' clothes at the cross (Matt. 27:35; Mark 15:24; Luke 23:24; John 19:24 — Ps. 22:19), or his being numbered with the criminals (Luke 22:27 — Isa. 53:12). Psalm 110 can be interpreted in a Christological context so that it testifies to Christ's sitting "at the right hand of God" (Matt. 22:24; Mark 12:36; Luke 20:42f.; Acts 2:34f.; Heb. 1:13).

This Christological use of the Old Testament is long and widely known. It has a place in almost every hermeneutical concept. For that reason, I took a closer look at this dimension of recontextualization. I discovered three clearly distinguished hermeneutical strategies. Apostles and evangelists use Old Testament words, images, theologies, and metaphors as words spoken *by Jesus,* words addressed *to Jesus,* and words *about Jesus.* It was therefore no surprise to learn that the church fathers connected the Psalms and Christ along the same three lines.[12]

---

10. "For Paul Christ was not only a factor, giving added meaning to the Old Testament but the only means whereby the Old Testament could be rightly understood" (Ellis 1985, pp. 115f.). Gerhard von Rad says that the exegesis of apostles and evangelists "often runs counter to our understanding of scripture; it nevertheless indicates that for Christians the Old Testament only has meaning in so far as it refers to Christ and was able to speak in the light of Christ" (1980b, p. 332).

11. "Language used to speak about Jesus is uniformly scriptural in origin" (Juel 1988, pp. 8, 23, 56).

12. "Der Psalter is für die Kirche der Märtyrer ein Christusbuch, dessen Lieder um den am Kreuz erhöten Kyrios kreisen, sei es, dass die von Ihm, sei es dass sie zu Ihm, sie es dass Er selbst in ihnen zum Vater redet ( ): *Psalmus vox de Christo/Psalmos vox Ecclesiae ad Christum/Psalmus vox Christi ad Patrem*" (Fischer 1982, p. 31).

## Words Spoken by Jesus

Apostles and evangelists quote the Old Testament as giving Jesus the role of the speaking (or acting) subject of the Old Testament text. That can be both a human and the divine subject. In Matthew 16:27, for example, Jesus gets the role of the divine "I" of Psalm 62:13. In this psalm, the LORD is the acting Subject who repays to all according to their work. In the Gospel of Matthew, Jesus is the one who does the repaying.

Jesus can also get the role of a human speaking (or acting) subject. The poet of Psalm 41:9 laments that even the bosom friend in whom he trusted and who ate of his bread has lifted the heel against his friend. John the evangelist uses this verse and its imagery in his description of the Last Supper (John 13:18). Jesus identifies himself with the "I" of this psalm the moment Judas betrays him. The one who eats the bread of the LORD nevertheless lifts his heel against his friend. The same pattern can be seen in the well-known words of Jesus at the cross, "My God, why have you forsaken me?" Jesus makes the complaint of the poet of Psalm 22 into his own prayer (Mark 15:22 and par.).

## Words Addressed to Jesus

The New Testament can also portray Jesus as the addressee, object, or receiver of Old Testament words or events. When Jesus entered Jerusalem, the crowds sing for him words taken from Psalm 118 (Matt. 21:9). In their original setting those words are addressed to God. Jesus is identified with the Subject of the psalm.

## Words about Jesus

In a third strategy, apostles and evangelists portray Jesus as the content, the theme, the subject matter, or the issue of the Old Testament text. We could also say that Old Testament words are used by others to describe or interpret the life and ministry of Jesus. When the disciples witness, for example, the cleansing of the Temple, they notice the passion of Jesus, which makes them recall Psalm 69:10 (John 2:17). The person who is praying in this psalm speaks to God about his or her zeal for the house of God (= content). The disciples use these words to describe the zeal of Jesus.

The early Christians listened to the words of Moses and the prophets and looked back over the patterns of God's words and deeds with his covenant people Israel in the past and saw that all those words and actions became flesh in the life and ministry of Jesus. Apostles and evangelists used these strategies in a varied and creative way for their Christological recontextualizations. The author of the letter to the Hebrews offers, for instance, a strong Christological interpretation of the cultic institutions[13] (e.g., 2 Sam. 7:14; Ps. 2:7/Heb. 1:5; Ps. 8:5-7/Heb. 2:6-8; Ps. 40:7-9/Heb. 10:5-7). Christ can get the role of priest, as appointed representative of the people (Heb. 5:6; 10:11, 21). But he can also be portrayed as the priestly representative of the God who reconciles (Heb. 7). That means that there is also a Christological key to the hermeneutical ring.

## 9.5. Written for Our Instruction

According to the apostles and evangelists, Christ is not the last station on the road of God's history with Israel, the nations, and creation. Heikki Räisänen concludes correctly that if "all God's promises are fulfilled in Jesus, their content has in the post-Paschal era been changed to such an extent as to be in effect nullified."[14] But the Old Testament can't be tied up to the Christological dimension. Moses and the prophets are, so to speak, not exhausted; they didn't finish their speaking in the Christ-proclamation. The interior of the Old Testament has more to say. God's way of salvation and judgment continues after the Christ-event. The Old Testament provided the disciples of Jesus — both Jews and gentiles — after the crucifixion and resurrection with words, images, metaphors, and theology to describe and interpret their lives *coram Deo*, both as a community and individually. This community was invited to "belong to the Way" (Acts 9:2).

After Easter and Pentecost, apostles and evangelists extended the expressiveness of the Old Testament kerygma to the context of gentile hearers and readers. Images, metaphors, theology, and paradigms of Moses and

---

13. Kistemaker 1961; A. T. Hanson 1964; Howard 1968; McCullough 1980.

14. Räisänen 1997, p. 63. This critical point could be raised against all the models discussed in part I. These concepts also maneuver the congregation into the role of mere spectators of a past-time event.

the prophets that seemed at first to be restricted to Israel now seemed to be absorbed in the second layer of meaning by the proclamation of Christ; they were, so to speak, raised and revitalized by apostles and evangelists to proclaim the salvation of the LORD for the gentiles. For them, it is obvious that "whatever was written in former days was written for our instruction, so that by steadfastness and by the encouragement of the scriptures we might have hope" (Rom. 15:4; cf. 1 Cor. 10:6, 11). And it is clear that for Paul, the "us" refers to the gentile community of faith. In doing so, Paul writes a continuation to the Christological "written of him" (Gal. 2:4; Eph. 5:32). For that reason Paul can use words and images from Isaiah to testify about Christ's mission (Acts 26:23), but he can use the same words to defend the legitimacy of his own mission (Acts 13:47).[15]

Paul testifies in Romans 4:16-22 about God's gracious concern with the history of Israel. He continues to say that those words "were written not for his sake [i.e., Christ's] alone, but for ours also. It will be reckoned to us who believe in him who raised Jesus our Lord from the dead" (Rom. 4:23f.). The apostles were convinced that the prophets were serving not themselves — also not exclusively Christ! — but the congregation of Christ (1 Pet. 1:12). The words of Moses and the prophets are inspired by God and are useful for teaching, for reproof, for correction, and for training in righteousness (2 Tim. 3:16).

That opened the possibility for apostles and evangelists to "read back" into the Old Testament the existence of the Christian community. Or do we have to say that they read the Old Testament "ahead" in the existence of the community of faith of both Jews and gentiles? From that point of view the "muzzled ox" refers to the "ministerial officers" in the congregation (1 Cor. 9:10; 1 Tim. 5:18 — Deut. 25:4). Jannes and Jambres, the adversaries of Moses, become a paradigm for those who oppose the proclamation of the gospel in the last days (2 Tim. 3:1, 8).[16] John depicts Cain as the archetype of those who don't love their neighbors (1 John 3:12).[17] Paul uses Habakkuk 1:5 as a warning for the congregation in Corinth in his ser-

---

15. "Paul finds in Isaiah a fellow preacher of the gospel, the message that reveals God's righteousness for all who believe, for the Jew first and also for the Greek. He uncovers in Isaiah's herald a veiled pre-figuration of his own mission to proclaim the good news to those among the Gentiles who have not yet heard news of the victory of Israel's God" (Wagner 2002, p. 356).

16. See Odeberg, *TDNT* III, pp. 193-94.

17. Schnackenburg 1984, p. 195.

mon in Antioch (Acts 13:40f.). "Beware, therefore, that what the prophets said does not happen to you." The proclamation of the apostles for their contemporary audience is molded time and again after Old Testament contours (1 Cor. 10:6, 11).[18]

The words of the prophet Joel become real and tangible for the young church on the morning of Pentecost (Joel 3:1-5/Acts 2:17-21). Those prophetic words become, as it were, flesh in the congregation as the body of Christ. After Pentecost, Luke quotes several psalms to describe what happened to Judas and to legitimize the choice of the new twelfth apostle (Pss. 69:26; 109:8/Acts 1:15-20). The original Jewish "we" from the psalms is in these cases broadened to the community of Christ, consisting of both Jews and gentiles (Ps. 44:23/Rom. 8:36).

The reaction of unbelief on the proclamation of God's salvation by Jesus and the apostles can in both cases be described and interpreted with Old Testament words and images (Ps. 69:5; Isa. 5:21; 6:9v.; 29:13; 53:1/Matt. 13:14f.; 15:8f.; Mark 4:12; 7:6f.; 8:18; Luke 8:10; John 12:38, 40; 15:25).

When apostles and evangelists open up the books of Moses and the prophets, they are not mere spectators of past events. They become aware that they too are a part of these stories and books. From that point of view the Psalms are also *their* hymns, and the prophecies give voice to their longings. Besides the abiding meaning of the Scriptures for Israel, and besides their Christological meaning, the Old Testament texts can also be opened as if they are written "for us." This ecclesiological recontextualization is thus also a key in our hermeneutical ring.

## 9.6. God All in All

As long as God's kingdom is not yet reality, the creation will long for ever-new fillings of Old Testament words and promises and will wait in eager expectation for consummation and fulfillment (Rom. 8:19). This will go on till the moment that God is all and everything (1 Cor. 15:28). The Old Testament offers the words, metaphors, images, theology, and paradigms for the proclamation of God's acts in the days to come. There are New Testament texts that quote the Old Testament in a longing, eschatological context.[19]

18. Childs 1974, p. 573.
19. Ellis is not correct when he identifies the eschatological re-application with a

The "self-presentation" of the LORD in Exodus 3:6 is quoted by apostles and evangelists to preach the resurrection of the dead in the age to come. God is a God not of the dead but of the living (Matt. 22:32; Mark 12:26; Luke 20:37).

The jubilation of Psalm 118:26-27 is not sung only on Palm Sunday, Jesus' triumphal entry into Jerusalem (Matt 21:1-11; Mark 11:1-11; Luke 19:28-40; John 12:12-19). The evangelists also discern an eschatological dimension in the words of the psalm. It will sound (again) at the return of Jesus (Matt. 23:39; Luke 13:35).

In the book of Revelation, texts from the Old Testament are set in an eschatological, or better, an apocalyptic perspective (e.g., Rev. 6:16/Hos. 10:8; Rev. 7:17/Isa. 25:8; Rev. 11:11/Ezek. 37:10; Rev. 15:3f./Deut. 32:4; Pss. 11:2; 145:17; Jer. 10:6).

Old Testament words that don't have an explicitly eschatological meaning or tone can acquire such a tone and meaning when apostles and evangelists quote these words in a context referring to events ahead of us. They recontextualize Scripture in an eschatological way.

There is a dimension in the words of Moses and the prophets that is continuously waiting for new fillings and ultimate fulfillment.[20] That means that Jews and Christians are both waiting communities. The New Testament opens with the announcement that the Word became flesh (John 1:1-7), the message that the kingdom of heaven is near (e.g., Matt. 4:17), and the proclamation of Jesus, saying, "Today this Scripture is fulfilled in your hearing" (Luke 4:21). But the New Testament as a whole ends with a prayer, "Come, Lord Jesus" (Rev. 22:20). That means that not only the books of Moses and the prophets but also the writings of apostles and evangelists are "waiting witnesses."[21]

## 9.7. Where Are We Thus Far?

We have discerned that the writers of the New Testament recontextualize the Old Testament in a fourfold way. We can organize the quotations un-

---

"'Christianized' summation or elaboration" of the Old Testament (Ellis 1977, p. 200). He thus restricts the surplus of the Old Testament exclusively to the Christological sense.

20. Zimmerli 1956, pp. 81, 87.

21. Zimmerli uses this expression for the witnesses of the Old Testament, but it is in fact true for both Testaments (Zimmerli 1978).

der the headings: Israel, Christ, the church, and the future.[22] The first dimension in interpretation points to the remaining and abiding meaning for Israel of the books of Moses and the prophets. In a next step, it seems that apostles and evangelists put all their Old Testament eggs in a Christological basket. The interpretation in this dimension of their proclamation of the Old Testament is determined wholly and entirely by the Christ-event. In my research I discovered that this Christological dimension is surely present, but the Old Testament is not subsumed in witnessing to Jesus Christ. The apostles and evangelists can pick up the Scriptures again and focus on the congregation of Jesus Christ, comprised of both Jews and gentiles. And even then, the meaning of the text is not exhausted. There is still a surplus of meaning latent in the text. The writers of the New Testament can project Old Testament images and metaphors in a fourth dimension on the back wall of history, where God will be all in all.

Throughout the history of interpretation and the practice of preaching, there was and still is the risk of letting the Old Testament take its hermeneutical end in the Christ-event. Texts that didn't fit at first sight within that paradigm were stretched or curtailed, in Procrustean fashion, so as to make them fit on the particular hermeneutical bed. It is obvious that such "tailoring" of the text violates the words of both Old and New Testaments. An exclusively Christological interpretation petrifies the words of Moses and the prophets. The Old Testament becomes truly old, in the sense of wrapped up and passed by. An exclusively Christological interpretation has, secondly, little or no eye for the remaining and abiding meaning of the Scriptures for Israel. In a Christian context we have to be aware of the fact that Israel not only was but still is the first addressee. Jesus lived with these words and from them, within that particular context. As such, he shares these words with us, the congregation from the gentiles. Because of him we are citizens with the saints and members of the household of God (Eph. 2:19). That means that the meaning of "testament" in Old Testament is that of a "last will," implying that the deceased has left his property to the legatee. But the words of Moses and the prophets are not entrusted into the hands of gentiles to renounce their meaning for the

22. Florian Wilk (1998) draws parallel conclusions in his thorough examination of the Isaiah-quotations in the undisputed letters of Paul. He organizes the apostle's interpretation of the prophet under four headings: "Israelfrage," "Christusbotschaft," "Selbstverständnis," and "Parusieerwartung" (see also Wilk 1999).

original audience. The Scriptures are waiting for "God all in all." And that promise is valid for both Jews and gentiles. The previous sections make clear that the New Testament doesn't quote Moses and the prophets in an exclusively Christological way. We can discern a "layered" reading of the Old Testament by apostles and evangelists. The apostles and evangelists have a ring with four hermeneutical keys. They use these keys creatively, and none of the keys is dominant. But there is still more to discover.

## 9.8. A Multiple Movement

When I took a closer look at the results of the biblical theological research, I discovered another remarkable phenomenon that underscored the results I had found thus far. There are Old Testament texts that are quoted more than once in the New Testament. I was really surprised to discover that apostles and evangelists can open these texts with more than one hermeneutical key in different situations. A few illustrations will elucidate.

a. In his speech to the council in Jerusalem (Acts 7:37), Stephen quotes some verses from Deuteronomy (18:15f., 18). He gives these words of Moses a place in a survey that reviews the *magnalia Dei,* the great events of God in Israel's history. We can say that the original context of Israel is preserved in the New Testament. Peter quoted the same verses from Deuteronomy in a Christological context in his sermon on the first day of Pentecost (Acts 3:22f.). The apostle identifies Jesus as the prophet about whom Moses was speaking.

b. Stephen quotes Exodus 3:6 in the just-mentioned speech to the council in Jerusalem (Acts 7:37). This verse also gets a place in the historical survey of the relation between God and Israel. That means that the words of Moses retain their place within the context of Israel. Matthew 22:32 and Luke 20:37 quote the same words but project them into the future, as part of an eschatological speech concerning the resurrection of the dead.

c. Apostles and evangelists report disbelief among the people of Israel on hearing the proclamation of the gospel, and they liken it to the disbelief of Israel vis-à-vis the proclamation of the prophets in former times. The words of Isaiah 6:9-13 describe and interpret the reactions to the proclamation of Isaiah in the first place. But those words also describe and interpret the reaction to the proclamation of Jesus (Mark 4:12 and par.; John 12:40) and of the apostle Paul (Acts 28:6f.). That means that the words of

Isaiah are not "exhausted" and did not come to their end in the ministry of Jesus. The same text can be used to describe and interpret the unbelief as reaction to the proclamation of the gospel through the apostles in the post-Easter era. The meaning and value of Isaiah 6:9-13 can be disclosed with more than one key.

d. The words of Isaiah 42:6 and 49:6 were originally addressed to the Servant of the LORD in the context of the exile. Luke applies those words and the imagery twice to Jesus (Luke 2:32; Acts 26:23).[23] In Acts 13:47 these words are also adopted to describe and interpret the role of Christian missionaries.[24] Words and images taken from the songs about the Servant of the LORD were thus used to describe and interpret not only the ministry of Christ but also of Christ's servants. Paul uses the wording and imagery of the first, third, and the fourth songs (Acts 13:46/Isa. 42:1-6; 2 Cor. 6:2/Isa. 49:8; Rom. 15:21/Isa. 52:15) to describe and interpret his own ministry among the gentiles.[25] And the apostle Peter points to the fourth song on the suffering servant to portray an example of a proper Christian response to unjust suffering (1 Pet. 2:22f.). Apostles and evangelists open the proclamation of the songs of the servant of the LORD with at least two hermeneutical keys.

e. Several words and images of Psalm 69 occur in the New Testament, and they do so in different contexts. The Gospel according to John identifies the "I" of the psalm with Jesus (2:17; 15:25). Paul too uses the words in a Christological context (Rom. 15:3). But the same apostle uses these words to describe and interpret the role and place of the Jews in their relation to the gentiles (Rom. 11:9f.). Luke uses the words of this psalm to describe and interpret the situation after the death of Judas (Acts 1:20). The psalm functions to legitimize the choice of the new twelfth apostle. The New Testament quotes this psalm several times but not in an exclusively Christological way. Apostles and evangelists recontextualize these words in an ecclesiological way, having in mind the situation of the young church.

23. Other words of Isaiah 42 were also used to describe and interpret the life and ministry of Jesus (Isa. 42:1/Mark 1:11; Matt. 3:17; 17:5; Luke 3:22; 9:35 — Isa. 42:4/Matt. 12:18-21 — Isa. 42:5/Acts 17:24-5).

24. Neil 1973, p. 161; Barrett 1994, p. 658. Calvin says that "many things which Scripture attributes to Christ do also appertain unto his ministers" (Commentary on Acts 13:47).

25. "It should be noted that the one definite quotation in Paul's epistles from the servant songs occurs in Romans but is used in a non-Christological way (Rom. 15:21 = Is. 52:15 LXX)" (Guthrie 1981, p. 266).

f. The hymn "Blessed is the one who comes in the name of the LORD" (Ps. 118:26) gets an evident Christological flavor when the evangelists describe Jesus' entrance into Jerusalem (Mark 11:9ff. and parallels). This hymn gets an eschatological outlook in Jesus' eschatological sermon (Matt. 23:39; Luke 13:35).

g. One can distinguish three dimensions in the way the New Testament refers to the Fatherhood of God, as described in 2 Samuel 7:8, 14, 1 Chronicles 17:13, and Ezekiel 11:20.[26] Hebrews 1:5 connects these words and images with Christ, and 2 Corinthians 6:18 connects them with the actual situation in the church. The words and images have an eschatological perspective in Revelation 21:7.

## 9.9. Evaluation

Biblical scholars are usually more uncomfortable in employing the hermeneutic of the New Testament than are laypeople. But there is no reason for such a scholarly hesitation. The abundance of explicit quotations and implicit echoes and allusions to the Old Testament in the New Testament is a sign that the connection with Moses and the prophets was not only "a" question among others but was a fundamental matter for apostles and evangelists. The concern of this chapter was therefore to explore the explicit or implicit hermeneutical strategy employed by apostles and evangelists to find meaning in the books of Moses and the prophets. The biblical theological research brought some new and surprising results.

1. It was an important eye-opener to discover that some Old Testament quotations in the New Testament occur within a context of abiding value and meaning for Israel. Even when those words can also be used to portray and interpret the Christ-event, those words did not stop having meaning for Israel. There was a hermeneutical confirmation of the explicit theological statements in the New Testament about God's ongoing loyalty to his firstborn son and covenant partner Israel. From this perspective it is also important to notice that apostles and evangelists nowhere call the church the "new Israel."

2. Apostles and evangelists use three clearly distinguished herme-

---

26. 2 Samuel 7:8, 14 refers to God being the Father of David; 1 Chronicles 17:13 refers to God as the Father of Solomon.

neutical strategies in their proclamation of Christ "according to the Scriptures." They use Old Testament words, images, theologies, and metaphors in a very creative way as words spoken *by Jesus,* words addressed *to Jesus,* and words *about Jesus.*

3. Another remarkable result is the fact that apostles and evangelists don't quote the Old Testament in an exclusively Christological way. Apostles and evangelists also use the Old Testament to portray and interpret the life and ministry of the early church in the post-Easter and post-Pentecostal period.

4. In the end, the Old Testament can be quoted to portray and testify to God's involvement with events in the days to come. Old Testament words that don't have an explicitly eschatological meaning or tone can get such a tone and meaning when apostles and evangelists quote these words in a context referring to events ahead of us. That's what I call the eschatological recontextualization. The Old Testament is continuously waiting for new fillings and ultimate fulfillment.

5. The New Testament quotes several Old Testament texts in more than one context. I was really surprised by the number of places where this phenomenon occurred. I could discuss only a part of the material in this chapter. None of the classical schemes and models give account of this phenomenon. As a result, those models and schemes cannot fully do justice to the colorful reality of the Old Testament in the New. They lose therefore much of the biblical material.

Apostles and evangelists alter the Old Testament creatively to facilitate four different recontextualizations or reapplications of specific Old Testament passages.[27] Interpreting Moses and the prophets is like entering a four-storied building. The interpretation of the words of Moses and the prophets is apparently not restricted to a single sense. Different contexts can bring forth different dimensions of meaning, and multiple "correct" senses. Those layers of interpretation don't exclude but enrich each other. There is no single master-key for opening up all the dimensions of the interior of the Old Testament. This reinforced my belief in the necessity of a hermeneutical model with a multidimensional character.

27. See for instance Barrera 1998, p. 491.

# 10. Literal Sense

## 10.1. Who Is a Republican?

When an inhabitant of the United States says he or she is a republican, we can imagine where we have to locate him or her on the political spectrum. You have more than a vague idea about his or her opinions about, for instance, moral standards or foreign policy. But when an inhabitant of one of the European kingdoms is called a republican, it means quite something else. Again, we have more than a vague idea about this person's political ideas. In the European context, those persons are probably to be found on quite the opposite side of the political spectrum. They oppose royalty, a king or queen by birth, and prefer an elected president instead. The "plain" or "literal" sense of the word "republican" is therefore dependent on the speaker's geographical context and nationality. Within the context of the United States the expression also has a historical dimension. A republican in the seventeenth century had different opinions and convictions than a supporter of the Republican Party in the twenty-first century. The "plain meaning" of words and expressions depends thus on the identities of both speaker and listener, on the setting in which words are spoken, and on whether they are used alone or accompanied by other words.

Scripture is the source and standard of preaching. That means that study of and reflection on the text of Scripture has a pivotal role in sermon preparation. The interpreter wants to do justice to that which the texts says and intends. Consequently, the literal sense and historical background of Scripture was and is considered to be of vital importance for the practice of preaching.[1] The process of sermon preparation starts therefore with a verbal analysis of a particular passage of Scripture text. The tools are the Hebrew Bible (or an interlinear Hebrew-English Bible), a concordance, a dictionary, and a grammar. The leading question is: Does the interpreter understand the words and expressions in this passage? Even at the height of the fourfold interpretation, the church upheld the importance of the literal sense as an indispensable reference point for interpretation. Thomas Aquinas (1224-1274) defined the literal sense of Scripture as "the meaning of the text which the author intends."[2] This "original" intention is seen as the anchor place for exegesis, exposition, and proclamation.[3] For that reason, almost every model for sermon preparation starts with a search for the literal or plain sense of the biblical text.[4] But what is meant by "literal sense" or "plain meaning"? These were and still are awkward questions. Brevard Childs rightly says that there "are few more perplexing and yet important problems in the history of biblical interpretation than the issue of defining what is meant by the literal sense of a text."[5]

At present we can discern three ways of considering the issue of the "literal sense."[6] The first approach restricts the "literal sense" to its literary and historical background and tries to dig therefore as far as possible into the genesis of the text. A second approach formulates the "literal sense" in terms of the kerygmatic contents or subject matter of a particular text as part of the canon as a whole. And the third track locates the "literal sense"

1. Greene-McCreight 1999.

2. For a good understanding, we have to add that for Thomas the author was primarily God and not a human person (*Summa Theologiae,* I, 1, 10).

3. "The most widespread theology, reigning from the mid-twentieth century and onward, led preachers to begin sermon preparation with the exegesis of a biblical text" (Buttrick 1994, pp. 5-32). "Der unauflösliche Zusammenhang unseres gegenwärtigen Verkündigungsauftrages mit dem überlieferten Zeugnis der Bibel ist Kern des reformatorischen Sola-scriptura Prinzip" (Ziemer 1990, p. 209).

4. See for instance Craddock 1985, chapter 6; Long 1989, chapter 3; Allen 1998, chapter 8; Dohmen/Stemberger 1996, pp. 196ff. Especially European scholars stress the importance of historical-critical research. "Die wissenschaftliche Art der Erforschung überlieferter Texte ist die historisch-kritische" (Ziemer 1990, p. 225; see also Schütz 1981, pp. 67f.; Hirschler 1988, pp. 108-16; Engemann 2002, pp. 20-33).

5. Childs 1977, p. 80. See also Greene-McCreight 1999; Wilson 2001, pp. 40-56; Büttner 2002, pp. 203-8. Vanhoozer speaks of a "checkered history" of the *sensus literalis* (1998, p. 307; cf. pp. 303-14).

6. Soulen/Soulen 2001, pp. 104-5.

in the contemporary interpretative community, the interplay between reader and text. These approaches are often intertwined and cannot be seen as subsequent steps in the process of sermon preparation. But in that process one has to discern somewhere and somehow these three elements. The next sections deal subsequently with these three approaches and their relevance for homiletics and the practice of preaching.

## 10.2. The "Tangibility" of the Text

The first approach is an examination of the so-called "world behind the text." It deals with issues such as authorship, date of origin, social, political, and geographical setting. It also examines the rhetorical elements and the literary structure. The tools for this approach are a substantial "introduction" on the Old Testament as literature, a detailed atlas of the ancient Middle East, a history of Israel, and a history of the religion of Israel. This kind of information can also be found in good biblical encyclopedias with entries on literary, historical, and geographical issues. The goal is to discern the intended sense of the original human author for an original audience in their historical contexts. However, within the process of sermon preparation, the examination of the "world behind the text" is not intended to uncover the deepest literary or historical layers of a given biblical text. In the context of preaching, this approach wants to become aware of the "tangibility" of the text. It is an attempt to taste, smell, touch, and feel the landscape of the text. This step tries to get "acquainted" with the persons or characters that walk around in or behind the text and to uncover the plot of the "play" they are acting in. The Old Testament is an earthy book; it speaks about physical goodness and suffering. You can smell and taste the earthiness on almost every page. R. Benjamin Garrison expresses this very well in a sermon on Deuteronomy 6:4-5, "Hear, O Israel: The LORD is our God, the LORD alone. You shall love the LORD your God with all your heart, and with all your soul, and with all your might." The sermon is titled "On Being an Honorary Jew."

> Old and New Testament are not bound together for the convenience of the bookseller. They are bound together because they belong together. Christians who talk about the New Testament being the fulfillment of the Old Testament are talking nonsense unless they know enough

about the Old Testament to know what it is that is being fulfilled. The older book is very earthy: Abraham having supper with God; Job arguing with God as if God were a quarrelsome old wife. The Bible is earthy and everyday because the Hebrews recognized that only in the concrete encounter of events does God become real to us.[7]

The same tone can be heard in one of the letters written by Dietrich Bonhoeffer (1906-1945) from the Tegel prison to his friend Eberhard Bethge. Bonhoeffer recognizes that the concern for God's tangible blessing is one of the core issues of the proclamation of the Old Testament.

> You think the Bible hasn't much to say about health, fortune, vigor, etc. I've been thinking over that again. It's certainly not true of the Old Testament. The intermediate theological category between God and human fortune is, as far as I can see, that of blessing. In the Old Testament — e.g. among the patriarchs — there's a concern not for fortune, but for God's blessing, which includes in itself all earthly good. In that blessing the whole of the earthly life is claimed for God and it includes all his promises.[8]

Moses and the prophets point to that which can and may be called God-given happiness, the happiness of sitting under your own vines and fig trees (Mic. 4:4). Preaching creates a space to enjoy our daily bread and to drink our wine with a merry heart (Ps. 104:15; Eccles. 9:7). The Sabbath leaves one open to moments of freedom and rest. The Sunday services leave in a comparable way moments that invite us to fix our eyes on the gifts of the Creator and to accept those gifts with a thankful heart. In his book *For All God's Worth: True Worship and the Calling of the Church*, N. T. Wright asks:

> What is the most beautiful thing you have experienced this week?
> Maybe something you heard. Maybe some beautiful music — perhaps in church, or in the cathedral. Maybe something in the world of nature: the sun breaking through the mist and making the autumn leaves luminous, the curl of a squirrel's tail as he sat nibbling a nut. It might be something you smelt: the scent of a rose perhaps, or the smell of a good meal cooking when you were very hungry. It might be some-

7. Garrison, in: Cox Vol. 1, pp. 176-77.
8. Bonhoeffer 1971, p. 374.

thing you taste: an exquisite wine, a special cheese, that same meal well seasoned and well cooked.

Maybe something you experienced in work: things suddenly coming together, an unexpected new opportunity. It might be something you experienced in human relationships: a quiet, gentle glance from someone you love dearly; the soft squeeze of a child's hand. (. . .)

I want to suggest to you ( ) that our ordinary experiences of beauty are given to us to provide a clue, a starting-point, a signpost, from which we move on to recognize, to glimpse, to be overwhelmed by, to adore, and so to worship, not just the majesty, but the beauty of God himself.[9]

Moses and the prophets invite us to accept physical life as a gift of the LORD. They also offer us the language, the metaphors, and the images to praise this gift and the Giver. This kind of doxology calls the congregation back to human standards. That is a curative message in a society where those standards are heavily under attack. Preaching sings a song for the gifts that simply fall into our lap, for all those moments when we experience that light is sweet (Eccles. 11:7) and that love and friendship are precious (1 Sam. 20:42 NIV). All those moments when we find refuge with God, moments when we are surprised by a deep joy. It has to do with all those experiences of the goodness of life, moments that inspired poets and seers, prophets and priests, narrators and judges to sing with a joyful heart. The liturgy sets the stage for making a reverence for our Creator, a gesture of profound respect to express our appreciation for God's gifts and honor the beauty of life. From a theological point of view, we examine the elements of creation and history in this step. For that reason, we have to investigate and examine the tangibility of the text.

## 10.3. Resonance-Box and Strings of Scripture

The second approach emphasizes the world of the text as part of Scripture as a whole. When the congregation of Christ opens the Scriptures we don't meet a collection of independent texts but an ingenious tapestry that came into existence in the course of a lengthy and complex process of tradition,

9. N. T. Wright 1997, pp. 5, 7.

redaction, and canonization. Originally independent texts became related to each other in a book of the community of faith. The new canonical whole creates a network of words, images, and motives where all kinds of internal rhymes can be heard between the once-independent but now related texts. This interrelatedness of canonical texts creates a surplus of theological meaning that transcends the grammatical and syntactical sense of individual passages. New meanings are called forth mutually; the resonance of the whole can be heard in the parts.[10] This surplus of meaning waits patiently for disclosure by later audiences and readers.[11] This reservoir of meaning can, so to speak, be tapped again and again.

Because of the canonical context, we cannot discuss independent words, events, institutions, or theological subjects. The oppression in Egypt and the exodus, the exile and the return, judgment and grace, death and resurrection are interdependent, and these words and events are only available in their mutual coherence. Exile and exodus resonate with each other. The exilic prophets interpret the return from Babylon as a new exodus (Isa. 43:16-21). And on the other hand, the exile is already present as a dark and threatening cloud in Deuteronomy 28. No text is thus available independently, as a separate entity.

All texts and the whole of Scripture are connected by the one acting and speaking Subject, the LORD, the God of Israel, known by Christians as the triune God. This God is the center of the Old Testament witness.[12] The church articulates this central Name in the weekly act of preaching in the context of the liturgy.

This approach advocates a theologically oriented exegesis that goes beyond the strict linguistic and historical boundaries of the letter of the text. But this kind of exegesis wants to stay expressly within the limits of the theological "elasticity" or "carrying capacity" of a given text.[13] Hughes Oliphant Old affirms that there "are times when we have to go beyond the literal meaning to a deeper meaning. Today, after several generations of nothing more than flat, literal interpretation there seems once more to be a quest for discovering a legitimate *sensus spiritualis*."[14] We can speak of "al-

---

10. Childs 1978, 1979, 1985, and 1992; Frei 1993, pp. 55-82.

11. Ellen F. Davis speaks about an "Abundance of Meaning" (Davis 2005, pp. 63-68).

12. Zimmerli 1978.

13. For this "theological exegesis" see Miskotte 1973, pp. 35ff.; Soulen/Soulen 2001, pp. 192-96. See also the entries in Vanhoozer 2005.

14. Old 1998a, p. 341.

legory within the fences of the letter of the text"[15] or a deeper sense "in the hollow of the letters."[16] Those expressions are vulnerable to misunderstanding and even to abuse. But such exegesis can free us from biblicism, because it can give wings to texts and stories so that they can reach us in our contemporary situation. This kind of exegesis is necessary if sermons are to be something other than a more or less successful exegetical lecture.

Preaching the Old Testament in the context of the Christian church can thus be likened to playing the violin. When the bow is pulled across one of the strings, it starts to vibrate and to generate resonances from all corners of the violin. In a similar way we can say that the individual texts are the strings on the resonance-box of the canon.[17] When we pull the interpreter's bow across the strings of a particular biblical text, it generates resonances from all corners of Scripture. Because of the canonical context, we can hear more resonances and echoes in a particular text than the strictly literal or historical context. A musician knows how to respect and maximize the character of both the resonance-box and the individual strings. Likewise, a skilled interpreter knows how to respect the boundaries of individual texts and maximize the dynamics of the canon. This image also clarifies the way that texts have not so much a multiple meaning in themselves but in the canonical context, which creates a resonance space so that we can hear a multi-voiced choir singing in a particular text. The interpreter listens to the reverberations and echoes that are called forth on the sound-box of the canon as a whole.

The resources for this approach are "theologies" of the Old and the New Testaments, a "biblical theology," one or two systematic theological textbooks, and two or three commentaries on a specific Bible book. These resources help us to get the scope or subject matter of the text into view as part of Scripture as a whole.

## 10.4. Physical and Figurative Interpretation

We have to consider another element of the second approach, because the "allegory within the fences of the canon" opens surprising windows on

15. This expression is from the Dutch theologian Oepke Noordmans (1979, p. 13).

16. This expression is from the French theologian Henri de Lubac (1997, p. 9).

17. For the image of the "sounding-box" see Barrera 1998, p. 480. See also Gregory the Great (Old 1998a, pp. 438ff.).

possible meaning(s) of a text. This window does not neglect or deny the "tangibility" of the text, but the meaning of the text is not restricted to its material character. When we do justice to the physical and tangible character of the Old Testament, we can also explore the possibility of its figurative or spiritual meaning. Moses and the prophets offer an enormous reservoir of images and metaphors to give language to both God's spiritual gifts and our own spiritual struggles. We even have to reckon with the possibility that the doors to a figurative interpretation were deliberately opened during the process of tradition and canonization. For example, apostles and evangelists often used persons, events, and institutions as "symbols." We can think of Cain and Abel, Sodom and Gomorrah, Jannes and Jambres, Jonah in the fish, Israel's rebellion in the desert, and much more besides.

We encounter this process of "symbolizing" already within the Old Testament. We are, for instance, not told about the original historical background of several psalms. They could have come from any number of circumstances. The poet in those psalms is an anonymous "I" or "we." And despite a vast number of thorough studies, the question about the identity of the "enemies" is still not answered in a satisfactory way.[18] We have to reckon with the possibility that the process of tradition made both the "I" and the "enemies" deliberately anonymous; concreteness was generalized.[19] As a result, future readers, singers, and hearers could imagine for themselves who or what could be meant. Paul Ricoeur stresses in the same way that a text has a life of its own over which the original author has no control (anymore). Texts have a (relative) autonomy in relation to their original socio-historical context. Interpretation is not necessarily bound to the point of formation.[20] Neither is the author privileged in any way with respect to the interpretation of his product.[21] This insight opens windows for interpretations that were not and could not be intended by the author but can yet be heard or read by a later audience in the new context of the canon. It invites future readers to identify themselves with the described persons and events. We can do that from a material or physical perspective, but we can also interpret persons and events in a figurative way.

18. B. W. Anderson 1983, pp. 82-87.
19. Brueggemann 1988, pp. 96-101.
20. Ricoeur 1976 and 1980.
21. J. B. Green 2000, p. 29.

Thomas G. Long offers a good illustration in a sermon on Jeremiah 17:5-8. The text reads, "Thus says the LORD: Cursed are those who trust in mere mortals and make mere flesh their strength, whose hearts turn away from the LORD. They shall be like a shrub in the desert, and shall not see when relief comes. They shall live in the parched places of the wilderness, in an uninhabited salt land. Blessed are those who trust in the LORD, whose trust is the LORD. They shall be like a tree planted by water, sending out its roots by the stream. It shall not fear when heat comes, and its leaves shall stay green; in the year of drought it is not anxious, and it does not cease to bear fruit."

> One summer a few years back, we went thirty-seven days without rain, and we called it a drought. My neighbor and I paced our front yards, pawing at the yellow spots, and raised our fists to the merciless heavens because we had lost a few boxwoods and patches of Zoysia. "We sure could use some rain," we would call to each other in the heat. "Yes, we could," the neighbor would call back. "My tomatoes are burned up." (. . .)
> But about drought, Jeremiah knows much. And Jeremiah has much to teach us — about drought in the human heart.
> In Palestine, drought is not merely a threat to backyard tomatoes and Zoysia lawns. It is a threat to all of life — human, animal, plant. When the harsh Judean sun turns its blazing wrath upon the land, fields are scored and cracked, cisterns become dry as sandpaper, towns grieve, farmers cover their heads in the morning, the crops shrivel, the doe abandons her fawn, and the donkeys pant like dogs in the torrid and killing heat (Jeremiah 14:2-6). About drought Jeremiah knows much.
> Jeremiah knows not only about the drought that affects the land, but also the drought that affects the human spirit.[22]

The preacher uses the physical drought as a metaphor for spiritual drought that makes the human spirit vulnerable to idolatry. It is clear that the spiritual interpretation is as real as the physical. The dangers and the seductive character of idolatry are not only an antiquated item in Bible encyclopedias and commentaries but a real threat and seduction in the lives of contemporary believers. Physical and spiritual realities are therefore not sepa-

22. Long 1998, pp. 9, 10.

rated by watertight walls. On the contrary, they cross and meet each other continuously. That means that preaching can use physical realities as metaphors for spiritual experiences and vice versa.

## 10.5. The Worlds in Front of the Text

The third approach locates meaning not in the text or in the author but in the readers or listeners. This approach assumes that a text possesses no fixed and final meaning or value; there is no one "correct" meaning. The meaning of a text is thus "transactional" and "dialogical"; it is created by the interplay between the reader and the text. The process of interpretation can be compared to a performative art. Each new interpretation is a performance, analogous to playing or singing a musical work or enacting a drama. Meaning is not a fixed datum or an abstract property of words but is discovered by noting the use of a word or expression in a certain contemporary context.[23] The world in front of a biblical text thus arises from the interplay of the text and the contemporary reader or listener.[24] Interpretation is a "reader-response" enterprise. Readers construct meaning based on the meaning potentials of semantic and rhetorical aspects of the text. Consequently, later readers may invent meaning in a text that is in fact not envisioned by the (alleged) original author. Every interpreter is invited to step into that ongoing creative process, finding time and again new meaning(s).

Using words and expressions in different contexts results in a shift in the meaning of these words or expressions. The verb "to justify," for instance, means different things when used by a printer, a lawyer, or a theologian. "Desert" has a meaning in the military different from its meaning in geography. Words can, so to speak, be tilted so that different meanings and images show up. There is no meaning of a text "as such" or "on its own." The meaning of a text is always the result of a process of interpretation in a specific context.

The final form of Scripture thus opens a field of meaning for individual texts, but there are boundaries for "legitimate interpretation." Trans-

23. Tracy 2000, p. 77 (referring to Wittgenstein).
24. "An exposition, no matter how true to the text, will die away ineffectively in a vacuum if there is no possibility of a responsive echo from those who hear it" (Barth 1991, p. 111).

gressing beyond these boundaries causes "overinterpretation."[25] The ancient church formulated the "Rule of Faith," a kind of outline of the basic Christian *kerygma* that has served through history as the chief guide for interpretation.[26] Christopher Seitz states rightly that the church "reads the final form of Christian scripture as canon, the parts informing the whole, the whole informing the parts, according to a rule of faith."[27] This rule of faith prevents the text becoming a "nose of wax" that can be shaped according to the whim of the interpreter.[28] The text is thus not an almost-empty container that can be filled with almost everything by almost everyone. The canon defines both the universe and the boundaries within which the reader can traverse between different texts. Interpretation has to respect the "fences" and at the same time use maximally the space within those boundaries.[29] The meaning that emerges in the interaction of reader and text thus contains an objective element (a text cannot simply mean anything) and a subjective element (a text cannot mean something without a reader making sense of it).

Chapter 9 made clear that the words of Moses and the prophets were heard by apostles and evangelists in four different contexts, four different worlds in front of the text: Israel, Jesus Christ, the church, and the eschatological expectations. Each of these contexts is able to call forth a different dimension of meaning and different reverberations in the canon as a whole. This brought me to the conclusion that there is a four-dimensional meaning "stored," "stacked," or "piled up" in the text that waits patiently for disclosure. My own proposal for a hermeneutical model is therefore not a single key but rather a bunch or ring with four keys. This implies that "meaning" is dynamic, but does not imply that it is unstable or indeterminate. The canon creates a sound-box, and we are invited to listen to the multi-voiced choir that sings in a particular text as part of the canon.

25. Eco 1990, pp. 2, 5, 9, 16, 141; Eco 1992, p. 43.

26. Kelly 1978, pp. 87-90.

27. Seitz 2001, p. 81; Von Rad 1980a, p. 118.

28. The expression is from Calvin (Greene-McCreight 1999, p. 154, note 51; see also p. 22).

29. See also Von Rad 1980a, p. 120.

## 10.6. The Preacher as Servant of the Word

Preaching doesn't fulfill its task and calling when a sermon informs the congregations only about the literal meaning and historical background of a text. When we read, for instance, the story about the calling of Abram from Haran (Gen. 12:1-6), the congregation is not interested only in the socio-historical situation of Haran in the second millennium BCE. The congregation is interested in questions like: How did Abram hear and recognize the voice of God? Can we hear and recognize that voice nowadays? Why did Abram believe a strange God? How did faith and trust in the LORD arise in him, as the story in Genesis 12:1-6 suggests? Can this story help us to overcome our own doubts and to handle the challenges we face? Scholars from the fields of the history of religion and Old Testament studies don't like these questions. But the ministry of preaching faces the calling and the obligation to answer these and related questions. When listeners don't hear anything about their own lives, when a sermon lacks relevance for our own questions and quarrels, our hopes and expectations, it fails its calling and task. The goal of Christian preaching is to build up the community of faith as people of God so that they are empowered to live and practice the good news from day to day. Karl Barth rightly said that "no exegete should stand in the pulpit wondering whether a word is to be understood this way or that. That is part of the preparatory work that belongs in the study. The congregation should be presented with the *results* of this careful preparatory work."[30] Martin Luther King evoked the imagery of the exodus to imbue the civil rights movement with Christian significance. It is difficult to imagine that he could have moved the people to action by offering a lecture on the authenticity of Moses' authorship or the architectural details of the ancient pyramids.

Sermons try to create an open space where the voice of God can be heard in the contemporary situation. If we don't try to achieve that, we will be stuck with archaeological and semantic data, dealing with the exterior of the words. Preaching has the calling to open up the kerygmatic interior of Scripture in such a way that it describes and interprets experiences of everyday life and faith in the light of the Word of God. For this task preachers have to use all of their skills in the areas of language, history, the-

---

30. Barth 1991, p. 128.

ology, and psychology. But preachers also have to use their empathy, imagination, and if necessary even their "faithful fantasy." That also gives preaching the possibility of interpreting Scripture in light of the experiences of a particular congregation. Scripture will remain a closed book and the God of Scripture will remain a hidden God if we don't succeed in connecting the worlds of Scripture and the congregation. "Frequently biblical preaching has told a biblical story replete with oodles of biblical background, a 'holy history,' but has not permitted God to step out of the biblical world into human history. The God of biblical preaching has been a past-tense God of past-tense God-events whose past-tense truth ('original meaning') may be applied to the world, while God remains hidden within a gilt-edged book."[31] It is clear that there are risks involved. But we must dare to make mistakes rather than quit before preaching ever becomes lively, recognizable, challenging, and exciting.[32]

Israel has opened the books of Moses for centuries expecting to be touched by its inward meaning. Stories, promises, institutions, commandments, and hymns are not locked up within the borders of letters and historical circumstances. The centripetal power of the words of Moses and the prophets extends in and through Jesus Christ to the gentiles.[33] Both Israel and the nations live from the trust that the LORD can use these words time and again. The power of the Most High can overshadow the words of Moses and the prophets time and again (Luke 1:35) so that these words become pregnant with meaning in a particular context.[34]

Concerning the content of the sermon, the preacher is completely dependent on the text of Scripture. But a simple repetition of those words or a simple literal or grammatical explanation cannot be called a sermon.[35] The kerygmatic power of the world "of" Scripture is constantly "in front"

31. Buttrick 1987, p. 18.

32. Karel Deurloo — a Dutch Old Testament scholar — speaks of the necessity of "exegetically controlled fantasy" in the process of sermon preparation. Expressions like "fantasy," "bright idea," and "intuition" play an important role in the homiletical work of the German homiletician Ernst Lange. The bright idea "ist eben doch ein Ergebnis der Intuition, der interpretatorischen Phantasie, er kommt oft überraschend und hat etwas Schöpferisches" (Lange 1982, p. 44).

33. "Because of its centripetal quality *as scripture* the Bible refuses over and over again to close itself as a book, to secure its connotations to a single self-referential tautology" (McClure 2001, p. 21).

34. Longenecker 1975, p. 48.

35. See Lange 1982, pp. 194f.

of the text and founded on the world "behind" the letters and words.[36] It is the responsibility of preaching to give voice to that ever-new and renewing word, brought forth by the resonance of the interior of the text.[37]

## 10.7. Summary and Conclusions

The process of sermon preparation faces at least three possible derailments of the meaning and role of "literal sense." There is in the first place a possible derailment from the side of the critical areas of biblical scholarship. This kind of exegesis runs the risk of dealing extensively with the sociohistorical backgrounds but hardly with the kerygmatic contents and contemporary relevance. As a result, sermons are under threat of ending up in a lecture on past things, institutions, and persons. They are like visits to a museum, interesting at best, but without relevance for the hearers' lives and faith at their worst. I don't want to ignore the results of critical scholarship in the quest for meaning, but the results of historical and literary criticism are as such insufficient for the practice of preaching.[38] We have to avoid the risk of a preacher diving deep into the text, staying under quite a while, but resurfacing as dry as possible.

The second risk of derailment comes from the conservative side, where "literal sense" too easily turns into "literalism." Despite the intended pious obedience to the "inspired letter," there is a risk of misunderstanding the "literal sense" as the meaning that is restricted to its one-dimensional exterior. Article VII of *The Chicago Statement on Biblical Hermeneutics* states: "We affirm that the meaning in each biblical text is single, definite, and fixed." This paradigm acknowledges only one legitimate meaning for a biblical text and therefore only one legitimate interpretation. In an explanation of this article Norman L. Geisler says, "What a passage means is fixed by the author and is not subject to change by

36. Ricoeur 1980, pp. 57-61.

37. The preacher "hat nicht das alte Wort des Textes nachzusagen, sondern das neue Wort zu wagen das jetzt und hier notwendig ist" (Lange 1982, p. 43). The expression "new Word" plays an important role in the thinking of the German homiletician Ernst Lange (Lange 1982, pp. 29, 35f., 51, 66).

38. Preachers became more and more dissatisfied with the meager results of the critical scholarship for the practice of preaching. See the contributions in Eslinger 1994 and Ochs 1993.

readers."[39] The notion that Scripture has only one meaning is, however, not advocated by the history of interpretation and not at all by the biblical writers themselves.

There is a third risk related to the post-Holocaust context. The quest for the literal sense is usually restricted to an exclusively Christian literal sense without taking Israel into account. That means that the Christian Old Testament's being in the first place the Holy Scripture of Israel disappears from the interpretative process. That does not imply that the words of Moses and the prophets don't have anything to say to the wider circle of the gentiles. But the congregation must be aware of the fact that such a Christological interpretation, however legitimate it may be, cannot claim exclusive rights.

Preaching cannot rest at the exterior of a text. For the practice of preaching we need a theological exegesis that is concerned with pointing out the meaning of a text within the context of canon and in front of contemporary hearers. An "objective" analysis of the text with some homiletical "applications," as a *donum super additum* above the alleged original meaning of the author, will not do. We need, as John Bright formulated, "an exegesis of the text in theological depth, an exegesis that is not content merely to bring out the precise verbal meaning of the text but that goes on to lay bare the theology that informs the text."[40] We need such a strategy to give voice to the kerygmatic interior so that contemporary hearers don't remain mere spectators but become participants of the God-event of the text. That is the objective of the interpretive strategy to be set out in the next chapters. This strategy originates in Scripture itself and allows the interpreter to get the different dimensions of the "literal sense" into view. The consideration of the "literal sense" is thus not so much an independent sense or layer of meaning but more the foundation or "anchorage place" of each of the four dimensions of meaning.

39. Geisler 1983, p. 6.
40. Bright 1967, p. 170.

# 11. Contours of a Hermeneutical Model

## 11.1. Tilting Images

Forging money has always been an interesting and sometimes profitable business for villains. There has always been a "cold war" between governments (and national or federal banks who are responsible for reliable and trustworthy money) on the one hand and forgers on the other. Citizens benefit of course from a winning government. In the "battle" against counterfeit currency the main European banks have for that reason endeavored to introduce the most up-to-date technical security features for the Euro banknotes. For some features a piece of equipment is needed, such as a magnifying glass, an ultraviolet lamp, or an infrared viewer. Other features can be checked using the naked eye. One of those features is a holographic image on each banknote that can help to check whether one is holding a genuine banknote or not. One has to hold the banknote up to the light and check the silver hologram. As the banknote is tilted, the image will shift from the value numeral to the euro sign (€5, €10, and €20 notes) or from the value numeral to an architectural motif (€50, €100, and €500 notes), and back again. At the surface you see one image (in this case the numeral sign) but when you tilt the banknote you can see another image (a Euro sign or an architectural motif). There is a different image hidden under the surface.

These stratified images in and on the European banknotes illustrate that multiple layers of meaning can be seen or heard in an object, depending on where you are in relation to that object. This stratified meaning is actually present in the European banknotes and requires only a little tilting to be seen behind or under the exterior. The multiple layers are actually a sign of trustworthiness!

The same can be said about the layers of meaning in the books of Moses and the prophets. Each time we listen from a different angle or in a different context, another layer of meaning or another image can be seen; other echoes reverberate. Each of the images has its own expression and expressiveness. At the same time, these different images are not completely independent of each other but are interrelated. The different strata of meaning are, we might say, part of the same family. So the interpretative question is: How can we tilt, topple, or turn over a text in such a way that potential images at different levels or from different angles can be seen or heard? We don't add those meanings to a text. We take different points of view to make the different layers of meaning visible that are enclosed or piled up in the text itself.

## 11.2. Stratified Meaning

This chapter sketches the contours of a hermeneutical model that enables preachers to hear the multi-voiced choir of the text and its reverberations in the canon as a whole, while respecting the "fences" that are given with the words of the text as part of Scripture. This model is the result of both theological reflection and intuition, both homiletical research and practice of preaching; it is founded in scholarly study and rooted in the practice of congregational life. It uses the richness of material from Scripture and the history of interpretation; it integrates the insights of laity and the fruits of theological thinking. The results of the biblical theological research were a rich source of inspiration (chapter 8). The inner-biblical multidimensional hermeneutical strategies are of homiletical importance because they can actually facilitate the practice of preaching. The patristic and medieval model of fourfold sense of Scripture offered a frame or grid that helped to organize my own understandings, intuitive thoughts, results of homiletical research, and scholarly analyses (chapter 9). The contents of the frame are provided by the results of contemporary biblical theological thinking and post-Holocaust theology. The result is a four-dimensional model that can serve the contemporary practice of preaching.

## 11.3. Sensus Israeliticus

In the classical model of the church fathers and the Middle Ages, the inter-preter steps directly from the *literal sense* to the *allegorical sense*. That sec-ond dimension of meaning had to do with the Christian tradition as it took shape in doctrine and creed. One of the conclusions of the first part of the present study was that we can discern the same pattern in actual ser-mons that are woven on the classical hermeneutical keys. The first part of this type of sermon starts with a kind of popularized exegesis of an Old Testament text and information on the "original" situation. The second part makes a direct move to an exclusively Christological interpretation. This second part is in fact presented as the most important part of the ser-mon. As a consequence, there is no attention given to the interpretation of Moses and the prophets within the context of the LORD's abiding loyalty to the covenant with Abraham and mercy for Israel. This hermeneutical pat-tern is already apparent in the structure of the Apostles' Creed. The con-fessing "I" jumps from the creation and the Creator immediately to the sal-vation in Jesus Christ.

> I believe in God, the Father almighty,
> Creator of heaven and earth.
> I believe in Jesus Christ, God's only Son, our Lord . . .

The LORD's way and covenant with Israel are hidden in silence. This hermeneutical "step and jump" strategy misses the point that Christians are not the first intended audience of the words of Moses and the prophets. That was, is, and will be Israel. Gentiles are an "engrafted branch" and play the "second violin."[1] It is for that reason that I propose to pay attention to Israel, to God's way with Israel, and to acknowledge Jewish contributions to the interpretation of Moses and the prophets in the first level or dimen-sion of meaning. I call this the *sensus Israeliticus*.[2] Preachers must them-selves be aware and make the congregation aware of the fact that Israel was not only the first addressee of God's message of merciful love from a his-torical point of view, but Israel is still the first addressee. Scripture testifies

---

1. Dohmen/Stemberger 1996, p. 196.
2. Pannenberg says that the doctrine of the church is in need of an *interpretation iudaica* (Pannenberg 1999, p. 273). Origen called the literal meaning of a text the "Jewish meaning" (Young 2003, p. 335).

about the abiding loyalty of the LORD to the covenant with Israel. That is not only antiquarian loyalty for Israel in Old Testament times.[3] God's faithfulness is eternal, in past, present, and future. A foundational step for a Christian interpreter of the Old Testament is an awareness that these words have abiding meaning and relevance for the Jewish community, being their Holy Scripture as Tanak.[4]

This does not mean that Christians must try to read the Scriptures as if they were Jews. Even if we would, gentiles can't listen with Jewish ears; we can't listen to Moses and the prophets from the perspective of the Oral Torah. But we can listen to the dimension of meaning of the words of Moses and the prophets in the context of the New Testament's witness of God's remaining loyalty to Abraham and his descendants (Luke 1:46-56; 1:67-80; 2:29-32; Rom. 9–11). And we can also listen to that which Jewish ears hear or have heard in a particular text. We can take notice of the Jewish contributions to interpretation. Paul's statement that the gospel is the power of God for salvation "to the Jew first and also to the Greek" has therefore not only theological consequences but also methodological implications in the process of sermon preparation. It means that sermon preparation has somewhere and somehow to attend to the meaning of these texts for Israel and the interpretation within the Jewish tradition. This *sensus israeliticus* is not an added meaning from a Christian point of view, but the "primary" or "original" meaning from a theological point of view.

At the same time, we have to take notice of the fact that the Old Testament does not speak about Israel purely and exclusively for its own sake. Israel is chosen to be a light for the nations (Isa. 42:6; 49:6). As N. T. Wright formulates, "Election, the choice of Israel, was the focal point of the divine purpose to act within the world to rescue and heal the world to bring about what some biblical writers speak of as 'new creation.'"[5] All the nations of the earth share in and benefit from Abraham's blessing (Gen. 12:1-3). Ruth makes clear that gentiles were from the beginning welcome under the wings of the LORD for refuge (Ruth 2:12). Jonah expresses almost cynically that he knew that the LORD's grace was not restricted to Israel. "O

---

3. "Die besondere Erwählung Israels ist nicht eine 'Perfektum.' Sie besteht auch *post Christum natum*" (Hoping 2004, p. 149).

4. Brueggemann says that the "Jewish character and claims of the text" are one of the four "insistent questions" of a theology of the Old Testament (Brueggemann 1997, pp. 107-12).

5. N. T. Wright 1999, pp. 101-2.

LORD! Is not this what I said while I was still in my own country? That is why I fled to Tarshish at the beginning; for I knew that you are a gracious God and merciful, slow to anger, and abounding in steadfast love, and ready to relent from punishing" (Jon. 4:2). Thus, when the Old Testament tells about Israel, it is never for its own sake alone. Moses and the prophets proclaim that God's way with Israel is meant beneficially for the whole family of man. God's acts on behalf of Israel are characterized by an expansive dynamic from the very beginning and onward.[6] The blessing of the LORD is therefore meant to be spread out on the whole creation, so that "the earth will be filled with the knowledge of the glory of the LORD, as the waters cover the sea" (Hab. 2:14).

The *sensus Israeliticus* does not contradict the Christological, ecclesiological, or eschatological dimensions of meaning the church hears or reads in those texts. It is on the other hand not correct to presuppose that the church knows about a richer or deeper meaning of the text after Christ, not to mention the misunderstanding that the church has a monopoly on the one and only true meaning of Moses and the prophets. The medieval model of fourfold sense of Scripture understood the first layer of meaning (literal sense) as fundamental. The other three (possible) meanings had to be built on this foundation. The literal meaning was the only valid foundation of faith, love, and hope.[7] The first layer of interpretation is also fundamental in my model. In this case we can say that the *sensus israeliticus* is the necessary foundation for Christian faith, love, and hope.

"Israel" can signify four related but distinct realities. It can refer to a *people* descended from the patriarchs and matriarchs, to a *religion* founded on the covenant established between the LORD and the patriarchs and renewed and extended to the whole people at Sinai, to a *land* promised by God to this people so that they would have a place in which to live in relationship with God and in accordance with the covenant, and to a *nation* in the region of the Middle East. None of these four elements can be excluded without losing the others. It is also not easy, and may not even be possible, to draw sharp lines between these four realities. That means that when I use the expression "Israel" in the present study, these four elements are echoing around in one way or another. The present Israel is accordingly included with all the complicated political and geographical issues. Included

6. Marquardt 1993, p. 455.
7. McGrath 1997, p. 192.

are Israel's suffering and stubbornness, the impressive loyalty to God and the godless agitating, the inferiority complexes and the feelings of superiority. But a miserable administration — led by an ancient king or a contemporary prime minister — didn't and doesn't mean an end of God's concern with and loyalty to the covenant with Israel.[8]

There is still a lot of work to be done in the field of practical theology and the ministerial disciplines to elaborate new insights as a result of the dialogue between church and Israel. Chapter 12 focuses on the implications for the practice of preaching using the (sometimes fragmentary) contributions that are already available in theological reflection and the practice of preaching.

## 11.4. Christological Sense

The Christian church lives from the "things about Jesus of Nazareth" (Luke 24:19). That means that theology and preaching have the task of reflecting on issues related to the Christological questions. Christology is at the heart of the church's creeds, hymns, rituals, and prayers. That means that the church has also to reflect on questions and issues related to the Christological dimension of preaching — not only for New Testament texts but also, maybe even especially, for Old Testament texts.

Christological interpretation of the Old Testament evaporated during the course of the twentieth century. The interpretation of church fathers and reformers was said to be superseded by the results of critical interpretation. As a result we can hear expressions to the effect that there were "of course" no historical or theological references between Mary, mother of Jesus, and the pregnant girl of Isaiah 7:14; speaking about the suffering servant of the LORD, Deutero-Isaiah pointed "obviously" to someone other than Christ; there were "evidently" no direct connections between the good shepherd of Psalm 23 and the one of John 10. Phrasings like these can be found in a substantial number of sermons delivered in mainline churches in the second half of the twentieth century, and some

---

8. We mean the Jews with "their suffering and struggle, their arrogance and their longing for peace, their feelings of superiority and inferiority complex, their loyalty to God and his promises (land!) and their godless agitating, the brute and also sensitive dynamism ( ). What is in our eyes a miserable polity and government does not mean a veto against God's presence among them" (Marquardt 2003, p. 9 — my translation).

still echo around at the beginning of the twenty-first. These phrasings are understandable and can even be legitimized from the background of a Christian and Christological absorption or "occupation" of the Old Testament. That kind of interpretation was common practice for a long time. The Jewish reproaches against this kind of Christian annexation were, generally speaking, correct and appropriate. It became apparent that Christian theology had to do some homework in clearing out those a-Semitic and sometimes even anti-Semitic elements from its hermeneutical strategies.

But while clearing out the house of theology from those kinds of elements, there is still a haunting question on the table of preaching and proclamation: In what way can we connect Old Testament texts with the testimony about Jesus Christ in a correct and legitimate way?

We have the fundamental fact that preaching on the Old Testament happens in an explicitly Christian liturgical context. In that context we say prayers and blessings, we speak and hear words of pardon, we sing the Apostles' Creed, and we celebrate Eucharist and baptism. We do all of that in the name of Jesus Christ. And even when the Scripture reading is taken only from the Old Testament, it happens in the liturgy of the Christian church. This liturgical context therefore sets the stage for Christian theological and hermeneutical reflection.

Chapter 13 offers a strategy to get the *Christological sense* into focus. Words, images, metaphors, and theology that refer to the God of Israel and those that refer to the Israel of God can be connected with the life and the ministry of Jesus Christ.[9] The way apostles and evangelists quote Old Testament texts provides us with a creative "grammar" for such a Christological recontextualization of Moses and the prophets (see §9.4). That doesn't mean that I simply copy the specific methods of exegesis and hermeneutics of apostles and evangelists. But I am intrigued by their fundamental attitude, i.e., their conviction of the unity of words and actions of the LORD in past, present, and future, the continuity and consistency of his words and actions in and for Israel, Jesus Christ, and the church.

I consider the hermeneutical strategy of apostles and evangelists as a creative challenge for the contemporary practice of preaching. We can therefore try to recontextualize texts from the Old Testament as words

---

9. Marquardt says that Moses and the prophets deliver the "elementary particles" for Christology (Marquardt 1990, pp. 52, 57).

spoken by, addressed to, or spoken about Jesus Christ. For each of these possibilities I offer an illustration taken from Jeremiah 17:5-8.

> Thus says the LORD: Cursed are those who trust in mere mortals and make mere flesh their strength, whose hearts turn away from the LORD. They shall be like a shrub in the desert, and shall not see when relief comes. They shall live in the parched places of the wilderness, in an uninhabited salt land. Blessed are those who trust in the LORD, whose trust is the LORD. They shall be like a tree planted by water, sending out its roots by the stream. It shall not fear when heat comes, and its leaves shall stay green; in the year of drought it is not anxious, and it does not cease to bear fruit.

The New Testament doesn't quote these words. That means that there are no existing hermeneutical patterns available. Yet, contemporary preaching can connect this text with Jesus Christ in the three ways described above.[10]

## Addressed to Jesus

Words, images, motives, and theology from this passage can in the first place be seen as addressed to Jesus. We can read the words from Jeremiah as words spoken by God to Jesus. They portray his calling and destination, i.e., we can portray Jesus as the righteous one who trusts the LORD and who doesn't cease to bear fruit.

## Spoken by Jesus

We can also listen to the words of Jeremiah as if they are words spoken by Jesus. We can take this passage, so to speak, as one of his sermons. In that case, Jesus appeals to his disciples to be like trees planted by water, to send out their roots by the stream, and to bear fruit.

10. This threefold division can also be heard in the way the young church connected the Psalms with Jesus Christ. "Der Psalter is für die Kirche der Märtyrer ein Christusbuch, dessen Lieder um den am Kreuz erhöten Kyrios kreisen, sei es, dass die von Ihm, sei es dass sie zu Ihm, sie es dass Er selbst in ihnen zum Vater redet . . . : *Psalmus vox de Christo/Psalmos vox Ecclesiae ad Christum/Psalmus vox Christi ad Patrem*" (Fischer 1982, p. 31).

*Spoken about Jesus*

A third window is opened when we see Jesus as the content of the text: He himself is the tree of life that brought forth fruit, for our benefit. From that point of view, the soteriological merits of Christ for the gentiles can be portrayed with the words, expressions, metaphors, and theology of this passage.

It might be clear that a preacher has to verify whether the Old Testament text has enough theological capacity to bear (one of) these possible connections between Old Testament and Jesus Christ. Exegesis, biblical theology, and systematic theology have the role of critical and controlling instruments. One could also say that in the process of sermon preparation, these disciplines are heard as witnesses for the defense of the theological integrity of the text.[11] Chapter 13 deals with possibilities and conditions of the Christological dimension using the strong elements of the existing hermeneutical keys, ingredients taken from theological reflection, and illustrations from published sermons.

## 11.5. Ecclesiological Sense

With the results of the first and second dimensions, preachers can return again to the text. They can listen again to the words and determine whether they can open another window, a dimension that offers a view in the direction of the church, the congregation from the gentiles. The resonance of the words of Moses and the prophets can be heard "till the end of the earth." In and through Jesus Christ, the centripetal power of words, images, metaphors, and theology of the text "must" cross the borders of Israel (John 10:16).

One of the surprising discoveries of the biblical theological research was that for apostles and evangelists the Old Testament did not take its end in Jesus Christ. The authors of the New Testament connect Moses and the prophets frankly and candidly with their own context, with the situation of the young church. In and through Jesus Christ, the Lord is not only the

---

11. The image of the preacher as "advocate on behalf of the Text" — with special interest for the forensic connotations — comes from the German homiletician Ernst Lange (1982, p. 30).

God of Israel but also the God of the gentiles (Rom. 3:29). The Spirit grants the gentile believers the joyful assurance of kinship that gives them the right to say "*Abba,* Father," an expression of the deepest experience of trust and affectionate intimacy on the part of the primitive church (Rom. 8:15; Gal. 4:6). Based on this gospel, contemporary preaching is mandated to extend the dynamics of Moses and the prophets to the farthest parts of the earth.

For that enterprise, the writers of the New Testament go further in the hermeneutical steps already visible in the Old Testament itself. We hear in Deuteronomy 5:3, "Not with our ancestors did the LORD make this covenant, but with us, who are all of us here alive today." Over the centuries, every generation was invited to understand themselves as if they had come out of Egypt. The questions and answers during the Passover *Haggadah* liturgy are composed in this key. "Why is this night unlike all other nights?" Year after year the answer begins by actualizing: "We were slaves to Pharaoh in Egypt, and the Lord freed us with a mighty hand. Had the Lord not delivered us from Egypt, we, our children, and children's children would still be enslaved." I expressed that in a sermon on Deuteronomy 5:3.

> Every time when we remember the exodus, we don't just talk about past history. At a deeper level, we engage the present and the future. To celebrate *Seder* is a remembrance. And the *Seder* liturgy makes clear what "remembrance" means.
>
> To remember means that a present community understands itself as contemporaneous to the people that left Egypt. To remember means that we present God's redeeming deliverance in the actuality of the present day.[12]

When the community of faith from the gentiles opens the books of Moses and the prophets, they join in this actualizing strategy that is already present in the Old Testament itself. Like Ruth the gentile, we are welcome to seek refuge under the wings of the God of Israel (Ruth 2:12; 3:9; cf. Pss. 17:8; 36:8; 57:2; 61:5; 63:8; 91:4).

> The Bible is the story of the faith of Israel. We, the gentiles, are invited to read this story as the story of our own faith and to understand the

12. Bos 2002.

exodus and the liberation of Israel as a promise for our own exodus and liberation. This story encourages dreaming of the "promised land" as a God-given future for us and our children. This story is given to interpret Israel's way through seas and deserts as our own way through life.

When we open the Scriptures, we are invited to test out our own personal experiences against the story of the faith of Israel. We are invited to listen to the stories to discover if there is a *torah*, a "teaching," that can clarify our own lives, that can open our lives for the presence of the LORD. We are thus invited to acknowledge this "teaching" as trustworthy for our lives.[13]

Hearers experience and value a sermon as a "good sermon" when a sermon pays attention to their life, their struggle and overcoming, their burden and joy, their fear and hope.[14] A sermon is good when the awareness is born in the listeners: this sermon is not only about a world that is far and gone, but connects my own world with the world of God. The kerygmatic interior of the text touches the heart of the listener in such "good" sermons.[15] Preaching connects the world of Scripture and the world of the congregation. It interprets the life of the hearers in the light of Scripture and vice versa. The Old Testament has an open eye for the fact that our experiences in life and faith are colorful and varied in shape and form. This variety can even be contradictory.[16] A "good" sermon deals in an authentic way with these complexities of our experiences. A sermon is "good news," gospel in the most fundamental sense, when the hearts of the members of a congregation are touched, when lives are put beneficially out of joint, when light is shed on dark secrets or misty ways of life. When a sermon — or just a part of it — resonates in the listener's heart or soul, when it brings movement in situations that are stuck, when it brings comfort to those who mourn, calls for repentance to those who have sinned, then the "good news" of a sermon can become "Good News" from heaven. The words of a preacher become the Word of God. The Story of God and the story of members of the congregation are woven together in such a way that the hearers feel included in the context of God's care for his creatures

---

13. Bos 1999.
14. See the contributions in Allen 2004 and 2005.
15. See the contributions in Childers 2004.
16. See Brueggemann 1997, pp. 333-58.

and his creation. Chapter 14 explores some human and divine threats of this sermonic tapestry.


## 11.6. Eschatological Sense

Eschatology is usually focused on something at the other side of life and death, things hoped for but yet to be revealed. Issues in this subdiscipline of theology are the state of the soul after death, the return of Jesus Christ, the end of the world, the resurrection of the dead, the final judgment, the renewal of the creation, the New Jerusalem, heaven and hell, and the consummation of all of God's purposes. The future to be expected is life in "another world." "This age" will be replaced by a "new age." And there will be a fundamental break or fracture in history before we enter that other world.

We notice not only prudence and caution but even hesitation and uncertainty during the second half of the twentieth and the beginning of the twenty-first centuries in the church and theology when it comes to matters concerning these issues: Is God really able and willing to make a decisive intervention in the course of history? As a result, all these classical eschatological issues have been gradually removed from the practice of preaching. The hesitation and uncertainty about God's active involvement in history was in the first place also fueled by a growing awareness of human responsibility for the course of history. And second, it was intensified by the postulated and experienced absence of God in catastrophes. If God did not or could not interfere in specific catastrophic situations in history, why do we believe that he will do so at the end of time? This question becomes even more troublesome in the face of the experience of the Holocaust. When God wasn't able or didn't have the power to save six million Jews from the gas chambers, why should we believe that he did so with that one Jew and with him also us?[17] The result has been a certain eschatological leanness in the practice of preaching.[18]

When we take a look at the Old Testament, we notice some important features. In the first place we hear that Israel never gave up the validity of God's promises, no matter how dark the future might have looked. Second, we hear that the prophets dream of "another world," but that "other

17. On this penetrating question, see for instance Van Gennep 1989.
18. See also Long 1995.

world" is not only, and may not be even primarily, a beatific life in the hereafter. The expected future can also be a restoration of existence in this world. It can mean, for instance, health after sickness or having enough food after a famine. The poet of Psalm 27 is convinced of the fact that he will see the goodness of the LORD *in the land of the living* (Ps. 27:13). And third, when Moses and the prophets speak and dream about the future, they focus their eyes not so much on *something*-to-come but primarily on *Someone*-to-come. They hope and long for "He that cometh" (Ps. 98:7-9; Isa. 40:10; 59:19-20). The prophets dream of a future event, of which the LORD is cause and center.[19] Sure, when God comes, tangible goodness can be experienced. But the coming of this God, the LORD of Israel, is the center of all the promises. He is both the content of the promises and the guarantor for the fulfillment. The ultimate promise is therefore given with the Name of God, "I am who I am," "I will be who I will be" (Exod. 3:13f.). It is the freedom of this God to choose new and surprising ways in the course of history, time and again, to reveal his name in words and events in the course of history.

Because of the LORD's faithfulness, Israel never ruled out the validity of the promises of this God. Not even when experiences in the course of history seemed to contradict God's given word. So, Israel has the right to raise her voice and invite the nations to hold on to God's pledges. These promises keep their value and are not exhausted when these words were filled with God's actions at a certain moment of history. The promise of "rest," for example, is not completely fulfilled when Israel enters Canaan after the exodus. There is still a certain credit or surplus on the account of the promise after the fulfillment, like the surplus on a credit note. We can discern different steps or stages in the fulfillment of the promised rest: the seventh day of the creation, the entrance into Canaan, the return from the exile, the rest promised by Jesus (Matt. 11:28f.), and the rest still to come in the New Jerusalem. The promised rest is constantly and dynamically longing for a completed fulfillment and consummation.

This crucial creed about the coming of the LORD fans out in a manifold testimony. The Old Testament confronts us with a multiple testimony concerning God's actions in days to come. Chapter 15 gives the possibilities of making the multiple and colorful eschatological witnesses of the Old Testament operable for preaching.

19. Zimmerli 1963, p. 85.

## 11.7. Summary and Conclusions

The model presented in this chapter honors the diversity and richness of meaning in a text while the words of the text function at the same time as "fences" to avoid interpretive anarchy. It thus avoids the Scylla of uncontrolled subjectivism but also avoids the Charybdis of historical positivism, with its restricted vision on a single meaning. The canon creates a four-dimensional context for a theological interpretation of individual texts. We listen in that theologically determined space to a particular text and its echoes from the different corners of the canon. Not every text contains the whole kerygma. But every text is a string on the sound-box of the canon that can cause reverberations from the four dimensions of the sound-box. Seen from the perspective of proclamation and kerygma, we can hear in a particular text more than it says "literally," in a grammatical sense or from a historical point of view. The discerned "levels of meaning" are therefore not the result of an interpreter's imposing a construction on the text but the result of careful listening to the four-voiced textual choir and its echoes in Scripture as a whole.

The development of the model outlined in this chapter is inspired by the way apostles and evangelists quote the words of Moses and the prophets.[20] Biblical scholars are usually more uncomfortable in employing the hermeneutic of the New Testament than are laypeople. Some scholars affirm that our world and worldview differ from that of the New Testament. For them the method of the New Testament differs therefore from a modern approach.[21] From that point of view the New Testament's use of the

20. Richard Hays describes three re-contextualizations of the books of Moses and the prophets in the letters of Paul. "No reading of Scripture can be legitimate if it denies the faithfulness of Israel's God to his covenant promises. That criterion binds Paul's interpretative freedom to a relation of continuity with Israel's story. ( ) Scripture must be read as a witness to the gospel of Jesus Christ. No reading of Scripture can be legitimate if it fails to acknowledge the death and resurrection of Jesus as the climactic manifestation of God's righteousness. That criterion binds Paul's interpretative freedom to a relation of faithfulness to the Christian *kerygma*. ( ) True interpretation of Scripture leads us into unqualified giving of our lives in service within the community whose vocation is to re-enact the obedience of the Son of God who loved us and gave himself for us" (Hays 1989, p. 191). Hays mentions thus three of the four described layers of interpretation.

21. Longenecker argues that we may follow the New Testament authors in their more literal approach to the Old Testament, but not when they approach it by other methods such as *midrash, pesher,* or allegory. The New Testament authors were inspired, we are not, when

Old Testament would be irrelevant for us.[22] These views usually arise from a concern that the hermeneutic of the New Testament writers occasionally finds meaning in the Old Testament that seems to go beyond what we can find by grammatical and historical interpretation.

It is clear, however, that this model is not a simple copy of the exegetical procedures of apostles and evangelists. I am interested in the way they testify to the unity of God and his loyalty to his covenant with Israel. This God does not forsake the work of his hands or the words of his mouth. That means that a Christian interpretation of the Scriptures must be aware of the abiding meaning of the words of Moses and the prophets for Israel. After that first and fundamental step in the process of interpretation, apostles and evangelists can pick up those words again to testify that they have seen the LORD at work in the words and ministry of the Lord Jesus Christ. After that, the meaning of the words of Moses and the prophets is still not exhausted. The writers of the New Testament can use the words, images, metaphors, and theology of the Old Testament and stretch out their impact and dynamics unto the gentile world. And after that, they can use those words for a fourth time when they hear in them a longing for and reaching out to the moment that the LORD will be all in everyone and everything.

It is also clear that this model is not identical to or a mere adaptation of the patristic and medieval model of the fourfold sense of Scripture. I only mention the fact that there is a completely different content and function of the first stratum of meaning in the ancient model and my own. However, the ancient models made me sensitive to the layered or multiple meaning that is "piled up" in a text.[23]

In the process of exploring the four dimensions, the preacher returns each time to the words of the text. That means that the starting point and anchorage of every step on the path of sermon preparation is the text itself. This model thus makes the fundamental insight of the Reformation operable in the process of sermon preparation: *sola Scriptura*. This repeated re-

---

they used these approaches to find meaning other than literal meaning (Longenecker 1975, pp. 218-20).

22. David Baker writes for instance, "We live in a different world from the authors of the New Testament, and our task is not to imitate the way they interpreted the Old Testament but to develop our own way" (D. L. Baker 1991, p. 268).

23. There is a widespread interest in and a revival of patristic exegesis and hermeneutics.

turn to the text is a methodical defense against hermeneutical one-way traffic, a common characteristic of the keys discussed in the first part of this book.

This model offers a pragmatic hermeneutic for preaching the Old Testament. It offers a model that does justice to the Old Testament as the Scripture of Israel, and it doesn't occupy the Old Testament in an exclusively Christological or Christian way. On the other hand, we have to say that this model does not avoid connections with the New Testament. It is a model that has proven to work in the practice of preaching. It has helped to get into view the layered theological meaning of the text. The next chapters may be seen as documenting a journey of exploration; they are therefore fragmentary in character and not a polished work of art. I hope to show the reader what I have discovered when I opened the words of Moses and the prophets with the described bunch or ring of keys. It is also an invitation for an open discussion about the results.

# III. A FOUR-VOICED CHOIR

# 12. The LORD Is Israel's God

## 12.1. *Ecclesia* and *Synagoga*

In front of the Cathedral of Strasbourg (Germany) stand two female sculptures personifying the Church *(Ecclesia)* and the Synagogue *(Synagoga)*. The cathedral was built about 1230 CE. *Ecclesia* is portrayed as a proud and victorious queen with an imperial robe on her shoulders. She looks like a vibrant, erect young woman, holding the cross and a chalice in her hands, signs of victory. *Synagoga* is shown with clear signs of defeat. Her head is bowed down, her crown fallen on the ground, her lance broken. The tablets of the law in her hands are cracked. She is also blindfolded, an implicit but clear and forceful message about the spiritual and moral "blindness" of the Jews and Judaism. In fact, this particular element of the image de-legitimizes any Jewish interpretation of the books of Moses and the prophets.

Those two images of *Ecclesia* and *Synagoga* were common in the sculptures, paintings, and stained-glass windows of European churches and cathedrals from the eleventh to the fifteenth centuries.[1] We can also find those images on bindings of Bibles and in prayer books.[2] When we

1. Similar images are found at the entrance of significant ecclesiastical buildings all over Europe, like the Cathedral of Reims, the *Nôtre Dame* in Paris, the *St. Séverin* church in Bordeaux in France, the cathedrals of Bamberg, Magdeburg, Worms, and Freiburg, and the *Liebfrauenkirche* at Trier in Germany. They figure (generally in mutilated condition) also in churches in Rochester, Lincoln, Salisbury, and Winchester in England. All these churches and cathedrals date from the thirteenth and early fourteenth centuries CE. For the pictures: Schreckenberg 1996; cf. bluffton.edu/~sullivanm/strasbourg/strasbourg.html).

2. In 1890 John Singer Sargent started a mural series in the Boston Public Library ti-

take into consideration that most people were unable to read in that period
of history, these images must have had a significant influence on both the
Christian self-understanding and on the Christian perception of Jews and
Judaism. The images of the "teaching of contempt" were not fueled in the
first place by reading textbooks but through the preached word and not at
least through the artistic imagery of the churches. Wherever you went you
saw, in a tangible way, that Christianity was triumphant; Judaism had no
reason and even no right to exist. These images affected without doubt the
congregation's conscience concerning Judaism and everyday attitudes toward Jews. They solidified the implicit or explicit opinion that not only
had the Jews forfeited their covenantal relationship with God for their failure to accept Jesus, but also that the church had replaced the Jewish people
in that relationship. These images of *Ecclesia* and *Synagoga* contributed
substantially to a theology of displacement and replacement. The church
came to view itself as the "new Israel" (opposed to the Israel of Old Testament times), the "spiritual Israel" (opposed to the "carnal Israel"), or the
"true Israel" (opposed to the "false Israel").[3] The name for this position is
"supersessionism." The term comes from two Latin words: *super* (on or
upon) and *sedere* (to sit), as when one person sits on the chair of another,
displacing the latter.[4]

When gentile Christians came to outnumber the Jews in the second
century, many of them held the view that the New Testament church had
replaced or superseded Israel as the people of God.[5] This opinion is still
present in the contemporary church. It is one of the great tasks of our age to
eliminate this supersessionist interpretation of Christianity in relation to
Judaism. The church has to say a definitive farewell to this theology of sub-

---

tled "The Triumph of Religion." It incorporated a panel depicting *Ecclesia* and *Synagoga*.
This panel caused a storm of protest from the Jewish community when it was unveiled in
1919. A vandal even threw ink on it. Three years later, the Massachusetts State Legislature
passed a law to remove it. But the state's attorney general eventually declared the act uncon-
stitutional. The protest dismayed Sargent so much that he never completed the final panel of
the mural (Sermon on the Mount). As for the charges of anti-Semitism, Sargent said, "My
intent was not to harm anyone."

3. Soulen 1996, p. 123.

4. Williamson 1993, p. 268 (note 9). The expressions "replacement theology" and "displacement theology" are also commonly used and are often viewed as synonyms for
"supersessionism." I use those expressions as synonyms.

5. Pannenberg points out that supersessionism "is still influential today" (Pannenberg 1993, p. 471).

stitution. The church cannot and must not pretend that she took over the role and place of Israel. A church that sees itself as the glorious successor of the synagogue denies her rootedness in Israel.[6] There is even a risk of inverting the relation between Jews and Christians. In such a construction the Jews are seen as part of the *corpus Christianum,* when in fact Christians are a grafted branch on the root of Israel (Rom. 11:17ff.)! Preaching has to prevent the impression that the church is the exclusive people of God and that the Jews are to be seen as outsiders who have only to do one thing, i.e., join the true (Christian!) people of God. This pretension can no longer be upheld when we consider the history of the church toward the Jews.

Gradually the church has come to the awareness that she never had any reason for such a triumphant or patronizing attitude toward Jews or Judaism. In the post-Holocaust era and after the establishment of the modern state of Israel we now have the solemn duty of fashioning new images of *Synagoga* and *Ecclesia* and contributing to a new, respectful relationship. The Old Testament not only deserves to be studied in its own literary historical context, as the Reformation rightly started to do. But the first step to be made in the interpretation of the books of Moses and the prophets is to consider their Jewish context. This chapter is an attempt at contributing to that effort in the area of preaching and proclamation.

## 12.2. What This Sense Is and What It Is Not

Before we continue, it is important to have a clear view of what we mean by *sensus Israeliticus* and also what we don't mean by it. To start with the last issue, the *sensus Israeliticus* does not mean that Christians must try to read the Scriptures as if they were Jews. I also don't mean that we have to copy, or even worse, imitate the Jewish exegetical methods. Even if we tried or wanted to try, we can't. We are Christians, gentile disciples of the Jew Jesus, and as such our sound-box is comprised of other materials. The sound-box of Christian interpretation has two parts, Old and New Testaments. The Jewish sound-box also has two parts: the Written and the Oral Torahs. In the years after the destruction of the Second Temple a basic outline of the Oral Torah was assembled into a series of books called the *Mishna* (second century CE). Over the next few centuries, additional commentar-

6. Tomson 2001.

ies elaborating on the *Mishna* were written down in Jerusalem and Babylon. These additional commentaries are known as the *Gemara*. The complete collection of the *Mishna* and the *Gemara* is called the *Talmud*. The Jewish interpretation of the books of Moses and the prophets happens in the context of the *Talmud*. This Jewish bi-partite sound-box creates its own reverberations that are not produced by or heard in the Christian sound-box. Gentile Christians cannot therefore listen to the books of Moses with Jewish ears. It is neither my intention nor pretension to do so.

Also, the *sensus Israeliticus* does not mean that we have to say only nice things about contemporary Jews or Israel. The strip of land between Asia, Africa, and Europe is for sure one of the most volatile locations on earth. It is a location with a complex and awkward mix of history, politics, and theology.[7] It is a place of both enriching ecumenical encounters and a complex multi-faith reality. There are several risks for preaching amidst these diverse and conflicting ingredients, such as an uncritical and romantic concept of the Holy Land, feelings of guilt over the church's anti-Semitic and anti-Judaistic past, and caricatures of Israelis and Palestinians or of Jews and Arabs. Amidst these risks, however, we have to say that criticizing the policy of a contemporary Israeli government doesn't necessarily mean that one is an anti-Semite. We hear the harshest things about the people and the rulers of Israel from Israel's own prophets, people such as Amos, Hosea, and Isaiah! We don't have to withhold therefore our critical questions when well-informed arguments raise disagreements about current social, geographical, and political issues. R. Kendall Soulen sets the stage for that kind of discussion by saying that since God's "promises include at a minimum the survival and security of the Jews as an identifiable people (see Luke 1:68-79), Christians should pray for and rejoice in everything that contributes to these ends in a manner consistent with the dignity and rights of the other families of the earth."[8]

Stated in a positive way, I mean with this first dimension of interpretation two things. The first is that in this dimension we start listening to the words of Moses and the prophets in the context of God's remaining loyalty to Israel, the eternal covenant with the children of Abraham.[9] We

---

7. For a good introduction in related issues for preaching see Mcpherson 2004.

8. Soulen 2000, p. 171.

9. This loyalty of the LORD is expressed in texts like Genesis 17:7, 13, 19, Psalm 105:8, 10, Isaiah 55:3, Jeremiah 32:40, and Ezekiel 16:60, 37:26.

look at an Old Testament text from the angle of the New Testament's confirmation of this loyalty. This angle is present in texts like Luke 1:46-56 (God's remembrance of divine mercy for Abraham and his descendants), Luke 1:67-80 (God's remembrance of the holy covenant with Abraham), Luke 2:29-32 (Jesus as the revelation of the light for Israel and gentiles), and Ephesians 2:11-21 (the "peace treaty" between Jews and gentiles).[10] James D. G. Dunn concludes, after broad and careful considerations, "that Jesus was understood by his first disciples to have been engaged on a mission to and on behalf of Israel as a whole. ( ) He had a special concern for the sheep separated from the flock of Yahweh."[11] Paul's testimony of God's remaining faithfulness to Israel in Romans 9–11 is also of importance. Those three chapters were for a long time a neglected "backyard" in the Pauline correspondence. But they have moved into the very center of scholarly debate in recent years. In this first dimension we thus listen to words from the Old Testament and their reverberations from the perspective of Romans 1:16 and 2:9, 10 — Paul's famous expression, *"first the Jew and also the Greek."* The leading question in this first layer of interpretation is: What can we hear in this text in relation to God's remaining loyalty to the covenant with the descendants of Abraham?

Good resources for answering this question are post-Holocaust studies like Thoma 1978; Van Buren 1980, 1983, and 1988; Peck 1982; Marquardt 1988, 1990/1991, and 1993/1994; Novak 1989; Williamson 1989 and 1993; Klenicki 1991; Charlesworth 1990; Fry 1996; Soulen 1996; Frymer-Kensky 2000; H. F. Knight 2000. The website of Jewish-Christian relations (jcrelations.net/en/) also offers much useful material.

We listen in the second place to the reverberations of Scripture that Jews hear on their two-part sound-box of the Written and the Oral Torahs. We do not listen with Jewish ears, but we listen to that which Jewish ears hear or have heard in a particular text on their sound-box. We can therefore listen to Jewish interpreters and commentators, read sermons from Jews, take note of Jewish novels and poems, and appreciate paintings or sculptures by Jewish artists. The things we hear in this dimension of interpretation can thus be typified as "hear-saying." And while that kind of reasoning is not valid in a court of justice it is, however, a necessary and ele-

10. See for this passage Marquardt 1992, pp. 444-54.
11. Dunn 2003, p. 516.

mentary step in the process (sic!) of sermon preparation. This leaves the possibility open that not everything that Jews hear or have heard is of importance or relevance for Christians. But when preachers have heard something that opens new and creative perspectives on a text, they can give that a place in a particular sermon. The leading questions here are: What have Jewish interpreters heard in this text? And is that of relevance for our understanding of the text?

> Good resources to answer these questions are the volumes in the series of commentaries published by Mesorah Publications (Brooklyn, NY).[12] Abraham Cohen is the chief editor of the fourteen-volume set *Soncino Press Books of the Bible* published by Soncino Press (London). Also worth mentioning are the *Midrash Rabbah,* edited by Harry Freedman and Maurice Simon (London: Soncino Press, 1961-63) and the multivolume set *Encyclopedia of Biblical Interpretation: A Millennial Anthology,* edited by Menahem M. Kasher (New York: American Biblical Encyclopedia Society, 1967).
>
> One can also think of the writings of Martin Buber and Elie Wiesel, and the artwork of Marc Chagall. The above-mentioned website on Jewish Christian relations also offers good material.

Listening to the *sensus Israeliticus* in the process of interpretation is to listen theologically to the primary dimension of meaning of Moses and the prophets. That doesn't mean that this dimension is necessarily the first step in the process of sermon preparation. But it is important that preachers listen to the *sensus Israeliticus* somewhere and somehow in that process.

## 12.3. Who Do People Say That the Son of Man Is?

Chapter 16 offers three elaborated illustrations to flesh out the four dimensions of meaning, i.e., Exodus 3, Psalm 22, and the songs of the servant of the LORD from Deutero-Isaiah. I will illustrate therefore (briefly) how the *sensus Israeliticus* can be worked out by means of Daniel 7, espe-

---

12. The series includes Avrohom Chaim Feuer on *Tehillim* (1995), Reuven Drucker on *Yehoshua* (1982), Hersh Goldwurm on *Daniel* (1988), Meir Zlotowitz on *Yonah* (2003), Meir Zlotowitz on *Kohelet* (1977), Meir Zlotowitz on *Ruth* (1986), Meir Zlotowitz on *Lamentations* (1989).

cially the reference to the "son of man." The meaning of this expression in Daniel 7:13-14 is heavily disputed. That is the more true because of all the Christological titles appearing in the New Testament, "Son of Man" is both the most significant and the most enigmatic. Gallons of ink have already been used to discuss the background, meaning, and use of this title. Theologies of Old and New Testaments as well as commentaries on Daniel and the Gospels struggle with at least four issues. First, does the figure of the son of man refer to a single person or to a collective (a "corporate personality")? Second, is the "son of man" coming from "above" or from "below"? Is his background divine or human? Third, can we discern a kind of "evolution" in the meaning of this expression in the period of the Second Temple (in, for instance, the Similitudes of Enoch)? And last, did Jesus consider himself to be "the" Son of Man? Connected with the last issue is the question of whether the son-of-man sayings in the Gospels go back to Jesus himself or have been incorporated at a later stage of the tradition's history.

For preachers, it is impossible to enter into the detailed debate and to oversee the ocean of literature that is available.[13] The model presented here does not solve these and related problems in an easy way. But this model offers a strategy for handling these issues in both a creative and a theologically accountable way for the practice of preaching. It prevents preachers from getting so paralyzed by the load of literature that they avoid this chapter in their preaching. And even though preaching on Daniel 7 requires a certain level of background information, one does not need a Ph.D. in apocalyptic literature before being able to preach properly and accountably on this chapter.

The following sections of this chapter offer several illustrations referring to that which Jews hear on their sound-box. At this moment I will therefore illustrate the first element discussed above: What can Christians hear on their "sound-box" in the expression "son of man" in relation to God's remaining loyalty to the covenant with Israel? Answering that question, the first thing to notice is that Daniel 7 is written in an apocalyptic language that flowered for about four centuries in Judaism and Christianity between 250 BCE and 150 CE. For the interpretation of this language we

13. A huge list of literature exists on the origin, particular features, influences from the ancient Near East and Mediterranean culture, and sources (Dunn 1996, p. 291 [note 2], p. 292 [note 14]; Goldingay 1989, pp. 137-93).

have to take notice of its representational character.[14] This means that the monsters represent nations, and the "son of man" represents the beleaguered and battered Israel. The "son of man" here may be seen as parallel with the "saints of the most High" (Dan. 7:18, 25, 27). That implies that the "son of man" clearly refers to Israel.[15] When the "Most High"/"the Ancient of Days" takes his seat, judgment is given in favor of the "holy ones of the Most High"/"one like a human being." The vision of Daniel 7 is about the suffering of Israel at the hands of the pagan monarch Antiochus IV Epiphanes (175-164 BCE), who desecrated the Temple. The passage expresses the hope and the trust that this enemy will be destroyed and that the LORD will again be faithful to his promises to the descendants of Abraham, and that Israel will be vindicated.[16] That was not only true for ancient Israel, it is and will be Israel's hope forever.

The next step is to listen to possible reverberations from the New Testament. We can discern two interpretative tracks in the Christian application of this chapter. The first is the interpretative "way ahead." The meaning of "Son of Man" as used by or ascribed to Jesus is "filled" with concepts taken from Daniel 7. The "gaps" and "blanks" in the Gospels are "filled" with theology and imagery taken from apocalyptic literature from the period of the Second Temple. The second track reads Jesus' references to the "Son of Man" back into Daniel 7. This track reads Daniel's vision as a "report in advance" on the ministry of Jesus Christ, mainly without reference to the "original" socio-historical setting before the common era. The "gaps" and "blanks" in Daniel 7 are "filled" with imagery and stories of the Gospels or with elements of Christological dimensions of creed and doctrine. Both tracks neglect completely the fact that "son of man" refers in the original context of Daniel to Israel, and that this chapter is about God's abiding loyalty to Israel. My model suggests therefore an alternative interpretative track.

The New Testament portrays Jesus as the legitimate representative of Israel (see further chapter 13 on this issue). We can interpret the expression "son of man" in the Gospels within that framework. But this interpretative coin also has another side. It allows us to listen to Jesus' use of this expres-

14. N. T. Wright 1992, pp. 289-91.
15. See the conclusion after the careful treatment of the issues by Dunn 2003, pp. 724-61.
16. That also parallels the lines of thought already present in Daniel 1-6 (N. T. Wright 1992, pp. 291-97).

sion, whether or not we can hear reverberations to describe and interpret the calling and identity of Israel as "son of man." An example taken from the Gospels illustrates how that works out. In Matthew 8:20 we hear Jesus saying, "Foxes have holes, and birds of the air have nests; but the 'son of man' has nowhere to lay his head." We can use this imagery, for instance, to describe and interpret the wanderings of Abraham. He indeed had no place to lay his head. He even had to buy a grave for Sarah and himself in the Promised Land (Gen. 23:19; 25:10; 49:31). This imagery also fits the story of Jacob. When Israel brings the offering of the first fruit of the ground before the LORD, they respond, "A wandering Aramean was my ancestor" (Deut. 26:5). But we can also use the wording and imagery of the Gospel to interpret the persecution and pogroms of the Jews in Europe during twenty centuries. They were often expelled from their homes, leaving them with no place to lay their heads. For this last reference we can also listen to Matthew 20:18: "See, we are going up to Jerusalem, and the son of man will be handed over to the chief priests and scribes, and they will condemn him to death; then they will hand him over to the Gentiles to be mocked and flogged and crucified; and on the third day he will be raised." How often was Israel handed down to the courts of the Inquisition, to the verdicts of church councils and synods, and to the gentile ideology of Nazism? How often were they mocked, flogged, condemned to death, and crucified? This perspective invites us to interpret the establishment of the state of Israel as the "son of man" being raised from the dead. This application of the Gospel fits well within the theological framework and proclamation of Daniel 7, i.e., Israel's vindication by the LORD.

A saying of Jesus in Luke 6:22 can serve as a second example. "Blessed are you when people hate you, and when they exclude you, revile you, and defame you on account of the son of man." The wording and imagery of this saying can be used to describe and interpret actions on behalf of Israel and Jews. *Yad Vashem* in Jerusalem is Israel's *Holocaust Memorial.* It embarked in 1963 upon a worldwide project to grant the title of *Righteous among the Nations* to non-Jews who risked their lives to save Jews during the Holocaust. In addition, *Yad Vashem* has been developing a comprehensive encyclopedia — *The Lexicon of the Righteous among the Nations* — that will eventually include the stories of those who received this title. Among others, several Dutch persons were granted the *Yad Vashem* award because they had hidden Jews during World War II. They risked their lives knowing that the Germans would send someone immediately to a concentration camp if they learned that he or she was hiding Jews. When a couple in a Dutch congregation were granted the *Yad Vashem* award, the local pastor read the quoted verse from Luke. These people were blessed because they tried to save Jews and took the risk of being hated by the Nazis, being excluded by them, and being defamed on account of the persecuted and oppressed son of man.

It may be the case that not every reference to the "son of man" in the Gospels contributes to the *sensus Israeliticus*. But this "reverse" hermeneutical step sheds new and creative light on the calling, the role, and the identity of Israel as the "son of man" seen in the light of this expression ascribed to or used by Jesus in the Gospels. My model does not deny the possibility or the legitimacy of a Christological interpretation of Daniel's "son of man." But it denies the exclusivity of such an interpretation. I therefore start to consider the *sensus Israeliticus* in this expression. Not only the text itself but Scripture as a whole invites us to make this initial interpretative step. The Most High was, is, and will be faithful to Israel as the "son of man." We can use the theology and the imagery of Daniel 7 to portray and interpret the story of Israel up to the present day. And we can listen to apostles and evangelists from the angle of this remaining loyalty of the LORD to Israel. So Jesus' question, "Who do people say that the son of man is?" (Matt. 16:13), and the question of the crowd, "Who is this son of man?" (John 12:34), are primarily to be answered by saying, "The 'son of man' refers to the people of the most High, to the Israel of God." That is true not only in the Old and New Testament times but also today.

## 12.4. Discovering Terra Incognita

World War II and the atrocities of Auschwitz revealed in a drastic way the ultimate consequences of the "teaching of contempt" inherent in the implicit or explicit theology of replacement. There was a reluctant beginning of an encounter and conversation between synagogue and church, Jews and Christians, Judaism and Christianity in the second half of the twentieth century. It became clear that (radical) changes in Christian theology and preaching were necessary.[17] The first fruits of this encounter became visible. Jews and Christians cooperated in research and the exegesis of the

17. See for instance the contributions in Frymer-Kensky 2000.

Scriptures, the books of Moses and the prophets as well as the writings of apostles and evangelists.[18] Jews requested that attention be given not only to the specific Jewish backgrounds of the New Testament but also to possible anti-Semitic tendencies in the writings of apostles and evangelists.[19] Christian theologians started a thorough research of the Jewish tradition and discovered the importance of the period of the Second Temple for the interpretation of the New Testament. Christians (re)discovered the Jewish roots of their worship and liturgy.[20] As a consequence of this encounter and conversation, some Christian theologians made an attempt to rethink and reconstruct the building of systematic theology,[21] based on the conviction that when the Lord reveals himself, he is wrapped up in Israelitic and Jewish clothing, in both the Old and New Testaments: the Lord, the *God of Israel,* is the *Abba* of the *Jew* Jesus of Nazareth.[22] Bruce Prewer expresses that conviction in a sermon on Exodus 12:1-14.

> The Christian Scriptures cannot be understood apart from the Hebrew Scriptures. The teaching of Jesus, and of the apostles, only makes sense in light of the story of the Jewish people. It is the same God with whom we are dealing. It is the same Creator and Savior and the same Holy Spirit who is at work. The God who called the Jews to be a servant people, calls the Christian community to be a servant people for the blessing of the world.
>
> It was a Jew whose love made new disciples. It was a Jew who taught us a loftier way to live. It was a Jew who gave us an appreciation of God's amazing grace. It was a Jew who died on the cross for us. It was a Jew who was raised from the dead and opened the minds of disciples to understand the Scriptures. It was a Jew who asked us to go into all the world, applying the Jewish practice of baptism to the people of all nations.
>
> And, many would claim that it was a Jewish Passover meal which became transformed into the new feast of salvation. That which we call

18. See for instance Holmgren/Schaalman 1995.
19. See for instance Tomson 2001.
20. See for instance Old 1998a.
21. Van Buren 1980, 1983, and 1988; Marquardt 1988, 1990/1991, 1993/1994, 1996, and 1997; Williamson 1993.
22. The course of history will show whether these changes are only superfluous and cosmetic in nature or if they will cause a real change at a deeper level.

the Lord's Supper, or the Holy Communion, or the Eucharist, is rooted in a Jewish Festival in which the glorious deliverance of God's people from slavery was celebrated.[23]

The church is rediscovering bit by bit that the Christian Old Testament not only was but still is and always will be the Holy Scripture (or Tanak) of Israel.[24] That awareness can be found in acts and pronouncements of synods and other official documents of the church, starting in the mid-sixties of the twentieth century. The first document of importance in this respect is the declaration *Nostra Aetate,* issued at the Second Vatican Council of the Roman Catholic Church in 1965. Protestant churches from all over the world followed subsequently with important statements, documents, and declarations.[25] Those documents were the result of both parallel developments in different denominations and of mutual influence.

But we have to say that the whole household of theology has barely started to reflect on the implications and consequences of these developments.[26] The underlying argument of these official ecclesial documents is strongly confessional and systematically theological in wording. That is possibly the reason that the "Israel theology" of these documents is ahead of the practices of congregational life. Liturgics is rediscovering the Jewish roots and in process of reconstructing the practice of worship.[27] But we notice only fragmentary attention given to this dimension in scholarly homiletics.[28] Homiletical handbooks pay scarce attention to Jewish contributions to this discipline. And when models for sermon preparation give, for instance, the advice to use commentaries, they mean in fact *Christian* commentaries. But why leave Jewish commentaries out? The practice of preaching depends on whether a particular preacher has affinity with this

23. Prewer 2004.

24. Büttner 2002, pp. 199f.; see also p. 21.

25. Examples of such church statements can be found in Croner 1977 and 1985; Brockway 1988.

26. Israel played no role whatsoever in systematic theological reflection up until the nineteenth century (Marquardt 1988, p. 376). That means that "the necessity of reconfiguring the churches' relationship to the Jewish people is not simply an act of theological reparation. The credibility and coherence of the Christian narrative demand a radical recasting to its foundational story" (Leighton 2000, p. 37; see also pp. 42-44).

27. Old 1998a, pp. 19-110.

28. Stäblein 2004, pp. 173, 182; see also Engemann 2002, p. 283; Marquardt 1992, p. 396.

subject. I noticed some positive and hopeful signs in the course of my research for this project. But there is still much work to be done, both in scholarly homiletics and in the practice of preaching. This is indeed a complicated matter, the more so because there are hardly any starting points or clues in the history of church and theology for the task of reconstruction, and we still work with a kind of interim-hermeneutic.[29] This chapter is an attempt at charting (parts of) this terra incognita.

## 12.5. First the Jew . . .

When gentiles in the congregation of Jesus Christ open the books of Moses and the prophets, the first one to be met is Israel. We meet the covenant partner of the LORD not only in matters of grammar, history, and geography, matters of the so-called "exterior" of the text. We also meet the *sensus Israeliticus* when we open the kerygmatic "interior" of the text. The fact that the Christian Bible opens with the integral Jewish Scripture[30] is not only an interesting historical detail but a fact with theological significance and hermeneutical implications.[31] The composition of the canon makes instantly clear that not the church but Israel is the first addressee of the books of Moses and the prophets.[32] The Old Testament doesn't give witness to a history of failure or a failed experiment.[33] Nor is Israel a kind of "dry run" on God's way to the church, like the work of a sculptor who first molds a design in clay before committing it to marble.[34] The original singing, confessing, telling, proclaiming, and lamenting "I" is a Jewish "I." The speaking and acting divine "I" about whom Moses and the prophets testify is the LORD, the God of Abraham, Isaac, and Jacob. So, we can't say that we

29. See the survey of the field of systematic theology in Marquardt 1992, pp. 374-97. For that reason some theologians even make a plea for nothing less than a total reconstruction of Christian theology as a whole (Eckhardt/Eckhardt 1982).

30. For the moment I will leave out the important question about the order and number of books.

31. Marquardt 1997, p. 412.

32. Dohmen/Stemberger, 1996, p. 196.

33. So the position of Bultmann 1964, pp. 313-36. He speaks about a "history of failure." Berkhof uses the expression "unfruitful experimental garden" (H. Berkhof 1986, pp. 243-45).

34. Soulen 2000, p. 171.

have dealt sufficiently and conclusively with Israel when we have studied
the Hebrew language or the history of events in the Old Testament text.
The "original" sense or first layer of meaning of a particular text has to do
with the remaining theological relevance for Israel.[35] That can be heard in
a sermon on Ezekiel 37:1-14, the vision of the dry bones. When we take into
consideration that this sermon by Robert McCheyne was first published in
1847 — long before the establishment of the modern state of Israel — the
power of the wording is even stronger.

> The first application made of this vision is to the restoration of the
> Jews. It teaches that at present they are like dry bones in the open val-
> ley — scattered over all lands. . . . God's ancient people shall yet stand
> up, and be an exceeding great army. . . . (It shall be as) when they
> marched through the wilderness, when God went before them in the
> pillar of cloud; that they shall then be led back to their own land, and
> planted in their own land, and not plucked up anymore.[36]

Almost a century before these words came true, in the years following the
atrocities of World War II, this preacher believed that no word that goes
out from God's mouth shall return empty, "but it shall accomplish that
which I purpose, and succeed in the thing for which I sent it" (Isa. 55:11).

That means that Paul's expression "first the Jew" is also valid for the
exposition of the "deeper grammar," the kerygmatic interior of the Old Testament text. Christian preaching about Moses and the prophets has to make
a clear statement that the text not only had value for Israel in Old Testament
times, but still has value for the contemporary Israel. It is an elementary in-
gredient of the *sensus Israeliticus* that the Jewish exposition of the Tanak has
its own right to existence after Christ and independent of the Christian interpretation. That kind of new theology needs nothing less than a conversion.[37] That is explicitly expressed in a sermon by P. Raniero Cantalamessa,
preacher to the Papal Household, also known as the Apostolic Preacher. Every Friday in Advent and Lent the Apostolic Preacher gives a meditation in
the presence of the pope, the cardinals, bishops, prelates, and general supe-

35. "Nur eine Predigt, die recht vor Israel redet, kann rechte christliche Bezeugung
des gnädigen Gottes bzw. seiner Treue und frohen Botschaft sein" (Stäblein 2004, p. 183).

36. McCheyne (Fant IV), p. 273.

37. The fundamental asymmetric relation between Israel and the church gives the
mortgage an abiding character.

riors of religious orders. In a sermon on Good Friday 1998 Cantalamessa refers to the relation between Israel and the Church, Jews and Christians.

> When I speak of the wrongs committed against the Jewish people, I have in mind not only the faults of others who belonged to generations before me, but of my own as well. I will always remember the beginnings of my own conversion in this regard. I was on a plane, returning from my first pilgrimage to the Holy Land. I was reading the Bible, and my eye fell on a phrase in the Letter to the Ephesians: "No one ever hates his own flesh" (Eph 5:29). I realized that this applies also to the relationship of Jesus with his own people. And all my prejudices, if not hostility, towards the Jewish people that I had unconsciously absorbed in my theological training, appeared to me to be an offense against Jesus himself.
>
> He became like us in all things, with the sole exception of sin. Since love of one's country and the bonds that bind us to our own people are not a sin, but rather a virtue, it follows that by the very fact of his incarnation, Jesus — let us call him by his Hebrew name, Yeshua — loved the people of Israel with a love stronger and purer than that with which any patriot in all the world has ever cherished his homeland. And so every sin against the Jews is also a sin against the humanity of Christ.
>
> I understood that I needed to be converted to Israel, "the Israel of God," as the apostle calls it, a reality not entirely identical with the "political Israel," but neither to be separated from it. I realized that this love need not threaten any other people, nor result in allegiances which exclude others, because Jesus taught us that our Christian heart must open itself to the entire universe and help Israel to do likewise. "Is God the God of the Jews only? Is he not the God of Gentiles also?" (Romans 3:29).[38]

The preacher's testimony about his "conversion" gives the sermon not only authenticity but also authority. The existential experience in the plane broke through the religious socialization and the theological training and made space for a new encounter with what is meant by "Israel." The preacher uses his own experiences without focusing exclusively on himself. He sets his own discovery and "conversion" at the disposal of the hearers.[39]

38. Cantalamessa 1998.
39. Engemann 2002, pp. 175-79.

## 12.6. . . . and Also the Greek

The LORD is not finished with Israel after Christ. Scripture assures us that Israel will show forth the LORD's praise (Isa. 43:21); that they are and remain a special people (Deut. 7:6). Moses and the prophets portray the LORD as One who maintains his "steadfast love and faithfulness" to his covenantal partner (Gen. 24:27; Exod. 34:6; Ps. 36:5).[40] Christian proclamation has the audacity to preach that "the Greek" is also encompassed by the LORD's love and faithfulness. This is even the ultimate foundation for preaching as such. In a day when it was unheard of even to consider such things, the Apostle Paul realized that the gentiles were to be fellow-heirs with the Jews in God's great plan of salvation (Eph. 3:6). He launched out on his vision to take the gospel to the gentile world. These tones can be heard in a sermon by James Van Tholen on Hosea 11:1-11.

> It's easy to think of God's power as all threat, because he can do so much. It's easy to think of power to judge, power to exile, power to kill. But that's wrong. The power of God is never more evident than it is here in Hosea 11, when he holds on to a son he has every justification for cutting off. "I will not execute my fierce anger, for I am God and no mortal."
>
> *There* is the hope of Israel. *There* is the gospel. He is God and not mortal. He is God and not a human being. In him there is power not to kill, and even when all the circumstances call for it. In him there is power to overcome his anger. Israel will return home, will know him, and will have their Father because that is what he has decided will happen:
>
>> They shall go after the LORD, who roars like a lion;
>> when he roars, his children come trembling from the west ( ).
>> And I will return them to their homes, says the LORD. (:10-11)
>
> "For I am God and not mortal." *There* is the hope of Israel.
> And *there* is the hope of you and me.[41]

The "there" is written four times in italics and probably spoken with emphasis. This sermon makes clear that the salvation for the gentiles did not

---

40. Soulen 1996, pp. 114-40.
41. Van Tholen 2003, pp. 177-78.

replace God's abiding loyalty to Israel. The preacher portrays the *sensus israeliticus,* i.e., God's abiding loyalty and faithfulness to Israel, as the ultimate and necessary foundation for the proclamation of God's salvation to the gentiles and thus to this congregation.

The tones of "first the Jew and also the Greek" can also be heard in a sermon by William Powell Tuck on Psalm 137, a poem filled with grief and anger, frustration and vindictiveness, homesickness and patriotism, love of Jerusalem and loathing of Babylon.

> Who of us has not been in some strange places and has not longed to go home again? But few of us have had the experience of being removed so quickly and drastically from home as he was. During World War II, however, some other Jewish people suffered that same kind of experience. They too, were ripped from their homeland and thrust into concentration camps. They too, wondered where God was. "Where is God now that I am in Dachau . . . in Auschwitz?" they asked. "Where is God? Where is God in this moment of my captivity?"
>
> In the eighteenth and nineteenth centuries blacks from Africa asked the same questions when they were snatched from their homeland, taken to foreign countries and sold as slaves. They too wondered where God was during those desperate moments of their lives. Many displaced persons have raised their voices wondering where God was in their time of need. The starving people in Somalia, in the inner cities, in the remote mountain regions of our own country have often raised the same cry.[42]

The words of the psalm are seen in the first place in the context of contemporary Israel but are surely not restricted to that context. The wording of the psalm gives voice to the absurd experiences of the Holocaust. In a next step, these words can also give voice to the humiliating experiences of the Africans who were sold as slaves or to the starving people who suffer from present-day atrocities of war.

---

42. Tuck (Klingsporn III), p. 118 (text slightly edited).

## 12.7. Glad Tidings

### Good News for the Nations

Paul sings with joy that the God of Israel is also the God of the gentiles (Rom. 3:29), the *Abba* of the nations (Rom. 8:15; Gal. 4:6). Paul traveled miles and miles to proclaim this good news all over the world. Contemporary preachers are invited to embroider their preaching on the pattern of that apostolic message: the gentiles are included in the proclamation of the mercy of the LORD (Lam. 3:22; Rom. 12:1); they are incorporated in the dynamics of his graceful company with humans, started with Israel.[43] "But now in Christ Jesus you who once were far off have been brought near by the blood of Christ" (Eph. 2:13). Both Israel and gentiles are invited and summoned to rejoice in the LORD, to celebrate his benefits, and to walk in the way of the instructions of this God. This is the foundation of Christian proclamation.

In and through Jesus Christ the gentiles also take part in the covenant of the LORD with Israel. Gentiles are fellow heirs and sharers in the promise in Christ Jesus through the gospel (Eph. 3:6). The nations are no longer the "godless," but are made friends through the holy love of the LORD, as made visible through the cross and resurrection of Jesus Christ. This proclamation is the very kernel of the preaching of Paul. For while the gentiles "were enemies, we were reconciled to God through the death of his Son" (Rom. 5:10).[44] The same melody can be heard in the letter to the Ephesians. "Remember that you were at that time without Christ, being aliens from the commonwealth of Israel, and strangers to the covenants of promise, having no hope and without God in the world" (Eph. 2:12). Paul sees a fulfillment of the promise that Abraham is not only the father of Israel but the father of many peoples, because Jesus died for those who were nearby and those who once were far off (Eph. 2:13).

Based on this theological and hermeneutical foundation of the

43. "Das ist eine der wichtigsten christlichen Heilsmaterien, daß wir, auch wenn wir keine Juden sind, in den Geschichtszusammenhang des jüdischen Volkes hineinberufen werden, um so am Drama, d.h. an der Spannung zwischen Verheißung und Erfüllung teilzunehmen, die ja die inneren Triebfeder der bisherigen Geschichte Israels und darum aller Geschichte ist; Christen sind solche Nichtjuden, die Gott am Drama der Geschichte des jüdischen Volkes beteiligt" (Marquardt 1990, p. 251).

44. Marquardt 1988, pp. 212-16.

*sensus Israeliticus,* a sermon according to an Old Testament text can include praise to the God of Israel. Such a doxology can make the joy and gratitude explicit that we, gentiles — i.e., the participants of that particular liturgy, listening to this particular sermon — share in the richness that is attested to in the books of Moses and the prophets: grace, comfort, and encouragement. The sermon can invite its listeners to join in the praise that has been sung for so many centuries by Israel. The hymn following the sermon can be a kind of doxological "Amen" to God's salvation.

## Humble Frankness

At the same time we have to say that Christian preaching can only join that jubilation in a humble way. Salvation did not arise nor was it born in the midst of the gentiles. Paul says "not many of you were wise by human standards, not many were powerful, not many were of noble birth" (1 Cor. 1:26). What the gentiles brought forth as good and honorable turns pale and becomes ashamed in the light of what God calls wise and strong (1 Cor. 1:27). The gentiles were alienated "from the commonwealth of Israel, and strangers to the covenant of promise, having no hope and without God in the world." It is through the Jew Jesus of Nazareth that we who once were far off have been brought nearby (Eph. 2:12). Consequently Christian preaching can only open and preach according to the books of Moses and the prophets with humble frankness. This attitude is not only a way of courteous, decent behavior or obligingness — although the church will have made substantial progress in her behavior when she brings that attitude into practice! The humbleness digs deeper than decency. We, gentile believers, play second violin in the orchestra of Israel's God. Israel is and remains God's firstborn (Exod. 4:22; Hos. 11:1).

The church can be seen as part of the "mixed crowd" that went up with Israel on their journey from Egypt, through the desert to the Promised Land (Exod. 12:38).[45] Believers from the gentiles are and remain aliens and exiles (1 Pet. 1:1, 17; 2:11). But we have to add that those strangers are also children and heirs of God (Rom. 8:17) who have the right to say *"Abba"* to the Father of Jesus Christ (Rom. 8:15). For this reason it is important that the humble attitude does not deteriorate into a kind of submissive-

45. Marquardt 1994, pp. 160-64.

ness, fueled by unhealthy feelings of guilt in relation to the Jews. We have to say that the believers from the gentiles indeed play "second violin." But being aware of that, we can play our part with self-confidence in the orchestra of Israel's God. We were reckoned as peoples registered on God's scroll (Ps. 87). "So then you are no longer strangers and aliens, but you are citizens with the saints and also members of the household of God, built upon the foundation of the apostles and prophets, with Christ Jesus himself as the cornerstone. In him the whole structure is joined together and grows into a holy temple in the Lord; in whom you also are built together spiritually into a dwelling place for God" (Eph. 2:19-22). Because of the primacy of the *sensus Israeliticus* the church has the obligation to be humble, but at the same time it has the right to be so in a frank and self-confident way.

## 12.8. A Mortgaged Relation

In the search for new images for *Synagoga* and *Ecclesia,* we have to be aware of the fact that the relation of those two is heavily mortgaged.[46] Christians cannot and may not ignore the fact that the church and theology have a history of nearly two millennia infected by anti-Judaism and anti-Semitism.[47] We also cannot and may not ignore the shadow of the Shoah.[48]

The "teaching of contempt," the "preaching of replacement," and the "theology of supersessionism" caused in fact implicit and even explicit verbal violence against the Jews. Dow Marmur, the former senior rabbi of Holy Blossom Temple (Toronto, Ontario), was born in Poland in 1935 and spent the years of World War II in the Soviet Union before returning to Poland in 1946. Two years later he moved to Sweden, where he went to school. He tells about his experiences as a little boy in a Swedish school, experiences that were fueled by a certain kind of Christian theology.

> But there were then no Jewish Day Schools in Sweden. In any case, our aim now was to be integrated as quickly as possible, not to remain

46. Thoma 1978, p. 44; Porter/Pearson 2000.
47. Katz 1961; Cohen 1991; Fisher 1993.
48. Marquardt 2003, pp. 152-55.

apart. That meant going to the local state school and thus, of necessity, learning a lot about Christianity. For despite the alleged secularism of the Swedish educational system, there was then still much Christianity on the curriculum, celebrated, for example, in the compulsory daily school assemblies.

I recall vividly the readings of the Passion Story before each Easter and how I — one of only two or three Jewish students in the school — would be made to feel personally responsible for having crucified Jesus. All eyes were on me each time the Jews — or the High Priest, or Judas — were mentioned. As I did not know the context, I was perplexed and very uncomfortable by the text. Some of that discomfort has stayed with me to this very day. There are times when I still have an exaggerated need to defend myself, my community and my Judaism before Christians.[49]

This story tells very personally the painful results of a Christian preaching based on replacement theology. The Jewish New Testament scholar David Flusser said that those Christian utterances had such a threatening impact for Jews that it could be reason to call the police and ask for assistance![50]

## 12.9. Attention to Jewish Exposition and Interpretation

Paul's statement "first the Jew and also the Greek" also has methodical consequences for the preparation of our sermons. We have to give methodical and systematic attention to the *sensus Israeliticus* somewhere and somehow in the process of sermon preparation. "First" refers necessarily to "first in order," but also to the fundamental awareness that Israel was and still is the "original" context for interpretation. That can be done in different ways and at different moments because the *sensus Israeliticus* affects and influences several steps and dimensions of the preparation process. But it is remarkable that this element is lacking completely in contemporary models for sermon preparation. The next six proposals and issues discussed in this section are also for that reason fragmentary.

49. Marmur 1998.
50. Quoted by Marquardt 1988, p. 93.

## Abiding Meaning for Israel

The congregation's awareness that the gentiles are not the first readers or listeners can be nourished by pointing regularly to the meaning of the words of Moses and the prophets in the context of Israel. That meaning has its place next to the meaning that a specific passage has in the Christian context. In a sermon on some verses taken from the book of Lamentations, Walter Brueggemann states clearly that these verses still have meaning for Israel.

> The book of Lamentation is just that, a lament, five long poems of sadness, grief over the ancient city of Jerusalem that was destroyed by the Babylonians in 587 BCE. The Jews cried over that destruction, because the holy city was the focus of all their dreams and hopes, the sign of God's presence and fidelity to them, the gathering of all things precious and treasured. And then it was gone, gone by Babylonian invasion, but they said, gone by the anger of God . . . in any case gone!
>
> And they wept. They wept for loss. They wept for abandonment. They wept in their deep hurt and despair. And the book of Lamentation lingers in the Bible, because Jews have never finished weeping over that loss that showed up again in the Nazi holocaust, and that likely is still at work in the present Israeli government with its fear and anxiety and brutality.[51]

The preacher points to the meaning of these words for the Christian congregation in what follows in this sermon. But that does not diminish the abiding meaning of these words for Israel until the present day. The preacher also gives a specific Christian interpretation to this passage in the next paragraphs of this sermon. But he does not oppose the Jewish interpretation and the Christian one. The tension between those two remains. As a result, there are some "loose ends" and there is no polished finale. But it is exactly this tension that prevents the laments from "disappearing" behind Christ.

51. Brueggemann 2004, p. 121.

## Attention to the Interpretation of Jews

Besides the use of specific Christian references, as commentaries, sermons, and theological literature, in the process of sermon preparation we can also use Jewish resources.[52] Taking notice of specific Jewish contributions can help to get the *sensus Israeliticus* into focus. Scripture and the Jewish tradition are together the "rich root of the olive tree," the nutrient medium or fertile soil that supports the engrafted, non-Jewish, Gentile-Christian branches (Rom. 11:17ff.). In the process of sermon preparation the material from this Jewish soil can help prevent Christian annexation and absorption.

Preachers can, for instance, tell explicitly that they used Jewish sources such as Talmudic commentary or Chasidic stories. In a sermon on Isaiah 42:1-9, Thomas G. Long tells about a rabbi who was captured by a group of Nazi brownshirts in World War II. The rabbi was in his study as he was preparing his Sabbath sermon at the moment of his arrest. The Nazis mocked and humiliated the rabbi by stripping and flogging him. As they did, they laughed and said: "This lash is for Abraham; this one is for Jacob; this one is for Isaac." When he was numb from the whipping, they took out scissors, sheared his locks and his beard, and mocked him the more. The sermon goes on as follows:

"Say something in Hebrew," the S.A. Captain ordered.

"Thou shalt love the Lord thy God with all thy heart," the Rabbi slowly pronounced the Hebrew words. But one of the other officers interrupted him. "Were you not preparing your sermon this morning?" he asked him.

"Yes," said the Rabbi.

"Well, you can preach it here to us. You'll never again see your synagogue; we've just burned it. Go ahead, preach the sermon," he cried out. "All quiet now, everybody. Jacob is going to preach a sermon to us."

"Could I have my hat?" asked the Rabbi.

"Can't you preach without a hat?" the officer asked him.

"Give him his hat!" he commanded. Someone handed the Rabbi his hat, and he put it on his head. The sight made the S.A. men laugh the more. The man was naked and he was shivering. Then he spoke.

52. Rendtorff 1995, p. 102; Büttner 2002, p. 200.

"God created man is his image and likeness," he said. "That was to have been my text for the coming Sabbath."

All of this destruction that human beings wreak on each other is an attack on creation and on the image of God in humanity. Whatever we wish God would do and be, the true God wills to repair creation, and God will not rest until justice has been established.[53]

It is important that preachers and their congregations develop sensitivity for this dimension in the interpretation of the books of Moses and the prophets. This sensitivity can help the congregation to be aware of the fact that the words of Scripture were not only relevant for Israel in Old Testament times but are still of relevance for contemporary Israel.

### Post-Holocaust Perspective

The *sensus Israeliticus* also invites the Christian interpreter to listen to the Old Testament from a post-Holocaust angle. Awful identifications can be made between biblical names and figures on the one hand and experiences of the Holocaust on the other hand. Henry F. Knight parallels the looking back of Lot's wife at Sodom (Gen. 19:12-29) with looking back at Auschwitz in a post-Holocaust context.

> Looking back at Sodom is dangerous. If there is any doubt, we need only inquire of Lot's wife. She turned to ponder Sodom and has remained frozen in her tracks ever since — a pillar of salt, the story proclaims. Do those who ponder Sodom's fate with lingering questions and their own resistance or reluctance to accept the fate of Sodom and her sister city (Gomorrah) risk a similar paralysis or ending to their pilgrimage of faith/life? Since, after all, that is what we are doing, we might be wise to begin with Lot's wife and ask of the story, Why was she punished for looking back, especially when we are told that Lot doubted and resisted the warning from the divine messengers? Lot was reluctant to heed their advice and leave. The story even tells that he had to be led away from Sodom (Gen. 19:15). Why was Lot's wife the one who faced the greater consequence?

53. Long (Klingsporn V), p. 21. The manuscript mentions Matthew 2:1-12 as a second Scripture-reading. The story is from Pierre van Paassen, *That Day Alone* (New York: Dial, 1941), p. 331.

Perhaps our post-holocaust circumstances in asking this question provide our first clue. We know that there are dangers in looking back at Auschwitz. More than once it has broken the spirits and claimed the lives of persons who turn to view its smoke and ashes. Even fifty years after, the danger still lurks in the darkness. As Elie Wiesel has said on more than one occasion, it is dangerous to study the Shoah. Through depression, loss of hope, suicide, through loss of faith, or world, or all of these combined, Auschwitz can transform those who gaze at its pillars of fire into pillars of salt.[54]

The awareness of the post-Holocaust situation can open new dimensions in the interpretation of an Old Testament text in a Christian context.

## Unfamiliar and Undeserved Acquittal

"Salvation is from the Jews" (John 4:22). Those words remind the faithful gentile that grace is both unfamiliar and undeserved. It is especially the Jew Paul who stresses the fact that humans are saved by God's unmerited grace. Justification is a gracious work whereby God, as righteous Judge, acquits us of accusations, guilt, and punishment and declares us to be members of his household and heirs of eternal life (Eph. 2:1-10). This acquittal is not founded on our own righteousness but on God's incomprehensible grace. We can neither achieve nor earn the acquittal in our own strength. Our righteousness is therefore "alien righteousness"; it comes from outside our possibilities and potentials. Evangelists and apostles testify that the LORD brought the gentiles too within the sphere and range of the influence of his grace.

The Subject of this "justifying acquittal" is Israel's God, who established his covenant in the first place with Abraham and his descendants. He chose Israel from all the peoples on earth to be his people, his treasured possession (Deut. 7:6ff.). After the coming of Jesus Christ, the LORD maintained covenant loyalty to the descendants of Abraham, Isaac, and Jacob and keeps the oath that he once swore (Rom. 11:25ff.). The LORD was, is, and will be Israel's God, also for gentile believers. The proclamation of Moses and the prophets was, is, and will be in the first place ("originally") di-

54. H. F. Knight 2000, p. 41.

rected to Israel. That adds an extra dimension to the "unfamiliar," "strange," and "alien" character of the acquittal for the gentiles.

### Curative Unrest

The Jews are, more than any other ecclesial or theological critics, a kind of curative unrest in the congregational life of the Christian church. And that is because the LORD does not and will not depart from Israel his firstborn son. The *sensus Israeliticus* gives voice to this unrest. Henry F. Knight recontextualizes the story of Jacob's wrestling at the Jabbok and his encounter with his brother Esau. The meeting between Jews and Christians can in fact be interpreted with the reverse of this story.

> The legacy of displacement and shame borne by Jacob vis-à-vis his brother Esau is not unlike that borne by sensitive Christians setting out to meet their Jewish siblings in the late twentieth century. Yet the journey to this modern Jabbok is a fearful and ironic twist to Jacob's story — indeed, it is a tragic parody. This encounter takes place on the other side of another night, not unlike Jacob's first night of wrestling. This time, however, the displacement is borne by those who have tried to usurp the place of Jacob in history, stealing birthright and name, as well as blaming the victim for the loss of sacred identity. After Auschwitz, any meeting between Christians and Jews over the biblical story of Jacob at the Jabbok calls forth an awareness of this other historical text and invites further wrestling with the issue of shame and the lifetimes brought to such an encounter.[55]

The "ironic twist" prevents us from dealing too easily and too romantically with this story. It calls forth a healthy unrest.

### Reproaches

A special word must be said concerning the reproaches, the wording of which is taken from Micah 6. Traditionally these reproaches were read on Good Friday to dramatize the accusations that God brings against the con-

---

55. H. F. Knight 2000, p. 4.

gregation in the light of the passion and death of Christ. The reproaches enlist questions that reveal our rebellion and complicity in the sufferings of Christ and in the evil and sufferings in the world. They are like an inversion of the holy history we recite and recall in the Great Thanksgivings at the Lord's Table. We must be aware, however, of the history of anti-Jewish sentiments that were fueled by these reproaches. This is abhorrent, especially in the light of consequences of anti-Semitism throughout history. The New *Handbook of the Christian Year* of the United Methodist Church offers for that reason a revised version.[56] The first verses follow the pattern of the "classical" text. In addition, several completely new verses have been composed, for example:

> I grafted you into the tree of my chosen Israel,
> and you turned on them with persecution and mass murder.
> I made you joint heirs with them of my covenants,
> but you made them scapegoats for your own guilt.
> I came to you as the least of your brothers and sisters;
> I was hungry and you gave me no food,
> I was thirsty and you gave me no drink,
> I was a stranger and you did not welcome me,
> naked and you did not clothe me,
> sick and in prison and you did not visit me.

The idea behind this text is of Christ speaking to his gentile followers from the cross. The *sensus Israeliticus* offers a number of possibilities for this part of the liturgy to prevent anti-Semitic or a-Semitic tendencies.

## 12.10. New Images for *Ecclesia* and *Synagoga*

The church has presented itself for a long time as the new covenant-partner of the LORD that took over the role and the place of Israel. In the slipstream of this theology, the church presented itself as the one and only true guardian and interpreter of the books of Moses and the prophets. The result was that those books were impropriated from the "veiled" synagogue.[57] But the church is not a "Plan B" that came onto the stage after the

---

56. Hickman 1992, pp. 187-89; see also *Book of Common Worship* 1993, pp. 288-91.

57. "Die Existenz und damit Realität des Judentums hat die Kirche zu allen Zeiten

failure of Israel as the original "Plan A." The grace of the new covenant does not mean that God has set the covenant with Israel aside. We are therefore in need of new "images" of *Ecclesia* and *Synagoga*[58] that are not placed in opposition to each other but side-by-side. That is not only a task for academic theology but also — may be even in the first place — for local congregations and their preachers. Because of the mortgaged relation between Jews and Christians, preachers have the task and calling to reflect on the questions and issues pertaining to their relation. This reflection will, without doubt, cause new and challenging insights.

Seen from a historical point of view, ancient Israel was just a puny nation amidst the superpowers of Egypt, Assyria, Babylon, and Persia. Seen from a geographical point of view, it was nothing more than a small strip on the borders of the Great Sea. But seen from a heavenly point of view, Israel was the covenant-partner of the LORD, called to be a blessing and a light for the world. The *sensus Israeliticus* makes us aware that this God reveals his intentions for humankind as a whole in his relationship with this puny nation. The gentiles are invited, challenged, and called to join this covenantal event between the LORD and Israel.[59] Karl Barth points to the simple fact of Israel when the question of a proof of God is raised.

> For in the person of the Jew there stands a witness before our eyes, the witness of God's covenant with Abraham, Isaac and Jacob and in that way with us all. Even one who does not understand Holy Scripture can see this reminder. And don't you see, the remarkable theological importance, the extraordinary spiritual and sacred significance of the National Socialism (Nazism) that now lies behind us is that right from its roots it was anti-Semitic, that in this movement it was realized with a simple demonic clarity, that *the* enemy is the *Jew.* Yes, the enemy in this matter had to be a Jew. In this Jewish nation there really lives to this day the extraordinariness of the revelation of God.[60]

---

begleitet, wobei sich das Verhalten von Kirche und Theologie hierzu im Großen und Ganzen unter Ignorieren oder Attackieren zusammenfassen läßt" (Büttner 2002, p. 188).

58. Two sculptures by Paula Mary Turnbull are a good illustration of how *Ecclesia* and *Synagoga* can be depicted as partners and co-workers (see bc.edu/research/cjl/metaelements/texts/cjrelations/resources/reviews/One_Blessing.htm).

59. Marquardt 1988, pp. 263-374.

60. Barth 1959, pp. 75-76.

Some pages earlier Barth had already affirmed that the man "who is ashamed of Israel is ashamed of Jesus Christ and therefore of his own existence."[61] The New Testament underscores God's affirmation of the promises given to Israel.

61. Barth 1959, p. 67.

# 13. Who Do You Say I Am?

## 13.1. Expiration Date

While surfing on the Internet, searching for sermons that could serve as illustration material for the present book, I discovered some sermons with a remarkable addition: "The best-before date of this sermon is expired."[1] The preacher was probably aware of the fact that those sermons were born in the midst of particular joys and burdens, happiness and sorrow. Both wording and construction of the sermon were dependent on a specific situation. That is not only true for this particular sermon but for preaching in general, because every sermon has a "best-before date." In a sense, sermons are disposable and each particular sermon is a one-shot event.

The metaphor of the "best-before date" fits especially for the Christological dimension of sermons on Old Testament texts in a gentile context. This dimension has a limited "life span" and is as perishable as the manna in the desert (Exod. 16:13-35). In our quest to preach Christ from the Old Testament, we can never proceed by building with assurance on questions that have already been answered. Preachers are directed every week to begin again at the beginning. It is after all Christ himself who raises this question time and again: "Who do you say I am?" (Matt. 16:13-20). This chapter describes a hermeneutical grammar that can provide us with words, theology, expressions, and images to formulate an answer to that question. We could also say that this chapter is a quest for keys to open up the Christological dimension of the interior of an Old Testament text. The playing field for this chapter is determined by two poles that are in a dialectical tension.

1. Van der Scheer 1996.

214

a. The Christological perspective doesn't close the window that offers a view on Israel. Everything to be said in this chapter will not and cannot deny the results of the previous chapter. We don't want nor can we open the Christological perspective of an Old Testament text at the expense of the abiding value of Moses and the prophets for Israel.

b. Apostles and evangelists give witness to Christ without hesitation, starting with Moses and the prophets. We sense the same open-hearted and uncomplicated frankness in the early church,[2] and this continues up until the period of the Reformation. Influenced by the results of the historical- and literary-critical research, theology and preaching have gradually lost that attitude. This chapter is an attempt to pick up the trail of the original frankness without ignoring or denying the results of modern biblical scholarship.

It is clear that there is a field of tension between these two poles. On the one hand, we have to say that the creed of incarnation is fundamental for the writers of the New Testament and for the Christian church. On the other hand, Jews do not share and cannot accept the narrative of God's incarnation in one Jew. Peter Ochs says that from a Jewish perspective, "the Christian doctrine of the Incarnation appears comprehensible but simply wrong."[3] This disagreement points to an irreducible tension and even to dispute and rivalry between Jews and Christians.[4] This chapter does not solve, deny, or diminish this tension but makes it operable for the practice of Christian preaching.

## 13.2. Confusion and Shyness

The frank and openhearted Christological dimension in the preaching and proclamation of the early church appeared to have an "expiration date" from a historical point of view. We have to locate this expiration date during the rise of historical- and literary-critical research, i.e., from the eighteenth century and beyond. At the moment that theology ate the fruit of

2. "The early Christian preachers could support their arguments only from the Old Testament when they began to proclaim the revelation of Jesus Christ" (Olivar 1998, p. 21).

3. Ochs 2000, p. 59.

4. Soulen 2000, p. 174.

the tree of critical research, eyes were opened, for the historical gap and proclamation became naked to critical inquiry. Preaching was driven out of the Paradise of uncomplicated Christology, and sermons had to sew homiletical and hermeneutical fig leaves together in order to clothe themselves. The flaming sword of the critical questions made it impossible to return to the Garden of Eden of insouciance.[5]

The results of scholarly research have affected not only those who are able to read the "theologian's Latin" as published, for instance, by the members of the *Jesus Seminar.* Popularized versions of much-discussed and high-profile publications have spread the results of this research widely in local congregations.[6] On the one hand, those publications meant a clearing out of layers of over-aged Christological varnish. But those publications caused on the other hand severe damage to the Christological images that had ornamented the ceiling of the Christian church for a long time.[7] Those familiar and trusted images — often with an origin going back to childhood — crumbled under the forces of critical questions.[8] The souls of the members of the congregation were set adrift in a sea of Christological confusion.

The result of the falling apart of trusted and well-known images resulted in a kind of uncertainty, shyness, and hesitation in preaching Christ that can be felt in the preaching of almost every mainline denomination.[9] The consequence is that congregations can no longer just move up a bit in the pew to avoid the rain of critical questions that comes through the hole of the damaged ceiling. That means that congregations, preachers, and theologians could not and cannot detach themselves from the results and questions of this Christological research.[10]

The (re)discovery of the Jewish tradition and the importance of this tradition for theology and proclamation added an extra dimension to this

---

5. Oeming 1987, p. 87.

6. See for instance Sanders 1993; Borg 1994; Theissen 2001.

7. For this metaphor see Troeger 1999, pp. 11ff.; for the post-Holocaust context see Schöttler 2001, p. 512.

8. The influence of children's Bibles on the implicit theology of the congregation can hardly be overestimated. That is true for both text and illustrations. See for instance Brown Taylor 2000.

9. For a list of issues related to preaching and Christology see Buttrick 1987, pp. 11-22.

10. It is from that point of view remarkable that — generally speaking — models and concepts for sermon preparation on Old Testament texts published in the last decades don't pay explicit attention to the soteriological dimension of Christology.

Christological shyness and uncertainty. That is especially true because this rediscovery originated in the theological reflection on the drama of the Holocaust. Some voices even made a plea for a period of silence to be used for a reorientation on Christology and the use of Christological titles like Messiah, Son of God, Son of Man, Lord, and Redeemer. In previous chapters I marked my position on the necessity of such a reorientation on these and related issues. And it is indeed a question as to whether Christians have the role of placing the subject of Jesus as the Messiah on the agenda of the dialogue with Jewish partners. However, for the discussion and the reflection within the church we cannot bracket out the Christological questions. The church lives from "the things about Jesus of Nazareth" (Luke 24:19), from "the Word that lived among us" (John 1:14). The crucified and risen Christ is at the heart of Christian faith and thus of Christian preaching (1 Cor. 2:2). For that reason the church, theology, and proclamation cannot withdraw from the task of continuous deliberation, consideration, and contemplation on Christological questions and issues. The church understands herself as a community of gentiles, called by the proclamation of the gospel of Jesus Christ to put their trust in the LORD, the God of Israel, and to seek and serve his kingdom. The name of Jesus and the confession of Christ play a pivotal role both in the community of the church and in the lives of individual members. They pray in Jesus' name, they celebrate his remembrance in bread and wine, they forgive sins in his name, they baptize in his name, and they are filled with — or hope to be filled with — his Spirit. Christology is thus at the heart of the church and marks everything she says and does. It is the responsibility and challenge of our days to see in Jesus' death and resurrection actions of the LORD that are in accordance with the Scriptures of Israel.[11]

## 13.3. Theological Presuppositions

How did the stories and accounts start concerning Jesus of Nazareth? A Jewish man walked through the Jewish land with a growing crowd of curious people as well as a group of honest believers. At first it seemed that the life of Jesus ended in a tragedy: he was convicted as a criminal, crucified with criminals, and buried in silence. But for his friends and disciples this was not the

---

11. Seitz 2001, p. 47.

definitive end. They even spoke of a decisive new beginning. They gave witness about an empty tomb and encounters with the risen Lord.

When Jesus' disciples and pupils searched for words, titles, images, and theology to describe and interpret what they had seen and heard, they found a rich source in the books of Moses and the prophets. They were familiar with those books because they were raised with them, just as Jesus was. Those books were also the primary source and foundation for his own teaching and preaching. Apostles and evangelists used the story and history of Israel to proclaim the good news of and about Jesus. All of Israel's stories and witnesses took place and occurred in the One from Nazareth. They realized that the things they had seen and heard in this "Stranger" (Luke 24:18) were exactly the things they had recited about the covenant between the LORD and Israel from generation to generation in psalms, stories, commandments, and prophetic utterances. For that reason they could describe and interpret Jesus with characteristic and crucial figures, stories, words, titles, and theological constructions from Israel's tradition: Moses and Elijah, David and Solomon, the servant of the LORD and the son of man, king and prophet, priest and anointed one. The books of Moses, the prophets, and David were the preeminent source for arranging, describing, and interpreting their remarkable and wonderful experiences with and concerning Jesus, the carpenter's son. The next two sections elaborate the basic theological presuppositions of apostles and evangelists for the benefit of contemporary preaching.

## Encounter with the God of Israel

The first theological presupposition is that believers from the gentiles encounter in Jesus of Nazareth the "form" of Israel's God (Phil. 2:6f.).[12] In Jesus we see the true image or *icon* of the invisible God of Israel (2 Cor. 4:4; Col. 1:15). Whoever has seen him has seen the Father (John 14:9; 6:46; 14:7). That does not mean that Jesus is a kind of second God besides the LORD. But he can be portrayed as the legitimate and mandated representative or agent of Israel's God. We hear the LORD speaking in the words of Jesus; we see the LORD acting in Jesus' ministry (John 1:1-4; 20:28; Titus 2:13; 1 John 5:20).[13]

12. "Jesus of Nazareth: The Presence of God" (Van Buren 1988, pp. 130ff.).
13. Marquardt 2003, pp. 276f.

From that perspective we can describe and interpret the life and ministry of Jesus Christ using the words and acts of the Lord as written in the books of Moses and the prophets (Acts 8:35).[14] That is the logical consequence of the confession of the unity of God in both Old and New Testaments. The Greek translation of the Hebrew Tetragrammaton (*YHWH*, translated as "Lord") is *kyrios,* in English "Lord." That translation became a prominent title for Jesus. Paul uses the *kyrios* title to apply concepts and functions to Christ that *YHWH* is expected to fulfill in the Old Testament context. After an accurate consideration of Paul's use of the Old Testament, David B. Capes concludes that Paul's application of the *YHWH*-texts to Christ "has significant Christological implications. It implies that he considered Jesus to be more than man. It suggests that he believed that Christ was in some sense Yahweh himself, manifested as Messiah."[15] So, we can say that we see Israel's God (the Lord) at work in the acts of Jesus Christ (the Lord). He is "the man in whom God does God."[16] Susan Bond rightly states that for "Christians, Jesus functions as God, representing or making God present to us."[17] John the evangelist formulated it in the well-known words, "The word became flesh and dwelt among us" (John 1:14).

Jesus performs, gives voice to, and impersonates the salvation of Israel's God. From that perspective we have to say that Jesus brings no plus above the revelation of the Old Testament. We hear in the Old Testament the full proclamation of God's grace and salvation. The New Testament witnesses don't bring a deeper or sounder message than Moses and the prophets did. Moses and the prophets give witness to the same God as the One we encounter in Jesus of Nazareth. It is this God who suffers because of the iniquities of man, a God who takes away the sins of the world, a God who was like a sheep led to the slaughter, and like a lamb silent before its shearer (Isa. 53/passion narratives). God was and is "reconciling the world with himself" (2 Cor. 5:19).[18] This Lord has compassion for the crowds who are like sheep without a shepherd (Ezek. 34/Matt. 9:36). The gentile nations encounter this God in the man from Nazareth.

The New Testament does not argue about this one and only God. Apostles and evangelists simply state that salvation in and through Christ

14. Fry Brown 2004, pp. 185-89.
15. Capes 1992, p. 164.
16. Forde 1990, pp. 99-105.
17. Bond 1999, p. 113.
18. Moltmann 1974 and 1993; Bauckham 1998.

is an act of this God, the LORD.[19] The particularity of the New Testament is the confession that we have seen the LORD in the flesh, in the embodiment of the Jew Jesus of Nazareth. And because of him, the God of Israel is also the God of the gentiles. The Old Testament provides us with the basic vocabulary and the conceptual framework within which to understand the nature and purpose of the LORD's presence in Christ.[20] Our challenge is therefore in fact the same as the challenge faced by the early church. Christopher Seitz rightly states that for them as for us, the question is not how to "square faith in Christ with an Old Testament regarded as outmoded, but the reverse. How, in the light of a scripture everywhere regarded as authoritative and a privileged witness to God and his truth, could it be said that Jesus was in accordance and one with the Father who sent him?"[21]

## Encounter with the Israel of God

The second theological presupposition for preaching Christ from the Old Testament is based on the testimony that the gentiles encounter the Israel of God in Jesus of Nazareth.[22] The way of Jesus is, so to say, Israel's history in a nutshell. Matthew tells the story of Jesus, not as an individual history but as the collective biography of Israel. From that perspective, the evangelists can connect and relate the story and the history of Israel to Jesus. So, they can tell about the return from Egypt (Hos. 11:1/Matt. 2:15), about King Solomon (1 Kings 10:1f./Matt. 12:42), and about Jonah in the fish (Jon. 1:17; 2:10/Matt. 12:38-41). Jesus is a son of Israel born under the Law (Gal. 4:4). He was circumcised "after eight days had passed" (Luke 2:21), becoming thus a partner of the covenant with Abraham. He went to the synagogue, as was his custom (Luke 4:16). He was sent to the lost sheep of the house of

19. Gunneweg 1978, p. 190.

20. Allen/Holbert 1995, p. 62. "The New Testament witness to Jesus the Christ, the Son of God, stands on the soil of the Old Testament and cannot be separated from it" (Barth, *CD* IV/1, p. 166). Marquardt says that Moses and the prophets provide the "elementary particles" for Christology (Marquardt 1990, pp. 52, 57). De Lubac argues that "the Old Testament was seen as the matrix of the New or as the instrument of its creation" (Marquardt 1997, p. 7).

21. Seitz 2001, p. 65.

22. Marquardt mentions Israel "the formal Christology" (Marquardt 1988, §7). And Van Buren speaks about the "re-presentational identity of Jesus with his people Israel" (Van Buren 1988, p. 250). That paragraph is called "Jesus as Israel" (Van Buren 1988, pp. 249-53).

Israel (Matt. 15:24), lived within the boundaries of Israel, the Law of Moses, the prophets, and the writings (Matt. 5:17-20). It is proper for him to fulfill all righteousness of the Law (Matt. 3:15). The songs of Mary and Zechariah sing about Jesus in the context of Israel's liberation (Luke 1:47-55, 68-79). He goes to Jerusalem to fulfill his *exodus* (Luke 9:31). Jesus calls forth expectations about the restoration of the kingdom of Israel even after his resurrection (Acts 1:6). Jesus reframes this expectation indeed, but he doesn't deny it.

Paul testifies that Christ was raised "in accordance with the Scriptures" (1 Cor. 15:3f.). That doesn't mean that the resurrection of Jesus is predicted in the Old Testament, but it means that "to resurrect" belongs to the very "nature" or character of God's actions on behalf of Israel. Paul draws an analogy between the resurrection and the repeated witnesses to the *toledoth* (i.e., the generations, descendants, genealogies; cf. Gen. 2:4; 5:1; 6:9; 10:1, 32) in the book of Genesis (Rom. 4:18-22). The God who opened and revitalized dead bodies of men and women in Old Testament times is the same God who doesn't leave his beloved Son in the realm of death.[23] That the Jew Jesus of Nazareth was raised "in accordance with the Scriptures" means therefore that the LORD acts in and with Jesus as this God has acted always and will act in the future with covenant partner Israel.[24] For that reason Christ "must" be risen again after three days (Matt. 16:21; Mark 8:31; Luke 24:26, 46; Acts 3:18; 17:3). Paul emphasizes that Christ is risen according to the Scriptures. That means that we are invited to interpret the Old Testament and the story of Israel as the "identity papers" of Jesus Christ.[25]

Jesus' calling, identity, and ministry are from that perspective the calling, identity, and ministry of Israel in a concentrated way. Because Christ opens the covenant with Israel for the gentiles, the gentiles for their part are gathered and grafted into the LORD's history with Israel. For that reason Jesus' life and ministry can be described and interpreted as Son of God, in accordance with the description and interpretation of Israel as son of the LORD (Exod. 4:22).[26] The intimacy of the covenant between the LORD and

23. Marquardt 1990, pp. 208-12.

24. Van Buren 1998.

25. Arnold A. van Ruler says that the Old Testament is the *legitimation* of Jesus as the Christ. What Jesus does and what takes place in him are in harmony with the structure of the LORD's relation with Israel (Van Ruler 1971, pp. 75-77).

26. As a consequence, the title "Son of God" does not fit exclusively in a "Christology

Israel has its parallel in the description of the intimate relation between the first and second persons of the Trinity. The One who is called *"Abba"* has a relation from heart to heart with the One who is called "Son." And this relation determines everything Jesus Christ is and wants to be as "truly God and truly human."[27] We can make this fundamental theological assumption homiletically operable. Words, images, motives, and theology used by Moses and the prophets to portray, describe, and interpret the story and history of Israel can be used to portray, describe, and interpret the story and history of Jesus Christ. Israel provides the church with patterns and frameworks for preaching Christ from the Old Testament.[28] The story and history of Israel thus provide the church with the "elementary particles" of the language for the Christological dimension of proclamation.[29]

## 13.4. Rearrangements

Old Testament images, expressions, and theological motifs had and have their original place in the covenant between the LORD and Israel. In the process of sermon preparation, we can rearrange or rephrase those images, expressions, and theological motifs and also use them to describe and interpret the life and ministry of Jesus Christ. This section makes the two theological presuppositions operable for the practice of preaching. It offers a hermeneutical grammar for that purpose and it offers at the same time a homiletical strategy for the process of sermon preparation. This grammar or strategy is inspired by the implicit hermeneutics of apostles and evangelists in their quoting of the Old Testament (§9.4.2). But it is not a simple copy of the interpretative methods of apostles and evangelists. This hermeneutical grammar should, however, be in accord with the deeper funda-

---

from above" but has its place more in a "Christology from behind." That is also true for other titles of Jesus like "son of Abraham," "Servant of the LORD," "son of David," "King," "prophet," and "priest."

27. Marquardt 2003, p. 292.

28. "Israel's story is the primary context that makes the Church's language about Christ intelligible. (. . .) It can ( ) therefore be said that Israel's Scriptures are the original context of the Church's talk and reflection on the things concerning Jesus of Nazareth" (Van Buren 1988, pp. 30, 31). "Every proper Christological statement will make clear that it is an affirmation of the covenant between God and Israel" (Van Buren 1988, p. xix).

29. Marquardt 1990.

mental theological conviction of the writers of the New Testament, i.e., the unity of the words and acts of the LORD in past, present, and future (Rom. 3:30; 1 Cor. 8:4-6; Gal. 3:20).

In the process of sermon preparation we can rearrange the words of Moses and the prophets in a Christological context in the way that colored stones are rearranged in a kaleidoscope. The same colored elements produce time and again different creative images.[30] We can discern three steps in the process of sermon preparation when we rearrange or rephrase the words, images, and theology of Moses and the prophets in a Christological context:

- The preacher starts to register the possible Christological rearrangements.
- In a second step, the preacher examines the letter of the text to see if it can carry the weight of (one of) these rearrangements.
- The preacher makes a choice for a specific rearrangement for a particular sermon.

The next sections offer several illustrations of how this model can function in the practice of sermon preparation.

## Discerning Possible Rearrangements

The biblical theological inquiry made clear that apostles and evangelists used three different rearrangements of the words of Moses and the prophets to give witness about Christ (see also §9.4.2). This hermeneutical strategy uses the New Testament rearrangements as a heuristic instrument to trace possible theological connections between Old and New Testaments for contemporary preaching. So we listen to the Old Testament text as if it were words addressed *to* Jesus (by God or humans), as if it were words spoken *by* Jesus, or as if it were words spoken *about* Jesus.

**Words Spoken *to* Jesus**   To find a possible Christological rearrangement of the text, we can consider the Old Testament words, images, and theological motifs as if they were spoken *to* Jesus. Jesus is seen as the representa-

---

30. Hays 1989, pp. 187-90.

tive of the LORD or of Israel and therefore as addressee of the words. Let's for example take a look at Isaiah 26:12f. Israel confesses trust in the LORD with these words:

> O LORD, you will ordain peace for us, for indeed, all that we have done, you have done for us. O LORD our God, other lords besides you have ruled over us, but we acknowledge your name alone.

We can use these words to express the trust of gentiles in the Jew Jesus. We can rephrase, or reformulate the prophetic words in relation to Christ, our Lord.

> O Christ, our Lord, you will ordain peace for us, gentiles. For indeed, all that we have, you have done for us. O Christ, our Lord, other lords besides you have ruled over us, but we acknowledge your name alone.

Thus formulated, we see Christ as the mandated representative of the LORD. A sermon on this Old Testament passage can weave together the original words and the rephrasing. It can be combined with New Testament images and theology, for instance, of Ephesians 2.

> We served under the regime of heathen gods and lords. And because of that, we were without Christ, being aliens from the commonwealth of Israel, and strangers to the covenants of promise, having no hope and without Israel's God in the world (Eph. 2:12). But in and through Jesus Christ our Lord, Israel's God has ordained peace for us so that we have access in boldness and confidence to our heavenly Father (Eph. 2:18; 3:12). For that reason, we gentiles acknowledge the Name of Israel's God for that gracious gift.

A sermon on this passage from Isaiah can elaborate the images and theological motifs — like the regime of other lords, the decree of peace, and the acknowledgment of God's name — in both soteriological and ethical ways. The ecclesiological dimension can be illustrated with stories and examples taken from concrete congregational life or from the creativity, wisdom, and experience of the preacher.

**Words Spoken *by* Jesus**   A second perspective comes into view when we listen to the words of the Old Testament as if they were spoken *by* Jesus.

We consider Jesus to be the Subject of the Old Testament text.[31] The first illustration is taken from Psalm 121. Israel sings and confesses that the LORD will neither slumber nor sleep but that this God will keep Israel's going out and coming in from this day forth and forevermore. In a sermon on this psalm we can make several connections with the testimony about Jesus Christ. It can be seen, for example, as Jesus' prayer in the garden of olives.

> I lift up my eyes to the hill of Calvary,
> from where will my help come?
> My help comes from you, my LORD,
> who made heaven and earth.
> You will not let my foot be moved,
> nor my bones be broken;
> You, who keep Israel,
> do not slumber or sleep in this moment.
> You, Father and LORD of Israel,
> You are my keeper and shade at my right hand.
> I trust that the sun shall not strike me by day,
> nor the moon by night.
> I trust you, Father,
> that you will keep me from all evil that is waiting for me;
> you will keep my life,
> even in the hour of suffering and death.
> You will keep my going out and your coming in
> from this time on and forevermore.

Thus rephrased, the psalm resonates with many elements in the passion narrative and can serve as a proclamation of God's presence in the crucifixion and resurrection.

Dietrich Bonhoeffer was impressed by the existential power of the psalms. But he wrestled with the psalms of innocence, the bitter, the imprecatory psalms, and also in part with the psalms of the Passion.

> One may have no desire to carp at the Word of Scriptures and yet he knows that he cannot pray these words. He can read and hear them as the prayer of another person, wonder about then, be offended by

---

31. Karl Barth uses this hermeneutical strategy in his sermons (see §6.3).

them, but he can neither pray them himself nor discard them from the Bible. ( )

Actually, however, this difficulty indicates the point at which we get our first glimpse of the secret of the Psalter. A psalm that we cannot utter as a prayer, that makes us falter and horrifies us, is a hint to us that here Someone else is praying, not we; that the One who is here protesting his innocence, who is invoking God's judgment, who has come to such infinite depths of suffering, is none other than Jesus Christ himself. He it is who is praying here, and not only here but in the whole Psalter.

This insight the New Testament and the Church have always recognized and declared. The Man Jesus Christ, to whom no affliction, no ill, no suffering is alien and who yet was the wholly innocent and righteous one, is praying in the Psalter through the mouth of his Church.[32]

Bonhoeffer hears the voice of Jesus Christ in and through the voice of the poet in the psalms. He calls the Psalter "the prayer book of Jesus Christ in the truest sense of the word."

The third illustration is taken from words originally spoken to the Pharaoh by Moses in the name of the God of Israel (Exod. 5):

Thus says the LORD, the God of Israel, "Let my people go, so that they may celebrate a festival to me in the wilderness."

We can rephrase these words as follows in a Christological context:

Thus says Jesus Christ, the Lord, to the powers, "Let the nations go, so that they may celebrate a festival to me."

I used this Christological rearrangement as follows in a sermon on this text:

Jesus of Nazareth, the Man of God, is mandated by his *Abba* to order and command the powers of evil, darkness, and guilt: Let the peoples and the nations go. We hear him speak to unclean spirits and powers, "Be silent and go out." He does not request. He orders with authority. And we ask amazed and astonished, "Who is this that even the powers obey him?"

We have to add that the powers don't obey voluntarily. They don't

32. Bonhoeffer 1954, pp. 45f.

capitulate instantly. They roar, "What have you to do with us and what do we have to do with you, Jesus of Nazareth? Have you come to destroy us?"

The first reaction of the powers is always the same: "Who is the Lord that I should heed him and let Israel go? Who is this man of God that I should heed him and let the gentiles go? I do not know the Lord. I do not know Jesus of Nazareth. I let no one go."[33]

A sermon can weave together words and images taken from Exodus 5 and theological elements of Mark 1:23-28, 4:35-41.

**Words *about* Jesus**    A third possible perspective is to listen to Old Testament texts as words, images, or theology uttered *about* Jesus. More than once, Israel thought that her history had come to an end. But time and again there was a gracious new beginning. That is the very kernel of the proclamation of the Old Testament. The prophet Micah speaks about judgment and decline (3:12). In the next chapter he testifies of hope and expectation (4:1). In a sermon on these verses, the experiences of Israel in history are connected with the New Testament witness about cross and resurrection.

Micah speaks about an end and a new beginning. Those two words are crucial to the messianic faith. Israel has experienced judgment and decline so often in her history. But there were also experiences of hope, of new beginning, and expectation of a new future.

The church proclaims "cross and resurrection." In the combination of those two words we can hear the echo of the history of Israel. Those two words that mark the history of Israel also mark the story of Jesus. His life, crucifixion, and resurrection reflect in a concentrated way the story of Israel.

We have to admit that the church has often neglected and even renounced those words, particularly in the relation with Israel. But those two words are worth treasuring in the heart of our proclamation and pondering in the heart of our faith.

Whenever we face the tremendous tension between decline and new beginning, between guilt and forgiveness, between being desperate and new hope, we are called and invited to give witness to these

33. Bos 1999.

two closely connected words about Christ, the crucified and risen Lord. And we cannot proclaim the one without the other.[34]

The sermon connects the prophetic testimony about the end and new beginning of Israel on the one hand and the witness of the apostles and evangelists about the cross and resurrection of Jesus Christ on the other hand.

The first three verses of Psalm 76 can serve as a second example of how we can rearrange words from the Old Testament in a Christological context.

> In Judah God is known,
> his name is great in Israel.
> His abode has been established in Salem,
> his dwelling place in Zion.
> There he broke the flashing arrows,
> the shield, the sword, and the weapons of war.

We can recontextualize these words and images to describe Jesus' ministry and to sing about his achievement. Again Jesus is seen as the representative of Israel's God.

> Jesus is known in Judah,
> his name is great in Israel.
> His abode has been established in Jerusalem,
> his dwelling place in Zion.
> There he broke the flashing arrows,
> the shield, the sword, and the weapons of the powers of death.

The preacher can connect the expression "dwelling place" with the words and theology of John 1:14 "The Word became flesh and dwelt among us" (KJV, ASV). The rearrangement of the last verse can invite the preacher to connect these words and images with a soteriological interpretation of the crucifixion. Christ broke the flashing arrows, the shield, the sword, and the weapons of sin and guilt by carrying them on the cross. And he did so "for us" (Rom. 5:8; 8:32; Gal. 3:13; Eph. 5:2; 1 Thess. 5:10; Titus 2:14; 1 John 3:16).

The image of the pillar of clouds that accompanied Israel on their way through the desert (Exod. 13:21f.) is a third illustration.

---

34. Bos 2003.

> The LORD went in front of them in a pillar of cloud by day, to lead them along the way, and in a pillar of fire by night, to give them light, so that they might travel by day and by night. Neither the pillar of cloud by day nor the pillar of fire by night left its place in front of the people.

The testimony about the LORD going ahead of Israel with a pillar of cloud in the desert can be used in our preaching to testify that the LORD guided the beloved son Jesus in the darkness of death.

> In the night of suffering, cross, and death, the LORD was like a pillar of cloud before his beloved Son to lead him along the way to the light of life. For that reason the angels ask on Easter morning, "Why do you look for the living among the dead? He is not in the desert of death. He is raised in the land of promise. The Father never left his place in front of his Son."

## Theological Verification of the Possible Recontextualizations

There are at least three criteria to verify the theological validity of a recontextualization. The first criterion says that we have to respect the fact that Jesus lived and believed as a Jew, as a member of the people of Israel. Therefore Christian preaching can't create an implicit or explicit antithesis between Jesus and Israel or between Jesus and the Old Testament. Israel and the books of Moses and the prophets are the context within which Jesus lived and fulfilled his ministry. Stanley Hauerwas expresses this well in a meditation for the period of Lent. He parallels one of the seven words from the cross ("I thirst," John 19:28) to Psalm 22:14-15 and Psalm 69:21.

> No doubt these Psalms shaped the memory of those who witnessed the crucifixion, but that they did so does not mean that Jesus actually did not thirst, that Jesus did not suffer. Jesus' thirsting, Jesus' suffering according with the Psalms is a reminder that this Jesus is Israel's son.[35]

The proclamation of the church has to emphasize that Israel's election and calling are still valid in the era after Jesus Christ. Jesus cannot therefore be

---

35. Hauerwas 2004, pp. 72-73.

229

played off against Israel. Jesus holds on to his people in his suffering, dying, and resurrection. The community of believers from the gentiles has its place beside Israel; the church is "a house next door to the synagogue" (Acts 18:7). The church lives and breathes within the "sphere of influence" of the promises and commandments once given to Abraham and his descendants. The church will therefore stay aware of the fact that she is an engrafted branch, with all the rights and obligations, with all the promises and commandments.

The second criterion has to do with respect for both the limits and the extension of the theological carrying capacity of a particular text. Preachers have to examine whether a possible recontextualization fits in the "theological profile" of the book and corpus. For that purpose, preachers can use the disciplines of exegesis, biblical theology, and systematic theology to check the theological elasticity or carrying capacity of the text.[36] In a certain way, we can say that these disciplines are called to the stand as witnesses to plea for the subject matter of the text in the process of sermon preparation. The expressions "witnesses," "plea," "called to the stand," and "process" can from this perspective be heard with an explicitly forensic connotation.[37] In the mentioned illustration of Exodus 5 (§13.4.1.b), for instance, the preacher has to find out if the healing stories in the New Testament have an analogous theological structure to the witnesses of Israel's exodus from Egypt. When research on the texts makes clear that the miracles of Jesus have their place within the same theological paradigm as Exodus 5, we can connect these images and texts in a legitimate way. It is clear that a certain subjectivism plays a role in this kind of interpretation. But that can only be rejected in principle by those who believe that interpretation without presuppositions is possible, and who at the same time cherish the conviction that every secret of a text can be revealed in an "objective" way.[38]

The Christian creeds, seen as summaries of the "Rule of Faith," offer a third criterion. These creeds have functioned through the ages as the "fences" or "guardrails" for sound theological interpretation in accord with

---

36. Seitz uses the expression "exegetical guardrails" (Seitz 2001, p. 8).

37. The German homiletician Ernst Lange introduced the image of the preacher as "attorney of the text" (*Anwalt des Textes*) deliberately including the forensic connotations (Lange 1982, p. 30). I also mentioned the fact that Karl Barth spoke about "die Sache," the subject matter of a text.

38. Miskotte 1973, pp. 50-51.

the apostolic proclamation and that which the community of the church has believed through the ages.

> A preacher needs good resources for this verification. Sections on Christology in systematic theological handbooks, theological dictionaries, and theologies of the New Testament are not only helpful but also of vital importance as background for this dimension of interpretation. (See, e.g., R. E. Brown 1994; Wright 1992 and 1996; Dunn 1996; Bauckham 1998; Bond 1999; C. D. J. Green 2003.) A preacher also needs one or two good monographs on Christology from the perspective of the Jewish-Christian relation, such as Van Buren 1988, Marquardt 1988 and 1990, Williamson 1993.

## Elaborating One Possible and Legitimate Rearrangement

In a third step, the preacher chooses a possible and legitimate hermeneutical rearrangement to connect Old and New Testaments in this particular sermon for this particular congregation. It is quite possible that more than one Christological rearrangement is theologically legitimate. After all, we have seen that apostles and evangelists give the same words of Moses or the prophets a place in different hermeneutical contexts (§9.8). For example, consider the words of Psalm 7.

> O LORD my God, in you I take refuge;
> save me from all my pursuers, and deliver me,
> or like a lion they will tear me apart;
> they will drag me away, with no one to rescue.

In elaborating the Christological dimension of these words, we can first of all listen to these words as if they were spoken by Jesus, as if he is the Subject of these words. In that case we can locate these words in Gethsemane and listen to them as the prayer of Jesus to his Father.

> O dear Father,
> I am deeply grieved, even to death.
> My betrayers will tear me apart like a lion;
> they will drag me away,
> with no one to rescue.

> If possible, remove this cup from me
> and save me from all my pursuers.
> Yet, not what I want, but what you want.
> In you I take refuge.

We can weave the words of Psalm 7 into the wrestling of Jesus with his Father and the things to come (Mark 14:32-41 and par.). In this prayer we can hear the echo of the individual psalms of lament.

Second, we can use this psalm to provide the congregation with words and images to deepen and enrich their own prayers to Jesus.

> Dear Lord,
> I take refuge in your salvation and atonement.
> Save me from all my pursuers, and deliver me,
> or like a lion they will tear me apart;
> they will drag me away, with no one to rescue.

In this case, we see Jesus as the object or addressee of the words of the psalm. Both options are valid from a theological point of view. That means that depending on the purpose and focus of a particular sermon, one of these two can legitimately be elaborated.

### The Process of Sermon Preparation

When two or three recontextualizations are legitimate, it is wise to choose one possibility for further elaboration. Otherwise the sermon will be overloaded from a communicative, theological, or pastoral point of view. A preacher can leave something for another sermon on the same text. The choice for one of the possibilities is determined by the theological competence, the spirituality, and the familiarity and acquaintanceship of the preacher with Scripture. The homiletical situation of the congregation is of course also an important element in taking this decision.

It can also happen that none of the hermeneutical rearrangements has a sound theological foundation. Or, more cautiously stated, it can happen that a particular preacher does not see a legitimate rearrangement for him- or herself. It may be clear that on such occasions it is far wiser to leave out any connection with the New Testament. If a preacher connects Old and New Testaments with a strong arm, Jesus appears in a sermon —

in the worst case — like a homiletical "bat out of hell" (sic!). The Christian identity and character of a sermon does not stand or fall by mentioning the name of Jesus or the title Christ when the theology of a sermon is embedded in a canonical context.

## 13.5. Hermeneutical Two-Way Traffic

The above-described hermeneutical and homiletical strategy opens new and surprising Christological perspectives on the Old Testament during the process of sermon preparation. There is nevertheless a "however." When we restrict ourselves to the above-described steps in the hermeneutical process, we still move forward on the hermeneutical one-way track between Old and New Testaments. And that was exactly one of the common weaknesses of the classical hermeneutical keys as discussed in chapters 2-6. We concluded that the outcome of this one-way track is not only an order of sequence in the construction of the sermon but that it also has consequences for the theological order of merit between the Old Testament and Jesus Christ. And that would mean that this new model turns out to be only an attempt at restoration, a concept ridden with all the mentioned weaknesses (§7.1-3). To meet those drawbacks, I suggest adding a hermeneutical and homiletical step to the process described in the previous sections. It is a step from the New Testament back to the Old.[39] And it is this second step that avoids having the Christological sense drowning the *sensus israeliticus*. I will give two possible hermeneutical elaborations of this step, using therefore the two theological presuppositions — the encounter with the LORD and with Israel in Jesus Christ.

### The God of Israel

Believers from the gentiles encounter the LORD in the Jew Jesus of Nazareth (see §13.3.1). We see in him the countenance and true *icon* of Israel's

39. "The New Testament writers are utterly unanimous in seeing ( ) in the history of Israel attested in the Old Testament Canon the connecting point for their proclamation, doctrine, and narrative of Christ; and *vice versa,* in seeing their proclamation, doctrine, and narrative of Christ the truth of the history of Israel, the fulfilment of the Holy Scripture read in the synagogue" (Barth *CD* I/2, p. 72). For this line of thought see also H. F. Knight 2000, pp. 85, 122, "From the Bush to the Vineyard (and Back)." See also H. Berkhof 1986, pp. 262ff.

God; the Son is *the* parable of the Father.[40] Based on that theological foundation, we listen to the resonance of the Old Testament in the witnesses of apostles and evangelists. Those New Testament resonances open up in their turn new perspectives on the books of Moses and the prophets. The way we encounter the LORD in Jesus Christ belonged from eternity to the character of this God.[41] The Shepherd-God of the Old Testament (Ps. 23; Ezek. 34) opens our eyes to see the Shepherd that gives himself as a Lamb that is led to the slaughter (Isa. 53:7; John 1:29; Rev. 5:6, 12; Heb. 7:27).

From that New Testament perspective on the suffering of Christ, we can hear in a next step echoes in the Old Testament about the suffering of the LORD. New light is thrown on passages that portray the LORD as despised (Num. 14:11) and reviled (Ps. 74:10).[42] Both Jew and gentile dishonor (Mal. 1:6) and mock the living God (Isa. 37:17). The word of this God seems powerless in the face of the threats and injustice of the nations. But his Name is also vulnerable in the hands of the people he has chosen to be his partner. His Word is defenseless in the hands and mouths of unreliable prophets, kings, and priests. This God is like a farmer whose cattle don't know its master's crib anymore (Isa. 1:3). He is like a husband who is cheated and forsaken by his wife. Despite that, the LORD remains faithful to his promises (Hos. 1:3). He has to accept that the people enter the sanctuary but have no real knowledge of God, no faithfulness or loyalty (Hos. 4:1; 5:4). This LORD is the rejected God, one whose love is despised, one who is often declared dead. But this God chooses to bear this rejection himself in great and everlasting endurance and patience. Time and again he takes the initiative to restore the covenant. James van Tholen expresses this in a sermon on Hosea 4:16-18; 11:1-11.

> God's people are not business partners with him. They are not acquaintances. They are not commodities. They are children. That's why he's pacing. That's why he is suffering. That's why he refuses to let them die. He is their Father, and this Father is God and no mortal. This parent has the power to forgive, to bring them back, to bring them home. . . .
>
> He's a God looking for ways to bring his children home, to keep

40. The expression "*the* parable of the Father" comes from Eduard Schweizer (1994, §II.5).

41. This track elaborates the theology of Karl Barth (§6.3).

42. For an Old Testament perspective on the suffering of God see Fretheim 1984.

them alive — even if it keeps him up at night, even if it means he must taste death himself.[43]

Without mentioning it explicitly, this sermon intertwines the imagery of the suffering and death of Jesus Christ with the proclamation of Hosea about the LORD.

## The Israel of God

We can also link back from the New to the Old Testament when we see the story and history of Israel in the testimony about Jesus of Nazareth. In his heart-wrenching and innocence-shattering book *Night,* Elie Wiesel tells of his experience as a teenager with his father in the concentration camps of Auschwitz, Buna, and Buchenwald. There was always the threat of the "selection," which meant the taking away of the weak to be killed and burned in the ovens. He tells of an old Rabbi, Akiba Dumer.

> Akiba Dumer left us, a victim of the selection. Lately, he had wandered among us, his eyes glazed, telling everyone of his weakness: "I can't go on. ( ) It's all over. . . ." It was impossible to raise his morale. He didn't listen to what we told him. He could only repeat that all was over for him. ( ) Suddenly his eyes would become blank, nothing but two open wounds, two pits of terror.

Then Wiesel makes this provocative link with Calvary:

> Poor Akiba Dumer, if he could have gone on believing in God, if he could have seen a proof of God in this Calvary, he would not have been taken by the selection.[44]

It is not clear what Wiesel means. But the link between Calvary and the concentration camp is impressive. Is it possible to think, not of linking Christ's passion to Auschwitz, but of Auschwitz leading to an understanding of Christ's passion? Would it be possible that the Jewish people, whose grandparents endured their own noxious crucifixion, might be able to help

---

43. Van Tholen 2003, pp. 178-79.
44. Wiesel 1982, pp. 72-73.

the Christian interpretation of Calvary? I leave it as an open and challenging question.

A second illustration is taken from African American preaching. This type of preaching has merged and brought together the proclamation of both Old and New Testaments in such a way that both Testaments do not compete but enrich each other mutually. The Old Testament story of the enslavement of the Israelites by the Egyptians told the story of the African American slaves. The story of the liberation of the Israelites by Moses fueled at the same time the hope for their own future liberation. They understood the account of the suffering of Jesus Christ as their own story of suffering and humiliation. And the same Jesus played a crucial role in the proclamation of atonement and forgiveness. African American preaching did not connect Moses and Jesus typologically or salvation-historically but fused or merged both figures.[45] Moses and Jesus were the two dimensions of both their existential and religious quests.[46] Thus preaching proclaimed a "Mosaic Jesus" and a "Messianic Moses." These images became effective vehicles for a vibrant spirituality on the one hand and political resistance and social reform on the other.[47] This hermeneutical merger or two-way traffic found its expression in African American preaching and in many impressive and moving spirituals, for example, in "O the Dying Lamb!"

> I want to get where Moses trod,
> O de dying Lamb!
> For Moses gone to de promised land,
> O de dying Lamb!
> . . .
> Brudder Moses promised for be dar too,
> O de dying Lamb!
> To drink from streams dat never run dry,
> O de dying Lamb!

45. Prothero 2003, p. 210; see also p. 213.
46. Genovese 1975, p. 253.
47. "Blacks embraced this God by the thousands in the eighteenth and nineteenth centuries after hearing the good news of God's promise of salvation from sin and death, but also after hearing of what God had done for the oppressed in biblical times" (Larue 2000, p. 15).

This spiritual merges the actions of Moses and the image of Jesus as the Lamb who was slain. Friend Jesus and liberator Moses were brought together in a dialectical tension.

## The Process of Sermon Preparation

Time is one of the major reasons that preachers don't make the described double hermeneutical movement. And even when preachers make this double movement during sermon preparation, there might be reasons for not giving this a place in a particular sermon. Coherence of line of thought is one of those reasons. But preachers have to be aware of the latent possibilities and the theological implications of this double movement. Such awareness will contribute to the "homiletical conscience" of the preacher, an awareness that can even be expressed in small sentences or a brief remark. That can be illustrated by way of this sermon introduction by C. Wayne Hilliker.

> I entitled this sermon — *"Hearing the Gospel of God"* rather than the phrase we are more used to, *"the Gospel of Christ."* It was an intentional change. For the gospel is about God. The message of the Gospel of Christ reveals something about God. It is, we believe, God who is the author of the gospel. After all, the story of Jesus Christ is set within a larger story, a story of God with Israel.[48]

This awareness will color the contents, the structure, wording, and presentation of the rest of the sermon even if there is no explicit attention to the movement back and forth between the Old and New Testaments.

## 13.6. The Jewish No

When we explore the possibilities of preaching Christ from an Old Testament text, we face the Jewish No to Jesus as the Messiah. Christian sermons usually spoke in a negative and even judgmental tone about this Jewish No. The post-Holocaust context, however, challenges Christians to elaborate this No in a positive and constructive way. Instead of interpret-

---

48. Hilliker 2000.

ing the Jewish No as the prelude for a "theology of substitution," "displacement theology," or "supersessionist theology," Christian proclamation has to try to understand this No as a challenging question to the church. And the latter without compromising our belief and creed that in Jesus Christ the Word became flesh. I give four suggestions for a constructive and positive elaboration.

## "Why Are You at Ease?"

Jews ask the church amazed and astonished: Why are you so tranquil and at ease? Haven't you got any questions anymore? If the Messiah has come, why is there so much evil in the world? Martin Buber formulated this Jewish objection to the Messiahship of Jesus in his discussion with the German New Testament scholar Karl-Ludwig Schmidt on January 15, 1933. The discussion took place in the Jewish school in Stuttgart. Buber formulated the incisive questions in such classic terms that it has been continually repeated ever since. Buber had a profound respect for Jesus, and even for Christianity. But his admission of his inability to see Jesus as the Messiah was determined by a still more profound experience:

> We know more deeply, more truly, that world history has not been turned upside down to its very foundations — that the world is not yet redeemed. We *sense* its unredeemedness. The church can, or indeed must, understand this sense of ours as the awareness that *we* are not redeemed. But we know that that is not it. The redemption of the world is for us indivisibly one with the perfecting of creation, with the establishment of the unity which nothing more prevents, the unity which is no longer controverted, and which is realized in all the protean variety of the world. Redemption is one with the kingdom of God in its fulfillment. An anticipation of any single part of the *completed* redemption of the world — for example the redemption beforehand of the soul — is something we cannot grasp, although even for us in our mortal hours redeeming and redemption are heralded. But we can perceive no caesura in history. We are aware of no center in history — only its goal, the goal of the way taken by the God who does not linger on his way.[49]

49. Quoted by Moltmann 1990, pp. 1021ff.

Buber's classic statement took on added intensity in the next few years, for 1933 was the year Adolf Hitler came to power in Germany. The Nazi regime put to rest any doubts about the unredeemed character of the world.

The Jewish No therefore asks of the Christian church, "If the Messiah did come, how is it possible that the world is still unredeemed?" And even more incisively, "How can you feel at ease in an unredeemed world?" These and comparable questions make it impossible for Christians to accept and live in peace with a status quo that is infected with injustice, poverty, hunger, and violence. This No keeps the prophetic and eschatological "balance wheel" going (see also chapter 15). It keeps the question of John the Baptist alive: "Are you the one who is to come, or are we to wait for another?" (Matt. 11:2f.) and puts this question under the highest eschatological tension. R. Benjamin Garrison expresses this awareness in a sermon on Deuteronomy 6:4-5, the Great Commandment. The title of this sermon is "On Being an Honorary Jew."

> The Christian faith is a healthier religion today because it lives under the constant cross-questioning of the Jewish faith.[50]

This Jewish "cross-questioning" can prevent us from giving easy answers to difficult questions. Chris Ward expresses this impressively in a sermon on Ezekiel 37:1-10, the vision of the valley of dry bones. The LORD raises a massive question in this pericope, "Mortal, can these bones live?" Ezekiel hesitates to answer this severe question.

> Why doesn't Ezekiel pour out his faith in God with a resounding, enthusiastic "yes" to that question? YAY GOD! Well, if the answer "no" lacks faith and hope, the answer "yes" lacks love, and fails to recognize the reality of sin, and of suffering and of pain. "Yes" is the answer of the quick, easy road; the road that would put God in our pockets to be pulled out in tough times like some magic pill. This easy answer devalues the situation and the sufferer, making both ultimately meaningless. "I'm sorry about your pain," we say, "but it's OK, God will make it all better in the end." This quick answer highlights God's power and ability, sure, but leaves no room for weeping, gives no recognition to sorrow and pain and loss. The easy answer has God standing back, clean and distant while we poor, pathetic creatures stumble around in

---

50. Garrison 1988, p. 180.

the muck of our existence; an existence that ultimately doesn't seem to have any value or meaning. It doesn't matter if you suffer or not, because it all comes out in the wash. Can you imagine saying to one of those survivors of Auschwitz, "You know, what you experienced in that horrible place . . . the evil, the inhumanity you witnessed . . . what you lived through . . . doesn't really matter in the long run, because God is just going to wave His mighty hands and make it all better."

Auschwitz was not some great cosmic game. Neither was Armenia. Neither is the reality of pain and suffering that ordinary people like you and I experience every day in this world. There are no easy answers; or, if there are, they are not satisfying, not complete. This short easy road, as attractive as it may be, leads to a shallow understanding of God and a devaluing of humanity. Can these bones live? The easy "yes" is no better an answer than the quick, hopeless "no."

But God's question still hangs before us. "Son of Man, can these bones live?" Is there a solution? Is there a way to redeem, to make sense of human suffering? "Oh Sovereign Lord, you alone know."

Ezekiel's answer tries to find a path between the two extremes. On the one hand, it recognizes God's power. "Oh Sovereign Lord," he says. He recognizes that God is indeed sovereign, Lord over all things including life and death. But he also recognizes that the situation is not simple or easy, and that any solution to it will have to come from God Himself. It is almost as if Ezekiel is bouncing back and forth between the two polar opposites. "Lord, I see no way of fixing this situation. But I know that you are God. But I see no way of fixing this situation . . . but I know that you are God." The two are held there in tension, and there is no easy answer to be had.[51]

"Son of Man, can these bones live?" The Jewish No invites and challenges us to find a path between the extremes of an easy "yes" and a quick, hopeless "no."

## No "for Our Sake"

The mission to the gentiles that Paul himself began is a result of the Jewish No. Paul emphasizes this to the Christian congregation in Rome, which was

51. Ward 2005.

made up of both Jews and Christians: "As regards the gospel they are enemies of God for your sake; but as regards election they are beloved for the
sake of their forefathers" (11:28). Paul seems to say that the Jewish No is the
"price" to be paid so that the gospel could come also to the Gentiles.[52] The
grace that we are no longer aliens from the commonwealth of Israel, no longer strangers to the covenant of promise, no longer without hope, and
above all no longer without God in the world, is due to the fact that the Jews
said No. That means this No is not a reason to blame the Jews but a reason
for gratefulness on the part of Christians. It is a "blessing in disguise."

## God's Presence in Jesus Is Not "Natural" or "Obvious"

The Jewish No underscores that God's presence in Jesus in not "natural" or
"obvious." We can never speak or preach in platitudes about a serving and
suffering God who is crucified by the world. A God who takes the image of
a suffering servant to save the world is and remains a stumbling block, a
*skandalon,* not only for Jews but also for gentiles (1 Cor. 1:23; Gal. 5:11). The
Jewish No expresses the resistance against the proclamation of a suffering
and crucified God, a resistance that can also be heard in our own hearts.

## Incomprehensible Grace

God's grace comes from outside our world and from beyond human possibilities. If we are faithless, God remains faithful, "for He cannot deny himself" (2 Tim. 2:13). This grace for the gentiles comes from a Jewish God.
The Jewish No underscores the graciousness but incomprehensibility of
the LORD (see also §14.7.5).

It is obvious that the respect for the Jewish No does not resolve the
tension between Jewish and Christian conceptions of the Messiah.

## 13.7. "Who Do You Say I Am?"

Jesus of Nazareth's ministry calls forth all kinds of questions and amazement by the crowd. "Who then is this, that even the wind and the sea obey

52. Marquardt 1981a.

him?" (Mark 4:41). "Where did this man get all this? What is this wisdom that has been given to him?" (Mark 6:2). "Is not this the carpenter's son? Is not his mother called Mary? And are not his brothers James and Joseph and Simon and Judas? And are not all his sisters with us?" (Matt. 13:55). "Is not this Joseph's son?" (Luke 4:22). "Can anything good come out of Nazareth?" (John 1:46). "How does this man have such learning, when he has never been taught?" (John 7:15). "Are you the one who is to come, or are we to wait for another?" (Matt. 11:3).

The questions about his origin and identity are, however, not only raised by people around Jesus; he calls forth these questions himself. He wants to know what kinds of thoughts and expectations are being raised by his ministry.

> Now when Jesus came into the district of Caesarea Philippi, he asked his disciples, "Who do people say that the Son of Man is?" And they said, "Some say John the Baptist, but others Elijah, and still others Jeremiah or one of the prophets." He said to them, "But who do you say that I am?" Simon Peter answered, "You are the Messiah, the Son of the living God." (Matt. 16:13-16)

It is remarkable that Jesus doesn't confirm but also doesn't correct any of the given answers. Jesus' question is more than just a springboard for Peter's allegedly more important answer.[53] It is after all Jesus himself who not only raises the Christological question but also denies every systematic fixing of answers and replies. Jesus is not keen on "Christological exactness" in this passage but is interested in the confessed answers of his disciples.[54] The relation between question and answer does not solidify into a theological one-way traffic. There is a constant movement from question to answer and backwards from answer to question. That theological and hermeneutical two-way traffic is constitutive for the books of Moses and the prophets. Every Christological utterance has an "expiration date" like the manna in the desert (Exod. 16). "Let no one leave any of it over until morning" (Exod. 16:19).

---

53. The calling for preaching is "daß die von der Kirche durch ihre lebendige Schriftauslegung neben dem Dogma ja auch überlieferten offenen Fragen wieder zu Gehör kommen, auf die Felsenworte einmal Antwort waren. ( ) Antworten ohne Fragen erbringen Orthodoxie — Fragen mit offenen Antworten helfen glauben, lieben und hoffen" (Marquardt 1990, pp. 31-32; see also pp. 337ff.).

54. Marquardt 1990, pp. 26ff., 34ff.; 2003, 272ff.; Moltmann 1993, p. 101.

The second remarkable element in this pericope is that Jesus apparently considers his disciples to be capable of answering the question. He mandates his disciples to answer it based on that what they know of and experience with him. Jesus thus creates space for ever-new answers. It is evident that Christological questions arise every time the gentile church gathers to open the books of Moses and the prophets. The congregation is invited and challenged to answer those questions every Sunday in prayers, hymns, Scripture-readings, and sermons.[55] Those weekly events don't pretend to give conclusive answers and also don't offer a watertight proof of Jesus' Messiahship. Those utterances can be characterized as confessions or witnesses. There are after all no direct, compelling, or imperative connecting links between the Old Testament and Jesus Christ. Within the Jewish community Moses and the prophets are continued in *Mishna* and *Talmud*. For that reason the connections that Christians draw between Old and New Testaments are temporary and provisional.[56] The church has nevertheless the task and is challenged to listen carefully to the words of Moses and the prophets, and to listen also to the reverberations of those words in the writings of apostles and evangelists. That process of listening provides us with the material to answer in a particular situation the question, "Who do you say I am?" (Matt. 16:13-20). Our confessions and witnesses have, so to speak, an expiration date; they are valid only until the coming Saturday. On the next Sunday when the congregation comes together, as their custom is, in "a house next door to the synagogue" (Acts 18:7), we are again challenged and invited to be a trained scribe for the kingdom of heaven, "like the master of a household who brings out of his treasure what is new and what is old" (Matt. 13:52).

The confessing character of the language of the sermons doesn't force the listeners.[57] It creates on the contrary a space of freedom between the preacher, the text, and the congregation. In that space each member of the congregation is invited and challenged to formulate an answer to the penetrating Christological question, "Who do you say I am?"[58] That is in line with the character of Moses and the prophets.[59] There we don't find

55. Moltmann 1993, p. 103; Marquardt 2003, pp. 272-75.

56. Schöttler makes a plea for a "fragmentary and open Christological sermon" (Schöttler 2001, p. 512).

57. Lose 2003, pp. 228ff.; see also McClure 2001.

58. Bos/Velema 2002.

59. Brueggemann 1997, pp. 117-44; Brueggemann 1997a, pp. 38-56.

solidified doctrine but a chain of ongoing interpretations and ongoing creedal utterances.[60] Listeners and readers of every generation are invited to add their own interpretative and creedal link to that chain.[61] Every confession is determined by situation and circumstances. That means that every confession is limited in its range and pretension. That situational character is not the weakness of the confession but, on the contrary, its strength. Every situation invites, calls, and challenges us to confess the LORD as our God, the One who is revealed in Israel and in Jesus Christ.

## 13.8. Evaluation

The whole proclamation of Moses, prophets, and writings centers on the covenant between the LORD and Israel.[62] The results of biblical theological research have made clear that apostles and evangelists describe and interpret the encounter with Jesus of Nazareth as an encounter with each of the two partners of the covenant. This twofold foundation of the inner-biblical hermeneutics opens perspectives for a contemporary hermeneutical strategy for the practice of preaching. Words, images, expressions, metaphors, theology, and motives referring to the LORD and those referring to Israel can both be recontextualized in relation to Jesus as words spoken by Jesus, addressed to, and spoken about him.

a. Gentiles encounter both the Israel of God and the God of Israel in Jesus of Nazareth. In Jesus Christ gentiles are partakers of the benefits of the covenant between the LORD and Israel. Both promises and commandments are valid for Jews and gentiles. The LORD invites the nations and urges them to join Israel on the path of righteousness.[63] This encounter is both a challenging and a complicated enterprise. It invites people to go to the land that he will show us. That is not a precisely described or specified future. There is the single but trustful promise that he will be our companion on that way.

b. This model presents a covenantal Christology — referring, that is, to

60. That is a fundamental element in the theology of the German Old Testament scholar Gerhard von Rad (1980a/b).

61. Lose 2003, pp. 189-232.

62. Oeming 1986.

63. Borg 1994, p. 30; H. Berkhof 1986, pp. 415ff.

the covenant between the LORD and Israel. Jesus represents both the God of Israel and the Israel of God. He is, so to speak, "the covenant made flesh" (Luke 1:72; Mark 14:24 and par.). Based on this fundamental conviction, apostles and evangelists can proclaim Jesus starting with the Scriptures of Moses and the prophets (Acts 8:35). The LORD extended the covenant with Israel to the gentile nations in the Jew Jesus of Nazareth (2 Cor. 3:6).

c. The history of theology shows and proves that Jesus is vulnerable and even defenseless in the face of all kinds of theological hypes and vogues. Jesus is clothed constantly with fashionable robes — from teacher of wisdom to revolutionary leader, from Gnostic seer to ethical ideal. However different these concepts may be, what these robes usually have in common is that Jesus is estranged from his Jewish origin and background. By taking the Old Testament text as the abiding anchorage place, the presented model can put a check on this phenomenon. The model can also serve as a medicine against annexation and absorption by triumphalistic Christianization.

d. The Christological part of a sermon is not the crown or apotheosis of the sermon. It has the character of a "crucial station in between." At the same time we have to say that the Christological element is the crucial and fundamental presupposition of Christian preaching of the Old Testament because it is Jesus Christ who hands over the words of Moses and the prophets to the gentiles. In him the nations are partakers of the covenant between the LORD and Israel.

The presented model does not restrict Christological connections between Old and New Testaments to some selected texts like the allegedly Messianic predictions, typological patterns of the coming Messiah, Angel of the Lord theophanies, or sayings about the "son of man" and the (suffering) "servant of the LORD." This strategy allows us to preach Christ from every corner of the books of Moses, the prophets, and David (Luke 24:27; Acts 8:35). The model also digs deeper than a superfluous verbal correspondence of "catchwords" or thematic linkages between Old and New Testaments. It offers a theologically founded and yet practical strategy to get the possibly Christological dimensions of an Old Testament text into view. The steps, described in sections 13.4-7, can easily be embedded in the process of sermon preparation and can be made by every preacher in a relatively short time. This hermeneutical strategy provides at the same time enough safeguards to do justice to the theological carrying capacity of the text.

Preaching can use the Old Testament to describe and interpret the Christ-event. That means that this chapter distinguishes between two interpretative actions. First, the Old Testament images can be used to describe what Jesus did or said. The Old Testament adds from that perspective words, expressions, and metaphors to the reservoir already available in the four Gospels. Second, the Old Testament provides us with words, theology, metaphors, and images to interpret the soteriological meaning and ethical implications of the ministry of Jesus the Christ. Both elements are intertwined and are not available independently, just as the historical Jesus and the Christ of faith are intertwined.

When I developed the model described in this chapter, I gratefully used the benefits of the existing hermeneutical models. Even though it is clearly not allegory in the classical sense of the word, I can describe my model as "allegory within the boundaries of the letter." The presented model, however, does more justice to the tangible history of the Old Testament, and Israel is still in view.[64] The model of Karl Barth was also an important source of inspiration. But it is nevertheless clear that this model takes a different hermeneutical and homiletical route. Barth ties the Father and the Son closely together in such a way that the Father (almost) disappears behind the Son. The model presented in this chapter differs on three important points from Barth's proposal. I stress that we encounter not only the God of Israel but also the Israel of God in Jesus of Nazareth. In Barth's sermons the second element misses completely. Second, the relationship between Jesus Christ and the God of Israel is in my model in fact the reverse of Barth's concept, where Jesus is in fact the one and only speaking and acting Subject of both Old and New Testaments. The Old Testament is thus for Barth in retrospect a Christian book. The presented model tries to interpret the New Testament "in accordance with the Scriptures." The third difference with Barth's concept is that I add an important step: take the way back from the apostles and evangelists' witness about Jesus to the books of Moses and the prophets. I have thus elaborated the strong elements of Barth's theology and have met at the same time the homiletical weaknesses. This model also elaborates the strong elements of typology and promise and fulfillment. But giving witness to Jesus Christ doesn't mean the theological

64. Wilson 2001, pp. 112-36.

end of Moses and the prophets, as is in fact the case in the classical models. The presented model listens to the texts as longing witnesses, waiting for the final and definitive word of the Lord, the God of Israel. We can say that Jesus of Nazareth has filled the words of the Old Testament, but Scripture as a whole is still waiting for the definitive ful(l)-fillment.

There are many Christological concepts. Of course, I have more affinity with some of these concepts and less with others. My preferences can be felt explicitly and implicitly in this chapter. But this chapter is not so much concerned with an appraisal or rejection of one or another Christological concept. It is my concern to offer a hermeneutical key — better: a ring of keys — to listen to possible Christological perspectives on the books of Moses and the prophets. It is my hope that the model described here can also be used by those who don't share my preferred Christological concepts. In any case, we can say that every Christological concept, whether from high or from below, sooner or later has to answer the question as to how it connects the Old and New Testaments, the Old Testament and Jesus Christ.

The aim and purpose of the Christological perspective of preaching the Old Testament is the glory of God. The God of Israel is the actual Subject of all the verbs in the New Testament.[65] Jesus is not a God besides, let alone over against, the God of Israel. Paul van Buren is correct when he says that "Every proper Christological statement, however 'high,' will make clear that it is giving the glory to God the Father."[66] Our preaching is about giving thanks to the God of Israel and the Lamb because we that were once far off are now members of the household of God. Those words express faith and trust in the God of Israel. It expresses at the same time our gratefulness that this God became flesh in the Jew Jesus of Nazareth. "Christology is therefore doxology, praise of God. It is an act of thanksgiving."[67] That characterizes the Christian creeds, Christology as the discipline of critical theological reflection, and our personal trust in Jesus Christ our Lord.[68] The acts of interpretation and proclamation have their end and ful-

65. Van Buren 1988. For the background in the Old Testament see Brueggemann 1997, pp. 145-212.

66. Van Buren 1988, p. xviii; see also Marquardt 2003, pp. 272-89.

67. Van Buren 1988, p. 35.

68. "For that reflection is concerned with an amendment of life or a reform of behavior to bring the life and actions of the Church more into conformity with Christ" (Van Buren 1988, p. 35).

fillment in the act of worship. "Were not our hearts burning within us while he was talking to us on the road, while he was opening the scriptures to us?" (Luke 24:32). Speaking about Jesus of Nazareth, apostles and evangelists give us the words and the theology to testify with confidence, "We have heard that God is with you."

# 14. You Who Once Were Far Off

## 14.1. Lines on the Playing Field

Year after year, students' first glimpse of the gymnasium floor at their junior high school causes them much confusion. They see a lot of lines in different colors and in all kinds of patterns. In the course of the first year, the gym teacher explains that each pattern of lines is linked with a different sport. Basketball, volleyball, and handball each have their own pattern and color of lines, related to the rules of the particular sport. In the course of time, that complex set of lines doesn't confuse the pupils anymore. When they play basketball, for instance, they see only the red lines on the floor. The other colors are still there, but the pupils don't notice them.

Whoever enters the landscape of the Old Testament discovers sooner or later that he or she uses different sets of interpretative rules. Reading a psalm differs from reading passages from the prophets. The Song of Songs is interpreted with another hermeneutical grammar than Ecclesiastes, even though both books belong to the so-called "five festival scrolls." Reading the books of Moses and the prophets, we encounter texts that are close to us, texts that speak with a more or less direct voice. The imagery of Psalm 23, for instance, hasn't lost its eloquence over the ages. The field of interpretation has, so to speak, only a few and clear lines on the floor. But there are also texts that sound as if they originate from a different and alien world. These are, as it were, texts with complex patterns on the interpretative floor and with complicated rules of the game. We can think of the extended rules for cultic institutions, the dietary laws, or the notorious stories about war and violence.[1]

1. Holladay 1995; Achtemeier 1998.

249

When we connect those texts directly with our own situation, we obviously get homiletical accidents. In those cases, we need several links in the interpretative chain between text and situation.

The Old Testament treats many different subjects and issues. We find patriarchal narratives in Genesis, purity laws in Leviticus, and chronicles of ancient kings of Israel and Judah in the books of Samuel and Kings. We have the poetry of the Psalms and love-songs in the Song of Songs. We hear the wearied reflections of Ecclesiastes as well as the impassioned preaching and dreams of the prophets. That means that we encounter a colorful spectrum of texts and testimonies in the Old Testament. Those differences in texts and textures make it necessary to draw different sets of interpretative patterns on the floor of the Old Testament.[2]

## 14.2. Experiences of Life and Faith

We can draw the image of the lines on the floor of the gymnasium a bit further when we focus on the two halves of the field. Both halves are the same, be it completely opposed. The two halves are in fact the home bases of two opposing parties. This feature of the image can serve as illustration for the structure of the Old Testament proclamation. When we listen to Moses and the prophets, we hear an ambivalent voice.[3] The poet of Psalm 8 asks, for example, in respectful amazement how it is possible that the Creator of heaven and earth is mindful of mortal beings (Ps. 8:3, 4).

> When I look at your heavens,
> the work of your fingers,
> the moon and the stars that you have established;
> what are human beings that you are mindful of them,
> mortals that you care for them?

Job is amazed by the same fact and utters the same question (7:17). But the meaning is completely reversed. The amazement of the psalm made place

---

2. Other hermeneutical studies with a homiletical orientation also offer awareness of the multi-colored character of the theological pattern of the Old Testament. They offer therefore a multidimensional hermeneutics for preaching (see for instance Allen/Holbert 1995; Greidanus 1988 and 1999; Goldingay 1981; Holladay 1995).

3. Brueggemann 1997, pp. 333-58; Bos 2005.

for severe complaint. God looks like a member of the secret service, leer-
ing at and hunting the human being.

> What are human beings,
> that you make so much of them,
> that you set your mind on them,
> visit them every morning,
> test them every moment?
> Will you not look away from me for a while,
> let me alone until I swallow my spittle?

In a similar way, Moses and the prophets can state on the one hand
that death is a definitive end from which there is no escape (2 Sam. 12:23;
Job 7:9f.; 10:20-22; 14:11f.). They testify on the other hand that God's loyalty
to creation defies the power of death (1 Kings 17:22; 2 Kings 4:32-37). The
LORD holds on to his creatures at the other side of life and death.

Or in another example, the LORD can be portrayed as the God who
destroys all instruments of war, the God who breaks the bow, shatters the
spear, and burns the shield with fire (Ps. 46:9). Israel dreams about peace,
tranquility, and the absence of war and violence in the name of this God
(Isa. 9:1-7; 11:1-9; Mic. 4:1-5). But Israel's God is also "the LORD of hosts"
(literally, "LORD of armies"). This expression is used more than two hundred times in the Old Testament. In the celebration of the exodus from
Egypt, this God is even called a "man of war" (Exod. 15:3). This God mus-
ters an army for battle (Exod. 14:13f.; Isa. 13:4) and he is celebrated as "the
LORD, strong and mighty, the LORD, mighty in battle" (Ps. 24:8).

We can discern this kind of dialectical treatment of every theological
issue or theme. Those two poles or positions are juxtaposed and sometimes even opposed to each other. While the two foci are opposed, they are
nevertheless always interrelated and interdependent because the canon as
a whole can give witness or offer proof for both positions or opinions. This
dialectical tension between two opposing opinions or positions is thus
something other than a contradiction. A magnet "works" because of the
field of tension between two "opposing" poles. Similarly, we come to arrive
at the meaning of a particular text within the field of tension between dialectical opposites or amidst the interplay of antiphonal voices.

For instance, the accounts of battles in the book of Joshua need to be
understood first of all in the context of other texts on war and violence.

But these texts in Joshua also need to be understood in relation to their counter-testimony about peace. Not only the two foci of this ellipse but the foci of every ellipse keep each other in balance and prevent possible radical opinions that center the attention on one focus only. Each position constantly asks questions to the companion voice. The complex tension between the foci of the elliptical witness of Scripture and the equal complexity of contemporary situations invite and require ongoing interpretative negotiations, not only between the different biblical texts, but between the biblical texts and the contemporary situation.

This chapter portrays in the following sections two fundamental sets of lines on the floor of faith and life: spirituality and ethics, or in other words, the inward and outward dimensions of our faith, the root and the fruits of faith.[4] The field of ethics and morality has to do with the practice of everyday life. There we meet on the one half of the playing field the pattern of fulfilled obedience to God's commandments, and on the other half of the field we learn about resistance against God's Law. The Old Testament portrays human beings in general and Israel in particular both as persons who break God's law and as persons who obediently fulfill the commandments of the LORD. Discussions on different ethical issues have their place in this hermeneutical ellipse. There are detailed studies on specific subjects like war and peace, sexuality, slavery, and family life. This chapter traces out the general interpretative ellipse for dealing with these kinds of particular subjects.

The second set of lines has to do with our experience of God, with our spirituality. We know of moments of intimacy and nearness, moments when we walk or speak with God almost "face to face, as one speaks to a friend" (Exod. 33:11). But there are also moments in which we experience a painful absence of the same God, moments when it seems as if God encounters us as an Adversary (like Exod. 4:24-26). Dealing with the issue of experience and spirituality has its place in this second hermeneutical ellipse.

The patterns of these two sets of lines cross each other sometimes, and at other times they seem so close they almost overlap; it is also possible that one set of lines seems to exclude another set. That complexity mirrors exactly the complexity of the colorful landscape of the Old Testament. And

---

4. The classical model of the fourfold sense of Scripture also dealt with these two issues.

that landscape in turn mirrors the multicolored and even paradoxical character of our experiences in everyday life, with all its heights and depths and the vast plains in between. That means that preaching the books of Moses and the prophets offers innumerable opportunities to bring ordinary life up to the face of God *(coram Deo)*.

## 14.3. Gentiles Included

When Moses and the prophets speak about Israel, they meant and still mean in the first instance Israel — both temporally and principally — as is set out in chapter 12. But they invite the gentiles to see themselves included in this name. In and through Jesus Christ these promises and commandments are valid "also for the Greek." The Pauline word "also" stresses the fact that Greeks cannot annex or absorb those words for exclusively Christian purposes. This apostolic "also" points to an open door in the words of Moses and the prophets, a door that is graciously opened for the gentiles in and through Jesus Christ. The Jew Jesus calls and invites the gentiles to join Israel and go up to the sanctuary of the LORD (Ps. 122:1), in that we are taught in his ways and walk in his paths (Isa. 2:3).[5]

This hermeneutical grammar of apostles and evangelists is the foundation and justification for the homiletical strategy to be outlined in this chapter. Because the nations are engrafted as a wild olive shoot, they are fed from the rich root of Moses and the prophets. It thus becomes clear that the lines of the *sensus Israeliticus* and the *Christological sense* can be extended to an *ecclesiological sense*. Hans Küng expresses this in his book *The Church.*

> Like Israel and following Israel, the Church sees itself as the journeying people of God, constantly being delivered from bondage, constantly wandering through the wilderness of this age, constantly maintaining the tension between thankful commemoration and hopeful expectation and preparing itself for its entry into the Promised Land, the messianic kingdom, the goal that always lies in the future.[6]

5. "Naturally the call had to come from where God had given his word, from a prophet of Israel" (Bornkamm 1969, p. 265).
6. Küng 1967, p. 148.

When the "Greeks" understand themselves as included when Moses and the prophets speak about Israel, it is clear that we cannot detach those books from Israel, the first addressee. It is, for example, quite obvious that the prophetic judgment "Not my people" (Hos. 1:9; 2:22) is meant in the first place for a discussion between the prophet and the people of Israel. The writers of the New Testament also hear in these words, after and beside the original *sensus israeliticus,* a surprising reference to the gentiles. Those that were formerly "not my people" are in and through Christ also called "God's people" (Rom. 9:25; 1 Pet. 2:10). Apostles and evangelists use the words of Moses and the prophets like the colored particles in a kaleidoscope that can be rearranged to show ever new, different, and creative patterns. Brian E. Daley formulates this well in an article on early Christian interpretation of the Psalms.

> Early Christian interpretation of the Bible generally assumed that the meaning of any given passage is not some self-contained intelligible entity, some intellectual content placed in it by its author or redactor, but that it also involves us — the reader, the hearer, the commentator or preacher, the church — precisely as the community that receives it, not simply as a historical document but as a revelation of God's will to heal and transform the hearer.[7]

The words of the text are not only addressed to the characters (individuals or groups) in or behind the text but in fact to all later readers and listeners, Jews and gentiles. The overarching narrative of Scripture is told and proclaimed in such a way that we ourselves figure or are figured as characters in the scene. That means that there is no unbridgeable gap between the "then and there" of the text and the "here and now" of preaching.[8]

## 14.4. Simultaneously Just and Sinner

This section deals with the hermeneutical ellipse of ethics and morality. Within that ellipse, it is not the task of preaching to proclaim, "I hereby decree that from this point forward everyone should be a bit nicer to each other." Such preaching becomes one-dimensional moralism. On the other

7. Daley 2003, p. 77.
8. Greene-McCreight 1999, p. 116.

hand preaching cannot and may not pretend that morality is of no importance at all. That means that preaching has to avoid the Scylla of judgmental and moralistic preaching and the Charybdis of preaching that is ethically indifferent. The books of Moses and the prophets offer us a playing field for a sound and healthy treatment of these issues. This playing field has indeed two halves: human beings as sinners and as righteous persons. This section deals with both "halves."

## Awkward Words

"Sin" and "guilt" are awkward words for several reasons. In the first place we have to say that these words have a thumb-marked history of misuse and manipulation, notably in the way that the church exploited the proclamation of forgiveness and atonement. When the words "sin" and "guilt" showed up in sermons, it was quite often in a mood of moralistic accusation and judgment. In that context, these words caused a lot of emotional damage. As a result, the words disappeared bit by bit from theological discourse and the practice of preaching in the second half of the twentieth century. Thomas G. Long asks almost rhetorically, "How long has it been since those of us who stand in the pulpits of polite and educated mainline churches have stimulated such a conversation [about sin]?"[9] Because of this silence in the pulpit, the role and place of "sin" in everyday language became prey to inflation and devaluation. Cornelius Plantinga rightly observes that the "awareness of sin used to be our shadow. Christians hated sin, feared it, fled from it, grieved it. But the shadow has dimmed. Nowadays the accusation you have sinned is often said with a grin, and with a tone that signals an inside joke."[10]

The second reason for the awkward character of the word "sin" has to do with the secularization of our culture. Contemporary ideologies teach that one can control his or her own destiny, determine their own characters, and reliably make choices based on instinct. That raises the question of how to preach about sin in a secularized age. Marsha G. Witten examined how the idea of sin has been faring in Protestant preaching in the United States. Her conclusion is that sin is still a central topic in sermons

9. Long 1996, p. 92.
10. Plantinga 1995, p. ix.

but that the content is highly contextualized, in the sense that the meaning is secularized.

> But a close examination of the sermons has shown the many ways in which the concept of sin has been accommodated to fit secular sensibilities. For while some traditional images of sin are retained in this pulpit speech, the language frequently cushions the listener from their impact, employing a variety of softening rhetorical devices: depersonalization (which renders notions of sinfulness vague and abstract, removed from specific members of the listening audience), rhetorical selectivity (which omits the foundational doctrine of original sin — a doctrine that would make inescapable the charge of personal sinfulness), deflection (through which sin is projected off of the listening audience and onto groups of outsider others), and therapeutic tolerance (in which sin is translated as errant behavior, explanations for misdeeds sought in the social context rather than in the individual, and judgment replaced by empathy). In its most extreme formulation, therapeutic tolerance applied to the idea of sin quashes even the possibility of authoritative religious speech, rendering the speaker silent on any matter except for the musings of one's own subjectivity.[11]

The Old Testament is realistic about human nature, aware of the horrific dimensions of sin, and cognizant of the longing for justice that lives in our hearts and minds. The proclamation about sin and guilt in the books of Moses and the prophets is therefore meant from the start for the sanitation of both the mind of the individual and the concrete relations and practices in community life. For that very reason contemporary preaching may not and cannot cease to speak in a theologically founded way about sin and guilt, about justice and righteousness.

*Theological Ingredients*

The biblical proclamation of sin and guilt digs deeper than talking about moral failure or giving an addition sum of wrongdoings. The appalling reality of sin refers to the incomprehensible fact that humans have cut themselves off from God's economy of grace and blessing and instead try to

11. Witten 1993, p. 253.

construct blessing and provide peace on their own. Genesis 3–11 tells us from the start that this enterprise is as dangerous as it is fruitless. These chapters frankly acknowledge the catastrophic power of sin, evil, and oppression on the one hand and the corresponding need for God's salvation and deliverance on the other. The story of the Flood (Gen. 6–9) can be seen as the culmination of the LORD's struggle with human wickedness.[12] The biblical proclamation of sin points to a fundamental deviation in our steering mechanism and not so much to one or more particular steering errors. The systematic theologian Hendrikus Berkhof rightly says that humans "are so made that we need to find the anchoring of our life in the holy love of God by seeking our security in him and by being obedient to him. Sin is the refusal to find our anchoring there."[13] This fundamental refusal expresses itself in concrete words and actions, in a blamable vandalism of the *shalom* of the LORD.[14] The refusal goes even so far that in the end we do not accept and tolerate the LORD in our midst. We remove and excommunicate him when he comes too near. That is the very core of sin in the biblical sense. Sin is the perplexing and bewildering reality that we deny both our origin and destiny in words and deeds. That is the message of Moses and the prophets when they testify about the suffering of the LORD in the history with Israel.[15]

Sin is therefore not just an anthropological category but a category from the realm of faith. Martin Luther was correct when he stated that he could not even know that he was a sinner unless the Holy Spirit taught it to him. As such the proclamation of sin is embedded in the proclamation of the canon as a whole. For that reason speaking about sin may not be the only topic and absolutely not the last word in a sermon, because it isn't God's last word. Moses and the prophets proclaim the urgent invitation, the permission, the command, and the freedom to look up to the LORD for forgiveness and liberation (Ps. 34:5). We have the freedom to know of, believe in, and hope for the grace and mercy of the LORD (Ps. 103:8-13). In the rising light of that proclamation, humans discover more and more who they are: sinful rebels. Maybe we have initially only a confused idea of guilt and sin. But the warmth of God's grace melts the soul, bringing clarity of

12. Soulen 1996, p. 117.

13. H. Berkhof 1986, p. 194.

14. Plantinga 1995, pp. 7-27. See also Van Deusen Hunsinger 1995 (*sub voce* "sin" and "guilt" in the index).

15. Fretheim 1984.

perception so that one is truly able to recognize oneself as sinner. This is not a crushing experience, however. Because exactly at that moment we may also discover who we are before the LORD: a beloved rebel, a justified sinner. Preaching is therefore urged to speak about sin and guilt only in dialectic with God's love and mercy.[16] Preaching tells the truth about our existence: we are sinners. But we can only hold that to be true when we, the gentiles, also hold it to be true that nothing can separate us from the love of Israel's God as revealed in the Jew Jesus of Nazareth, the Christ (Rom. 8:37-39).

The God of Israel comes to visit our injured and alienated existence; he visits his rebels. Preaching gives witness about the disclosing and at the same time graceful coming of God. Preaching keeps the awareness alive that our hearts are devious (Jer. 17:9) and that we want to keep God away from us. And preaching knows too about the deep joy because of God's gracious intervention and saving and redemptive word. Preaching lives from the promise that God's Spirit will enter the hearts of individual hearers and in the midst of congregational life. When that happens, light from heaven is thrown on our lives and we come to know that we are known by God. Our sins are forgiven and though our souls are injured, we are known by God as loved ones.

## Disclosure of Sin and Guilt

According to Moses and the prophets, sin is not a mere misunderstanding, a mistake, a thing that happened unfortunately. Scripture addresses us in our freedom and responsibility: "You are that man," "You are that people" (Gen. 3; 2 Sam. 12:7; Mic. 6). Preaching extends the range of these disclosing voices so that they also reach our contemporary situation, the lives of gentile believers (Eph. 2:1, 5; Col. 2:13).

That is the more necessary in a world where news bulletins on radio and television announce almost every day that groups and individuals hurt and damage each other. *Amnesty International,* for example, reports regularly about oppression, mistreatment, and torture. And how many are mistreated in their offices, their factories, or their schools? For instance, ac-

---

16. See the chapter on God's "holy love" (H. Berkhof 1986, pp. 126-40; see also Barth, *CD* II/1, §30.1).

cording to the U.S. Department of Justice, somewhere in the United States of America a woman is raped every two minutes. Regretfully, we have to say that we can add to the list of wrongdoings and injustice almost endlessly. And we have to say even more regretfully that those lists and statistics don't exclude church members.

In all those cases there are perpetrators and victims. Sermons often put perpetrators and victims in the same box. They do that in proclaiming general forgiveness and even combine it with a generally formulated call for repentance. This equal treatment of victim and perpetrator is hurting and even offensive for most of the victims. Preaching the Old Testament can help to distinguish and differentiate between persons responsible for evil and those who suffer from it. A good example can be heard in a sermon by the African American preacher Babydoll Kennedy. She refers to rapper Tupac Shakur, who addresses the issue of gang rape in his song "Baby Don't Cry: Keep Your Head Up." The song is about a thirteen-year-old who is on the verge of suicide due to her emotional pain after being gang-raped. Tupac said,

> You gotta find a way to survive
> cause they win when your soul dies.
> Baby, please don't cry, you gotta keep your head up.
> Even when the road is hard, never give up.

After having quoted this song, Babydoll Kennedy continues her sermon on Judges 19:16-30, the story about a Levite's concubine who was raped and abused "all through the night until the morning" (19:25).

> This is what the church needs to be doing — offering a hopeful word and help the victims and survivors of abuse. We can't stay silent. We need to speak and act on behalf of those who have been broken by life and tell them that they are not alone. We need to stop making them feel as though the beatings, the verbal abuse, and the rapes are their fault. We all need to look at ourselves and see if we have played a role in this story. Did we play the role of the father who didn't care for his daughter? Did we play the role of the husband who pushed his wife out the door, of the neighbors who turned away, or of the Benjamites who sexually assaulted a woman?
> The people in Judges 19:30 were told to think about it. Think about the countless victims of sexual and physical abuse. Those who received

the man's message had half the story. We now know the whole story! Consider it (see then) then give your verdict (act on it!)! Speak about these issues at little league practice, at the fraternity/sorority functions, at the office, at church meetings, from the pulpit, and at home![17]

The Old Testament confronts us with shocking and troubling stories that turn our stomachs. But it is exactly these stories that give names to destructive words and actions. In doing so, the Old Testament discloses sin in its bare existence. That gives preaching the opportunity of disclosing contemporary destructive words and actions and naming them not only as wrongdoings but as sin. The Old Testament also provides us with stories that enable us to distinguish between perpetrator and victim. Preaching about these issues therefore faces both the challenge and the responsibility of calling the perpetrators to remorse, to repentance, to a change of behavior. Radical evil requires a radical sermonic response.[18] Victims on the other hand have to count on support, empathy, solidarity, and encouragement.

### Pastoral Preconditions for Preaching of Sin

The awareness of guilt and sin is not one-dimensional cerebral knowledge but knowledge in the context of faith, and it thus has a strong emotional dimension. Addressing the issues of sin and guilt in a sermon — curatively and not condemningly or judgmentally — requires careful handling from the preacher-as-pastor. A preacher therefore needs elementary insights in pastoral theology and pastoral psychology. Those insights can help us to move healthily and constructively in the fields of tension between the poles of human sin and divine forgiveness, the poles of victims and perpetrators, the pole of calling to repent and the pole of support. Preachers need to know, for example, some elementary things about the differences between "real" and "neurotic" or "false" guilt, between a (healthy) sense of guilt that needs to be confessed and (unhealthy) feelings of guilt that need therapy.[19] That can help contribute to a healthy-minded and sound theological awareness about sin and guilt so that the hearers are not belittled

17. Kennedy 2001, p. 67.

18. Smith 1992; C. L. Campbell 2002.

19. Stein 1968, pp. 103f.; Leech 1987; Pattison 2000, pp. 145-68 (= chapter 7, Failure in Pastoral Care).

but addressed as responsible creatures of God and accountable members of the body of Christ.

Preaching has a redemptive purpose and invites the congregation to engage in redemptive practices.[20] We have to be aware of the fact that the proclamation of sin and guilt in the past may have caused emotional and spiritual damage to members of the congregation. Keeping that in mind, sermons will not be based on blaming the people in the pews, on creating unhealthy feelings of guilt, or on moralistic directives. Clear and lucid illustrations of liberation and redemptive practices invite the congregation to reflect on their own particular context and on how they can become living members of the body of Christ. Barbara Brown Taylor exemplifies this in a sermon on 2 Samuel 11:26-27, the story of the conversation between King David and the prophet Nathan, who had to confront the king with his wrongdoings against both Uriah and his wife Bathsheba. Nathan was sent by God to confront the king. But Nathan did not preach like a fire-and-brimstone preacher. He came in sideways, with a story. Why did the prophet take an indirect route?

> Because he had not come to condemn David. That would have been easy enough to do, given the facts at hand, but Nathan was up to something much more profound than that. He had come to change David's life, if he could — to help the king see what he had done so that his conscience was revived and his sense of justice restored. Then Israel might have the king she was supposed to have instead of this handsome hero whose power had begun to stink.
>
> If David could see that — if he could pronounce judgment on himself — the impact would be a hundred times greater than if Nathan did it for him. But it called for real restraint on Nathan's part. He had to contain his anger and resist the temptation to do David's work for him. He had to remember why he had come — not to demolish the king but to bring him back to God — which in this case called for an incredibly light touch.[21]

And because of this "light touch" we have to say, last but not least, that preachers themselves must know why and how to humble themselves be-

---

20. So several contributions in Childers 2004 (C. L. Campbell 2004, p. 28; Fry Brown 2004, p. 65; Hogan p. 2004, p. 75; Smith 2004, p. 93).

21. Brown Taylor 1997, p. 14.

fore the Lord; they must know from their own experience about confession and repentance; they need to know what it means to regret wrongdoings as sin. When preachers never experience things like that, they had better be silent about these subjects in the pulpit.

## I Have Walked in Integrity

The Old Testament does not only proclaim that humans are sinners. There is also a remarkable but strong voice of another kind. In several psalms we can hear a poet testifying that he had walked in integrity, in relation to both humans and the Lord. Psalm 26 is a striking example.

> Vindicate me, O Lord,
> for I have walked in my integrity,
> and I have trusted in the Lord without wavering.
> Prove me, O Lord, and try me;
> test my heart and mind.
> For your steadfast love is before my eyes,
> and I walk in faithfulness to you.
> I do not sit with the worthless,
> nor do I consort with hypocrites;
> I hate the company of evildoers,
> and will not sit with the wicked.
> I wash my hands in innocence,
> and go around your altar, O Lord,
> singing aloud a song of thanksgiving,
> and telling all your wondrous deeds.
> O Lord, I love the house in which you dwell,
> and the place where your glory abides.
> Do not sweep me away with sinners,
> nor my life with the bloodthirsty,
> those in whose hands are evil devices,
> and whose right hands are full of bribes.
> But as for me, I walk in my integrity;
> redeem me, and be gracious to me.
> My foot stands on level ground;
> in the great congregation I will bless the Lord.

In many psalms we can hear and read the poets declaring themselves innocent and just before the Lord and other human beings (e.g., Pss. 1, 5, 6, 7, 15, 31, 34, 35, 38, 59, 66, 69, 73, 109). Psalms 17, 18 (with a parallel in 2 Sam. 22), 26, and 44 are the five that are most discussed because of the bold statements of innocence. The poets of these psalms affirm that they aren't criminals. They stand justly before God and that's why they are convinced they are entitled to God's aid and deliverance. These voices raise a problem for theology and proclamation.[22] Because how can sinners, ungodly human beings who are totally dependent on God's forgiveness, argue that they are innocent? How can they argue that their words and deeds are righteous and just? Isn't that Pharisaic?

Preachers use different strategies to answer these and related uncomfortable questions. One strategy is to simply ignore the clear and bold statements about the poets' innocence. Those sermons pick from the psalms words and expressions that fit within their own theological paradigm or bend the wording so as to make it fit. The utterances about the psalmists' incorruptibility are simply left in silence. Another strategy is to point to the poet's insufficient awareness and sense of sin and guilt. Seen from the theological perspective of the preacher, the poets are still dependent on God's grace and forgiveness, despite the psalmists' clear testimony about their innocence. Such sermons need the New Testament to "correct" and to "complete" the deficit of the Old Testament. So, for instance, the commentary of James Luther Mays on Psalm 26.

> The theme sounds theologically wrong and the occasion unlikely. To pray for vindication on the basis of one's own righteousness contradicts what we have learned from Jesus and Paul. It sounds like the prayer of the Pharisee (Luke 18:11f). It conflicts with Paul's doctrine that "all have sinned" (Romans 3:23). Surely it is incredibly presumptuous to pray that God investigate and vindicate us. Perhaps the only use we can make of Psalm 26 is to take it as a negative example, an Old Testament contrast to proper prayer and faith.[23]

It should be clear that when we preach this way, Marcion is knocking loudly at the door. There are, however, at least two reasons to give the psalms of innocence a place in the practice of preaching. First of all,

22. Holladay 1995, p. 14.
23. Mays 1994, p. 127.

preaching must do justice to this bold language of Scripture. The LORD sanctifies human beings so that they are holy (Lev. 11:44f.; 21:8; Pss. 34:10; 89:6). We hear about kings who did what was right in the sight of the LORD (1 Kings 15:5; 22:43; 2 Kings 12:2; 14:3; 15:3 and 34; 18:3; 22:2). This kind of testimony about practiced justice, faith, hope, and love is not a privilege of the Old Testament. Such voices can also be heard in the books of apostles and evangelists (Matt. 25:21, 23; Col. 1:2; 1 Pet. 1:15f.; 2:5, 9). When Paul was suspected and challenged in his mission and faith, he claimed that he had a good conscience before God (2 Cor. 1:12; 4:2; Acts 23:1; 24:16).

The second reason is that sermons can't treat their hearers' situations under the exclusive heading of guilt and sin. Preaching has to do justice to the practiced sanctification and the respectful obedience fulfilled by the hearers, however fragmentary it may be. Sermons can thus name and make explicit the fulfilled righteousness and justice by the members of the congregation. In doing so, sermons interpret the reality of the congregation *coram Deo* so that their "alternative consciousness"[24] is nurtured from the perspective of the realm of God. That can be done by pointing to traces of God's kingdom and righteousness in everyday life.[25] For example, the reformer Martin Luther read Psalm 26 when he faced accusations of disloyalty to the church. Scripture offered him the wording to express his trust that God knows the mind and heart, even if others don't. God will vindicate the righteous even if the world doesn't. That kind of interpretation can help to "articulate a clear and coherent perception of how the Bible, feelings, and other resources can contribute to the congregation's understanding of God's presence and purpose for the world," as Ron Allen rightly formulates.[26] The next questions can be helpful during the process of sermon preparation:

- Do you know about stories, situations, or events of individuals or groups that, seen from the perspective of a particular text, can be called "footprints" of the LORD?
- Are there testimonies of men and women, children and adults, about the passing of God's glory, even if only "the back of the LORD" is seen (Exod. 33:18-23)?

24. Brueggemann 1978, p. 14.
25. Allen 1998, p. 133.
26. Allen 2005, p. 18.

We encounter this line of thought in a sermon by George Arthur Buttrick (1892-1980) on Jeremiah 22:16. The text reads, "He judged the cause of the poor and needy; then it was well. Is not this to know me? says the Lord" (RSV).

> The footprints of God are hidden in a growing concern for social justice and personal love. This contention surely has biblical warrant. In the Old Testament is the story of a king who could not forget the poor: "Was not this to know me, saith the Lord?" In the New Testament the words are etched in fire: "Inasmuch as you have done to one of the least of these, you have done it to me." At long last we begin to own men of another skin as brothers. ( ) Slowly the light breaks on us. A city stops work to rescue one trapped child. Another man and another ask, "If I had been born black or Chinese . . . ?" Another and another says, "If I lived in a colonized land and the white man took my land and paid me far less in wages than the sale in his homeland, and exported my land's wealth . . . ?" No, we do not yet finish the sentence, but we begin it.[27]

We are aware that in this life even the holiest have only a small beginning of this obedience[28] and that God himself is and remains the Subject of our sanctification. But this sanctification influences the practice of everyday life in such a way that even the bells of the horses and the cooking pots become holy to the LORD (Zech. 14:20). God's holiness is a power that pulls, lures, and even seduces us to participate in God's way of righteousness.

In our liturgy we can sing songs of thanks and praise for such accomplished righteousness. Such a doxology is a medicine against both legalism and moralism.[29] Thus, we can make room for a Christian form of "Rejoicing in the Torah."[30] God's gift of the Torah was and is not in vain but it sanctifies life. God's Torah is as it were a power station with a high level of energy to empower human beings to resist the evil and destructive powers, to sustain in times of crisis, and to hold against opposition.[31] The syna-

27. Buttrick, in: Fant Vol. X, p. 270.
28. Heidelberg Catechism, Lord's Day 44, Q and A 114.
29. Josuttis 1966.
30. Marquardt 2003, pp. 313-27.
31. See Procksch/Kuhn 1978.

gogue goes ahead of the church to make us sensitive to the true nature and character of the Law of the LORD: a God-given charter of liberty, first for the Jew, and through Jesus Christ also for the Gentiles.[32] It is this Law-of-life that sets us free from every other law of sin and death.[33] It was Luther who said in his *Large Catechism* that "anyone who knows the Ten Commandments perfectly knows the entire Scripture."[34]

## Social Engagement

The prophetic voices advocate personal loyalty to the LORD's commandments on the one hand and to the ethical health of the community on the other. And when one of these two is under threat, the "lion starts roaring" (Amos 3:8). The Old Testament therefore has proven to be a rich source for relevant preaching on social issues. Just think of the role of the book of Exodus in African American preaching and the impact of that preaching on the civil rights movement. The proclamation of Moses and the prophets is still an invitation and a challenge to resist evil powers, inhumane ideologies, and systems of tyranny. It is a call to stand up for the worth and dignity of every human being. Walter Brueggemann expresses this in a sermon titled "A Loser's Powerful Footnote." The readings from Scripture were taken from Psalm 1, Acts 15:12-22a, 1 Corinthians 15:1-11, and Matthew 13:54-58.

> Biblical faith has arisen out of moral passion which we claim to be rooted in God's own heart. The courage of Moses in Egypt voiced God's sense that injustice that violates human possibility in the long run cannot prevail. At Sinai, as Moses went on and on in Leviticus and Deuteronomy, Israel's moral passion grew and expanded, until it occupied all of life, every meal, every sexual act, every bird's nest, every prayer tassel, every homeless slave, every corpse. All belong to God, all are visited by God's holiness, all must be guarded and attended to and honored.[35]

32. Christian Old Testament preaching has therefore to prevent drawing caricatures of Jews and Judaism. We have to be especially aware of the risk of portraying Judaism as a legalistic religion (Novak 2000, pp. 115f.; Von der Osten-Sacken 1982).

33. Marquardt 2003, p. 326.

34. Quoted by Hauerwas 2000, p. 137.

35. Brueggemann 1996, p. 159.

And just as the gentiles are included in the proclamation of grace, they are also included when the prophets address Israel in their call for justice and righteousness. That can be heard in a sermon by James R. van Tholen on the last words of Micah 3:9-11. That text reads:

> [Jerusalem's] rulers give judgment for a bribe,
> its priests teach for a price,
> its prophets give oracles for money;
> yet they lean upon the LORD and say,
> "Surely the LORD is with us!
> No harm shall come upon us."

After the preacher explained the meaning of those words in their historical context, he then points out the relevance of this passage for his listeners.

> But now what are we to do with this information? If we are not Israel, if Micah is not speaking to us, then what should we hear in these words?
> We should hear that the good will of the LORD is no sure thing just because we hang out at the temple. We should hear that one time a prophet of the LORD said all of Jerusalem would pay because its leadership misplaced their job descriptions. We should hear that one time, when the leaders of God's people, in his capital city, placed wealth above justice, when their politics were determined by their bank books, when their religion was used to help out the big shots, then at least one time, God turned himself off. We should hear that, and we should let it speak to us. We should hear that when the leaders of Jerusalem lived on the backs of the poor people from Moreshet, Jerusalem turned into a scrap heap. Before we assume that God's blessing is upon us, before we assume that his voice is with us, ( ) we should think about Micah 3.[36]

The proclamation of the Old Testament focuses on the benefit, the *shalom*, of both community and personal life, with local as well as global dimensions. Preaching on Old Testament texts thus sharpens our eyes for social issues. The proclamation of Moses and the prophets is never out of date or irrelevant because the wrongs of the past are still alive. On this planet there exists no perfect community. Bus as Fredrick C. Holmgren rightly con-

36. Van Tholen 2003, pp. 204-5.

cludes, "We learn from the Israelites that if a community opens itself to critical review and takes part in self-criticism, it can be a place, despite its flaws, where people can live and find blessing."[37]


## Justified Sinner

The poles of human sin and righteousness and divine forgiveness and empowerment create a field of tension that enables us to preach soundly and relevantly on the issues of sin, guilt, confession, remorse, and repentance. It offers the opportunity to encourage the congregation to put away their "former way of life, their old self, corrupt and deluded by its lusts, and to be renewed in the spirit of their minds, and to clothe themselves with the new self, created according to the likeness of God in true righteousness and holiness" (Eph. 4:22-24). The field of tension also creates a space for ethical reflection by the members of the congregation. As a result of that, the sanctification of life will not turn out in moralism but in encouragement to mature in the relation with the LORD. The call to repent is not a swing with the sword of God's judgment but an invitation to rediscover the way of God's commandments and promises. That tone and atmosphere create indeed a healthy space for real "joy in the Torah."

Our awareness of sin and guilt is "knowing in part" (1 Cor. 13:9). Consequently, it is not appropriate to use absolute utterances or an accusing tone. It is a real risk that sermons using such a tone will turn out to be an indictment of the hearers. But the preacher is shepherd and not prosecutor. The most appropriate mood for speaking and preaching about sin and guilt is therefore a prayer. Daniel Dillard expresses that tone in a sermon on the topic "Praying for Forgiveness."

> Now, to pray this prayer is to admit our real and actual sins, and our real and actual guilt before God, and perhaps to other people, if those sins have been sins against others. That is to say, we need to be specific. Surely it is appropriate to confess to God our sinfulness because we do not even know all of our sins. But, when we are asking God to forgive us, we need to state what it is that we are asking God to forgive us of. Faulty prayers for forgiveness are not prayers at all. C. S. Lewis put it

37. Holmgren 1999, p. 6.

this way, "Forgiveness needs to be accepted as well as offered if it is to be complete, and a man who admits no guilt can accept no forgiveness." So, when we ask God to forgive us our sins, we need to specify what those sins are. (. . .)

(T)o accept responsibility for, to name and acknowledge our sin as sin, is the beginning of repentance and the beginning of a turning away from those sins.[38]

This preacher helps the congregants to get a clear view of sin and forgiveness. He helps them to understand that these expressions and the reality of these expressions are not shallow or superficial, but touch the world of God. And the world of God touches our world in the proclamation of these words. The preacher encourages the listeners to be specific in their prayer so that they can experience the concrete reality of forgiveness.

## Penance

Too often, forgiveness is understood as a whitewashing of past wrongdoings. But forgiveness is not a "detergent with a unique double active formula" for our iniquities. It is a gracious gift of God to make a new start. Forgiveness is therefore not so much a finish line but a starting place. The church long practiced penance to mark such new beginnings. We meet the same attitude in the Old Testament regulations for offerings with restitutions (see, for instance, Lev. 5:14-19). This restitution or penance is not an effort to buy or earn God's love and forgiveness, nor is it meant to somehow influence God. On the contrary, penance is the humble and logical consequence of the gift of God's gracious forgiveness. The verb that Leviticus 5 uses for "restitute" can also be paraphrased as "to bring (back) *shalom*."[39] Doing penance is therefore closely linked with conversion. To convert always involves taking a new path, a turning from evil to the LORD. Conversion is turning from sin, injustice, lies, selfishness, and guilt, to salvation, justice, peace, truth, and the pardoning of others. Our thoughts are changed to be in harmony with God's thoughts and our ways are changed to his ways. Conversion means turning away from idols and coming home

38. Dillard 2005.
39. Gerlemann 1978, p. 923.

to the LORD. It means a turning away from the reigning idolatries back to the living God. The Old Testament regulations concerning restitutions teach Israel about very concrete realities. Penance makes the conversion tangible; it is a visible sign that a conversion is seriously meant. There is a change in all relationships: to God, to this world, to possessions, to the poor and marginal, to war and violence, to friends and enemies, to the false gods of society.

Barbara Brown Taylor says in her book *Speaking of Sin: The Lost Language of Salvation* that a lot of people would rather feel bad about the damage they have done than get estimates on the cost of repair. They would rather learn to live with guilt than face the hard work of new life.

> While penance has all but disappeared from our vocabulary, it was once the church's best tool for getting over that hump. Once a person had confessed her sins and received assurance of pardon, she voluntarily took on specific acts of penance, which were baby steps in the direction of new life. If she had stolen vegetables from a neighbor's garden, then she might volunteer to weed the garden every other day for a month. If she had slandered someone, then she might revisit all the households where she had done that and set the record straight.[40]

This illustration makes clear that a fresh approach to the instructions of the Old Testament for sacrificial and offering practices can uncover a healing capacity for broken and damaged relations. The proclamation of the Old Testament holds up the tension between the message of Nathan when he addressed King David after his adultery with Bathsheba ("You are that man") and the promise of forgiveness and the proclamation of grace by the same prophet ("You shall not die"). The "glad tiding" that is borne in that tension creates a space to live our everyday life. In that life we meet the consequences of our own sins and of the sins of other people. God's forgiveness does not create a storm-free area, but God's grace is every morning new (Lam. 3:22-24) and can renew a steadfast spirit within us to renew our lives (Ps. 51:10). A Nicaraguan prayer can be seen as an elaboration of this line of thought. It became loved around the globe.

> Sent by the Lord am I
> my hands are ready now

40. Brown Taylor 2000, pp. 90-91.

to make the earth a place
in which the kingdom comes.
The angels cannot change a world of hurt and pain
into a world of love of justice and of peace.
The task is mine to do, to set it really free.
O help me to obey, help me to do your will.

This poetic prayer understands that God calls our hands and eyes to do justice when we receive the gracious gift of forgiveness.

## 14.5. God Nearby and Far Off

The second interpretative ellipse deals with spirituality, the "inner room" of faith, the intimate dimension of the relation with the LORD. The Old Testament expression for this "inner room" of faith is "fear of the LORD" (Ps. 110:10; Prov. 1:29; 2:5; 9:10). This expression has a double meaning. First of all it is a respectful shiver, a kind of awesome and pervasive reverence for the holiness of God. The "fear of the LORD" expresses the awareness of the qualitative distance between God and humans. This reverence is something other than *being afraid of God*. In the expression "fear of the LORD" we hear above all the melody of respectful confidentiality and love. The "fear of the LORD" has to do with an intimate relationship. However, the spirituality in this melody never turns into an unworldly mysticism or esoteric knowledge. A spirituality that is characterized by the "fear of the LORD" always has both feet on the ground.

Preaching calls and encourages the members of the congregation to persist in this intimate relation with the LORD. Moses and the prophets call this "walking with the LORD." Sermons give a sketch of what can be seen and experienced on that walk. They explain that one has to climb and clamber now and then, but that there are also relaxed moments with panoramic views. There are moments of awareness of inner peace and rest, awareness that this peace is anchored and embedded in the eternal God and in eternity. There are also moments when our lives are without color and flat, without height or depth. Humans don't always have "mountain-top" experiences in faith. Thank God, it is also true that we don't always live in the valley. There are also lowlands and mediocrity in life. But there are moments amidst that mediocrity when we are lifted up from everyday experiences, from the flatness, the conventional and bourgeois life, moments in which the Eternal touches our lives. Those are moments of deep joy.

Decades ago sermon listeners in both the United States and Europe were more likely to have a certain biblical and theological competence. But in the twenty-first century we are no longer part of Christian lands. There is a biblical illiteracy. People no longer have scriptural language, images, or metaphors to express their experiences in religious terms, experiences *coram Deo* (i.e., "before the face of God" or "in the presence of God"). This situation urges preachers to provide the congregation (again) with language to express their everyday life experiences in the light of God's walking with us, and of our walking with him. The Old Testament is a rich source for naming, portraying, interpreting, and nurturing the reverent and confidential relation with the LORD. The Old Testament is thus also the "language school" for a biblically oriented spirituality. The books of Moses and the prophets provide us with the tools of language to utter and nurture the interior dimension of our faith.

This section deals with the two halves on the field of that interior dimension. Moses and the prophets were aware that "walking with the LORD" does not lead to a safe haven or to some remote area where we can withdraw from the reality of everyday life. Those who live in a confidential relation with the LORD know about the paradoxical experiences of both close community with God and abandonment by him. The Old Testament tells and proclaims that the LORD can be encountered as Friend and as Adversary. The next sections deal with both halves on the field of spirituality.

## A Friend and a Friend

Moses and the prophets tell us that the LORD speaks face to face with humans and that they can "see" this God with the eyes of the heart (for instance, Ps. 34:5-6). The poets, storytellers, and prophets give witness to a surprising and unexpected encounter with the Most High. They came to understand themselves as a "you" addressed by a divine "I."[41] They experienced this encounter as very real and very personal, like friends meeting and encountering each other. For that reason, they speak and testify con-

41. Buber 1958.

cretely and humanly about these experiences. In this relation of promises and faith, of loyalty and trust, the LORD turns to us — graciously and freely — to make us members of the divine household.[42]

This encounter goes deeper than that which can be touched or seen. Such an encounter is experienced as if the Creator touches his creatures beneath the skin. In our quest for the secret of life and the mystery of being, we discover that we are found and known by God (Ps. 139). There are no reasons anymore for self-importance, conceit, and arrogance. We no longer need to prove or justify ourselves at the expense of others. God justifies and accepts us apart from our "works." So we are set free before God, with respect to other people, and for the future. We are set free for walking with the LORD in a frank and open relation. When we allow ourselves to enter into this relation with the LORD, we encounter fundamental experiences of liberation, joy, release, and refuge.

From that perspective the sermon can acquire the character of a sanctuary where humans can grasp the horns of the altar (Exod. 21:13; Num. 35:9-15; Deut. 4:41-43). The context of the liturgy invites us to "remove the shoes from our feet" in a spiritual safe haven (Exod. 3:5). The awareness can be born that a particular experience is a holy moment on holy ground. Such moments invite us to close our eyes, bow our heads, kneel down, or murmur a prayer. I once tried to express that awareness in a sermon on Exodus 33:18-23.

> Moses said, "Show me your glory, I pray." And God meets the request. And God said, "I will make all my goodness pass before you, and will proclaim before you the name, 'The LORD.'" The reality of God is not only something to believe. Neither is it only something that is handed over in texts. God's glory is not only mediated in thoughts and feelings. Humans can experience the reality of God itself. This text portrays both the preconditions and the limitations of such an encounter with God's glory.
>
> "I will be gracious to whom I will be gracious, and will show mercy on whom I will show mercy." To see the LORD is not the result of a method. We cannot switch on or off God's glory as if was it an electronic device or a program on TV. Whoever really wants to see or en-

---

42. H. Berkhof 1986, pp. 113-26; "It was made clear at the outset that faith of the Old Testament knows Yahweh only as the God who bestows his favor on this world" (Zimmerli 1984, p. 59 — my translation).

counter the LORD must prepare himself and herself. But when such an encounter presents itself, it is clearly not the result of those preparations. When a human being is allowed to see something of the glory of the LORD, it is a gracious gift. And we can experience such an impressive moment only once or twice in a lifetime.

"But," he said, "you cannot see my face; for no one shall see me and live." To see God's face is not the same as and cannot be compared with the way we see the face of a fellow human being. God's face is holy. We cannot survive even one glimpse of this face. The fact that God's face is hidden is therefore also a gracious hiddenness. It is even a gracious precondition of staying alive!

"See, there is a place by me where you shall stand on the rock; and while my glory passes by I will put you in a cleft of the rock, and I will cover you with my hand until I have passed by." To talk about God can be done everywhere. But one can see God only in specific places. And those are usually places where life hurts, in the desert for instance, or on the bank of a stream, in the mountains, or on a cross. Whoever is brought to such a place sits down, and covers the head with a mantle, so that he or she can survive the encounter with God. "Then I will take away my hand, and you shall see my back; but my face shall not be seen."[43]

*God Nearby*

Preaching tries to nourish the trust of the members of the congregation that they don't have to hide from the LORD. We don't have to conceal our questions, laments, complaints, or vulnerability. We don't have to sew fig leaves together or make loincloths for ourselves in order to veil our guilty past or vulnerable present. Such efforts make no sense (Gen. 3) because God knows about our going out and our coming in (Ps. 121). This God hems us in, behind and before (Ps. 139). The LORD knows us better than we know ourselves because God knows how we were made (Ps. 103). This God is even present when we are on our way to the ends of the earth (Jon. 1). We can't run away from this God, but we don't have to run away either. When we become exhausted by our escape behavior, Scripture invites us to agree

43. Inspired by Josuttis 1999, pp. 89f.

with the voice from the heart of God, maybe even in a cynical way: "I knew that you are a gracious and merciful God" (Jon. 3). This proclamation is valid for our own life, and to our astonishment — sometimes to our irritation — also for others.

The Old Testament offers a rich variety of images and metaphors for naming, describing, and interpreting our shelter in the refuge of the LORD. With the LORD we are as safe as on a rock (Ps. 18:3, 47; Isa. 44:8). He hides us in his shelter and conceals us under the cover of his tent (Pss. 15:1; 27:5; 91:10). The LORD is our shade at our right hand (Ps. 121:5). In and through Jesus Christ, the gentiles are allowed to say with Israel: the LORD has inscribed us on the palms of his hands (Isa. 49:16). The LORD bears us up and even makes us escape from death (Ps. 68:20f.). Our souls shall be bound up in the bundle of the living under the care of the LORD (1 Sam. 25:29). This knowledge of the LORD can revitalize the lost life of the inner self and can develop and empower counter-forces in a flattened culture.

## God's Absence

Life has more to offer than just quiet waters and green pastures. There are moments when we don't experience the comforting rod and staff of the LORD (contra Ps. 23). There are times when we have no reason to sing a song of joy (Ps. 137:1f.). There is so much that contradicts God's promises, so much that causes physical or spiritual pain. There are so many bitter questions that go beyond the understanding of our head and heart. The listeners have to deal with sickness, temptations, difficulty, suffering, and tribulation. They know from their own experience how humans can be crushed between the millstones of bureaucracy and technocratic systems and thus become prey to the "raging of the enemies" (Ps. 2:1f.). And where is God in the moments when it hurts? Sometimes it seems that God is asleep (Ps. 44:23f.).

> Oh, that I knew where I might find him,
> that I might come even to his dwelling!
> If I go forward, he is not there;
> or backward, I cannot perceive him;
> on the left he hides, and I cannot behold him;

I turn to the right, but I cannot see him.
If only I could vanish in darkness,
and thick darkness would cover my face! (Job 23:3, 8-9, 17)

The prevalence of this motif in the Old Testament raises a point of importance for preaching. Israel's struggle with God's hiddenness is not an insignificant footnote to an otherwise optimistic faith. Israel suffered more than once under the experience of God's hiddenness. And the French philosopher Blaise Pascal (1623-1662) said, "Every religion which does not affirm that God is hidden, is not true."[44] The tension between trust in the LORD and the reality of actual hurting experiences of God's absence caused and causes time and again a painful paradox.[45] Sometimes Israel had the impression that God hid himself without reason, and felt engulfed by the "presence of an absence." Samuel Balentine expresses this well in his book *The Hidden God.*

> Doubt and despair are not mere side-steps in an otherwise optimistic faith. They are in fact integral to the faith experience. One indication of this is Israel's basic honesty in bringing these feelings before God. With questions and petitions, accusations and complaints Israel candidly gave expression to the frustration of being abandoned by God. In effect the prayers of lament give form to even the darkest experiences and so guarantee their legitimacy in the life of faith.[46]

God's hiddenness is not only the result of human sin or the result of human limitations. Sometimes that is the case but not always. The LORD can choose to be a hidden God just as he can choose to be a known God. This God can be far away and come nearby. "Truly, you are a God who hides himself, O God of Israel, the Savior" (Isa. 45:15). Both elements of the paradox are uttered in one sentence: God who hides and saves. He is not only a "hidden God" understood in a passive sense. We have to recognize the full force of the verbal reflexive in the Hebrew original: the LORD is a "self-concealing God."[47] God is indeed not a "kindly old uncle" (Søren

44. Pascal 1955, p. 195.
45. Balentine 1983, pp. 13-21, 49, 51-56, 56-62.
46. Balentine 1983, p. 173; see also Terrien 1978, p. 83.
47. Terrien 1978, pp. 251, 321. Gerhard von Rad could even say that "all true knowledge of God begins with the knowledge of his hiddenness" (von Rad 1980b, p. 377; see also Barth *CD* II/1, p. 183).

Kierkegaard). The God of Israel can never be reduced to a smooth or simple formula. Speaking and preaching about the hiddenness of God is not exactly what we expect to hear in sermons. But perhaps for that very reason it is a word we need to hear. Allen C. McSween picks up this question in a sermon on Exodus 33:12-13, 17-23 and John 12:27-40.

> We preachers are too often tempted to iron out all the wrinkles of life. Sometimes we give the impression that faith in God is the most obvious thing in the world. How could anyone not believe in God, surrounded by all the beauty of the world? On Sunday morning we sanitize the world of its darkness. We cross out its tragedy and terror, and offer a comic-book version of the gospel that sooner or later proves as useless as an umbrella in a hurricane. Faith that is real must find expression in a world of rough edges — a world that hides God every bit as much as it reveals God. To pretend otherwise would be to turn faith into a Sunday School pageant and rob it of its power. ( )
>
> To speak of the "darkness of faith" is a way of saying that whatever else God is, in a world like ours God is not obvious. God is deeply hidden — hidden by our human limitations, hidden by our sin. God is no show-off. The God revealed in the pages of Scripture is a hidden God, who dwells in deep darkness. Isaiah exclaims, "Truly thou art a God who hidest thyself."[48]

It is touching and impressive how intensely realistic the books of Moses and the prophets are about the hiddenness of the LORD. This God is not obvious in our world like a billboard on the highway. That hiddenness is not solved in the New Testament. On the contrary, the tension between revelation and hiddenness is only intensified. That can be heard in a sermon by Maurice K. Mickles on Isaiah 45:15 and Mark 7:24. The title of the sermon is, "God Are You Still Here?" The preacher doesn't say that Jesus is the answer to an Old Testament problem. Neither does he say that Jesus reveals the hidden God. It is exactly in Jesus Christ that we encounter the hiddenness of God.

> Isaiah's cryptic words may likewise be applied to Christ. The father hid himself in his son, for God was in Christ reconciling the world to himself. The most wonderful veiling of the Almighty is associated

---

48. McSween, in: Cox Vol. 7, pp. 96-97.

with Jesus, who alone gazed upon the father. "No man can see Me and live" was God's pronouncement through Moses (Exod. 33:20). It is only as we see God in Christ that we can live, presently and eternally. "No man hath seen God at any time; the only begotten Son, which is in the bosom of the Father, He hath declared Him" (John 14:9). Again, "He that hath seen me hath seen the father." Often in the Old Testament, God veiled Himself in angelic form or appeared as a man. In the Gospels he was incarnate in Jesus; "Veiled in flesh the Godhead see."[49]

Sermons express a cry to the hidden God and spread out the need of the world before God's eyes, just as the praying community in the Old Testament spreads out their wrinkled and damaged existence before the LORD. Preaching spreads out the letters from the hand of life's adversaries before the LORD: "Incline your ear, O LORD, and hear; open your eyes, O LORD, and see; hear the words which ( ) mock the living God" (2 Kings 19:14-19). Because of the raw experiences in life, Israel cries, "How long?" (Pss. 6:4; 13:2ff.); "Where is God?" (Exod. 17:7; Pss. 42:3; 44:24; 79:10; 115:2); "Why?" (Pss. 10:1; 22:2; 43:2; 74:1; 88:15; 115:2); "Are you asleep?" (Ps. 44:23); "Rise up" (3:8; 7:6; 9:19); "Wake up" (35:23; 59:5); "Hear" (17:1; 27:7; 30:10); and "See" (9:13; 80:14).[50] Those prayers are all strong verbal forms and therefore more like admonitions than humble petitions. Israel teaches the gentiles not to speak always "softly and tenderly"[51] in our communication with an absent God.

### God as Adversary

Israel experienced God as absent, but also as acting more robustly with creation and humans than romantic idealism wants to be true. Instead of God's "mild, fair-fingered hands,"[52] people can experience the LORD as a "hard-handed" God. The God of Israel is not a nice, sweet, easygoing God. He is a God who defeats enemies, a God who punishes sins, who oppresses people. And even if the last is not his intention, he is oppressing neverthe-

49. Mickles 2003.
50. Brueggemann 1997, pp. 319ff.
51. The expression is from a well-known hymn by Will L. Thompson.
52. The expression is taken from the Apocalypse of Sedrach, XI.

less. It is the God who refuses to give account to Job, the God who tests Abraham on Mt. Moriah (Gen. 22), a God who judges Israel when they turn their backs.[53]

The LORD can even be encountered as someone who is out for someone's blood, as we read in the strange and awkward story of Exodus 4:24-26. The story tells of Moses' return to Egypt: "On the way, at a place where they spent the night, the LORD met him and tried to kill him." The significance of this passage remains enigmatic.[54] There are parallels between this story and the wrestling of Jacob at the Jabbok in the night (Gen. 32). In a sermon on this text, the Dutch preacher Nico ter Linden points to the fact that angels are waiting for Jacob when he enters the Promised Land again. After a period of exile, Jacob returns to Canaan in hope of blessing.

> Will God, the Lord of this land, let him enter immediately? Over there lies Bethel, the place where he left the land long ago. At that time angels had escorted him out of it. In his last night in God's land they had unveiled to him the mystery of that land, in a dream in which he saw heaven opening. The dream had comforted him all those years.
>
> And look, in a new vision the same angels are actually standing waiting for him. An army of God! Why is that army standing there? Is it a guard of honor for a lost son who is returning? Does heaven still have a bone to pick with him? Is this Esau's army, ready to advance in attack? (. . .)
>
> Suddenly a figure appears in the dark. Someone grabs Jacob and they begin to wrestle.
>
> Who is this someone? Who is this dark frontier guard who watches over this area? What kind of river demon is this which shuns the light? Is it the creditor of his soul who comes to him this night to make the reckoning? Is it Esau who is pressing hard upon him? Is Jacob at odds with himself, and is this a fight with his own shadow? Or is this mysterious form an angel? Is Jacob wrestling with God?[55]

This preacher doesn't rule out any of the mentioned possibilities, not for Jacob and not for the hearers. Robert W. Jenson rightly comments on this

---

53. Brueggemann has a chapter on the subject "Ambiguity and the Character of Yahweh" in his theology (Brueggemann 1997, pp. 359-72).

54. Childs 1974, pp. 95-101, 103f.

55. Ter Linden 1999, pp. 135, 137.

text that "Israel preserves something essential to her initial experience of God — that God is *dangerous*."[56]

Job is the most well known of those who met and experienced God as an Adversary. Jacob had reasons to fear God's "critical evaluation." But Job was blameless and upright, one who feared God and turned away from evil (Job 1:1, 8; 2:3). And it is exactly for that reason that God's reign is a complete mystery for Job. In 16:9-17 he accuses God with bitter complaints.

> He (= God) slashes open my kidneys,
> and shows no mercy; he pours out my gall on the ground.
> He bursts upon me again and again;
> he rushes at me like a warrior.

The book of Job doesn't answer these penetrating questions, nor does the rest of Scripture. The testimony of Moses and the prophets is restricted to posing the difficulty with great strength. But even when we cannot solve these complexities, in naming and mentioning these taunting questions, preaching can entangle the strangling force of these dark experiences and kindle a hopeful light in the shadow of these difficulties. We can hear that tone in a sermon by Lyle E. McKee titled "Trying the Patience." The readings from Scripture were taken from Isaiah 35:1-10, Psalm 146:5-10, Matthew 11:2-11, and James 5:7-10.

> We generally speak of the "patience" of Job. But patience is far too passive a word. There is a sense in which Job was anything but patient. As we read the tremendous drama of his life, we see him passionately resenting what has come upon him, passionately questioning the conventional arguments of his so-called friends, passionately agonizing over the terrible thought that God might have forsaken him. Few men have spoken such passionate words as did Job; but the great fact about him is that in spite of all the agonizing questionings that tore at his heart, he never lost his faith in God. "See, he will kill me; I have no hope" (Job 13:15). "My witness is in heaven, and he that vouches for me is on high" (Job 16:19). "I know that my redeemer lives" (Job 19:25). This is not some kind of unquestioning submission; he struggled and doubted, and sometimes even defied, but the flame of his faith was never extinguished.

56. Jenson 1997, pp. 53-54, note 81.

The word used of him is a word that describes, not a passive patience, but that gallant spirit which can bear the tides of doubt and sorrow and disaster and come out with faith still stronger on the other side. There may be a faith which never complained or questioned; but still greater is the faith that is tortured by questions and still believes. It was the faith which held steadfastly on that came out on the other side, for "The Lord blessed the latter days of Job more than his beginning" (Job 42:12).

There may be moments in life when we think that God has forgotten, but if we cling to the remnants of faith, in the end we, too, discover anew the kindness and the mercy of God.[57]

This God of kindness and mercy is also an incomprehensible God. Humans can stumble harshly on this element of God's character. The congregation from the gentiles takes the freedom to quarrel with this God just as Israel did and does. The preacher takes the role of a lawyer who defends the case of the hearers before this God.[58] Proclamation becomes the partner of Job, of the poet of Psalm 22, of the suffering servant of the LORD, and of Jeremiah in their closing arguments before God. The covenant between God and humans is surely one-sided in its origin but is definitely two-sided in its existence.[59] That mutual character of the covenant gave and gives Israel the frankness to communicate robustly with the LORD.[60] Job, for instance, does not submit to the facts and the fate of life.[61] He debates extensively, not only with his friends but also with God.

This tone and pattern of communication between the LORD and Israel mandates Christian preaching to speak freely and frankly to, with, and about the LORD. Preaching asks God to give account; it makes an appeal to God against God (Job 16:20f.). We have to reckon with the possibility that there will come a moment that we have to lay our hands on our mouths. "Shall a faultfinder contend with the Almighty? Anyone who argues with

---

57. McKee 2004.

58. Lange 1982, p. 28.

59. "The covenant is a gracious disposition from God, yet involving two parties who relate to each other as subjects and whose attitude and behavior are always mutually co-determinative" (H. Berkhof 1986, p. 252).

60. Marquardt states that humans need not only be justified by God but that God must also be justified by humans (1996, pp. 194ff.).

61. Holbert 1999, especially chapter 8, "On Becoming a Joban Preacher."

God must respond" (Job 40:2). But as long as humans are put through the wringer of life, preaching may not anticipate that judgment of God. Preaching may not be muzzled by anyone or anything. Maybe there will come a moment that God forces us to put our hands on our mouths. But we will not do that before God himself urges us to do so.

Until that moment, Moses, the prophets, and David provide the Christian congregation with the language to communicate robustly with the God of Israel. In giving voice to this kind of experience in the midst of the congregation, preaching also enforces mutual solidarity. Because "if one member suffers, all suffer together with it" (1 Cor. 12:26). Preaching can also break through present-day myths inspired by TV series, movies, and commercials. It is the myth of the perfect, glamorous, and undamaged life on the one hand and the myth of hedonism on the other hand. Preaching can nurture a healthy sense of the finiteness and vulnerability of human life. That can be combined with an equally healthy celebration of the gifts of God's blessings in life. From that perspective, preaching according to the Old Testament offers a healthier message for the contemporary culture than contemporary modish gurus do.

### Dialectical Tension

The Old Testament weaves together the voices of dissent and confession; it juxtaposes affirmation and denial. The testimony of God as Friend and Adversary, the experiences of God nearby and far off, are juxtaposed and yet always interrelated, interdependent. Each of these words needs to be understood amidst the interplay with their antiphonal word. We find meaning in these contradictory witnesses within the dialectical tension of opposites. David Leininger makes this explicit in a sermon on Psalm 13. He quotes the fourth and fifth verses in his sermon,

4. My enemy will say, "I have overcome him,"
   and my foes will rejoice when I fall.
5. But I trust in your unfailing love;
   my heart rejoices in your salvation.
   I will sing to the Lord, for he has been good to me.

There is quite a shift in tone between these two verses!

Here is that shift we spoke of earlier. Read it this way: "My enemy will say, 'I have overcome him' and my foes will rejoice when I fall." Sigh! "But I trust in your unfailing love; my heart rejoices in your salvation. I will sing to the Lord, for he has been good to me." In between verses 4 and 5, something changes. It is the arrival of hope that is born of memory. Yes, things are awful, but I can remember a time when they were not awful, when God's care for me was much more evident, and I am convinced that such a day will come again. (. . .)

It seems to me that the church, when it is at its best, lives its life between verses 4 and 5. We hear that deep sigh when words cannot come. We hear the laments from both within and without as people feel free and safe to speak to their anguish. All by itself, that listening ear helps the healing process because, as psychotherapy has taught us, there is catharsis in voicing the pain. Between verses 4 and 5 tears are shed, because when the church is at its best, we rejoice with those who rejoice, but we also weep with those who weep. Between verses 4 and 5 we remember the despair of Good Friday that was answered by the delight of Easter. Between verses 4 and 5, we hear again Tony Campolo's wonderful phrase, "It's Friday, but Sunday's comin'." Between verses 4 and 5 is where the church finds its most meaningful life.[62]

We trust our chaotic life experiences in the hands of God. We don't see or experience the LORD every moment, but this God has left enough footsteps in the course of history that we can trust God even after we have pressed charges against this God. Amidst the dark experiences in the concreteness of life, preaching gives testimony about the dwelling place in the shadow of the Almighty (Pss. 90:1; 91:1). Scripture wants to assure us of that gracious good news even if we don't experience anything of this dwelling place. On the foundation of this promise preaching nurtures the spiritual and mental determination of the hearers, and empowers the congregation to endure the night and maintain their humanity in trials, tribulations, and temptations. To see dimly in a mirror, to know only in part, to live in enigmatic riddles is an intrinsic part of walking with God. And those blurred reflections of God's reality will only disappear when perfection comes, when we shall see face to face, and shall know and understand fully and clearly (1 Cor. 13:12f.).

Preaching the Old Testament can thus offer a counter-voice to the

---

62. Leininger 2002.

myth of unbroken and undamaged life as it is presented in TV series, movies, and commercials. We meet the same myth in sugar-coated romantic Christianity. Thomas H. Troeger is correct when he says that the "primary condition for becoming an effective preacher is not homiletical technique and method, as helpful as these may be, but is rather a willingness to acknowledge and struggle with humanity's paradoxical relationship to God."[63] The Old Testament is aware of the fact that life isn't perfect. The Old Testament testifies of the stark reality that Israel's life was lived from beginning to end under the shadow of countless threats.[64] The books of Moses and the prophets struggle with God on this issue. That can be heard in a sermon by Charles E. Crain on Psalm 88, titled, "The Suffering Man and the Silent God." In this psalm there are no flashes of light. There is only gloom and unrelieved darkness.

> Is it too much to suggest that it is only as the psalmist continues his prayer of protest that there is hope of recovery? I do not mean recovery from his illness, or from his isolation, or even from interrogation of God, but a recovery of the sense of God's presence in the midst of them all.
>
> The silence of God does not mean the absence of God. God is present even in and through his silence. God stands "within the shadow, keeping watch above his own." There is no proof of this. There is only the cry of faith, "Lord, I believe, help thou my unbelief."
>
> > O Lord, my God, by day I call for help,
> > by night I cry aloud in *thy presence.*
> > Let my prayer come *before thee,*
> > hear my loud lament. . . .[65]

The citation of the words of the father of the son with a dumb spirit (Mark 9:24) doesn't absorb the psalm in an exclusively Christian way. The prayer of the father deepens the meaning and proclamation of the psalm. The words in italics (probably spoken with emphasis) give the sermon the tone of a prayer and not of a bold statement.

---

63. Troeger 2004, p. 115.

64. B. W. Anderson 1963, pp. 63-105 (§3. "The Trials of Faith"); Kraus 1986, pp. 125-36 (§5, "The Enemy Powers").

65. Crain, in: Cox Vol. 1, p. 124.

## 14.6. The Old Testament, Christ, and the Congregation

The bi-focal language and theology on ethics and spirituality discussed in the previous two sections is particularly true of the Old Testament. The tension between the poles rises when we come close to Israel's core-testimony: the LORD is Israel's God and they are the people of this God. This crucial element in Israel's testimony is reason for songs of joy. But when Israel lacks the experience of this God or lacks the righteousness that belongs to this covenant, the same testimony is reason for critical, skeptical, or protesting voices as counter-testimony.[66]

The gentiles read the Old Testament as a witness with a power of expression that reaches beyond the borders of Israel. In and through Jesus Christ, the gentiles are incorporated in the story of salvation and judgment, in the prayers of lament and the songs of joy, in the call for justice and the joy of the Torah. These pairs of words are the foci of ellipses that hold each other in a dialectical tension. Preaching offers the opportunity to deal with matters of ordinary day-to-day life exactly because of this dialectical and sometimes paradoxical character of the testimony of Moses and the prophets.

The Christian church recognizes the different foci of the ellipses in the life and ministry of Jesus Christ. We can hear the counter-testimony in Jesus' lament from Psalm 22 on Good Friday (Matt. 27:39-44). On Easter morning we hear the jubilation: "This is the day that the LORD has made; let us rejoice and be glad in it" (Ps. 118:24). Good Friday, Holy Saturday, and Easter Sunday have indeed a particular — (salvation) historical — order, but from an existential perspective these are not once-for-all sequenced events.[67] This *Holy Triduum* determines the faithful existence of the everyday life of every believer.

The remaining and ongoing tension between praise and lament, between the presence and absence of God, between burden and joy, between resistance and submission, leaves no room for a triumphalist church or concepts that portray faith as panacea or remedy against grief, suffering, and sorrow. The world with its barbarism, its grief and sorrow, its alienation between humans, between God and humans, and between humans

---

66. "The tension between the core testimony and the counter-testimony is acute and ongoing" (Brueggemann 1997, p. 400).

67. Brueggemann 1997, p. 401.

and creation makes hard-handedly clear that the victory of Easter waits for its completion. This awareness of brokenness is also present when we sit at the Lord's Table. We celebrate the suffering and resurrection of Jesus Christ for our salvation. But the closing prayer is a longing Maranatha, "Come, Lord Jesus" (Rev. 22:20). Not only Moses and the prophets but also apostles and evangelists are still waiting — confidently and trustfully but nevertheless waiting.

The movement back and forth played an important role in the previous chapters. The same is true for the present chapter. It goes back and forth between trust and doubt, resistance and submission, righteousness and guilt, the awareness of nearness and absence of God, material and spiritual well-being. This mutuality has yet another dimension. In the process of sermon preparation we try to open windows on the text so that the dialectical character of the proclamation of Scripture can be heard. We try to open the grammatical surface of the words but also the meaning of the kerygmatic interior. Bruce Shields is correct in saying that preaching "wants to mediate between Scripture and the everyday world of the hearers in such a way that the hearers become participants of the world of Scripture and the world of God. (. . .) Our task is not to explain the gospel; it is not to describe the gospel; it is not even to contextualize the gospel. Our task is to actualize the gospel so that people can do more than just listen to it; our task is to help people to enter into it."[68]

Preaching can thus provide the members of the congregation with a spiritual vocabulary and grammar that help them to name, describe, and interpret their lives again or for the first time *coram Deo.* That doesn't mean that the "purpose of preaching is primarily to scratch where people already itch or to give names to what the culture already knows and feels," as Thomas G. Long rightly says.[69] Sermons function sometimes as an "abrasive" for the soul, as a curative resistance for thought, or as a challenge for action. Preaching offers the opportunity to weave personal experiences into the larger context of God's redemptive purposes for humanity and creation. Every human being spins his or her own thread of life. Every thread has its place in God's cloth of the coming realm of *shalom.* And it is this theological context that gives meaning and purpose to our lives. Sermons weave together the story of humans and the Story of God, so that each individual

68. Shields 2000, pp. 158-59.
69. Long 1996, p. 96.

can find himself or herself back in God's story. Preaching makes contemporary situations and issues translucent so that we can see and hear words, images, and theology from Scripture behind or under our own experiences. Preaching also makes the reverse movement: making words, images, and theology of Scripture translucent so that the members of the congregation can discover and discern their own lives in it and (re)interpret their lives within the framework of the scriptural proclamation.

Doing that, we can also experience a movement in the opposite direction. When we read and interpret Scripture, we can become aware of the mystery that Scripture reads and interprets *us*. In those moments, the witnesses of Moses and the prophets break through our lines of defense and open the inside of our lives. The lines on the floors of our hearts and souls are read by the Spirit of God. In those moments, sermons bring nearby those who were once far off.

# 15. Life in the World to Come

## 15.1. The Future: Labyrinth or Maze?

Images of labyrinths are found in ancient cultures around the world, and designs found on pottery, tablets, and tiles date as far back as 4,000 years. The image has its origin in a famous Greek myth in which Theseus killed the Minotaur on the island of Crete and escaped from its labyrinth with the help of Ariadne's thread.

Although the words "labyrinth" and "maze" are frequently confused, they are not the same. Mazes contain cul-de-sacs and dead ends. They have more than one entrance and also more than one exit and are designed to make us lose our way; they're a game. Labyrinths have the opposite purpose: they are designed to help us find our way. They have only one path from the outer edge into the center and back again. There are no tricks and no dead ends. Through the act of trusting the path, of giving up conscious control of how things should go and being receptive to our inner state, we can be opened up to a whole new world. The labyrinth thus became a metaphor for human life in general. Being in the labyrinth is like taking a thoughtful walk or going on a sacred journey. From that perspective the labyrinth also acquired a religious meaning, especially during medieval times. Walking the path of a labyrinth while praying and meditating implied a spiritual dimension. For that reason, in many churches one can find labyrinths beside specific Christian symbols like cross, lamb, and fish. In Europe, as many as twenty-two of the eighty Gothic cathedrals contain labyrinths. Many modern churches too, along with other institutions around the world, have either indoor or outdoor labyrinths.

Images of the labyrinth and the maze can also serve the start of a discussion on eschatology. The coming of God's realm has played an important role in proclamation, creeds, and systematic-theological reflection since the origins of Christianity. But since that beginning there have also been many disagreements among Christians on this issue. Questions were raised such as, How will God's reign be established? When will God come? What sort of realm will God establish? These questions are brought into sharp focus when interpreters give their explanation of such passages as Daniel 2 and Revelation 20, where the text speaks of a coming period of peace, the so-called millennium. Attempts to relate these texts to the course of human history have led to a number of different concepts. The reader is almost dazzled by the labeling of these models: historic premillennialism, dispensational pre-millennialism, post-millennialism, and a-millennialism.[1] A multitude of options and models is offered of pre-, post-, or mid-tribulation rapture concepts, and about different dispensations. There is also a multitude of possible persons and institutions that can or could be identified with the mysterious number 666, the beasts from the sea and the earth, the Antichrist, or Armageddon. It is material that makes for real science-fiction or horror page-turners like the *Left Behind* series or favorite movies like *Armageddon* and *The Matrix*. In all these cases the subject of the future is interesting and intriguing at the same time.

History sometimes looks like a maze, with more than one entrance and also more than one exit and several dead-ends in between. Moses and the prophets testify, however, that history is a labyrinth: there is a beginning and an end.[2] On our journey through the paths of life we often ask, "Is there a way out? Does this path lead to something or somewhere?" Scripture testifies that it leads to God's kingdom and that this way is led by God. The Old Testament testifies in manifold and colorful ways about the life in the world to come. This chapter makes that testimony operable for preaching.

1. For good introductions in the different options of dispensationalism, see Clouse 1979 and Erickson 1987.
2. "We should consider that the brightness of the Divine countenance, which even an apostle declares to be inaccessible (1 Tim. 6:16), is a kind of labyrinth, — a labyrinth to us inextricable, if the Word do not serve us as a thread to guide our path; and that it is better to limp in the way, than run with the greatest swiftness out of it" (Calvin, *Institutes* I, 6, 3).

## 15.2. Last Things — Latter Days

Sections on eschatology in systematic theological textbooks usually deal with the so-called "last things." One can think of subjects like the last judgment, heaven, hell, the new heaven and the new earth, the new Jerusalem, and the so-called "intermediate state" (about the condition and the place of our loved ones between the moment of their deaths and the last day). In short, eschatology has to do with things at the other side of the line between life and death.[3] This future-to-be-expected comes after a total caesura with this world. The present era will be replaced by a new era.

The Old Testament testifies extensively about the future. But Israel's eschatological hope is not exclusively concerned with transcendent redemption as expressed in the Christian dogmas, creeds, and confessions. Israel's hope is concerned with wholeness, health, fullness of life, peace, and blessing as realities to be experienced in this world. The expression "at the end of days" refers primarily to the future, a subsequent time or the time of descendants (Gen. 49:1; Deut. 4:30; 8:10; Isa. 46:10). Even the word "end" means primarily a temporal or spatial distance (Job 28:3; 2 Kings 19:23). N. T. Wright says that when Jews died in their fight for the restoration of Israel, "they hoped not to 'go to heaven,' or at least not permanently, but to be raised to new bodies when the kingdom came, since they would of course need new bodies to enjoy the very much this-worldly *shalom*, peace and prosperity that was in store."[4]

We have, however, to keep in mind that Moses and the prophets don't speak about "last things" but about "latter days." "Last things" are gravestones or shrouds. During World War II concentration camps and boxes with the murderous gas *Zyklon B* (the insecticide used for gassing the Jews) were "last things" in the most horrible sense of the word. Nowadays we face the threat of weapons of mass destruction, "last things" that can destroy all life on earth.[5] Old Testament eschatology is not only interested in events at the end of history but also and even more so on renewal of life in the "latter days" — days within the limits of our human history.

We have to consider, furthermore, that the Hebrew language makes

---

3. See for instance H. Berkhof 1986, §§ 57-59. Pannenberg identifies for instance "eschatological hope" explicitly with "hope beyond death" (Pannenberg 2002, p. 3).

4. N. T. Wright 1992, p. 286.

5. Marquardt 1993, p. 17.

no distinction between "future" and "end," between "later" and "latter."[6] A substantial part of the eschatological references are thus explicitly earthly in character (German: *diesseitig*). Indeed, prophets dream of another world, a world to come. But that other world is not only a life hereafter. The prophets give witness that both restoration and judgment will take place within the limits of their own socio-historical context.

We also have to say that the Old Testament testimony about the future is more determined by the coming of Someone than Something. The prophets give witness to a coming event, but the LORD is the actual cause and "kingpin" of those events.[7] The Old Testament testimony about promise and fulfillment points to "He that comes" (Ps. 98:7-9; Isa. 40:10; 59:19-20). And in the "slipstream" of "He that comes," tangible goodness and salvation can be experienced for his people and for the whole creation.

Partners who promise to be faithful to each other on their wedding day don't predict the future. They make a solemn and authentic commitment of loyalty. Promise in the Old Testament context also has less to do with a predictable future than with the LORD's commitment to creatures and creation. As a consequence, fulfillment cannot be fixed chronologically. Promise is the word for the LORD's commitment of loyalty to covenant-partner Israel, to humanity as a whole, and to creation.

## 15.3. Development in Old Testament Eschatology

Future in the Old Testament means that the LORD is coming to the creation, the land given to Israel, to the capital where God dwells, or to Israel as the covenant-partner. This God is continuously on the way to realize the realm of justice and peace.[8] The Old Testament witnesses about the future point to this coming of God. That means that the LORD is the actual core of the promises about the future. He is both the content of the promises and the One who guarantees the fulfillment of the promise. The *eschaton* is therefore not a thing but a person. The ultimate promise about the future

6. Vriezen 1978, p. 120.

7. Zimmerli 1963.

8. Westermann points to the fact that the semantic structure of the Old Testament is more focused on verbs than on nouns (Westermann 1982, p. 17). Moses and the prophets are not primarily focused on creation as such but on the creating acts of the LORD; they are not focused on blessing as a "thing" that can be possessed but on God who blesses.

is given in the Name of God: I am who I am and who I will be (Exod. 3:14). It belongs to the freedom of God to choose new and creative ways to reveal this Name in the concreteness and the reality of history. And because this God is the core and center of the testimony of Moses and the prophets, the Old Testament remains therefore a waiting, a longing, an open book.[9] That is not a deficit or shortcoming of the Old Testament but rather, its waiting and longing character is its ultimate strength and dynamic power.

The Old Testament testifies that history is safe in the hands of the LORD. This God is the actual content of the future. Based on that confession, Moses and the prophets speak in various shapes and forms about the future and God's participation in future events. It isn't easy to systematize that variety. But within that rich variety of the Old Testament we can discern a certain stratification in the testimony about the future and God's being involved in it.[10]

### Tangible Goodness after a Crisis

In the period before the classical prophets, the longing for the LORD's interference with the future has to do with the restoration of Israel after concrete crises. The political and national character of the prophetic dreams and visions is predominant. The "day of the LORD" is a day of goodness and prosperity for the land and its inhabitants. It will mean liberation from enemies, having enough food after a famine, becoming healthy again after sickness, the restoration and rebuilding of the land and the nation as it was in the (idealized) period of the government of David and Solomon. Eschatology means in this case that there is concrete, this-worldly goodness waiting after the crisis. The expectation of God's coming goodness has its focus in everyday life.

### Crisis as Judgment

The scene changes dramatically during the period of the prophets Amos, Isaiah, and Jeremiah. The "day of the LORD" is no longer announced as a

---

9. Zimmerli 1978, p. 214.
10. See for the following Vriezen 1978, pp. 122ff.

day of redemption but as a day of judgment. The prophets speak about the end of history. The announced crisis will not only mean judgment for Israel's neighbors but also (and even primarily) for Israel itself.

> Alas for you who desire the day of the LORD!
> Why do you want the day of the LORD?
> It is darkness, not light;
> as if someone fled from a lion,
> and was met by a bear;
> or went into the house and rested a hand against the wall,
> and was bitten by a snake.
> Is not the day of the LORD darkness,
> not light, and gloom with no brightness in it? (Amos 5:18-20)

The pre-exilic prophets recognized that sin and the failure to obey God's Torah broke up the way to *shalom*. The penalty for these transgressions had to be paid (Isa. 40:2). The crisis says that God's patience has come to an end and that the crisis has to be understood as judgment. This judgment was experienced as a palpable reality in this world and this history.

## A New Perspective after a Crisis

Deutero-Isaiah and Ezekiel prophesy during the time that the crisis of exile was a reality. Jerusalem becomes like a widow and Judah can find no resting place (Lam. 1:1, 3). These prophets say, however, that the crisis is not the end and that judgment it is not the last word of the LORD. The exile also means that the penalty is paid and that Jerusalem has served her term (Isa. 40:1, 2). Thus, a new chapter in history can be written. The future redemption that is at hand is meant not only for Israel but has all-embracing and worldwide dimensions. The re-creation comes into sight (Isa. 65:17-19). The rebuilding of the temple is not a means in itself but part and herald of a universal new future.

> For thus says the LORD of hosts:
> Once again, in a little while,
> I will shake the heavens and the earth
> and the sea and the dry land;

and I will shake all the nations,
so that the treasure of all nations shall come,
and I will fill this house with splendor,
    says the LORD of hosts.
The silver is mine, and the gold is mine,
    says the LORD of hosts.
The latter splendor of this house shall be greater than the former,
    says the LORD of hosts;
and in this place I will give prosperity,
    says the LORD of hosts. (Hag. 2:6-8)

Eschatology is now understood as God planting his goodness in an unexpected new way and astounding scale after the radical, judgmental crisis.

### Everything New

The fourth and last step in this development of future redemption has transcendent features. The prophets announce that the present world has no future. There will come a radical and drastic caesura. And God will personally make a completely new beginning at the other side of that caesura. The difference between eschatology and apocalyptic is now vague. But the "earthly" dimension does not vanish and hope does not turn into an escape from the present reality. N. T. Wright stresses the continuum of experience and theology that gave rise to the apocalyptic writing. "At one end of the scale are the full-blown mystics. At the other are those who write about socio-political events in colourful metaphor. In between, there were most likely pious Jews who, without dramatic visionary experiences, nevertheless wrote from a full and devout belief and longing, in words highly charged with religious emotion."[11]

Theology has usually interpreted this layered testimony about the future from the perspective of development and evolution. The earlier steps were interpreted through the lens of the last step. That means that the different dimensions were interpreted on a hermeneutical one-way road. The fourth transcendental step was seen as the ultimate step, as the overture to the proclamation of apostles and evangelists. The particular voice of the

11. N. T. Wright 1992, p. 287.

other three elements disappeared more or less behind metaphysical and meta-historical concepts of the future.

That is regrettable, because the Old Testament's layered testimony about "the world to come" can be very fruitful for relevant contemporary preaching. The following sections of this chapter offer ingredients for an interpretative grammar for opening the four eschatological windows on Old Testament texts, for interpreting the layered testimony concerning the "world to come." This grammar is based on the outlined inner-biblical stratification of the prophetic proclamation. We can open these windows on texts that are explicitly eschatological in character. But we will also try to open these windows on other texts.

## 15.4. Tangible Goodness after a Crisis

For a long time preaching gave hardly any attention to the "this-sided" dimension of eschatology. The proclamation of the future was restricted to issues like heaven and the last judgment. And when sermons dealt with the issues of the "good life," it was mainly understood within a salvation-historical paradigm. That meant the "good life" was something that was buried in an inaccessible past (paradise) or was yet to be revealed in the new creation. God's grace for the here and now was a strictly spiritual matter, completely "stripped" of physical elements. This spiritualization doesn't do justice to the evidently material dimension in the proclamation of Scripture about the future. The church confessed her trust in the Creator and the goodness of creation, but its mind was often closed to the "earthly" character of the Old Testament's promises and eschatology — even though Moses and the prophets proclaimed that in the wake or slipstream of the coming of the LORD, tangible goodness will be experienced. That is not only a peculiarity of Old Testament proclamation. We hear the same message in the New Testament. The stories about cleansings and healings (Mark 1:40-45; 2:1-12; 3:1-6), the feedings of the thousands (Mark 6:34-44; 8:1-10), the exorcisms (Mark 3:7-12; 9:14-29), and the miracle at the wedding at Cana (John 2:1-11) give witness to the fact that the coming of God's kingdom in our reality has a tangible and material dimension.[12] God's redemption is not only

12. "Das Wunder ( ) ist der unüberhörbare Hinweis, daß Heilsgeschehen ein reales und wirkliches Ereignis in dieser unserer sichtbaren und greifbaren Welt bedeutet" (Schütz 1981, pp. 93-96; see also Vos 1996b, pp. 89-97).

and exclusively material, but according to the Scriptures it has an explicitly material dimension.

It is regrettable that the "this-sided" dimension of the proclamation of the future is underexposed in preaching. That is all the more true because this dimension offers important opportunities for relevant preaching to present-day listeners. This dimension nurtures and nourishes the hope that (new) life is possible after a crisis. The LORD promises not to forsake the work of his hands. We are therefore not only allowed to hope, we are even called to give account for the hope that is in us (1 Pet. 3:15). Joseph R. Jeter Jr. introduces a sermon by Gina Rhea with a particular personal coloring of this hope.

> The following sermon was preached on the first Sunday after a marital separation had occurred between the author [= Gina Rhea] and her husband. The two had served together as co-pastors for eight and a half years in the congregation where the sermon was delivered. On the previous Sunday evening, the co-pastors met with the elders to announce their separation. At the meeting the author's husband resigned the co-pastorate, effective immediately, and the author expressed her desire to renegotiate the call with the congregation in order to remain as the pastor. The elders, in a unanimous recommendation to the Official Board, affirmed her desire to remain. A letter from the co-pastors was sent to the active membership of the congregation, sharing information about the marital separation, the resignation, and the author's hope to remain. The sermon reflects the tension the author experienced between acknowledging her own pain and caring for the congregation in their grief.[13]

The readings from Scripture for the sermon of Gina Rhea were taken from Ecclesiastes 3:1-8 and 2 Corinthians 4:5-10.

> I can get through because I know that I am not alone. There are people who are standing here with me this morning, who are holding me and you in their thoughts and prayers. I can feel their strength from across town and across miles.
>
> And ultimately I can get through because I know there is Someone standing with me at this very moment who knows the pain better than

13. Jeter 1998, p. 159.

I know it myself and who shares the burden of this time in the most profound way. That same Someone, God, is sitting with you right now, too, and is aware of your sadness and anger and bewilderment and disillusionment and embarrassment. ( )

We will continue to strive and to thrive not because of who we are but because of Whose we are. And God has the power to turn even this crucible experience into the dawning of a new day. I believe that. I hope you do, too.[14]

This preacher declares in an impressive way that anger, bewilderment, disillusionment, and embarrassment are not "last things." She hopes for "latter days" where tangible hope is revived, both for the congregation and for herself. This is eschatological proclamation.

The next illustration has a broader scope. On April 19, 1995, in the week after Easter, Oklahoma City was startled by the bombing of the Federal Building. The loss of so many lives caused a national shock. J. Philip Wogaman was scheduled to preach just a few days later, on April 30. A year before he had already planned to preach on the words from Psalm 30, "You have turned my mourning into dancing." But how to read and interpret those words in the aftermath of what happened in Oklahoma City? Wogaman did not change his plans for the Scripture reading. In the introduction of the printed version of this sermon he says,

> The bombing also had a sobering effect on public opinion. For years the airwaves had been saturated by mean-spirited extremism. The bombing led many people to see the relationship between such extremism and the loss of civility in public life, and I felt it important to touch upon that relationship in this sermon.

Almost at the end of his sermon Wogaman says,

> In spite of the tragedy and the mourning, I sense some turnings. I sense in the aftermath of this awful event in Oklahoma City a deeper pondering of the nation's soul by the nation's people. ( ) And we have been served by [political] leaders in both parties who have set aside their differences and acknowledge together that our common vision as a people, our being a community of mutual caring, is vastly more im-

14. Jeter 1998, pp. 163-64.

portant than any partisan issue or partisan gain. I sense a new appreciation of that, a new struggle with that.[15]

Wogaman senses a turning for the good, for tangible goodness after a crisis. The Old Testament offers us words, images, and theology to name and
to interpret this turning from particular oppression or need to goodness,
hope, and salvation and to see this turning as a gift from the LORD.

Opening this hopeful and tangible window on a text, the preacher
can weave together hopeful stories of the congregation and the redemptive
Story of God so that the sermon turns out to be communal pastoral care as
well as a prophetic appeal. In weaving together stories and Story we can
encourage and challenge the congregation to live in hope and expectation
that there will come a day that they can salute the light again because the
sun has risen upon us again (Gen. 32:31).

## 15.5. Crisis as Judgment

### Uncomfortable Words

For several decades, words and expressions like "last judgment," "punishment," "the wrath of God," and "hell" have disappeared slowly and silently
from the vocabulary of the proclamation of the mainline churches in Europe and the United States. For that reason there are scarcely any sermons
from so-called "hard texts" from prophetic books, as Debra K. Klingsporn
comments.

> I could probably count on one hand the number of times I've read
> from the book of Amos — and I'd be willing to bet that I'm not alone.
> The book of Amos is not one to inspire comfort and hope.
>
> Amos has never been a very popular fellow. Few prophets are. The
> Israelites didn't like what Amos had to say; modern listeners like his
> words even less. Amos has been making people uncomfortable for
> centuries.
>
> Nearly every preacher struggles with what it means to be "pro-
> phetic." When faced with texts filled with judgment, condemnation,

---

15. Wogaman 1998, pp. 165-66.

and very little hope, how does one proclaim the good news, or for that matter, what is the good news? ( )

Not surprisingly, when lectionary readings direct our attention to this Old Testament doomsayer, most ministers choose an epistle or Gospel reading for their sermon text.[16]

This "homiletical ignorance" of words about judgment, wrath, and punishment of the biblical "doomsayers" is understandable and can even be justified because of the judgmental and moralistic derailment of preaching on these subjects. This kind of proclamation caused unnecessary fear and was surely in need of a retouch. But, as in every reaction, this counter-movement also had some (unwanted) side effects. And above all, we have to ask what there is to proclaim after the retouch. We are left with a flattened, one-dimensional message of "I'm OK — You're OK." Indeed, the "toothless God" doesn't threaten anymore, but that God cannot comfort or bring liberation either. This image of God can be compared with the lions in a circus. They look dangerous through children's eyes, but adults know that they are tame and domesticated. Some decades ago H. Richard Niebuhr already sharply criticized this kind of "therapeutic Christianity." "A God without wrath brought men without sin into a Kingdom without judgment through the ministrations of a Christ without a cross."[17]

## Preconditions and Precautions

Contemporary preaching is therefore again challenged to give the awkward words of (last) judgment, punishment, and wrath a place in actual sermons. With the help of words, images, metaphors, and theology of a given text, preachers can explore the concrete situation of the listeners, as to whether there is an element of judgment in it. It is obvious that such an exploration is precarious because there are no logical or translucent causal connections between sin and guilt on the one hand and misfortune, suffering, and crisis on the other. But we have to say at the same time that there are no watertight shots between those words and the realities of those words, as will become clear in the following sections. We have to take into

16. D. K. Klingsporn in a comment on a sermon of Robert T. Snell in Klingsporn 5, pp. 223-26 (223).
17. Niebuhr 1937, p. 193.

account some necessary preconditions for that endeavor, because preaching on God's judgment is vulnerable to mistakes and even to manipulation, as is shown by the history of the church and its proclamation.

The first consideration is that words like *sin, guilt, judgment,* and *punishment* can't be seen on their own but only within the broader framework of the proclamation of Scripture as a whole. These words must be seen in their relation with *repentance, forgiveness, atonement,* and *new beginning.* Judgment and exile, for instance, cannot and may not be loosened from the notions of new beginning, return to Jerusalem, and the rebuilding of the Temple. This is very impressively expressed on what remains of the *Karl-Wilhelm Gedächtnis Kirche* in the heart of Berlin, Germany. This church was bombed and heavily damaged in one of the innumerable Allied raids on the German capital during World War II. The council of the church decided not to rebuild the church after the war. An inscription on a plaque on the remains of the church tells why not.

> To remember Wilhelm I, the German *Kaiser* and King of Prussia, this church was constructed in the years 1891-1895. It was financed by the donations of the whole German people. This church was destroyed during the WW II on the night of November 11th 1943 in an air attack. The damaged tower of the church shall be a memorial of God's judgment that fell on our people during the war.[18]

Even after so many years, these words move every visitor when they stand before the remains of what was once an impressive building. The words of the plaque utter a humble confession. The authors of the plaque also had the courage to interpret the history of the German people during World War II from the perspective of judgment. A plaque at the other side of the former entrance hall says that the remains of the church were reopened in 1987 as a memorial, as a place of reminder against war and destruction, and as a call for reconciliation. The texts on these two plaques at either side of the entrance hall make clear that we can only talk about the dimension of judgment when it is — in this case literally — juxtaposed by the call for repentance and the possibility of reconciliation.

A second consideration is the fact that Israel's prophets never spoke in general terms or to abstract situations about guilt, sin, remorse, and re-

18. My translation.

pentance. When they spoke of judgment, Moses and the prophets always addressed very specific behavior and particular situations. This means for contemporary preaching that we have to address these topics clearly and concretely. Sermons must be specific when they deal with evil, remorse, and repentance. Speaking in general terms will only fuel unhealthy feelings of guilt or even activate feelings of depression.

There is, thirdly, also the dangerous possibility that preachers will abuse the pulpit and their own calling by saying things in a sermon that they wouldn't dare to say in a private conversation with one or more members of the congregation. This abuse violates both Scripture and the listeners. Preachers must consider this danger with complete honesty.

And every preacher must, fourthly, be aware of the fact that the prophetic mantle does not fit everybody. It fits only those who are actually called by God. Speaking and preaching about judgment was always against the will of a particular prophet. Moses claimed a speech impediment (Exod. 4:10-13), Isaiah confessed the impurity of his lips (Isa. 6:5), and Jeremiah made an appeal to his inexperience (Jer. 1:6). He felt enticed and overpowered by the LORD and thus wanted to keep God's word to himself (Jer. 20:7-9). Speaking about judgment can therefore not be done in an "eager" tone.

And last but not least, we have to keep in mind that when the LORD speaks about judgment, it is never a verdict of an unmoved, emotionless, and impersonal power. The LORD is a God who is committed to creatures and creation. Dealing with God's judgment in sermons requires a comparable attitude on the part of preachers and a suitable intonation in their voices. Preaching on the issue of God's judgment asks for authentic solidarity between preacher and listeners. In their wording and tone preachers must show that God's judgment has also touched their own existence, that they have felt the sword of the living and active word of God, judging the thoughts and intentions of their own hearts (Heb. 4:12-13). They must feel the burning fire shut up in their bones (Jer. 20:7-9).

When these precautions and preconditions are observed as "safety fuses," they create a space in which we can ask for careful attention to the judgment-dimension in a particular crisis.

## *The Dimension of Judgment in a Crisis*

When people experience a personal crisis they need comfort and help, especially when it concerns a severe illness or the loss of a loved one. But there are also crises that give rise to the question of whether there is — not exclusively but also — a dimension of judgment in that which happened or occurred. Those are usually crises on a larger, i.e., communal (nationwide or global) scale. Herbert O. Edwards Sr. has an eye open for the dimension of judgment in a national crisis in a sermon on Genesis 19:23-24, "The sun had risen on the earth when Lot came to Zoar. Then the LORD rained on Sodom and Gomorrah sulfur and fire from the LORD out of heaven."

> A crowd gathers outside Lot's house, demanding that he send the strangers out so that they might have some sport with them. The people themselves did not think this unusual; apparently they had done as much many times before. But there is a point beyond which the patience of God cannot go. Lot refused their request, and when the mob clamored outside Lot's door a sudden blindness fell upon them, and they did not realize that they had already passed "the hidden boundary between God's patience and his wrath."
>
> This night seemed no different from any other. No trumpet of wrath has shattered the stillness; no earthquake has shaken the hills; no threatening wave has rolled upon the shore of the peaceful lake; no cloud of vengeance darkens the coming day. But things are not always what they seem.
>
> Nations and individuals tend to believe that they see no evidence of approaching doom, that because God does not seem to be doing any more today than He did on days and weeks gone by they can continue in the old way. So often we fail to see the gathering clouds of disaster until they are overheard ready to rain down trouble. (. . .)
>
> In the winter of 1955, an insignificant and unimportant woman took a seat on a city bus in Montgomery, Alabama. Rosa Parks was not known beyond her immediate circle of family and friends, and her continued insignificance was assured by the color of her skin. When the bus driver asked her to give up her seat to a white man, the bus driver never dreamed that something was about to happen that would change the course of this nation's history. He was only doing what he had done on so many previous occasions. Why should this be any different? But things are not always what they seem.

What happened in Montgomery, Alabama, on that fateful day in 1955 might well have been God's way of giving this country another chance to redeem itself and urge itself, to repent, to make amends, and to be saved. But few were sensitive enough to receive and understand the message, and subsequent opportunities, too, have been largely ignored.[19]

This is a sound and sincere voice. But it is obvious that preaching on these political and social issues has risks in itself. It can easily derail and be swayed by the issues of the day.[20] It is not easy to strike the right chord.[21] But silence on these and related matters leaves the victims again alone in their suffering, pain, and injustice. Preaching is called to support the "rebellion of the justice of the kingdom of God" and nurture beneficial alternatives for an unjust status quo.


## "Vengeance Is Mine"

Judgment means revenge and retribution against the perpetrators of injustice. Moses and the prophets can announce God's wrath. And the poets of the Psalms pray explicitly for God's fury. Wrath is God's response of antipathy toward the unholy behavior of his covenant-partner. For many members of the congregation these prayers belong to the indigestible ingredients of the Old Testament proclamation.[22] But we have to keep in mind that those prayers ask for a reproof not of humans in general but of the perpetrators of injustice. The bottom line is the request and longing for justice for the victims. These prayers express the longing and the hope that the wicked will not have the last word. That can even be heard in "notorious" words like the last three verses of Psalm 137.

> Remember, O LORD,
> against the Edomites the day of Jerusalem's fall,
> how they said,
> "Tear it down! Tear it down! Down to its foundations!"

19. Edwards 1994, pp. 200, 201.
20. Burbach 1990; Walbrunn 1995; Engemann 2002, pp. 382-91.
21. Allen 2005, pp. 91-110 ("Controversy and Challenge in the Preaching Moment").
22. See for instance Holladay 1995, pp. 71-87 (The Wrath of God).

> O daughter Babylon, you devastator!
> Happy shall they be
> who pay you back what you have done to us!
> Happy shall they be
> who take your little ones and dash them against the rock!

The poets of this psalm do not suppress their anxiety and aggression. In his book *A Theological Introduction to the Book of Psalms,* J. Clinton McCann says this about this particular psalm,

> The structure of Psalm 137 teaches us that the crucial act of remembering is energized by the strong and inseparable emotions of grief and anger. ( ) In the face of monstrous evil, the worst possible thing is to feel nothing. What must be felt is grief, rage, outrage. In their absence, evil becomes an acceptable commonplace. To forget is to submit to evil, to wither and die, to remember is to resist, be faithful, and live again.[23]

Words like Psalm 137 are in fact prayers not to submit to evil. The words about revenge offer therefore enormous chances and challenges for contemporary preaching. Not in the sense that preaching invites or encourages the members of the congregation to take revenge. But this dimension of the proclamation of Scripture can serve as a means to channel emotions and feelings of revenge, grief, and anger and convey these experiences to God. These prayers ask indeed for God's revenge, but that implies at the same time the abandonment of revenge by the one who prays! The preacher nurtures the awareness that God is the ultimate Subject of revenge. "Vengeance is Mine; I will repay, says the LORD" (Deut. 32:35; Rom. 12:19; Heb. 10:30). These words thus keep vengeance out of the human domain. On the other hand, these words make clear that justice will be done and that even vengeance will come — but not vengeance because of offended pride, affronted egos, or ill feelings. Judgment aims for a restoration of justice and *shalom.* The other side of God's favor for the ill-treated is revenge for the perpetrator. The "woe to you" and the "blessed are those" are inextricably connected (Luke 6:20-26).

God's judgment and revenge are, however, meant to be curative and not destructive. Preaching can thus nurture the sensitivity of justice and

---

23. McCann 1993, p. 119.

righteousness of the members of the congregation. The deprived may count on the solidarity and loyalty of the congregation. Preaching has to be hesitant in using the cloak of charity or love on the issue of (in)justice. When we preach forgiveness and atonement in Christ too quickly, we are in danger of silencing and even legitimizing injustice instead of tackling unholy practices. The South African homiletician Cas Vos expresses this quite well in his homiletical commentary on the Psalms.

> The Psalms also firmly express that the biblical God does not exhibit false neutrality when there is injustice and suffering. The psalms do not tell the oppressed to have brotherly love for their oppressors. Instead, the Psalter exposes the mechanisms of oppression and calls on God to change the lot of his people, so that his kingdom can grow in righteousness and solidarity.[24]

Those who pray for God's vengeance lay their understandable longing for revenge down before God in prayer. The prayer names and makes explicit the feelings of vengeance, fear, rage, and anger, and it brings them thus out of a dark silence and anonymity. These kinds of emotions can be channeled when they are uttered with their proper names or descriptions. That is important because when feelings of vengeance are silenced, they go spiritually "underground" and can consequently emerge in an uncontrolled way. The psychological and social health of a community therefore requires that these feelings and emotions are no longer imprisoned in silence but liberated, made explicit, and channeled in a curative way. This can open doors to new beginnings, to liberation, and to salvation for persons who struggle with such feelings. Preaching offers listeners the possibility of reframing their emotions in a liberating and salvific way.

God's judgment is not only an event at the end of time. Just as God's judgment is not reserved to eternity, God's redemption can likewise be experienced in the here and now. God's vengeance can appear, however, in surprising ways. That can be illustrated by means of an impressive quote from the book *Letters to My Grandson*, by the Dutch Zionist Abel Jacob Herzberg (1893-1989).[25] He wrote plays and novels, many about biblical characters. But he is best known for his highly personal essays and the memoirs of his experiences in the Bergen-Belsen concentration camp. His

24. Vos 2005, p. 40.
25. The original Dutch title is *Brieven aan mijn kleinzoon* (= *Letters to my grandson*).

work was distinguished with the Constantijn Huygens Prize (1964) and the
P. C. Hooft Prize (1972), the highest Dutch awards for literature.

> On a beautiful Saturday afternoon in August 1945 we sat on the patio
> of the villa of a Jewish family in Amsterdam. The villa had fallen into
> the hands of a well-known member of the *National-Socialist Move-*
> *ment*[26] [= the most important Nazi party in Holland during World
> War II] when the war started. These collaborators were now impris-
> oned. His wife was ill and the doctor prescribed the eating of green
> prunes. Because she had lived in the villa for some years, she knew that
> there was a tree with green prunes in the garden of the Jewish family.
> She also knew that these prunes were ripe in August. So she sent her
> maid with the request to bring her a basket with these prunes.
>
> Jews call that a *chotspe* (a brutality). This request caused a general
> and enormous indignation.
>
> But my father would have commented in this way. "Imagine that in
> the bitterest hours of the war, we went dreaming about our revenge af-
> ter the liberation. One would have suggested a hatchet day and some-
> one else would have suggested another, even crueler revenge. But the
> most successful proposal would have been made by the one who de-
> scribed what we are experiencing right now. It is peace. They are be-
> hind bars. His wife is ill and asks us for help. Why don't we give her the
> help she is asking for? Give her the best prunes you can find." And who
> knows my father would have been right? Vengeance must be sweet,
> not bitter.[27]

"Vengeance is Mine; I will repay, says the LORD."

## 15.6. To Dream Dreams and See Visions

When crisis and judgment are endured, when Israel has served her term
and her penalty is paid, God creates a new perspective to dream dreams and

26. In Dutch, the *Nationaal-Socialistische Beweging* (NSB). After the German occupation (May 1940) this party collaborated with the occupier. After December 1941, when other
Dutch Nazi parties were absorbed, it was the only one. The NSB wanted to unite Holland
and a part of Belgium (Flanders) and give it the name *Dietsland*. This new country would be
part of the larger "Germanic League" of which Germany would of course be the leader.

27. Herzberg 1990, p. 22 (my translation).

see visions (Isa. 40:3-5; 51:21–53:12). The language born from that perspective is both poetic and prophetic in nature. The language is also subversive because it does not restrict the future to a merely extended present.[28] Preachers are therefore invited and challenged to open windows on realizable utopias.[29] A well-known example of that kind of language is Martin Luther King Jr.'s *I have a dream*.[30] King dreamed of a world after the abolition of discrimination.

> I have a dream
> that one day this nation will rise up
> and live out the true meaning of its creed:
> "We hold these truths to be self-evident: that all men
>     are created equal."
> I have a dream
> that one day on the red hills of Georgia
> the sons of former slaves and the sons of former slave owners
> will be able to sit down together at a table of brotherhood.
> I have a dream
> that one day even the state of Mississippi,
> a desert state, sweltering with the heat of injustice and oppression,
> will be transformed into an oasis of freedom and justice.
> I have a dream
> that my four children will one day live in a nation
> where they will not be judged by the color of their skin
> but by the content of their character.
> I have a dream today. ( )
> I have a dream that one day every valley shall be exalted,
> every hill and mountain shall be made low,
> the rough places will be made plain,
> and the crooked places will be made straight,
> and the glory of the Lord shall be revealed,
> and all flesh shall see it together.

God-given dreams share one feature: the prophets all dream about elementary goodness in everyday life. They dream about daily bread, sharing

28. H. Berkhof 1986, p. 521. See also Brueggemann 1978; Troeger 1999.
29. Marquardt 1997.
30. See Lischer 1995, pp. 30f., 116f., 178f.

clothes, sitting under their own vine in peace, children walking hand in hand, and tears being dried. Isaiah, Micah, John the Baptist, Martin Luther King Jr., and Bishop Desmond Tutu all share the same dream about ordinary happiness. But don't be mistaken: dreaming such "ordinary" dreams is anything but daydreaming. Longing for daily bread and sharing clothes is anything but an innocent pastime. The way prophets were and still are oppressed and even killed makes that all too clear. To dream dreams asks total commitment and has everything to do with social and economic justice. That can be heard in a sermon by James Earl Massey titled "Songs in the Night." It is a sermon on Psalm 77:3, 6, "I think of God, and I moan; I meditate, and my spirit faints. I commune with my heart in the night; I meditate and search my spirit."

> There are those times of inward struggle when music is our best release and our readiest resource. ( ) All humans suffer, and all humans sing — either a song of faith or the blue notes of fate. Traverse the world, taking notice of the music of the masses, and you will come back home aware that songs are often profiles of the soul in crisis, indications, like our text, of some dark experience during which some soul communed with itself.
>
> Such is the story behind the Negro spiritual. Through the long night of enslavement here our forefathers and mothers played the lyre, communing with their hearts, anxious that their spirits might be healed. The Negro spirituals are songs from the night; they are shafts of light for those who watch and wait for the expected new day.[31]

It is clear that longing for that "new day" has nothing to do with flying away from the harsh reality of this world. That is also clear in Massey's sermon. He continues:

> Although these songs are universally known as "spirituals," songs with a religious character, they cannot rightly be understood or regarded until we recognize many of them as *honest documents of social protest.*

A "spiritual" song and liberation in the concreteness of history are inseparable. Eschatological preaching thus breaks the "old" world open, the world that can be seen and touched, and it offers a view on surprising

31. Massey in: Cox Vol. 1, p. 350.

images of possible "new" worlds of peace, freedom, justice, and abiding joy. To dream dreams aims for nothing less than the sanctification of life as it is lived in the concreteness of reality. As Walter Brueggemann puts it:

> Poetic speech is the only proclamation worth doing in a situation of reductionism. The only proclamation that is worthy of the name preaching is not moral instruction, or problem solving, or doctrinal clarification. It is not good advice, nor is it romantic caressing, nor is it a soothing good humor. It is rather the ready, steady, surprising proposal that the real world in which God invites us to live is not the one made available by the rulers of this age.[32]

The eschatological dimension of preaching fuels the longing for new fulfillments of the classic promises, i.e., the restoration of inter-human relationships so that righteousness and peace can kiss each other (Ps. 85:11). We long for a world where no training camps for terrorists will be found, where no one shall learn war anymore, where no suicide attacks will be planned, where swords and spears will be beaten into constructive tools, and where nations will not wage war against each other (Isa. 2:1-4; Mic. 4:1-5). We long for a society where the slaves and the oppressed will be free people (Lev. 25:10), where international relations will be stable (Isa. 19:23). All these promises say that God is worried about this world and this history, and that God urges us to do the same. These promises therefore nurture our dreams and visions of possible "worlds to come."[33]

## 15.7. The New Heaven and the New Earth

The Old Testament prophets dream about a world to come, a world without abuse of power and responsibilities. We hear dreams about a world without exploitation of our fear by swindlers and pseudo-healers, a world without the arrogant games of politicians and journalists, a world without cheap dreams of pseudo-messiahs (or are those dreams in fact very expensive?!), a world without hunger, violence, attacks, humiliation, and repression. The consummation of God's promises, the restoration of the creation, and a general resurrection of the dead — i.e., the ultimate advent of

32. Brueggemann 1989, p. 3.
33. Van Ruler 1971, pp. 88-93; Marquardt 1994, pp. 16, 25.

the kingdom of the LORD — require a new heaven and a new earth. The full advent of the realm of God will bring the perfect realization of the ultimate destiny of humans for a life in intimate communion with God, with creation, and among themselves. Such a communal life is conditioned by justice, righteousness, and peace.[34]

Who will bring all of that to an end, God or humans? That question unites promise and commandment. We live from the promise that the initiative and the consummation of *shalom* are ultimately in God's hands. And his Spirit touches humans in concrete and particular situations, stimulates and challenges them to rise above their problems, and to give witness to the Living God in words and deeds. God's promises about the new heaven and the new earth never absolve us of responsibilities in everyday life. One of the best-known legends attributed to Martin Luther is the famous saying, "If I knew that tomorrow was the end of the world, I would plant an apple tree today!" (But we have to take into consideration that the first written evidence of this saying is as recent as 1944!)

Taking that into consideration, we are allowed to listen to the Old Testament dreams and also to hear echoes and reverberations from the New Testament that testify about the resurrection of the dead. The canonical context allows Christians to listen to the promises of the Old Testament not exclusively and not "originally" but nevertheless also from the perspective of being united with Christ in the life hereafter. Roy Fowler expresses this very carefully in a prayer at a funeral service. The reading from Scripture in that service was taken from Lamentations 3:31-33. The prayer uses the wording, imagery, and theology of these verses and connects them with the promise of eternal life.

> Almighty God, in your keeping there is shelter from the storm, and in your mercy there is comfort for the sorrows of this life. Hear now our prayer for those who mourn and are heavy laden. Give to us strength to bear and do your will. Lighten our darkness with your love. Enable us to see beyond the things of this mortal world and by faith see the promise of the eternal world. Help us to know that your care enfolds all your people, that you are our refuge and strength, and that underneath are your everlasting arms.[35]

34. Pannenberg 2002, pp. 5, 11.
35. Fowler 2004.

In doing so, we have to keep in mind that even the New Testament's promise of the house of the Father with its many dwelling-places (John 14:2) never turns into a longing for some Platonic sphere of eternal happiness enjoyed by disembodied souls after the end of this earthly reality. Our faith in "the life everlasting" in the Apostles' Creed is preceded by the trust in "the resurrection of the body." Our faith in life hereafter has therefore also a tangible dimension.

It should be clear that the "language" of art and music, and the metaphorical and figurative language of poetry, are more adequate than conceptual language for "speaking" about this element of eschatological longing.[36] Eschatological proclamation calls forth worlds that are not yet reality, but the realization of those worlds is hoped for. For that reason the eschatological proclamation also needs music, imagination, and poetic language as resources.

## 15.8. Partial Fulfillment of Promises

The books of Moses tell us that Israel is constantly underway. It is the frequently repeated refrain of breaking up, going on, taking a rest, and breaking up again. Moses speaks about going on a journey (literally: road or way) of days (Exod. 3:18; 8:27; Deut. 5:33). Scripture counts the age of a human life not in years but in days. And because those days are vulnerable (Pss. 90:5-6; 103:15-18), the poet prays, "O my God, take me not away in the midst of my days" (Ps. 102:24, KJV). Living day by day is therefore walking by faith and not by sight (1 Cor. 5:7). That means that our faith in "the world to come" is provisional in character. We are still waiting for the definitive coming of the realm of God, a realm of peace and justice. We still await full-fillment. That means that every fulfillment within our history is partial and provisional in character.

The Epistle to the Hebrews emphasizes the unfinished state of the "new age" that started with the ministry of Jesus. The author portrays Jesus as the "pioneer" or "forerunner" of a people still on the way to fulfilled redemption (Heb. 12:1-3). As a result, there is an awareness growing among Christians about the "provisional nature" of the kingdom announced and established by Jesus.[37] The church becomes aware of the fact that we live in

36. H. Berkhof 1986, p. 521.
37. Moltmann 1967.

"the meantime." That is the title of a sermon by James van Tholen on Habakkuk 3:17-19.

> The word of the Lord to Habakkuk is the word of the Lord to every person who knows that this is their Father's world but at the same time knows just as well that the way things are is not the way they're supposed to be. Habakkuk is about living in the tension of those two truths. It's about seeing destruction and violence but knowing the God of hope and peace. Habakkuk is about living in the meantime.
>
> And the way to do that, the way to live between the promise of God and its full display, is also found in Habakkuk:
>
> > Look at the proud!
> > Their spirit is not right in them,
> > but the righteous live by their faith. (2:4)
>
> Faith is the way to live in the meantime. ( ) Faith gives us hope, so that, even when the wrong seems so very strong, we know this is our Father's world.[38]

This partial character of the fulfillment has some implications. It makes Christians in the first place humble. It is an anti-serum against every form of spiritual or religious pride.[39] Next, the awareness of the partial fulfillment of the promises underscores the vulnerable character of the creed "Jesus is Lord." The image of V-day and D-Day says in its own way that the definitive fulfillment and consummation are yet to come. The question raised by the Jews — "If the Messiah has come already, why is the world still not redeemed?" — remains a curative tickle in the throat of Christianity. And third, the fragmentary fulfillment urges the congregation to long for the definitive coming of God's reign. This longing is not only an attitude of the heart but also the dynamic source of concrete actions for justice and righteousness. The congregation thus yearns actively for the consummation of all things. Our soul thirsts for the living God (Ps. 42). That longing is borne in the tension between God's promises on the one hand and the rough experiences in the concreteness of history on the other. That is the reason that

---

38. Van Tholen 2003, p. 220.

39. "One should pursue the quest for the single correct interpretation under the aegis of hope and its reminder 'not yet.' That the meaning and significance is never a present possession, but a partially fulfilled promise, is perhaps sufficient antidote to the poison of prideful interpretation" (Vanhoozer 1998, p. 465).

we pray, "Maranatha, come Lord Jesus."[40] Jason Patrick expressed this well in a sermon delivered on October 7, 2001, just a few weeks after 9/11, an event that shook not only the foundations of the United States but of the whole world. The reading from Scripture was taken from Psalm 137 and the sermon is titled "Pretending Everything Is Okay."

> During the Thirty Years' War in the 17th century, German pastor Paul Gerhardt and his family were forced to flee from their home. One night as they stayed in a small village inn, homeless and afraid, his wife broke down and cried openly in despair. To comfort her, Gerhardt reminded her of Scripture promises about God's provision and keeping. Then, going out to the garden to be alone, he too broke down and wept. He felt he had come to his darkest hour. But in the midst of his despair, with no viable hope for a future, Gerhardt simply remembered. He remembered the peace of knowing God and wrote the following words to a hymn which would later give countless others comfort.
>
> > *Give to the winds thy fears,*
> > *Hope and be undismayed.*
> > *God hears thy sighs and counts thy tears,*
> > *God shall lift up thy head.*
> >
> > *Through waves and clouds and storms,*
> > *He gently clears thy way;*
> > *Wait thou His time; so shall this night*
> > *Soon end in joyous day.*
>
> Gerhardt's words were not a proclamation that everything was okay. Everything was miserable, but he refused to forget God in the midst of his weeping. He would hold on to God and hope even when both were hidden in the shadows.[41]

## 15.9. Dispensations or Dimensions

Hal Lindsey's book *The Late Great Planet Earth* was the best-selling non-fiction work of the 1970s.[42] The book presented an interpretation of bibli-

---

40. Marquardt 1996, p. 33; Van de Beek 1990, pp. 119-23.
41. Patrick 2001.
42. Grand Rapids: Zondervan, 1970.

cal prophecy that saw the founding of the state of Israel in 1948 as a sign that the end of the world would come in the generation to follow. Lindsey outlined how Russia would attack Israel, based on (among other texts) Ezekiel 38–39. He also argued, based on the books of Daniel and Revelation, that the European Common Market would be a tool in the hands of the Antichrist. Lindsey was soon followed and copied by a multitude of marketplace theologians who sold their connections between newspaper headlines and a particular concept of biblical prophecies concerning the End Time. Tim LaHaye and Jerry Jenkins, for example, have been stocking bookstores with their apocalyptic *Left Behind* series for more than a decade. During these years the series and its related books have sold over 62 million copies and have cumulatively spent hundreds of weeks on every major best-seller list in America, including the *New York Times* list. The authors cherish the so-called "pre-Tribulation" concept, the notion that those who believe in Christ will be "raptured," or taken straight to heaven at a certain moment in history. Everyone else is "left behind" to suffer through a seven-year period of Tribulation during which the Antichrist emerges. This period culminates with the return of Christ to earth, his triumph over the Antichrist, and the beginning of a thousand years of peace. From a certain perspective the *Left Behind* series may be labeled as "horror," because the books tap into contemporary uncertainties and even exploit people's fears of the future, evoking terrifying emotions.

These books all stand in the tradition of "dispensationalism," the belief that God deals with humanity in seven successive so-called "dispensations," or epochs of history — beginning in Genesis 3 and eventuating in the millennium. This system of biblical interpretation arose in the nineteenth century and remains influential in certain areas of contemporary Christianity.[43] Dispensationalism merges a specific biblical theology and a specific philosophy of history. The prophetic dreams, apocalyptic visions, and eschatological discourses are read as if they provide a linear and detailed map of the future. International circumstances are viewed in light of biblical prophecy, whether it be World War I or II, the formation of the modern state of Israel in 1948, the oil crises, or environmental problems.

My model presents the stratification of the witnesses of Moses and the prophets not as referring to distinguishable periods in history or as

43. This is especially true for the United States. "Dispensationalism" has hardly any supporters in Europe.

four subsequent stages on a historical one-way road. This stratification is seen as dimensions, as possible windows on a text. And, as discussed in this chapter, there is an interpretative two-way traffic between these four windows. This two-way traffic creates a four-dimensional eschatological space of meaning in the canon as a whole. We live every day in this four-dimensional space, and none of these dimensions is therefore behind us. This model invites us, for instance, to examine whether there is a dimension of judgment in a particular crisis. But a crisis is never exclusively a judgment, because every crisis also offers the possibility of starting over again. And every crisis also fuels dreams about a possible other, newer, world to come. It is exactly this multidimensional character that offers preaching the possibility of reframing horror-scenarios about the future into hopeful and curative scenarios.

In and through Jesus Christ the gentile nations are invited to trust themselves to the promise that the last word in history is not given to death and destruction but to the God of Israel. For that reason we are called to rebel against all possible powers and principalities, against all institutions and organizations that serve death. The eschatological dimension of preaching nurtures the love for life and the living.[44] From this theological perspective, preaching can encourage the congregation to win back terrain on the influence of the powers of death, rulers, the powers, the worldly forces of darkness, and the spiritual forces of wickedness (Eph. 6:12).[45]

## 15.10. Evaluation

Preaching deals with worlds to come, with new territory for the realm of God, with a future world as a gift of God. Preaching calls to prepare the way of the LORD, to make straight in the desert a highway for our God, to lift up every valley, to make low every mountain and hill, to level the uneven ground, and to make the rough places plain (Isa. 40:3-4). This can be understood in both a tangible and a metaphorical way. It thus opens the possibility of referring to the valleys of grief and to the rough places of social injustice. There are worlds waiting in the texts of Scripture, scenarios

44. Moltmann 1996.
45. The word "death" has different meanings in the Old Testament (see Childs 1985, pp. 231ff.; Brueggemann 2002, pp. 47-50).

of God's *shalom* to come — not scenarios for a "privileged few" but concrete scenarios for establishing justice, righteousness, and liberation for those who actually need it. That means that this fourfold hermeneutical pattern derived from the proclamation of the Old Testament can help to bring all kinds of end-time fantasies literally down-to-earth. In his book *Roll, Jordan, Roll: The World the Slaves Made*, Eugene D. Genovese describes how all these eschatological elements are present in the slave-spirituals.

> Did the slaves sing of God's Heaven and a life beyond this life? Or a return to Africa? Or a Heaven that was anywhere they would be free? Or of an undefined state in which they could love each other without fear? On any given occasion they did any one of these; probably, in most instances they did all at once. Men and women who dare to dream of deliverance from suffering rarely fit their dreams into neat packages.[46]

Dreaming about and hoping for the world to come, Christian eschatology has to integrate all of creation into the conception of the final destiny of our world and humankind. We have heard that God is not only with Jews and Greeks but there will come a moment when God is all and in everything. The church rests in the hope that in the world to come, the anguished divisions will be overcome definitively.[47] Both the Jewish and the Christian communities are waiting and longing communities. The New Testament ends therefore with the same prayer as the Old Testament: "Come, Lord Jesus!" (Rev. 22:20). Will that be the first or the second coming of the Messiah? Elie Wiesel reports in his memoirs, *All Rivers Run to the Sea*, that Martin Buber told a group of priests the following anecdote.[48]

> What is the difference between Jews and Christians? We all await the Messiah. You believe He has already come and gone, while we do not. I therefore propose that we await Him together. And when He appears, we can ask Him: "Were you here before?"

Then Buber paused for a moment and added:

46. Genovese 1975, p. 252.
47. Leighton 2000, p. 37.
48. Wiesel 1995, pp. 354-55.

And I hope that at that moment I will be close enough to whisper in his ear, "For the love of heaven, don't answer."

Till that moment, both Jews and Christians live from the same promise, "I am coming" (Zech. 2:10; John 14:18; Rev. 22:20).

# 16. Preaching the Old Testament — Chances and Possibilities

## 16.1. Walking in the House of the King

A Chassidic story expresses what it means to walk around and be a guest in the house of the king.

> Once when many wise men were gathered about his board, the rabbi of Rizhyn asked: "Why are the people so set against our master Moses ben Maimon?" A rabbi answered: "Because in a certain passage he asserts that Aristotle knew more about the spheres of Heaven than Ezekiel. So why should we not be set against him?"
>
> The rabbi of Rizhyn said: "It is just as our master Moses ben Maimon says. Two people entered the palace of a king. One took a long time over each room, examined the gorgeous stuffs and treasures with the eyes of an expert and could not see enough. The other walked through the halls and knew nothing but this: "This is the king's house, this is the king's robe. A few steps more and I shall behold my Lord, the King." [1]

We can compare walking in the house of the king with walking in the house of Scripture. The LORD is the ultimate subject of the words, stories, psalms, commandments, and promises. The model presented in the previous chapters offers four keys for opening the rooms in this house of the King. When preachers "examine the gorgeous stuffs and treasures" of the King, they indeed do so "with the eyes of an expert." But that is not enough for proclamation. Preachers must also have the awareness, "This is the King's house."

1. Buber 1947, p. 58.

The next sections take the reader for a walk in the "house of the King" and elaborate the four dimensions of meaning that can be heard in Exodus 3, the songs of the servant of the LORD from Deutero-Isaiah, and Psalm 22.

## 16.2. Exodus 3

The book of Exodus is foundational for the understanding of the identity of Israel as the people of God and the identity of the LORD as the God of Israel. The LORD identifies himself as the God who observes the misery of Israel, who hears their crying, and who knows their suffering. This God identifies Israel as "my people" (Exod. 3:7). He comes down to bring up his people to a good and broad land (Exod. 3:8). God's name is therefore not a definition but a program of salvation and redemption. The LORD is not a "neutral" God who treats all and everyone the same. This God is a partisan advocate of the weak, the poor, the oppressed, the afflicted, and the helpless. That was, is, and will be the character of the LORD. He continues his liberating "strategies" and goes on to work exoduses in the course of history. Israel is the primal "landing-strip" for these strategies. The LORD did not set his heart on this people because they were more numerous, more important, or more culturally developed than any other people. There is only one reason for Israel's election: "It was because the LORD loved you and kept the oath that he swore to your ancestors, that the LORD has brought you out with a mighty hand, and redeemed you from the house of slavery, from the hand of Pharaoh king of Egypt" (Deut. 7:7-8).

God's self-revelation to Moses at the burning bush (Exod. 3) is of pivotal significance for this proclamation.[2] The fact that God gives his name opens the possibility of a true encounter and an authentic communication between this God and Israel. Both can address each other; they are "accessible" to each other. Yet, even if the LORD gave his name, it is at the same time enigmatic. Israel does not possess this name and cannot manipulate God with this name. There remains an "otherness," an opaqueness, and even a mysterious dimension in this name and in the communication with this God. This is also true when we recognize Jesus Christ as the Word

---

2. Childs 1974, pp. 47-89; Ochs 2000, pp. 129-42; Fretheim 1991, pp. 143-54; Brueggemann 1997, pp. 155-72; H. F. Knight 2000, pp. 85-122; Seitz 2001, pp. 131-44; Brueggemann 2002, pp. 238-40.

made flesh. Christians and the church can never possess the name of this Jesus and this Lord, just as Israel can never possess the name of the LORD.

## Sensus Israeliticus

When we listen to Exodus 3 on the sound-box of the Christian canon, we can hear reverberations that confirm God's loyalty to his people. We can, for instance, rephrase Mary's *Magnificat* in such a way that it describes and interprets the exodus as an event that fits into the LORD's redemptive strategy on behalf of Israel (Luke 1:71-73).

> The powerful pharaoh was brought down and the lowly slaves were lifted up. The Mighty One did great things to this small and unimportant nation. The name of this God is therefore indeed holy. He shows strength with his arm and scatters the proud and so-called "wise" Egyptians in the thoughts of their hearts. This God looked and looks in favor on the low status of his servant Israel. He acted toward this nation according to the promises made to the ancestors.

We are allowed to rephrase the *Magnificat* in this way because Israel was not only the first addressee of the proclamation of Moses and the prophets but also of the preaching of Jesus.[3] His preaching and ministry call forth the expectation about the restoration of Israel. Jesus reframes this expectation but does not deny its legitimacy (Acts 1:6).

What do Jews hear in this chapter on their sound-box? This story served to formulate Israel's identity. The LORD made a covenant with this threatened and oppressed people. The exodus-event reveals the very kernel of the LORD's intention for his covenant-partner. Israel is therefore commanded to celebrate this event, year after year (Exod. 13:3-5). This story provides the script for the liturgy of the Feast of the Passover, from the moment Israel arrives in the Promised Land up until this day. The story fuels hope for a possible liberated future beyond an oppressing status quo. The Passover feast nourishes courage to persevere; it nurtures resistance against oppressive "pharaohs." This line of thought can also be heard in a commentary from the *Midrash* on the story of the burning bush.

3. Dunn 2003, pp. 506-16.

Why did God show Moses such a symbol? Because he [Moses] had thought to himself that the Egyptians might consume Israel; hence did God show him a fire which burnt but did not consume, saying to him: "Just as the thorn bush is burning and is not consumed, so the Egyptians will not be able to destroy Israel."[4]

The bush is treated as a metaphor for Israel's existence in the world. And, unfortunately, Egypt was replaced in the course of history by Assyria, Babylon, Persia, Greece, Rome, Christian anti-Semitism, Hitler, and suicide-bombers. But the LORD will keep his promises to his thorny bush Israel, and therefore no one will "be able to destroy Israel."

## Christological Sense

Exodus is not only a book and a story but a fundamental theological paradigm. The story of Exodus is also the theological pattern or grid of the proclamation of apostles and evangelists.[5] Matthew starts his Gospel by saying that Jesus is called from Egypt (Matt. 2:13-15). And Luke uses the explicit word "exodus" when he tells about the transfiguration (Luke 9:31). Jesus is portrayed as the representative of Israel; his story is their story. Jesus' ministry can be expressed with words, images, and theology taken from the story of Exodus. From the beginning, his ministry is focused on the good news that is brought to the poor (Luke 7:22). When we proclaim Christ according to the apostles and evangelists, we do so on the theological plot or grid of the exodus-story.

The apostles and evangelists also portray Jesus as the representative of the God of Israel. The "I am" sayings in the Gospel of John[6] are explicit references to the revelation of the holy Name in Exodus 3:16.[7] John is saying that the same God who revealed himself to the Israelites in the exodus

---

4. *Midrash Rabbah*, Vol. 3, London: Soncino Press, 1939, p. 55.

5. The theological structures of the books of Moses and the prophets are the presuppositions and the foundations of the *kerygma* of apostles and evangelists (Van Ruler 1971, pp. 80-83).

6. I am "the bread of life" (6:35), "the light of the world" (8:12; 9:5), "the door of the sheep" (10:7, 9), "the good shepherd" (10:11, 14), "the resurrection and the life" (10:25), "the way, and the truth, and the life" (14:6), and "the true vine" (15:1, 5).

7. R. E. Brown 1966, pp. 533-38.

is now revealing himself in the Jew Jesus of Nazareth. The "I am" sayings can thus be seen as the Johannine way of saying that the words and deeds of Jesus were "according to the Scriptures." The holy Name can also be heard in other Johannine expressions. For example, Jesus addresses the Samaritan woman at Jacob's well near the town of Sychar by saying (literally), "I am, the one speaking with you" (John 4:26). Another example can be heard in the words to the disciples in the boat while Jesus is walking on the Sea of Galilee: "It is I (literally: "I Am"); do not be afraid" (John 6:20; see also 8:23, 24, 28; 13:19; 18:5, 8).

One of the consequences of this line of thought is that these "I am" sayings do not refer in the first place to a spiritual redemption but are to be understood in the context of the (tangible) exodus event. Jesus' comfort for the crowds and his feeding of the five thousand are to be understood as liberating, redemptive acts and not just as material illustrations for the more important spiritual redemption. Healings and miracles are "embodied" redemptive acts. Reading about Jesus as the light of the world or as the bread of life means that Christ conquers every palpable power of darkness and all the principalities that prevent the world from having enough food. "I am the true vine" means that Christ opposes all those powers that cause sadness and grief, and supports those actions that make hearts glad as with wine so that their hearts shall exult in the LORD (Ps. 104:15; Zech. 10:7). Our contemporary proclamation of the life and ministry of Jesus has thus to fit within the paradigm and the theological grid of the exodus. Jesus Christ does not loose Christians from the story of Exodus but puts us right in the kerygmatic center of it. This point of view makes it possible that Old and New Testaments may enrich each other and that the Christological sense does not drown the *sensus Israeliticus*.

## Ecclesiological Sense

The story of Exodus defines the identity of "first of Israel and also the Gentiles." The New Testament church is not the "new Israel" but rather the "mixed crowd" or "great rabble" (Exod. 12:38, NRSV and Young) that went up with Israel. Gentiles have therefore a double identity seen from the perspective of the proclamation of the Old and New Testaments. We do not become Jews but remain gentiles, "aliens and transients," "strangers and sojourners" (1 Pet. 1:1; 2:11). But the proclamation of the canon as a whole invites gentile Christians to redefine their identity as members of the household of the God of Israel (Eph. 2:19), partakers in the promises and commandments first and originally given to Israel. We also have a double identity seen from the perspective of the gentile world. As Christians we are full members of the society of "this world" and at the same time we no longer belong to "this world" (John 15:19). We no longer belong to the sphere of influence of the gods-who-are-silent (Acts 17:16-32). Jesus Christ liberated us and set us free to serve the God of Israel and his kingdom. This call does not take believers out of the world but instead calls them to affirm and to enter more deeply into their world, though knowing of "another homeland" (Heb. 11:14-16).

When we join Israel in the exodus-event and go up to the sanctuary of their God (Ps. 122:1), we are taught in the ways of the LORD and walk in God's paths (Isa. 2:3). Consequently, the story of Exodus 3 has served and serves as source of inspiration, hope, and encouragement — not only for Israel but for innumerable gentiles — to withstand all kinds of "pharaohs." This story was the inspiration of Martin Luther King Jr. in both his actions and his preaching. The story can also be seen as the background for Nelson Mandela's opposing of *apartheid* in South Africa. The story will time and again challenge and encourage people who survive oppression, who keep hope alive amidst tyranny, and who keep their pride alive amidst humiliation.

Redemption, liberation, and vindication belong to one of the two interpretative foci of the ellipse of this event. Exodus is not only the story of the survivors and the victors. Preaching this story therefore also has to focus on the victims, those who died under Egyptian oppression and their contemporaries, those who don't survive all kinds of slavery, those who are tortured and killed by dictators and oppressive regimes. John McClure correctly directs the preacher's eye to "characters, ideas, and narrative actions that hover in the margins of the biblical texts. They will tend to ask questions such as: Who doesn't speak? Who's missing? Who goes nameless?"[8] The story of Exodus reminds us therefore of two stories, both of the survivors and of the victims. And it is because of these victims that we have to walk carefully on the ground of Exodus 3, on the ground before the burning bushes of history, and on the ground of those who suffer from or die under oppression. Preaching still has to remove the sandals from our feet to honor and respect these victims.

---

8. McClure 2001, p. 139.

## Eschatological Sense

There is still more to hear in this story, and we go back for a fourth time to
the text. The story of Exodus will always remind us that God's redemption
is not only something in a spiritual realm. Redemption nourishes the hope
for "another world," for a palpable "good and broad land." Deliverance and
redemption from Egypt are not only *from* something but also *to* something. And that is to live in a concrete "good land," not in a wishful Utopia.
Israel is actually on its way to "the garden of the LORD" (Gen. 13:10).[9] The
palpability can also refer to a mental or psychological recovery after a crisis, just as "pharaoh" can become a metaphor for oppressing and humiliating powers in or around us. But it is clear that this story longs for tangible
goodness after a crisis, be it physical or mental goodness.

The fact that the LORD names not Egypt but Israel "my people" is at
the same time a judgment on "Pharaoh and all his host," on every oppressive or humiliating person or system. Exodus 3 calls the Christian reader
therefore to join Moses in his "availability" for service to the LORD and his
redemptive intentions and strategies. The story of the exodus is an ongoing cry to resist every form of oppression and humiliation, whether it takes
place in some remote area of the globe or in the neighborhood of our
homes, offices, schools, and even in our churches. It is a call and a challenge to act for the benefit of those who are oppressed, for those who are
called "the least of the members of Jesus' family" (Matt. 25:41).

Exodus 3 fuels the longing for the moment that the home of God is
definitively among us, that he will dwell with us as our God and that we
will be his peoples (Rev. 21:3). John of Patmos uses the word "peoples" in
the plural. All the peoples and nations of the earth look forward to the moment that the promise of Exodus 3 defines the identity of every nation, so
that every knee shall bow to the LORD and every tongue shall give praise to
this God (Isa. 45:23; Rom. 14:11).

### 16.3. Songs of the Servant of the LORD

The second illustration is taken from Deutero-Isaiah, the four well-
known songs of "the servant of the LORD" (42:1-4; 49:1-6; 50:4-9; 52:13-

9. Fretheim 1991, p. 59.

53:12). There has been and still is a long and heavy discussion on the identity and meaning of this figure.[10] Theologies of Old and New Testament and commentaries on Second-Isaiah and the Gospels struggle with the question of whether the figure of the (suffering) servant of the LORD refers to a single person or to a collective (corporate personality). And another question is whether Jesus actually considered himself to be "the" (suffering) servant of the LORD. The presented model does not solve these problems from a historical or exegetical point of view. But it does offer a strategy for handling these issues in a theologically accountable way for the practice of preaching. It prevents preachers from getting paralyzed by the immense biblical-theological problems and the load of literature on these issues to the point that they avoid preaching on these crucial passages from Deutero-Isaiah.

## Sensus Israeliticus

The figure of "the servant of the LORD" is introduced in Isaiah 41:8. Israel/Jacob is designated as servant, the elect one, the friend, the offspring of Abraham. Israel has not been abandoned in exile, but rather, God promises to uphold his servant in Babylon with his victorious hand (41:10). Seen from the angle of the larger literary context, we thus have to say that Israel is the servant who is named in the introduction of the first poem (42:1).[11] This suggestion is reinforced by the reading in the LXX of this verse: "Jacob is my servant, I will help him; Israel is my chosen, my soul has accepted him." This meaning is stressed again in the third poem where the LORD says, "You are my servant, Israel, in whom I will be glorified" (Isa. 49:3). This is such a noteworthy reference that some commentators have argued that "Israel" is not a part of the original text and consider it to be a gloss. But there is no evidence for this consideration in the text or in the manuscripts.[12]

When it comes to the interpretation of these poems in a Christian context we notice that scholars seem to wrestle only with the question

---

10. For literature on this subject see Janowski/Stuhlmacher 2004 and Bellinger/Farmer 1998.

11. Childs 2001, p. 325.

12. Whybray 1975, pp. 136-38.

about the relation between the figure of the servant and Jesus Christ. But none of them seem interested in relating this figure to Israel in the *post Christum natum* context. Even the interpreters who pay attention to Israel as the servant of the LORD in the context of Deutero-Isaiah pay hardly any attention to the consequences of this reference for the church in the *Common Era*,[13] even though Mary sings explicitly about God's "servant Israel" in her *Magnificat,* a clear reference to Isaiah 41:8-9. Consequently, Christian theology has to be aware that Israel was, is, and will be the first dimension of meaning in the expression "servant of the LORD." That is also true when we hear about the suffering of the servant of the LORD in Isaiah 52:13–53:12. This fourth poem portrays the fate of Israel in the course of history, culminating in the atrocities of Auschwitz. The German New Testament scholar Franz Mussner addresses this issue sharply.

> Jesus of Nazareth with his atoning suffering and death is in the view of the primitive Church the "servant of God" seen by the prophets. ( )
>
> The Church must ask itself when it reads the sentence of Paul in Col. 1:24: "Now I rejoice in my sufferings for your sake, and in my flesh I complete what is lacking in Christ's afflictions for the sake of his body, that is, the Church," whether Israel, who is seen with the servant of God in Deutero-Isaiah in a mysterious joint view, must not also endure a "supplementary" atoning suffering in the world, not only for its own sins, but also for the sins of the whole world.
>
> There are enough Jewish voices who understand the frightful suffering of Auschwitz and elsewhere as representative atoning suffering for the sins of the Gentiles. ( )
>
> Can the Christian remain indifferent to such explanation? If according to the apostle there is a supplementary participation in the afflictions of Jesus, with what right then dares the Christian exclude a participation of Israel in such a "supplement"? The Christian should be filled with reverence when the Jews understand the fearful suffering which has come over Israel in the course of the centuries as "the suffer-

13. See for instance the treatment of this expression in the monumental *Theological Dictionary of the New Testament,* Vol. 5, pp. 654-717. Walther Zimmerli pays explicit attention to the Old Testament reference to Israel (p. 662). But Joachim Jeremias neglects this reference completely in the section on the New Testament (pp. 700-717). The same is true for Lindsey 1985, pp. 6-9. He focuses on the Christological interpretation and neglects completely that the proclamation of the apostles also uses these poems in an ecclesiological way.

ings of the servant of God" by which they assist in the redemption of the world.[14]

This illustration makes clear that a Christian interpretation of the servant of the LORD in general and the interpretation of Isaiah 53 in particular can no longer ignore Israel and offer an exclusively Christological interpretation. Israel is not only the "original" meaning from a historical point of view, a collective meaning that gradually evolved into a more singular and representative meaning. The collective meaning "Israel" is piled up in the text and waits time and again to be respected, by both Jews and gentiles.[15]

That answer can also be heard from Jewish interpreters. Commentaries interpret the servant as referring to the ideal Israel, the pious Israelites, or the faithful remnant. Ibn Ezra comments for instance as follows on the identity of the servant: "The singular 'my servant' is used because the prophet speaks of every one that is a servant of the Lord and suffers in exile, or because ( ) 'my servant Israel' refers to the whole nation." The commentator holds the last option as the more probable one.[16]

## Christological Sense

When we respect the *sensus Israeliticus,* Christians can also — but not exclusively — listen to a Christological echo in the four poems. We can, just like Philip, "start with this scripture and proclaim the good news about Jesus" (Acts 8:35). Our theology and liturgy, our hymns and proclamation, can be enriched with the imagery and theology of the songs of the servant.[17] I offer some illustrations of how we can listen to the poems as words of Christ, as words addressed to him, and as words about him. We can rephrase the words, images, and motives of, for instance, the third poem as if they were *addressed to Jesus* to describe his calling and ministry.

14. Mussner 1984, p. 43.

15. That gives us possibilities of interpreting these songs on the (suffering) servant of the LORD in Deutero-Isaiah not only forward in history (in relation to Christ) but also backward (in God's history with Israel). That means that we can, for instance, describe and interpret the lives of Moses, Elijah, and Jeremiah with the words, metaphors, images, and theology of these poems.

16. Friedländer 1873, pp. 186, 240.

17. Melugin 1998, p. 59.

> The Lord God gave you
> the tongue of a teacher,
> that you may know how to sustain
> the weary with a word. (50:4)

When we intertwine the passion story of the Gospels with words and images of the four poems, it is possible to read words from the third poem as God's answer to Jesus' prayer in Gethsemane.

> Who will contend with you?
> Let them stand up together.
> Who are your adversaries?
> Let them confront you.
> It is the Lord God who helps you;
> who will declare you guilty?
> All of them will wear out like a garment;
> the moth will eat them up. (50:8-9)

From a second perspective we can listen to these poems as if they were *spoken by Jesus*. We can, for instance, listen to Isaiah 42:1-2 as words of Jesus reinstating Peter after Easter (John 21:15-19).

> You are my servant, whom I uphold,
> my chosen, in whom my soul delights;
> I have put my spirit upon you;
> you will bring forth justice to the nations.

And the third perspective is opened when we listen to these poems referring to *Jesus as the contents* of the words.

> The Lord made his mouth like a sharp sword,
> in the shadow of his hand he hided him;
> he made him a polished arrow,
> in his quiver he hid him away. (49:7)

Jesus' "sharp sword" and "polished arrow" can be heard in the disputes not only with his adversaries but also with his disciples (Mark 8:33).

The presented illustrations in this section were not explicitly quoted in the Gospels, but this step in the hermeneutical strategy offers the possi-

bility of listening to these poems and hearing different Christological reverberations that can enrich and deepen the proclamation of Jesus Christ.

## Ecclesiological Sense

In a third step we go back again to the text and listen to the words in the
context of the contemporary congregation of Jesus Christ. The text of the
book of Isaiah invites us already to do so because when the LORD restored
Israel after the exile to its previous status as God's servant, foreigners were
also invited to become servants of the LORD (Isa. 56:6). Through Christ we
no longer serve sin which leads to death, but we serve obedience which
leads to righteousness. Sin no longer exercises dominion over us but we
are brought under the rule of grace and invited to present our members as
instruments of righteousness (Rom. 6:12-17).

Jesus' death on the cross established an ethical pattern for his disciples to follow. The call to discipleship is ipso facto (literally: by that very
fact) a call to take up the cross (Matt. 16:24-25). Richard B. Hays says that
there is not the slightest hint "that the requirements of God must be pru-
dentially tailored or 'realistically' limited because of human weakness.
Rather, the demand for self-sacrificial discipleship is uncompromising."[18]
We hear that Jesus blesses those who suffer for the sake of righteousness
(Matt. 5:10-12). The poems on the servant of the LORD provided from that
perspective an ethical challenge not only for Israel but also for the gentiles.
Jesus invites his disciples to take up their crosses and blesses those who
suffer for the sake of righteousness (Matt. 5:10-12). The apostle Peter uses
the image of the suffering servant to encourage his readers who endure
pain while suffering unjustly. "For to this you have been called, because
Christ also suffered for you, leaving you an example, so that you should
follow in his steps" (1 Pet. 2:22-25).[19]

However, we have to consider the risks of misuse of the imagery and
the theology of the (suffering) servant of the LORD.[20] The first risk is that
of glorifying suffering and death. This risk can be heard from those who

18. Hays 1996, pp. 82-83.
19. Brox 1979, pp. 136-40.
20. For the following see Smith 1992, pp. 152-62; Stratton 1997; Bond 1999, pp. 75-108;
S. A. Brown 2005.

draw an aura of the sacred around those "servants" who sacrifice themselves as suicide-bombers. But it can also be heard in those who casually justify the loss of young lives in senseless battles around the world. The second risk is to sentimentalize the suffering of the "servants" as heroic martyrdom. The third risk is that the image of the "suffering servant" is misused to legitimize the suffering caused by oppressive systems and humiliating communal practices. Derailed images and theologies of the suffering servant are disastrous for persons and groups who suffer because of their race, gender, sexual orientation, age, or physical disabilities. How many have been forced to "serve" in the kitchen, the cotton fields, or the battlefields? "Servant" becomes synonymous with "slave." Different strands of post-colonial hermeneutics and ideological criticism unmasked the oppressive dimension in the interpretation of the servant songs. The portrayal of self-sacrifice as a virtue and a characteristic of the true faithful has done a lot of harm, both physical and psychological.

To counter these risks, preaching has to stress that the servant of the LORD in Deutero-Isaiah opposes death and the powers of death. He loves life in righteousness and freedom. He will not break the bruised reed or quench the dimly burning wick. But he will faithfully bring forth justice. It is for that reason that the servant suffers and bears the iniquities. That is not to romanticize suffering but exactly the opposite: it calls for rebellion against oppressive and humiliating powers and principalities. We have therefore to proclaim the suffering servant in elliptical tension with the "whole armor of God" so that the congregation may be able to stand against the wiles of the devil (Eph. 6:10-17). The LORD makes the mouth of his servants therefore like a sharp sword and a polished arrow (Isa. 49:2). We can also read the poems in Deutero-Isaiah in dialectical tension with the "rebellious uproar" of God's kingdom, which drives out everything and everyone that makes the Word of God into a hiding place for oppressors and abusers (Isa. 59;[21] Mark 11:15-19 and parallels). Christ indeed left us an example in his suffering, but also in his rebuking of evil spirits and overturning the tables of evildoers. We have therefore to consider both focuses of this interpretative ellipse.

21. "The basic content of this poem is then that Yahweh looks after his own, in this case to see that righteousness and justice receive their due. That means that when they are flagrantly abused or their demands ignored, Yahweh can be counted on to punish his enemies and to vindicate the victims, as he is recognized and remembered to have done so often in the past" (Neufeld 1997, p. 38).

## Eschatological Sense

The "original" meaning of the songs of the servant of the Lord lies not in the past but is in fact always ahead of us. We therefore return again to the text in order to listen to the eschatological challenges. The first song can help to express our gratitude for accomplished justice, for the healing of bruised reeds and dimly burning wicks in hospitals, shelters, schools, and homes.

> Here is my servant, whom I uphold,
> my chosen, in whom my soul delights;
> I have put my spirit upon him;
> he will bring forth justice to the nations.

The "servants of the Lord" who accomplish these things usually don't cry out or lift up their voices on TV talk shows, nor do they appear on the front pages of newspapers. But these servants are chosen ones in whom God has delight. This first song provides preachers with strong and powerful words and imagery to interpret from a theological viewpoint the concrete acts of justice accomplished by members of the congregation — to make clear and to proclaim that the servants of the Lord indeed have names, like Nelson Mandela and Martin Luther King Jr. But there are also many servants of the Lord with names that can be found on every page of any phonebook, names of persons in the pew. These servants bring tangible goodness and justice in situations of crises, and spread light in the places where they live and work. The Lord has given them the tongue of a teacher, that they may know how to sustain the weary with a word.

We also meet the servants of the Lord in those persons who raise their voices against economic or social injustice. They may be well-known or Pulitzer Prize–winning journalists, but they may also be a neighbor or a colleague who stands up for the cause of righteousness.

> The Lord made their mouth like a sharp sword,
> the vulnerable can hide in the shadow of their hands;
> their words are like a polished arrow. (49:2)

And in the end, we long for the ultimate consummation of God's promises. The awareness that Deutero-Isaiah itself does not refer to such a final consummation, to a Christian concept of *parousia,* has to make the preacher careful in his wording on this issue. The proclamation of the vindication of the servant of the LORD cannot carry the whole load of Christian eschatological dogma. But because these four poems are part of the canon as a whole, they can surely serve to nourish and nurture hope for the ultimate defeat of the LORD's enemies, evil and death. These songs can thus also serve the proclamations of the ultimate vindication of all the peoples of God (Isa. 65:17-25; Rev. 21).

## Two Complementary Questions

Luke tells in Acts 8 about an Ethiopian eunuch who was returning home after visiting Jerusalem to worship. On his way back, he was reading from the book of Isaiah, the passage from chapter 53 on the suffering servant of the LORD. The eunuch asked Philip a penetrating question: "About whom does the prophet say this, about himself or about someone else?" (Acts 8:34). I answered this question multidimensionally in a sermon on that passage.

> First of all we have to say that the prophet speaks about Israel, the first-born of God who was and is led to the slaughter like a lamb, so many times in history, up until this very day — voiceless, humiliated, without vindication. (. . .)
>
> According to the passage from Isaiah, Philip can also proclaim Jesus, the son of Israel. He gave himself for the bruised and the wounded, for those that are weary and are carrying heavy burdens. Just as his people, this servant was led to slaughter like a lamb, humiliated and without vindication.
>
> In Jesus Christ, the LORD takes the form of a lamb; he humiliated himself to the bottom of life. And there, at the bottom, there did the God of Israel find all those voiceless people with their wounds, their humiliation, and their guilt. (. . .)
>
> And last but not least, Philip could proclaim the gospel that the Ethiopian eunuch was included in the reading of Isaiah. Being a eunuch, he was in fact not allowed to enter the temple in Jerusalem. The books of Moses say clearly that "he who is emasculated by crushing or mutilation shall not enter the assembly of the LORD" (Deut. 23:1, NKJV). But that is not the last word of God. All the bruised reeds, all

the lambs that were led to the slaughter are welcome, proclaims the servant of the LORD. Who knows? The Ethiopian eunuch may have discovered that for himself as he continued reading in the book of Isaiah (56:3-5).

> Do not let the foreigner joined to the LORD say,
> "The LORD will surely separate me from his people";
> and do not let the eunuch say,
> "I am just a dry tree."
> For thus says the LORD:
> To the eunuchs who keep my sabbaths,
> who choose the things that please me
> and hold fast my covenant,
> I will give, in my house and within my walls,
> a monument and a name
> better than sons and daughters;
> I will give them an everlasting name
> that shall not be cut off.

Maybe this good news was the reason why "he went on his way rejoicing" (Acts 8:39).[22]

This sermon-example gives voice to three of the four different possible reverberations that can be heard on the sound-box of the fourth song of the servant of the LORD. None of these dimensions has priority over the others. Nor is any dimension excluded.

We can therefore ask a similar but reversed form of the Ethiopian eunuch's question. After asking "About whom does the prophet say this?" we can ask the complementary question: "The lamb that takes away the sins of the world, about whom do the apostles and evangelists say that? About Jesus or about someone else?" We can answer that question, saying, "Starting with the gospel of Jesus Christ, he proclaimed the good news about the LORD whose steadfast love for Israel extends to the heavens" (Ps. 36:5).

Because of this double movement, the *sensus Israeliticus,* the Christological sense, the ecclesiological sense, and the eschatological sense are mutually connected and enrich each other; they don't remain in independent compartments. It should also be clear that exegesis, and biblical and systematic theology, are intertwined in this hermeneutical strategy.

22. Bos 1998.

## 16.4. Psalm 22

The opening of Psalm 22, with its desperate accusation, "My God, my God, why have you forsaken me?" resonates with Jews and Christians alike. For Christians, it is the final lament that escaped Jesus' lips. For Jews, it is a cry that the persecuted Hebrews, whose history of oppression is as long as their history as a people, have often had cause to raise to the LORD. Yet, despite the universality of human suffering, this psalm has not unified Jews and Christians, but has instead been a "bone of contention between the synagogue and the church."[23] There is also no consensus among Christian interpreters. The church fathers state almost unanimously that the Christological interpretation is the most appropriate one. The church fathers read Psalm 22 mainly and exclusively as Christological, sometimes disregarding the literal and historical context of the Old Testament. Among historical-critical scholars there is also a widespread consensus: they deny that Psalm 22 is a prediction of Jesus Christ. There is also agreement among these scholars that this psalm is not "messianic" because the form or the genre of Psalm 22 is neither a prophetic oracle nor a royal psalm. The commentators thus conclude that the psalm has no intention of pointing forward to a coming messiah in general let alone the particular suffering and resurrection of Jesus Christ. The loyalty to the "world behind the text" of these interpreters means at the same time that the link to the New Testament is (almost) lost. So, the classical reading restricts the meaning of Psalm 22 to Christ, and the historical-critical reading restricts the meaning to a particular situation in ancient Israel. What both approaches have in common is that they fail to see any meaning in the text for contemporary Israel. Both models see no direct but only indirect meaning of this psalm for members of the contemporary Christian church. Also, the eschatological longing of this psalm is absent in both approaches. The different dimensions of meaning in the presented model combine the strengths of the patristic and the modern approach and meet their weaknesses at the same time.

23. Vall 2002, pp. 175-200.

## Sensus Israeliticus

Psalm 22 may be located within theological circles of the exilic and early post-exilic periods. The spiritual dimension of Psalm 22 can be associated with the piety of the *anawim* (i.e., afflicted, lowly, humble ones; the singular is *ani*). These *anawim* are those who "fear" and "seek" the LORD (vv. 24, 27). The *anawim* describe and interpret their lives and experiences from the perspective of what it means to be Israel.[24] The "I" who laments, petitions, and praises God represents Israel as a collective. This psalm therefore still functions as a provider of words, imagery, and theology to express and interpret the experiences of Israel's *anawim*.

As a Jew, Jesus was undoubtedly familiar with this psalm, with its wording, its theology, and piety. Using words of this particular psalm at the cross in his ultimate moment, Jesus identifies himself with the "I" of the psalm and thus with Israel. The most fundamental relation between Psalm 22 and Jesus Christ starts not with a Christology from "above" or "below," but with the fact that Jesus prayed this psalm as a suffering Jew among Israel's *anawim*. Gregory Vall is right when he says that

> it would be a grave mistake to minimize or omit from consideration the Israelite context of the sufferings described in Psalm 22 and the Israelite context of Jesus' own sufferings. If Jesus enters into human suffering, he does so as an Israelite who enters into Israel's sufferings. Indeed, by taking up the prayer of the *anawim* he identifies himself as one who assumed and is living out of Israel's true identity and vocation. (. . .)
>
> (T)he *ani* is one who is keenly aware of his total lifelong dependence on God. Yahweh is, as it were, the midwife who pulls him "from the womb" (v. 10) and the undertaker who lays him "in the dust of death" (v. 16). And for the entire intervening period he is "thrown upon" God (v. 11).[25]

That means that the *sensus Israeliticus* makes us aware of the fact that Jesus prays the prayer of Israel and that he identifies himself with the innumerable Jews before and after him who have prayed and pray these words. Jesus is thus the representative of Israel. That perspective also challenges us to use words and imagery of the passion narratives to portray and in-

24. Mays 1994, pp. 111-12.
25. Vall 2002, p. 191.

terpret the suffering of the Jews through the ages. This line of thought makes it therefore impossible to claim this psalm exclusively for a Christological interpretation.

Jews listen to the reverberations of this psalm on their own soundbox and they connect this psalm with the person and the story of Esther. That can be read for instance in the commentary of Rabbi Avrohom Chaim Feur.[26]

> This Psalm, although entitled "A song of David" primarily deals with events which were destined to occur hundreds of years after David's time. David with his "holy spirit" foresaw the bleak Babylonian and Persian exiles in general, and in particular, the terrible threat of Haman and Ahasuerus against the entire Jewish nation, personified by Queen Esther.

Rabbi Feur interprets this psalm subsequently and consequently in the context of Esther's trials and tribulations. That offers Christian preaching several interpretative opportunities even if we don't share this connection from a historical point of view. The first is of course to intertwine the wording, the imagery, and the theology of Psalm 22 with the story of Esther. This queen was in her situation the key representative of her people. The Jewish interpretative connection also offers the possibility of connecting the story of Esther with the ministry and suffering of Christ. Psalm 22 can, so to speak, serve as the interpretative "interface" between Esther and Christ. We can see Esther as a "type" of Christ and Jesus as an "embodied" Esther. Seen from that angle, we can intertwine words and imagery of the Gospels with the story of Esther and vice versa.

## Christological Sense

The Gospels not only quote several words and expressions from Psalm 22,[27] but the passion narrative as a whole is heavily influenced by this psalm.[28]

26. Feuer 1979, p. 267.

27. Jesus was sneered at and mocked (Ps. 22:7/Luke 23:11, 35-39); he was pierced through hands and feet (Ps. 22:16/Luke 23:33; 24:36-39; John 19:18; 20:19-20, 24-27); his bones were not broken (Ps. 22:17/John 19:31-33, 36), men gambled for his clothing (Ps. 22:18/Matt. 27:35; Mark 15:24; Luke 23:34; John 19:23, 24).

28. N. T. Wright 1996, pp. 600-602; Dunn 2003, pp. 777-81.

That doesn't mean, however, that we have to read this psalm as a "report in advance" of the suffering and crucifixion of Jesus Christ. The presented model offers a deeper hermeneutical grammar than that. When we consider Jesus as the representative of Israel, as an *ani* amidst of *anawim*, we can read this psalm as a petition that Jesus makes to God, even those words and verses that are not explicitly quoted in the New Testament. This can be illustrated by means of an episode taken from the Gospel of Luke. After Jesus told his disciples about his death and resurrection, he "went up on the mountain to pray" (Luke 9:28). What would Jesus have prayed? Maybe some words taken from Psalm 22.

> Many bulls encircle me,
> strong bulls of Bashan surround me;
> they open wide their mouths at me,
> like a ravening and roaring lion.
>
> But you are holy,
> enthroned on the praises of Israel.
> In you our ancestors trusted;
> they trusted, and you delivered them.
> To you they cried, and were saved;
> in you they trusted, and were not put to shame. (Ps. 22:12-13, 4-5)

Some verses later in the Gospel of Luke we can hear that Jesus headed for Jerusalem to accomplish his *exodus* (Luke 9:31).

This interpretative grammar makes it possible that we are not strictly bound to the way that apostles and evangelists quote Psalm 22. We can rearrange words from the psalm and listen from another angle. Hebrews 2:11-12 applies Psalm 22:23 as if these words were spoken by Jesus Christ. The presented model offers the possibility of rearranging these words in a "homiletical kaleidoscope." We can, for instance, listen to these words as if they are spoken by someone else *about Jesus*. For instance, the story of the cleansing of a leper (Mark 1:40-45) might come to mind. Despite the fact that Jesus prohibited the man from saying anything, the man "began to proclaim it freely, and to spread the word." What would this man have said and proclaimed? We can use Psalm 22 to answer that question.

> I will tell of His name to my brothers and sisters;
> in the midst of the congregation I will praise Him:

> You who fear the LORD, praise Him!
> All you offspring of Jacob, glorify Him;
> stand in awe of Him, all you offspring of Israel!
> For He did not despise or abhor
> the affliction of the afflicted;
> He did not hide His face from me,
> but heard when I cried to Him. (Ps. 22:22-24)

Consequently, we can use these words in our own prayer to praise Jesus Christ as our Lord. We can insert some gentile "editorial additions" in verse 23:

> All you offspring of Jacob, glorify Him
> and praise Him, all you engrafted branches;
> stand in awe of Him, all you offspring of Israel,
> and be amazed, you gentile nations!

These formulations respect the abiding meaning for Israel and at the same time open the proclamation of the psalm for the benefit of the gentiles.

### Ecclesiological Sense

Listeners know of moments when God is nearby but also moments when they don't experience the comforting rod and staff of the LORD. And where is God in moments of pain? The question itself hurts, especially concerning the God who had promised "I will be there." Psalm 22 is part of the "language school" for our communication with this God. This psalm says that we don't have to edit our prayers; we don't have to protect God from our protest and our grumbling. This prayer gives us permission to be honest before God with our pain. We do not have to respond to the crises of life with a false piety that denies our questions, doubts, and despair. When our heart hurts, we can go to God openly with that hurt.

Psalm 22 provides the means of expression for our anguish at the prospect of betrayal and abandonment. But in this psalm we can also find the psalmist's characteristic insistence on looking beyond our anguish, as well as on looking that anguish in the face. Therefore we have to read the psalm from the beginning to the end. It is honest to give voice to questions, laments, and complaints in addressing God. But that honesty requires that we also listen to the rest of the psalm, including the already-quoted verses 22-24. Dennis Batcher considers these verses to be the "heart of the psalm." What caused the change in tone between verse 1 and verses 22-24?

> The transformation of the Psalmist is complete here. He has moved from the dark despair of verse 1 to a point where he can talk about embracing a future filled with possibilities, even proclaiming those possibilities to others!
>
> Not only has his own perspective changed, he is now calling on others to praise God. The one who began by questioning where God is now calls on others to stand in His presence! Where he had earlier complained that God had not heard him, he now affirms that God has heard him.
>
> Again we must ask what has happened since verse 1. What great event of deliverance has occurred that caused such a radical turnaround for the Psalmist?
>
> And we will be surprised at the answer. Nothing! Nothing has changed! No miracle. No great vision of God. No promise of a solution. No hint of resolution of the problem. He is still in the midst of his crisis. Nothing has changed.
>
> *Except, the Psalmist has worshipped God from the midst of his pain.* He has brought his pain honestly to God. He has prayed for God to intervene. And he has left his hurt in God's hands. He has trusted God. He has been totally, authentically human before God. And it has brought healing and a renewed faith.
>
> The change has not come because God has changed, or because circumstances have changed. It has come with the Psalmist as he has faced his pain honestly, and released it to God in prayer, with God's help, and strength, and grace. He has laid his burdens at God's feet, with all the force that his emotions honestly require. And he has left them there.
>
> He has found newness and hope simply by coming into the presence of God as a needy human being. No pretense. No nice words. Just the Psalmist, and his pain. And God! That is praise in its purest form. That is worship at its most honest level. That is being authentically human before God. There God does some of His best work![29]

29. Bratcher 1997.

That kind of "worship in its most honest level" can also be heard in a famous spiritual of Louis Armstrong:

> Nobody knows the trouble I've seen,
> Nobody knows but Jesus.
> Nobody knows the trouble I've seen,
> Glory Hallelujah.

Both Jewish and gentile *anawim* know how "the trouble I've seen" can be combined with the "Glory Hallelujah." The pronoun "my" in the expression "my God" (Ps. 22:1) provides the bridge between utter despair and hope. As a member of the covenant people Jesus recalls the LORD's promises to be their God — and therefore also the God of the one who prays. In his commentary on the Psalms, Arnold A. Anderson refers to an expression of Martin Luther, who, "when he was assailed with doubts, used to say 'I am baptized' ( ) which as an unchangeable fact provided a ray of light in the dark night of anguish."[30]

*Eschatological Sense*

The eschatological dimension of Psalm 22 is closely related to what has been said in the previous sections. The God who heard the cry and saw the affliction of his people opened a way to the future (Exod. 3). The appeal out of a situation of distress and the jubilant cry of redemption and deliverance go hand in hand. Through the whole of Scripture, we can discern a pattern from distress to jubilation, from humiliation to exaltation. This pattern can be traced especially in liturgical materials like the Song of Moses (Exod. 15), the Song of Deborah (Judg. 5), the Song of Hannah (1 Sam. 2:1-10), and the *Magnificat* of Mary (Luke 1:46-55).[31] Psalm 22 weaves together the experiences of God's absence and presence in the same pattern as the existing liturgical material. The utterances of God being nearby and being far off are juxtaposed and yet interrelated. Claus Westermann declares that in the Psalms "there is no petition ( ) that did not move at least one step ( ) on the road to praise," as "there is also no

30. A. A. Anderson 1972, p. 186.
31. B. W. Anderson 1983, pp. 50-51.

praise that was fully separated from the experience of God's wonderful intervention in time of need."[32]

It is for that very reason that the suffering of the poet calls for a protest against the perpetrators, those who are responsible for this suffering, those who create the hell where the desperate cry of this psalm can be heard. Ernesto Cardenal rephrased Psalm 22 from the perspective of contemporary victims.

> My God, my God, why did you abandon me?
> I am a caricature of a man,
> despised by everyone.
> They make fun of me in their newspapers.
>
> Their armored cars close in on me,
> their machine-guns point at me,
> and I am surrounded by barbed wire,
> by electric fences.
>
> I am just a name in their files,
> they burned a number into my skin
> and took photos of me behind bars.
>
> My ribs may be counted
> as in a radiography.
> They put me without clothes in their gas chambers,
> they divided my clothes and shoes among themselves. ( )
>
> But one day I will tell my brothers and sisters about you.
> I will praise you in our gatherings,
> my hymns will resound from a great people.
> The poor will be fed,
> our people celebrate,
> the new people that will be reborn.[33]

This is indeed a stark and comprehensive description of the devilish reality that can be witnessed under dictatorial regimes all over the world. This rephrasing denounces every abuse of power, in accordance with the "enemy"

32. Westermann 1981, p. 154.
33. Cardenal 1969.

descriptions of Psalm 22. This deadly and oppressive reality must be un-masked, combated, and overcome in the name of the LORD.

The same Psalm 22 thus fuels the hope for "another world," for a "good and broad land." Walter Brueggemann combines very powerfully the implications of the story of Exodus 3 and the perspective of Psalm 22. The element of praise can thus also be read as a prayer: come LORD, come soon.

> A life alternative to Pharaoh and alternative to the gods of Pharaoh de-pends on alternative, subversive praise, and on the particular subject to whom praise is sung. Through that powerful, passionate, pain-informed praise, Israel
> - hosts the living, transforming God in the face of the idols,
> - envisions a world of truth, righteousness, and equity in the face of a powerful, hostile ideology,
> - invites and evokes genuine covenant persons in the face of regi-mented automatons or rootless, self-sufficient persons,
> - legitimates the urgent practice of justice against all the cover-ups of fear and the denials of uncritical order,
> - watches the powerful emergence of a missional community in the face of a human community nearly voiceless and passionless in de-spair.
>
> Israel's praise is a dangerous, joyous witness of a different world, a world "this age" does not suspect, permit, or credit. No wonder, the rulers of this age want to stop the singing, or pollute it with ideology and managed slogans! But Israel has not stopped singing and Yahweh has not stopped governing, enthroned on the praises of Israel (Psalm 22:3).[34]

## 16.5. The Practice of Sermon Preparation

Sermon preparation is a complex process and a melting pot of several dis-ciplines: exegesis, biblical theology, systematic theology, rhetoric, psychol-ogy, pastoral care, and education. These disciplines both inspire and ac-company each other critically in the landscape of interpretation. Each of these disciplines requires a level of knowledge and skills that cannot rea-

34. Brueggemann 1988, p. 159.

sonably be expected from preachers. Consequently, they have to move in this complicated landscape with a certain "dilettantism." But preachers are also invited to move with a certain easygoing and untroubled joy in all those fields.

The genesis of a sermon also has to do with the person and personality of a particular preacher, with his or her gifts and talents, with limitations and shortcomings, with areas of interest and blind spots. One preacher is a passionate storyteller; another is more a poet. One preacher works systematically and another associatively. Every preacher therefore has to find a strategy that fits his or her specific gifts and limitations. The illustrations given here are woven on a grid that can be used by every preacher and in different strategies for sermon preparation.

## Sensus Israeliticus

- On the sound-box of Old and New Testaments, what can we hear in a particular text in relation to God's remaining loyalty to his covenant with the descendants of Abraham?
- What have Jewish interpreters heard in this text? Is that of relevance for our understanding of the text?

### Christological Sense

Listen to the Old Testament text as if it were

- words addressed to Christ;
- words spoken by Christ;
- words about Christ.

### Ecclesiological Sense

Discern the location of the text on the scale between the two foci of the theological "elliptical" system of ethics and spirituality. Be aware of the counter-position or dialectical voice within the whole of the canon.

*Eschatological Sense*

Open one or more eschatological windows on Old Testament texts, i.e., that of

- tangible goodness after a crisis;
- the dimension of judgment in a crisis;
- a new perspective after a crisis;
- the vision of everything new.

The model presented in this book is not meant as a generally applicable bone-structure for every sermon. The four dimensions of meaning don't provide four subsequent "points" of a sermon, nor are these dimensions four subsequent steps in the process of preparation. The four dimensions are also not meant as a "hermeneutical lasagna" with the *sensus israeliticus* at the bottom and the eschatological dimension as the topping. Sermons prepared in that way will become very predictable.

The "grid" presented in this book therefore has a heuristic function for getting the multidimensional character of the text into view; it enables the interpreter to listen to the four-voiced choir singing in the text as part of the canon as a whole. The text is allowed to unfold its multi-colored kerygmatic interior, in the way that peacocks display their multi-colored fans. Preachers tell in sermons what they have heard and seen in the multi-dimensional landscape of Scripture (Luke 2:20; 7:22; Acts 4:4), and they often rearrange and rephrase the words of Scripture in a "homiletical kaleidoscope." The presented "grid" can serve as a kind of "checklist" during the process of sermon preparation in that it makes preachers aware of the multidimensional character of the meaning of Scripture. In that process preachers can choose to focus on a single dimension, or, on reflection, to leave out one or two dimensions. Such a choice can be made because of the lack of time for deeper and broader preparation. It can also be made because of the preacher's disposition or because of the congregation's "homiletical situation." And even when all four dimensions get attention in the preparation-process, it may still happen that only two or three of them fit into the chosen composition or plot of a particular sermon. The reason for this limitation may be, for instance, that preachers don't want to overstretch a sermon's theological capacity. Consequently, it isn't necessary that all four dimensions get a place in the preparation process or in the actual sermon. But preachers should still be aware of the multidimensional character of a text's meaning, so that what they say in a particular sermon leaves an implicit space for what they don't say.

## 16.6. Postscript

The homiletical and interpretative model presented here is characterized by the notions of encounter and engagement, mutuality, and abiding anchorage place — all of which embrace the meaning of "old" in Old Testament.

### *Encounter/Engagement*

Gentiles meet both the Israel of God and the God of Israel in Jesus of Nazareth. In Jesus Christ gentiles are partakers of the benefits of the covenant between the LORD and Israel. The promises and commandments are valid for both Jews and gentiles. The LORD invites the nations and urges them to join Israel on the path of righteousness.[35] This encounter is both a challenging and a complicated enterprise. It invites people to go to the land that he will show us (Gen. 12:1-3). It is not a precisely described or specified future. There is only one promise: He will be our companion on that way. The act of interpretation overflows in the act of worship. "Were not our hearts burning within us while he was talking to us on the road, while he was opening the scriptures to us?" (Luke 24:32).

### *Mutuality*

The back-and-forth movement between the two Testaments and the enriching movement between the four dimensions of meaning stress the theological mutuality between Old and New Testaments and thus meet the disadvantages of the linear one-way hermeneutical traffic. As a result, there is a continuous two-way traffic between Old and New Testaments, between Israel and the LORD, between Jesus and Israel, between the LORD

---

35. Borg 1995, p. 30; Berkhof 1986, pp. 415ff.

and Christ, between question and answer. Interpreters can move back and forth. The way of Jesus is the way of both Israel and the LORD and vice versa. There is no later or earlier in this hermeneutical strategy, no more or less. All the texts testify to one and the same God, the LORD of Israel who became flesh in Jesus Christ.

## Abiding Anchorage Place

The text of Scripture is the anchorage place of this model. The model centers around the text of Scripture, its theological context, its genre, and its wording. The text is allowed to speak for itself on the sound-box of Scripture as a whole. Thus two elementary hermeneutical rules are combined: *sola Scriptura* and *Scriptura sui interpres.*

Herb Gardner once wrote a wonderful play called *A Thousand Clowns.* The title comes from a metaphor the chief character uses in a conversation with his nephew. The adult wants to help the boy to understand the wonders of being alive.

> Every day is like going to the circus. You remember how a little car always drives into the middle of the ring, and it looks so tiny, and then all of a sudden, all of the sides open up and out pop a thousand clowns? You never dreamed that all those people could be in such a tiny vehicle, but somehow they were.
>
> This is the shape of life, my boy. There is always so much more to any event than we humans can see on the surface. Do not ever assume you know everything about anything. Every day is a little car filled with a thousand clowns — learn to be humble and a friend of mystery, and who knows how you will be surprised?[36]

When we want to understand the wonders of the words of Moses and the prophets, we have to reckon with the possibility that even a tiny text is filled with a multidimensional meaning. And when the mystery happens and this abundance of meaning pops out of the text, who knows how we will be surprised? The biggest and most gracious surprise is, time and again, in hearing the multi-voiced proclamation of Immanuel, the good news that the LORD is with us.

36. Gardner 1962.

# Literature

**Elizabeth R. Achtemeier**

1998    *Preaching Hard Texts of the Old Testament* (Peabody: Hendrickson).

**Peter R. Ackroyd/Christopher Francis Evans, eds.**

1980    *The Cambridge History of the Bible. Vol. 1: From the Beginnings to Jerome* (Cambridge: Cambridge University Press).

**Ronald J. Allen**

1998    *Interpreting the Gospel: An Introduction to Preaching* (St. Louis: Chalice).

**Ronald J. Allen et al.**

2004    *Listening to Listeners: Homiletical Case Studies* (St. Louis: Chalice).

2005    *Believing in Preaching: What Listeners Hear in Sermons* (St. Louis: Chalice).

**Ronald J. Allen/John C. Holbert**

1995    *Holy Root, Holy Branches: Christian Preaching from the Old Testament* (Nashville: Abingdon).

**Arnold A. Anderson**

1972    *The Book of Psalms 1* (New Century Bible) (London: Oliphant).

**Bernhard W. Anderson, ed.**

1963    *The Old Testament and Christian Faith* (New York: Harper & Row).

1963a   "Introduction," in: Anderson 1963, pp. 1-7.

1983    *Out of the Depths: The Psalms Speak for Us Today* (Philadelphia: Westminster Press).

**Gleason L. Archer/Gregory Chirichigno**

1983    *Old Testament Quotations in the New Testament* (Chicago: Moody).

**Otto Bächli**

1987    *Das Alte Testament in der kirchlichen Dogmatik von Karl Barth* (Neukirchen: Neukirchener Verlag).

1988    "Das Alte Testament in der Passions- und Osterzeit 1931. Zu Karl Barths Andachten. Ein Beitrag zur Hermeneutik," in: *Theologisch Zeitung*, vol. 44.

## Raymond Bailey
1992a    "Hermeneutics: A Necessary Art," in: Bailey 1992, pp. 7-26.

## Raymond Bailey, ed.
1992    *Hermeneutics for Preaching: Approaches to Contemporary Interpretations of Scripture* (Nashville: Broadman).

## David L. Baker
1991    *Two Testaments, One Bible: A Study of the Theological Relationship Between the Old & New Testament.* Revised Edition (Downers Grove: InterVarsity).

## Samuel E. Balentine
1983    *The Hidden God: The Hiding of the Face of God in the Old Testament* (New York: Oxford University Press).

## Hans Urs von Balthasar
1992    *The Theology of Karl Barth: Exposition and Interpretation* (San Francisco: Communio Books/Ignatius Press).

## Willem Barnard
1979    *Op een stoel staan 3 (Herfst en winter)* (Holland: Haarlem).
1992    *Stille omgang. Notities in het dagelijks verkeer met de Schriften* (Brasschaat: Buitink).

## James Barr
1966    *Old and New in Interpretation: A Study of the Two Testaments* (London: SCM Press).

## Julio Trebolle Barrera
1998    *The Jewish Bible and the Christan Bible: An Introduction to the History of the Bible* (Leiden/Grand Rapids: Eerdmans).

## Charles Kingsley Barrett
1980    "The Interpretation of the Old Testament in the New," in: Ackroyd/Evans 1980, pp. 377-411.
1994    *A Critical and Exegetical Commentary on the Acts of the Apostles I* (International Critical Commentary) (Edinburgh: T. & T. Clark).

## Karl Barth
1936-77    *Church Dogmatics I/1–IV/4,* authorized translation of *Kirchliche Dogmatik* by George Thomas Thomson (Edinburgh: T. & T. Clark).
1959    *Dogmatics in Outline,* translated by George Thomas Thomson (New York: Harper).
1968    *The Epistle to the Romans,* translated from the sixth edition by Edwyn C. Hoskyns (New York: Oxford University Press).
1968a    "Nachwort," in: Schleiermacher 1968, pp. 290-312.

1978       *The Humanity of God* (Atlanta: John Knox).
1978a      "Evangelical Theology in the Nineteenth Century," in: Barth 1978.
1981       *Letters 1961-1968,* edited by J. Fangmeier and H. Stoevesandt, translated by Geoffrey W. Bromiley (Grand Rapids: Eerdmans).
1991       *Homiletics* (Louisville: Westminster/John Knox).

**Richard Bauckham**
1998       *God Crucified: Monotheism and Christology in the New Testament* (Carlisle, UK: Paternoster).

**Friedrich Baumgärtel**
1952       *Verheißung: Zur Frage des evangelischen Verständnisses des Alten Testaments* (Gütersloh: Gütersloher Verlag).

**William H. Bellinger/William R. Farmer**
1998       *Jesus and the Suffering Servant: Isaiah 53 and Christian Origin* (Harrisburg, PA: Trinity Press International).

**Hendrikus Berkhof**
1986       *Christian Faith: An Introduction to the Study of Faith* (Grand Rapids: Eerdmans).

**Louis Berkhof**
1950       *Principles of Biblical Interpretation: Sacred Hermeneutics* (Grand Rapids: Baker).

**Karl-Heinz Bieritz et al.**
1990       *Handbuch der Predigt* (Berlin: Evangelische Verlagsanstalt).

**Harold Bloom**
1987       *The Bible* (New York: Chelsea House).

**Rudolph Bohren**
1986       *Predigtlehre,* 5th ed. (München: Kaiser).

**L. Susan Bond**
1999       *Trouble with Jesus: Women, Christology and Preaching* (St. Louis: Chalice).

**Dietrich Bonhoeffer**
1954       *Life Together* (New York: Harper).
1971       *Letters and Papers from Prison* (enlarged edition) (New York: Macmillan).

**Marcus J. Borg**
1994       *Jesus in Contemporary Scholarship* (Valley Forge, PA: Trinity Press International).

**Heinrich Bornkamm**
1969       *Luther and the Old Testament* (Philadelphia: Fortress Press).

**Rein Bos**
1992       *Identificatie-mogelijkheden in preken uit het Oude Testament* (Kampen: Kok).
2005       "American Football or European Soccer Ball: On the Shape of Scripture's Core Commitment," paper for the Academy of Homiletics in Williamsburg (December).

**Rein Bos/Arjen W. Velema**
2002    "Christologie en prediking," in: *Verbum et Ecclesia*, November, pp. 274-91.

**Karel Bouhuijs/Karel A. Deurloo**
1981    *Gegroeide geschriften: Dichter bij het ontstaan van de bijbelboeken* (Baarn: Ten Have).

**Carl E. Braaten/Robert W. Jensen, eds.**
2002    *The Last Things: Biblical and Theological Persepctives on Eschatology* (Grand Rapids: Eerdmans).

**John Bright**
1967    *The Authority of the Old Testament* (Nashville: Abingdon Press).

**Allan Brockway et al.**
1988    *The Theology of the Churches and the Jewish People: Statements by the World Council of Churches and Its Member Churches* (Geneva: WCC Publications).

**Roger Brooks/John J. Collins, eds.**
1990    *Hebrew Bible or Old Testament: Studying the Bible in Judaism and Christianity* (Notre Dame: University of Notre Dame Press).

**Raymond E. Brown**
1966    *The Gospel According the John I–XII* (Garden City, NY: Doubleday).
1994    *An Introduction to New Testament Christology* (New York: Paulist Press).

**Sally A. Brown**
2005    "Negotiating the Shifting Semantics of Sacrifice in Preaching," in: *Homiletics* 30, no. 2 (Winter): 1-8.

**Barbara Brown Taylor**
1997    *Bread of Angels* (Cambridge, MA: Cowley Publications).
1998    *When God Is Silent* (Cambridge, MA: Cowley Publications).
2000    *Speaking of Sin: The Lost Language of Salvation* (Cambridge, MA: Cowley Publications).

**Norbert Brox**
1979    *Der erste Petrusbrief* (Zürich etc.: Benziger Verlag).

**Frederick Fyvie Bruce**
1982    *The Epistle to the Galatians* (Grand Rapids: Eerdmans).

**Walter Brueggemann**
1978    *The Prophetic Imagination* (Minneapolis: Fortress).
1988    *Israel's Praise: Doxology Against Idolatry and Ideology* (Philadelphia: Fortress).
1989    *Finally Comes the Poet: Daring Speech for Proclamation* (Minneapolis: Fortress Press).
1997    *Theology of the Old Testament: Testimony, Dispute, Advocacy* (Minneapolis: Fortress).
1997a   *Cadences of Home: Preaching Among Exiles* (Louisville: Westminster/John Knox).

2001    *Testimony of Otherwise: The Witness of Elijah and Elisha* (St. Louis: Chalice).

2002    *Reverberations of Faith: A Theological Handbook of Old Testament Themes* (Louisville: Westminster/John Knox).

**Martin Buber**

1947/48    *Tales of the Hasidim, Vols. 1/2: The Later Masters* (New York: Schocken Books).

1958    *I and Thou* (New York: Scribner).

**Matthias Büttner**

2002    *Das Alte Testament als erster Teil der christlichen Bibel: Zur Frage nach theogischer Auslegung und "Mitte" im Kontext der Theologie Karl Barths* (Gütersloh: Kaiser/ Gütersloher Verlagshaus).

**Rudolf Bultmann**

1963    "Prophecy and Fulfillment," in: Westermann 1963, pp. 50-75.

1964-65    *Glauben und Verstehen 1* (Tübingen: J. C. B. Mohr).

1964a    "Die Bedeutung des Alten Testaments," in: Bultmann 1964, pp. 313-36.

**Christine Burbach**

1990    *Argumentation in der "politischen Predigt"* (Frankfurt am Main/New York: P. Lang).

**Eberhard Busch**

1994    *Karl Barth: His Life from Letters and Autobiographical Texts* (Grand Rapids: Eerdmans).

**David Buttrick**

1987    *Homiletic Moves and Structures* (London: SCM Press).

1994    *A Captive Voice: The Liberation of Preaching* (Louisville: Westminster/John Knox).

**Barry L. Callen, ed.**

1995    *Sharing Heaven's Music: The Heart of Christian Preaching* (Nashville: Abingdon Press).

**John Calvin**

1960    *Institutes of the Christian Religion,* edited by John T. McNeill, translated and indexed by Ford Lewis Battles (Philadelphia: Westminster).

1979    *Commentaries* (Philadelphia: Westminster).

**Alistair V. Campbell, ed.**

1987    *A Dictionary of Pastoral Care* (London: SPCK Press).

**Charles L. Campbell**

2002    *The Word Before the Powers: An Ethic of Preaching* (Louisville: Westminster/John Knox).

2004    "Resisting the Powers," in: Childers 2004, pp. 23-38.

**David B. Capes**

1992    *Old Testament Yahweh Texts in Paul's Christology* (Tübingen: J. C. B. Mohr).

**Ernesto Cardenal**

1969    *Salmos* (Buenos Aires: Ediciones Carlos Lohle).

**James N. B. Carleton Paget**

1996    "The Christian Exegesis of the Old Testament in the Alexandrian Tradition," in: Saebö 1996, pp. 478-543.

**Anna Carter Florence**

2004    "Put Away Your Sword! Taking the Torture Out of the Sermon," in: Graves 2004, pp. 93-108.

**John Cassian**

2002    "The Fourfold Reading," in: Lischer 2002, pp. 182-87.

**James H. Charlesworth, ed.**

1990    *Jews and Christians: Exploring the Past, Present, and Future* (New York: Crossroad).

**Jana Childers, ed.**

2004    *Purposes of Preaching* (St. Louis: Chalice Press).

**Brevard S. Childs**

1974    *Exodus* (Old Testament Library) (London: SCM Press).

1977    "The Sensus Literalis of Scripture: An Ancient and Modern Problem," in: Donner 1977, pp. 80-93.

1978    "The Exegetical Significance of Canon for the Study of the Old Testament," in: *Vetus Testamentum Supplementum*, vol. 29.

1979    *Introduction to the Old Testament as Scripture* (London: SCM Press).

1985    *Old Testament Theology in a Canonical Context* (London: SCM Press).

1992    *Biblical Theology of the Old and New Testament: Theological Reflection on the Christian Bible* (London: SCM Press).

2001    *Isaiah* (Louisville: Westminster/John Knox Press).

**Carsten Claußen**

1999    "Alttestamentliche Gestalten als negative Beispiele," in: Öhler 1999, pp. 204-18.

**Robert G. Clouse**

1979    *The Meaning of the Millennium: Four Views* (Downers Grove: InterVarsity Press).

**Jeremy Cohen, ed.**

1991    *Essential Papers on Judaism and Christianity in Conflict: From Late Antiquity to the Reformation* (New York: New York University Press).

**Fred B. Craddock**

1985    *Preaching* (Nashville: Abingdon).

**Helga Croner**

1985    *More Stepping Stones to Further Jewish-Christian Relations* (New York: Stimulus Books).

**Helga Croner, ed.**

1977    *Stepping Stones to Further Jewish-Christian Relations* (New York: Stimulus Books).

**Oscar Cullmann**

1964    *Christ and Time: The Primitive Christian Conception of Time and History* (Philadelphia: Fortress Press).

1967    *Salvation in History* (Philadelphia: Fortress Press).

**Mary B. Cunningham and Pauline Allen, eds.**

1998    *Preacher and Audience: Studies in Early Christian and Byzantine Homiletics* (Leiden: Brill).

**Brian E. Daley**

2003    "Is Patristic Exegesis Still Usable? Some Reflections on Early Christian Interpretation of the Psalms," in: Davis/Hays 2003, pp. 69-88.

**Philip R. Davies**

2003    "Biblical Interpretation in the Dead Sea Scrolls," in: Hauser/Watson 2003, pp. 144-66.

**Ellen F. Davis**

2005    *Wondrous Depth: Preaching the Old Testament* (Louisville: Westminster/John Knox).

**Ellen F. Davis/Richard B. Hays, eds.**

2003    *The Art of Reading Scripture* (Grand Rapids: Eerdmans).

**H. Grady Davis**

1958    *Design for Preaching* (Philadelphia: Fortress Press).

**Axel Denecke**

1989    *Gottes Wort als Menschenwort: Karl Barths Predigtpraxis — Quelle seiner Theologie* (Hannover).

**Elisabeth Dhanens**

1973    *Van Eyck: The Ghent Altarpiece* (London: Lane).

**Gijs D. J. Dingemans**

1991    *Als hoorder onder de hoorders . . . Een hermeneutische homiletiek* (Kampen: Kok).

**Charles Harold Dodd**

1928    *The Authority of the Bible* (London: Nisbet).

**Christoph Dohmen/Günter Stemberger**

1996    *Hermeneutik der Jüdischen Bibel und Alten Testaments* (Stuttgart-Berlin-Köln: Kohlhammer).

**Herbert Donner et al., eds.**

1977    *Beiträge alttestamentlicher Theologie* (Göttingen: Vandenhoeck & Ruprecht).

**Reuven Drucker**

1982    *Yehoshua: A New Translation with a Commentary Anthologized from Talmudic, Midrashic, and Rabbinic Sources* (Brooklyn, NY: Meshorah Publications).

**Michael Duduit**

1992    "The Church's Need for Old Testament Preaching," in: Klein 1992, pp. 9-16.

**James D. G. Dunn**

1996-2002  *Christology in the Making: A New Testament Inquiry into the Origins of the Doctrine of the Incarnation* (Grand Rapids: Eerdmans, 1996-2002).

2003    *Jesus Remembered (Christianity in the Making, Vol. 1)* (Grand Rapids: Eerdmans).

**Gerhard Ebeling**

1954    *Die Geschichtlichkeit der Kirche und ihrer Verkündigung als theologisches Problem* (Tübingen: J. C. B. Mohr).

1959    "Hermeneutik," in: *Religion in Geschicht und Gegenwart III* (Tübingen: J. C. B. Mohr, Sp. 242-62).

**Arthur Roy Eckardt**

1974    *Your People, My People: The Meeting of Jews and Christians* (New York: Quadrangle).

**Arthur Roy Eckardt/Alice L. Eckhardt**

1982    *Long Night's Journey into Day: Life and Faith After the Holocaust* (Detroit: Wayne State University Press).

**Umberto Eco**

1990    *The Limits of Interpretation* (Bloomington: Indiana University Press).

1992    "Interpretation and History," in: *Interpretation and Overinterpretation*, ed. Stephan Collini (Cambridge: Cambridge University Press).

**Otis Carl Edwards Jr.**

2004    *A History of Preaching* (Nashville: Abingdon).

**Earle E. Ellis**

1977    "How the New Testament Uses the Old," in: Marshall 1977, pp. 199-219.

1985    *Paul's Use of the Old Testament*, 2d ed. (Grand Rapids: Eerdmans).

**Wilfried Engemann**

2002    *Einführung in die Homiletik* (Tübingen/Basel: A. Franck Verlag).

**Millard J. Erickson**

1987    *Contemporary Options in Eschatology: A Study of the Millennium* (Grand Rapids: Baker).

**Richard L. Eslinger, ed.**

1994    *Intersection: Post-Critical Studies in Preaching* (Grand Rapids: Eerdmans).

**Edward Farley**

2002 *Practicing Gospel: Unconventional Thoughts on the Church's Ministry* (Louisville: Westminster/John Knox).

**Frederic J. Farrar**

1961 *History of Interpretation* (Grand Rapids: Baker).

**Stephen Farris**

1998 "The Binding of Isaac," in: Papers for the Meeting of the American Academy of Homiletics 1998, pp. 149-58.

**Al Fasol**

1992 "Preaching in the Present Tense: Coming Alive to the Old Testament," in: Klein 1992, pp. 225-39.

**Leonhard Fendt**

1970 *Homiletik*, 2. Auflage (Bearbeitet von Bernhard Klaus) (Berlin: De Gruyter).

**Avrohom Chaim Feuer**

1979-82 *Tehillim* (Brooklyn: Mesorah Publications).

**Balthasar Fischer**

1982 *Die Psalmen als Stimme der Kirche: Gesammelte Studien zur christlichen Psalmenfrömmigkeit* (Trier: Paulinus Verlag).

**Michael Fishbane**

1996 "Inner-Biblical Exegesis," in: Saebö 1996, pp. 33-48.

**Eugene Fisher, ed.**

1993 *Interwoven Destinies: Jews and Christians Through the Ages* (New York: Paulist Press).

**Gerhard O. Forde**

1990 *Theology Is for Proclamation* (Minneapolis: Fortress Press).

**Stephen Fowl**

1997a "Introduction," in: Fowl 1997, pp. xii-xxx.

**Stephen Fowl, ed.**

1997 *The Theological Interpretation of Scripture: Classic and Contemporary Readings* (Cambridge: Blackwell).

**Harry Freedman/Maurice Simon, eds.**

1939 *Midrash Rabbah* (Vol. 3) (London: Soncino Press).

**Hans W. Frei**

1993 "The 'Literal Reading' of Biblical Narrative in the Christian Tradition: Does It Stretch or Will It Break?" in: Ochs 1993, pp. 55-82.

**Terence E. Fretheim**

1984 *The Suffering of God: An Old Testament Perspective* (Philadelphia: Fortress Press).

1991    *Exodus* (Interpretation: A Bible Commentary for Teaching and Preaching) (Louisville: John Knox Press).

**Michael Friedländer**

1873    *Commentary of Ibn Ezra on Isaiah* (New York: Philip Feldheim).

**Heinrich Fries et al., eds.**

1981    *Klassiker der Theologie I* (München: Verlag C. H. Beck).

**Karlfried Froehlich, ed.**

1984    *Biblical Interpretation in the Early Church* (Philadelphia: Fortress Press).

**Kurt Frör**

1961    *Biblische Hermeneutik* (München: Kaiser).

**Helen P. Fry**

1996    *Christian-Jewish Dialogue: A Reader* (Exeter: University of Exeter Press).

**Teresa L. Fry Brown**

2004    "The Action Potential of Preaching," in: Childers 2004, pp. 49-66.

**Tikva Frymer-Kensky et al., eds.**

2000    *Christianity in Jewish Terms* (Boulder: Westview Press).

**Harry Gamble**

2003    "The Formation of the New Testament Canon and Its Significance for the History of Biblical Interpretation," in: Hauser/Watson 2003, pp. 409-29.

**Herb Gardner**

1962    *A Thousand Clowns: A Comedy in Three Acts* (New York: S. French). Quoted after John R. Claypool, "Good Luck Bad Luck — Who Is to Say?" in: Klingsporn Vol. 1, pp. 31-38.

**Hans van der Geest**

1981    *Presence in the Pulpit: The Impact of Personality in Preaching* (Atlanta: John Knox).

**Norman L. Geisler**

1983    *Explaining Hermeneutics: A Commentary* (Oakland, CA: International Council on Biblical Inerrancy).

**Harmut Genest**

1995    *Karl Barth und die Predigt: Darstellung und Deutung von Predigtwerk und Predigtlehre Karl Barths* (Neukirchen: Neukirchener Verlag).

**Frederik O. van Gennep et al.**

1989    *Waarlijk opgestaan! Een discussie over de opstanding van Jezus Christus* (Baarn: Ten Have).

**Eugene D. Genovese**

1975    *Roll, Jordan, Roll: The World the Slaves Made* (London: Deutsch).

**Ginnis Gerlemann**

1978 *"ms*," in Ernst Jenni/Claus Westermann, eds., *Theologisches Handwörterbuch zum Alten Testament I* (München: Chr. Kaiser Verlag), pp. 922-25.

**John E. Goldingay**

1981 *Approaches to Old Testament Interpretation* (Downers Grove: InterVarsity Press).

1989 *Daniel* (Word Biblical Commentary: Volume 30) (Dallas: Word Books).

**Hersh Goldwurm**

1988 *Daniel: A New Translation with a Commentary Anthologized from Talmudic, Midrashic, and Rabbinic Sources* (Brooklyn, NY: Mesorah Publications).

**Leonard Goppelt**

1978 "Typos," in: *Theological Dictionary of the New Testament VIII* (Grand Rapids: Eerdmans), pp. 246-60.

1982 *Typos: The Typological Interpretation of the Old Testament in the New* (Grand Rapids: Eerdmans).

**Friedrich Wilhelm Graf**

1990 "Kulturprotestantismus," in: *Theologische Realenzyklopädie Band 20* (Berlin/New York: De Gruyter), pp. 230-43.

**Robert McQueen Grant**

1980 "The New Testament Canon," in: Ackroyd/Evans 1980, pp. 284-307.

1984 *A Short History of the Interpretation of the Bible* (Philadelphia: Fortress Press).

**Mike Graves, ed.**

2004 *What's the Matter with Preaching Today?* (Louisville: Westminster/John Knox Press).

**Colin J. D. Green**

2003 *Christology in Cultural Perspective: Marking Out the Horizons* (Grand Rapids: Eerdmans).

**Joel B. Green**

2000 "Scripture and Theology: Uniting the Two So Long Divided," in: Green/Turner 2000, pp. 23-43.

**Joel B. Green and Max Turner, eds.**

2000 *Between Two Horizons: Spanning New Testament Studies and Systematic Theology* (Grand Rapids: Eerdmans).

**Kathryn E. Greene-McCreight**

1999 *Ad Litteram: How Augustine, Calvin, and Barth Read the "Plain Sense" of Genesis 1–3* (New York: P. Lang).

**Rowan A. Greer**

1989 "The Christian Bible and Its Interpretation," in: Kugel/Greer 1989, pp. 145-47.

## Sidney Greidanus

1970    *Sola Scriptura: Problems and Principles in Preaching Historical Texts* (Kampen: Kok).

1988    *The Modern Preacher and the Ancient Text: Interpreting and Preaching Biblical Literature* (Grand Rapids: Eerdmans).

1999    *Preaching Christ from the Old Testament: A Contemporary Hermeneutical Method* (Grand Rapids: Eerdmans).

## Robert H. Gundry

1967    *The Use of the Old Testament in St. Matthew's Gospel* (Leiden: Brill).

## Antonius H. J. Gunneweg

1978    *Understanding the Old Testament* (Philadelphia: Fortress Press).

1983    *Sola Scriptura: Beiträge zu Exegese und Hermeneutik des Alten Testaments* (Göttingen: Vandenhoeck & Ruprecht).

1983a   "Über die Prädikabilität alttestamentlicher Texte," in: Gunneweg 1983, pp. 159-83.

## Donald Guthrie

1981    *New Testament Theology* (Leicester: InterVarsity Press).

## Anthony T. Hanson

1964    "Christ in the Old Testament According to Hebrews," in: *StEv* 2: 393-407.

## Richard P. C. Hanson

1980    "Biblical Exegesis in the Early Church," in: Ackroyd/Evans 1980, pp. 412-54.

## Roy A. Harrisville/Walter Sundberg

1995    *The Bible in Modern Culture: Theology and Historical-Critical Method from Spinoza to Käsemann* (Grand Rapids: Eerdmans).

## Gerhard Hasel

1979    *Old Testament Theology: Basic Issues in the Current Debate* (Grand Rapids: Eerdmans).

## Stanley Hauerwas

2000    "Christian Ethics in Jewish Terms," in: Frymer-Kensky 2000, pp. 135-41.

## Alan J. Hauser/Duane F. Watson

2003    *A History of Biblical Interpretation, Vol. 1. The Ancient Period* (Grand Rapids: Eerdmans).

## Richard B. Hays

1989    *Echoes of Scripture in the Letters of Paul* (New Haven: Yale University Press).

1996    *The Moral Vision of the New Testament: A Contemporary Introduction to New Testament Ethics* (San Francisco: HarperSanFrancisco).

## Jan Hermelink

1987    "Predigt und Predigtlehre bei Karl Barth," in: *Praktische Theologie* 76: 440-60.

**Abel Jacob Herzberg**

1990    *Brieven aan mijn kleinzoon* (Amsterdam: Querido).

**Hoyt Leon Hickman et al.**

1992    *The New Handbook of the Christian Year: Based on the Revised Common Lectionary* (Nashville: Abingdon).

**Horst Hirschler**

1988    *Biblisch predigen,* 2nd ed. (Hannover: Lutherische Verlagshaus).

**Lucy Lind Hogan**

2004    "Alpha, Omega, and Everything in Between," in: Childers 2004, pp. 67-82.

**John C. Holbert**

1991    *Preaching Old Testament: Proclamation and Narrative in the Hebrew Bible* (Nashville: Abingdon Press).

1999    *Preaching Job* (St. Louis: Chalice).

**William L. Holladay**

1995    *Long Ago God Spoke: How Christians May Hear the Old Testament Today* (Minneapolis: Fortress Press).

**John Hollander**

1981    *The Figure of Echo* (Berkeley: University of California Press).

**Fredrick C. Holmgren**

1999    *The Old Testament and the Significance of Jesus: Embracing Change — Maintaining Christian Identity* (Grand Rapids: Eerdmans).

**Frederic C. Holmgren/Herman E. Schaalman**

1995    *Preaching Biblical Texts: Expositions by Jewish and Christian Scholars* (Grand Rapids: Eerdmans).

**Helmut Hoping**

2004    *Einführung in die Christologie* (Darmstadt: Wissenschaftliche Buchgesellschaft).

**George Howard**

1968    "Hebrews and the Old Testament Quotations," in: *Novum Testamentum* 10: 208-16.

**Deborah van Deusen Hunsinger**

1995    *Theology and Pastoral Counseling: A New Interdisciplinary Approach* (Grand Rapids: Eerdmans).

**David Instone-Brewer**

1992    *Techniques and Assumptions in Jewish Exegesis Before 70 CE* (Tübingen: J. C. B. Mohr).

**Manfred Jacobs**

1991    "Liberale Theologie," in: *Theologische Realenzyklopädie Band 21* (Berlin/New York: De Gruyter), pp. 47-68.

**Bernd Janowski/Peter Stuhlmacher, eds.**

2004    *The Suffering Servant: Isaiah 53 in Jewish and Christian Sources* (Grand Rapids: Eerdmans).

**Robert W. Jenson**

1997    *Systematic Theology (Vol. I: The Triune God)* (Oxford: Oxford University Press).

**Joseph R. Jeter**

1998    *Crisis Preaching: Personal and Public* (Nashville: Abingdon Press).

**Henk J. de Jonge et al.**

2003    "De titels 'Oude Testament' en 'Nieuwe Testament,'" in: *Met Andere Woorden* (December).

**Manfred Josuttis**

1966    *Gesetzlichkeit in der Predigt der Gegenwart* (München: Kaiser).

**Donald H. Juel**

1988    *Messianic Exegesis: Christological Interpretation of the Old Testament in Early Christianity* (Minneapolis: Fortress Press).

2003    "Interpreting Israel's Scriptures in the New Testament," in: Hauser/Watson 2003, pp. 283-303.

**Eberhard Jüngel**

1980    "Karl Barth," in: *Theologische Realenzyklopädie,* Band 5 (Berlin/New York: De Gruyter), pp. 251-68.

**Jacob Katz**

1961    *Exclusiveness and Tolerance: Studies in Jewish-Gentile Relations in Medieval and Modern Times* (Springfield, NJ: Behrman House).

**Werner Keller**

1956    *The Bible as History: A Confirmation of the Book of Books* (New York: W. Morrow).

**John N. D. Kelly**

1978    *Early Christian Doctrines* (rev. ed.) (San Francisco: HarperCollins).

**Søren Kierkegaard**

1990    *For Self-Examination* (Princeton: Princeton University Press).

2002    *Provocations: Spiritual Writings of Kierkegaard,* compiled and edited by Charles E. Moore (Farmington, PA: The Bruderhof Foundation).

**John Killinger**

1996    *Fundamentals of Preaching* (Philadelphia: Fortress Press).

**Simon Kistemaker**

1961    *The Psalm Citations in the Epistle to the Hebrews* (Amsterdam: VanSoest).

**Bernt Klappert**

1980    *Israel und die Kirche: Erwägungen zur Israellehre Karl Barths* (München: Kaiser).

**George L. Klein, ed.**
1992    *Reclaiming the Prophetic Mantle: Preaching the Old Testament* (Nashville: Broadman Press).

**William W. Klein et al.**
1993    *Introduction to Biblical Interpretation* (Dallas: Word Books).

**Leon Klenicki**
1991    *Towards a Theological Encounter* (New York: Paulist Press).

**Douglas A. Knight/Gene M. Tucker, eds.**
1983    *The Hebrew Bible and Its Modern Interpreters* (Philadelphia: Fortress Press).

**George A. F. Knight**
1982    *Psalms* (The Daily Study Bible) (Philadelphia: Westminster Press).

**Henry F. Knight**
2000    *Confessing Christ in a Post-Holocaust World: A Misdrashic Experiment* (Westport, CT: Greenwood Press).

**Emil G. Kraeling**
1955    *The Old Testament Since the Reformation* (London: Lutterworth).

**Hans-Joachim Kraus**
1970    *Die Biblische Theologie: Ihre Geschichte und Problematik* (Neukirchen: Neukirchener Verlag).
1982-83 *Geschichte der historisch-kritischen Erforschung des Alten Testaments* (Neukirchen: Neukirchener Verlag).
1986    *Theology of the Psalms* (Minneapolis: Augsburg).

**Georg Kretschmar**
1981    "Origenes," in: Fries 1981, pp. 26-43.

**James L. Kugel/Rowan A. Greer**
1989    *Early Biblical Interpretation* (Philadelphia: Fortress Press).

**Werner G. Kümmel**
1961    "Schriftauslegung III," in: *Religion in Geschichte und Gegenwart,* Vol. V (Tübingen: J. C. B. Mohr [Sp. 1517-20]).

**Hans Küng**
1967    *The Church* (New York: Sheed & Ward).

**George Eldon Ladd**
1974    *A Theology of the New Testament* (Grand Rapids: Eerdmans).

**Geoffrey W. H. Lampe/Kenneth J. Woollcombe**
1957    *Essays on Typology* (London: SCM Press).

**Ernst Lange**
1971    "Neue Praxis," in: *Predigtstudien VI/1* (Stuttgart: Kreuz Verlag), pp. 89-112.

1982     *Predigen als Beruf: Aufsätze zur Homiletik, Liturgie und Pfarramt* (München: Kreuz Verlag).

**Cleophus Larue**

2000    *The Heart of Black Preaching* (Louisville: Westminster/John Knox).

**Kenneth Leech**

1987    Confession, in: A. V. Campbell 1987, pp. 44ff.

**Christopher M. Leighton**

2000    "Christian Theology After the Shoah," in: Frymer-Kensky 2000, pp. 36-48.

**Gotthold E. Lessing**

1967    "On the Proof of the Spirit and of Power," in: *Lessing's Theological Writings,* translated and edited by Henry Chadwick (Stanford: Stanford University Press).

**F. Duane Lindsey**

1985    *The Servant Songs: A Study in Isaiah* (Chicago: Moody Press).

**Richard Lischer**

1995    *The Preacher King: Martin Luther King Jr. and the Word That Moved America* (New York: Oxford University Press).

**Thomas G. Long**

1989    *The Witness of Preaching* (Louisville: Westminster/John Knox Press).

1995    "Preaching God's Future: The Eschatological Context of Christian Proclamation," in: Callen 1995, pp. 191-202.

1996    "Learning to Speak of Sin," in: Long/Farley 1996, pp. 91-103.

2004    "No News Is Bad News," in: Graves 2004, pp. 145-58.

**Thomas G. Long/Edward Farley, eds.**

1996    *Preaching as a Theological Task: Word, Gospel, Scripture* (Louisville: Westminster/ John Knox Press).

**Richard N. Longenecker**

1975    *Biblical Exegesis in the Apostolic Period* (Grand Rapids: Eerdmans).

**David J. Lose**

2003    *Confessing Jesus Christ: Preaching in a Postmodern World* (Grand Rapids: Eerdmans).

**Andrew Louth**

1983    *Discerning the Mystery: An Essay on the Nature of Theology* (New York: Oxford University Press).

**Henri de Lubac**

1997    "Spiritual Understanding," in: Fowl 1997, pp. 3-25.

1998a/b  *Medieval Exegesis I/II* (Grand Rapids: Eerdmans).

**Martin Luther**

1958    *Luther's Works,* Vol. 33 (Philadelphia: Muhlenberg).

1969    *On the Bondage of the Will,* in: Rupp/Watson 1969.

1982    *The Babylonian Captivity of the Church* (Works of Martin Luther 2) (Grand Rapids: Eerdmans).

**Ulrich Luz**

1989    *Matthew: A Commentary (Vol. I)* (Minneapolis: Fortress Press).

**Joel Marcus**

1992    *The Way of the Lord: Christological Exegesis of the Old Testament in the Gospel of Mark* (Louisville: Westminster/John Knox Press).

**Friedrich-Wilhelm Marquardt**

1981    *Verwegenheiten, Theologische Stücke aus Berlin* (München: Kaiser).

1981a   "Feinde um unsretwillen," in: Marquardt 1981.

1988    *Von Elend und Heimsuchung der Theologie: Prolegomena zur Dogmatik* (Gütersloh: Gütersloher Verlagshaus).

1988/1990    *Das christliche Bekenntnis zu Jesus den Juden. Eine Christologie,* Vols. 1 and 2 (Gütersloh: Gütersloher Verlagshaus).

1993/1994/    *Was dürfen wir hoffen, wenn wir hoffen dürften? Eine Eschatologie,* Vols. 1-3
1996    (Gütersloh: Gütersloher Verlag).

1997    *Eia, wärn wir da — eine theologische Utopie* (Gütersloh: Gütersloher Verlag).

2003    *Bij de slip van zijn kleed . . . Een christelijke theologie na Auschwitz* (Baarn: Ten Have).

**I. Howard Marshall**

1980    *The Acts of the Apostles: An Introduction and Commentary* (Grand Rapids: Eerdmans).

**I. Howard Marshall, ed.**

1977    *New Testament Interpretation: Essays on Principles and Methods* (Grand Rapids: Eerdmans).

**James Luther Mays**

1994    *Psalms* (Louisville: John Knox Press).

**J. Clinton McCann**

1993    *A Theological Introduction to the Book of Psalms* (Nashville: Abingdon).

**John S. McClure**

2001    *Other-Wise Preaching: A Postmodern Ethic of Homiletics* (St. Louis: Chalice).

**Bruce L. McCormack**

1995    *Karl Barth's Critically Realistic Dialectical Theology: Its Genesis and Development 1909-1936* (New York: Oxford University Press).

**John C. McCullough**

1980    "The Old Testament Quotations in Hebrews," in: *New Testament Studies* 26: 363-79.

**Alister E. McGrath**

1997    *Christian Theology: An Introduction* (Cambridge: Blackwell).

**Duncan Mcpherson**

2004    *Pilgrim Preacher: Palestine, Pilgrimage, and Preaching* (London: Melisande).

**Roy F. Melugin**

1998    "On Reading Isaiah 53 as Christian Scripture," in: Bellinger/Farmer 1998, pp. 55-69.

**Esther Menn**

2003    "Inner-Biblical Exegesis in the Tanak," in: Hauser/Watson 2003, pp. 55-79.

**Carol A. Miles**

2000    *Proclaiming the Gospel of God: The Promise of a Literary-Theological Hermeneutical Approach to Christian Preaching of the Old Testament* (Princeton: Unpublished Ph.D. dissertation).

**Kornelis Heiko Miskotte**

1967    *When the Gods Are Silent* (New York: Harper & Row).

1973    *Om het levende woord: Opstellen over de praktijk der exegese*, 2d ed. (Kampen: Kok).

**Jürgen Moltmann**

1967    *Theology of Hope: On the Ground and the Implications of a Christian Eschatology* (London: SCM Press).

1974    "The Crucified God," in: *Theology Today* 31, no. 1: 6-19.

1990    "The Way of Jesus Christ," in: *The Christian Century*, November 7.

1993    *The Crucified God: The Cross of Christ as the Foundation and Criticism of Christian Theology* (Minneapolis: Fortress Press).

1996    *The Coming of God: Christian Eschatology* (London: SCM Press).

**Robert Morgan/John Barton**

1988    *Biblical Interpretation* (New York: Oxford University Press).

**Stephen Motyer**

2000    "Two Testaments, One Biblical Theology," in: Green/Turner 2000, pp. 143-64.

**Hans Martin Müller**

1996    *Homiletik: Eine evangelische Predigtlehre* (Berlin/New York: De Gruyter).

**Klaus Müller**

1994    *Homiletik: Ein Handbuch für kritische Zeiten* (Regensburg: Verlag Friedrich Pustet).

**Franz Mussner**

1984    *Tractate on the Jews* (Philadelphia: Fortress Press).

**Eberhard Nestlé/Kurt Aland et al., eds.**

1979    *Novum Testamenten Greace*, 26. neu bearbeitete Auflage (Stuttgart: Deutsche Bibelstiftung).

*Literature*

**Tom Yoder Neufeld**

1997    *Put on the Armour of God: The Divine Warrior from Isaiah to Ephesians* (Sheffield: Sheffield Academic Press).

**H. Richard Niebuhr**

1937    *The Kingdom of God in America* (New York: Harper).

**William Neil**

1973    *The Acts of the Apostles* (NCB) (London: Oliphant).

**Oepke Noordmans**

1979    *Verzameld Werk 2* (Kampen: Kok).

**David Novak**

1989    *Jewish-Christian Dialogue: A Jewish Justification* (Oxford: Oxford University Press).

2000    "Mitsvah," in: Frymer-Kensky 2000, pp. 115-27.

**Peter Ochs**

2000    "The God of Jews and Christians," in: Frymer-Kensky 2000, pp. 49-68.

**Peter Ochs, ed.**

1993    *The Return to Scripture in Judaism and Christianity* (New York: Paulist Press).

**Hugo Odeberg**

1978    "Jannes" and "Jambres," in: Gerhard Kittel et al., eds., *Theological Dictionary of the New Testament* (Vol. III) (Grand Rapids: Eerdmans), pp. 192-94.

**Manfred Oeming**

1985    *Gesamtbiblische Theologien der Gegenwart. Das Verhältnis von AT und NT in der hermeutischen Diskussion seit Gerhard von Rad* (Stuttgart: Kohlhammer).

1986a   "Unitas Scripturae? Ein Problemskizze," in: Oeming 1986, pp. 48ff..

**Manfred Oeming et al.**

1986    *Jahrbuch für Biblische Theologie. Band 1: Einheit und Vielfalt Biblischer Theologie* (Neukirchen-Vluyn: Neukirchener Verlag).

**Hughes Oliphant Old**

1998a   *The Reading and Preaching of the Scriptures in the Worship of the Christian Church, Vol. 1. The Biblical Period* (Grand Rapids: Eerdmans, 1998).

1998b   *The Reading and Preaching of the Scriptures in the Worship of the Christian Church, Vol. 2. The Patristic Age* (Grand Rapids: Eerdmans, 1998).

**Alexander Olivar**

1998    "Reflections on Problems Raised by Early Christian Preaching," in: Cunningham/Allen 1998, pp. 21-32.

**Grant R. Osborne**

1988    "Typology," in: *The International Standard Bible Encyclopedia* (Vol. 4) (Grand Rapids: Eerdmans), pp. 930-31.

**R. Larry Overstreet**

2001    *Biographical Preaching: Bringing Bible Characters to Life* (Grand Rapids: Kregel).

**Wolfhart Pannenberg**

1959    "Heilsgeschehen und Geschichte," in: *Kerygma und Dogma V*, pp. 259-88.

1993    *Systematic Theology III* (trans. Geoffrey W. Bromiley) (Grand Rapids: Eerdmans).

1999    *Beiträge zur Systematischen Theologie I: Philosophie, Religion, Offenbarung* (Göttingen: Vandenhoeck & Ruprecht).

2002    "The Task of Christian Eschatology," in: Braaten/Jensen, 2002, pp. 1-13.

**Erwin Panofsky**

1953    *Early Netherlandish Painting: Its Origin and Character* (Cambridge, MA: Harvard University Press).

**Blaise Pascal**

1955    *Thoughts: An Apology for Christianity* (Cleveland: World Publishing Co.).

**Stephen Pattison**

2000    *A Critique of Pastoral Care*, 3rd ed. (London: SCM Press).

**Abraham J. Peck, ed.**

1982    *Jews and Christians After the Holocaust* (Philadelphia: Fortress Press).

**Rudolf Pesch**

1986    *Die Apostelgeschichte* (EKK V/2) (Neukirchen: Neukirchener Verlag).

**Josef Pietron**

1979    *Geistige Schriftauslegung und biblische Predigt: Überlegungen zu einer Neubestimmung geistiger Exegese im Blick auf heutige Verkündigung* (Düsseldorf: Patmos Verlag).

**Cornelius Plantinga**

1995    *Not the Way It's Supposed to Be: A Breviary of Sin* (Grand Rapids: Eerdmans).

**Stanley E. Porter/Brook W. R. Pearson, eds.**

2000    *Christian-Jewish Relations through the Centuries* (Sheffield: Sheffield Academic Press).

**Gary G. Porton**

2003    "Rabbinic Midrash," in: Hauser/Watson 2003, pp. 198-224.

**Wilhelm Pressel**

1967    *Die Kriegspredigt 1914-1918 in der evangelischen Kirche Deutschlands* (Göttingen: Vandenhoeck & Ruprecht).

**James Samuel Preus**

1969    *From Shadow to Promise: Old Testament Interpretation from Augustine to the Young Luther* (Cambridge, MA: Belknap Press).

**Horst Dietrich Preuß**

1984    *Das Alte Testament in christlicher Predigt* (Stuttgart-Berlin-Köln-Mainz: Kohlhammer).

**Horst Dietrich Preuß, ed.**

1978    *Eschatologie im Alten Testament* (Darmstadt: Wissenschaftliche Buchgesellschaft).

**Otto Procksch/Karl Georg Kuhn**

1978    "*Hagios* etc.," in: Gerhard Kittel et al., eds., *Theological Dictionary of the New Testament* (Vol. I) (Grand Rapids: Eerdmans), pp. 88-114.

**J. F. Procopé**

1996    "Greek Philosophy, Hermeneutics and Alexandrian Understanding of the Old Testament," in: Saebö 1996, pp. 451-77.

**Stephen Prothero**

2003    *American Jesus: How the Son of God Became a National Icon* (New York: Farrar, Straus and Giroux).

**Gerhard von Rad**

1963    "Typological Interpretation of the Old Testament," in: Westermann 1963, pp. 17-39.

2001a/b Old Testament Theology, Vols. I/II (Louisville: Westminster/John Knox, 2001).

**Heikki Räisänen**

1997    *Marcion, Muhammad and the Mahatma: Exegetical Perspectives on the Encounter of Cultures and Faiths* (London: SCM Press).

**Rolf Rendtorff**

1995    "Die Bibel Israels als Buch der Christen," in: Dohmen/Söding 1995, pp. 97-113.

**Paul Ricoeur**

1976    *Interpretation Theory: Discourse and the Surplus of Meaning* (Fort Worth: Texas Christian University Press).

1980    *Essays on Biblical Interpretation* (Philadelphia: Fortress Press).

**Naomi H. Rosenblatt**

1995    *Wrestling with Angels: What the First Family of Genesis Teaches Us About Our Spiritual Identity, Sexuality, and Personal Relationships* (New York: Delacorte Press).

**Arnold A. van Ruler**

1971    *The Christian Church and the Old Testament* (Grand Rapids: Eerdmans).

**Ernest Gordon Rupp/Philip Saville Watson, eds.**

1969    *On the Bondage of the Will*, cited in *Luther and Erasmus: Free Will and Salvation* (Philadelphia: Westminster).

**Magne Saebö, ed.**

1996    *Hebrew Bible/Old Testament, Vol. 1. From the Beginnings to the Middle Ages (Until 1300)* (Göttingen: Vandenhoeck & Ruprecht).

**Ed Parish Sanders**

1993    *The Historical Figure of Jesus* (London: Penguin Press).

**David Fox Sandmel**

2000    "Israel, Judaism, and Christianity," in: Frymer-Kensky 2000, pp. 159-67.

**Wolfgang Schildmann**

1983    "Wandlungen im Predigtverständnis bei Karl Barth," in: *Praktische Theologie* 72: 208-23.

**Peter Schmidt**

1996    *Het Lam Gods* (Leuven: Davidsfonds).

**Rudolf Schnackenburg**

1984-87  *Die Johannes-Briefe* (HThKNT XIII/3) (Freiburg-Basel-Wien: Herder).

**Gerhard Schneider**

1982    *Die Apostelgeschichte* (HThKNT V/2) (Freiburg-Basel-Wien: Herder).

**Heinz-Günther Schöttler**

2001    *Christliche Predigt und Altes Testament* (Ostfildern: Schwabenverlag).

**Wolfgang Schrage**

1995    *Der Erste Brief an die Korinther 2* (EKK VII/2) (Neukirchen: Neukirchener Verlag).

**Heinz Schreckenberg**

1996    *The Jews in Christian Art: An Illustrated History* (New York: Continuum).

**Werner Schütz**

1981    *Probleme der Predigt* (Göttingen: Ehrenfried Kloz Verlag).

**Eduard Schweizer**

1994    *Jesus, the Parable of God: What Do We Really Know About Jesus?* (Allison Park: Pickwick Publications).

**Jean Louis Segundo**

1983    "Faith and Ideologies in Biblical Revelation," in: Gottwald 1983, pp. 482-96.

**Christopher R. Seitz**

1998    *Word Without End: The Old Testament as Abiding Theological Witness* (Grand Rapids: Eerdmans).

2001    *Figured Out: Typology and Providence in Christian Scripture* (Louisville: Westminster/John Knox Press).

**Bruce E. Shields**

2000    *From the Housetops: Preaching in the Early Church and Today* (St. Louis: Chalice).

**Moisés Silva**

1987    *Has the Church Misread the Bible? The History of Interpretation in the Light of Current Issues* (Grand Rapids: Eerdmans).

**Oskar Skarsaune**

1996    "The Development of Scriptural Interpretation in the Second and Third Centuries," in: Saebö 1996, pp. 373-442.

**Rudolf Smend**

1995    *Das Alte Testament im Protestantismus* (Neukirchen-Vluyn: Neukirchener Verlag).

**Christine Smith**

1992    *Preaching as Weeping, Confession, and Resistance: Radical Responses to Radical Evil* (Louisville: Westminster/John Knox).

2004    "Hospitality, De-Centering, Re-Membering, and Right Relations," in: Childers 2004, pp. 91-112.

**R. Kendall Soulen**

1996    *The God of Israel and Christian Theology* (Minneapolis: Fortress Press).

2000    "Israel and the Church: A Christian Response to Irving Greenberg's Covenant Pluralism," in: Frymer-Kensky 2000, pp. 167-74.

**Richard N. Soulen/R. Kendall Soulen**

2001    *Handbook of Biblical Criticism* (Louisville: Westminster/John Knox Press).

**Charles H. Spurgeon**

n.d.    *The Treasury of David I* (McLean, VA: MacDonald Publishing Company).

**Christian Stäblein**

2004    *Predigen nach dem Holocaust: Das jüdische Gegenüber in der evangelischen Predigtlehre nach 1945* (Göttingen: Vandenhoeck & Ruprecht).

**Edward V. Stein**

1968    *Guilt, Theory and Therapy* (Philadelphia: Westminster Press).

**David C. Steinmetz**

1980    "The Superiority of Pre-Critical Exegesis," in: *Theology Today* 37, no. 1 (April); reprinted in: Fowl 1997, pp. 26-39.

**John R. W. Stott**

1982    *Between Two Worlds: The Art of Preaching in the Twentieth Century* (Grand Rapids: Eerdmans).

**Beverly J. Stratton**

1997    "Engaging Metaphors: Suffering with Zion and the Servant in Isaiah 42-53," in: Fowl 1997, pp. 219-38.

**Samuel Terrien**

1978    *The Elusive Presence: Toward a New Biblical Theology* (San Francisco: Harper & Row).

**Gerd Theissen**

1995    *The Sign Language of Faith: Opportunities for Preaching Today* (London: SCM Press).

2001    *The Shadow of the Galilean* (London: SCM Press).

**Theology and Worship Ministry Unit of the Presbyterian Church (USA)**

1993    *Book of Common Worship* (Louisville: Westminster/John Knox Press).

**Clemens Thoma**

1978    *Christliche Theologie des Judentums* (Aschaffenburg: Paul Pattloch).

**Peter J. Tomson**

2001    *"If this be from heaven . . .": Jesus and the New Testament Authors in Their Relationship to Judaism* (Sheffield: Sheffield Academic Press).

**Elmer Towns**

1998    *How to Create and Present High-Impact Bible Studies* (Nashville: Broadman & Holman Publishers).

**David Tracy**

2000    "God as Trinitarian," in: Frymer-Kensky 2000, pp. 77-84.

**Joseph Trigg**

2003    "The Apostolic Fathers and the Apologists," in: Hauser/Watson 2003, pp. 304-33.

**Thomas H. Troeger**

1999    *Preaching While the Church Is Under Reconstruction: The Visionary Role of Preachers in a Fragmented World* (Nashville: Abingdon).

2004    "Why Homiletics Is Always More Than Method," in: Childers 2004, pp. 113-30.

**Gregory Vall**

2002    "Psalm 22: *Vox Christi* or Israelite Temple Liturgy?" in: *The Thomist* 66, no. 2: 175-200.

**Paul M. van Buren**

1980    *Discerning the Way: A Theology of the Jewish-Christian Reality (Part 1)* (New York: Harper & Row).

1983    *A Christian Theology of the People Israel: A Theology of the Jewish-Christian Reality (Part 2)* (New York: Harper & Row).

1988    *Christ in Context: A Theology of the Jewish-Christian Reality (Part 3)* (New York: Harper & Row).

1998    *According to the Scriptures: The Origins of the Gospel and of the Church's Old Testament* (Grand Rapids: Eerdmans).

**Abraham van de Beek**

1990    *Why? On Suffering, Guilt, and God* (Grand Rapids: Eerdmans).

**Willem VanGemeren**

1983    "Israel as the Hermeneutical Crux in the Interpretation of Prophecy," *Westminster Theological Journal* 45, no. 1.

**Kevin J. Vanhoozer**

1998    *Is There a Meaning in This Text? The Bible, the Reader, and the Morality of Literary Knowledge* (Grand Rapids: Zondervan).

**Kevin J. Vanhoozer, ed.**

2005    *Dictionary for Theological Interpretation of the Bible* (Grand Rapids: Baker).

**Arjen W. Velema**

1991    *God ter sprake: Een homiletisch onderzoek naar de vooronderstellingen van de prediking bij Karl Barth in vergelijking met Hans Joachim Iwand, Ernst Lange en Rudolph Bohren* ('s Gravenhage: Boekencentrum).

**Geza Vermes**

1980    "Bible and Midrash: Early Old Testament Exegesis," in: Ackroyd/Evans 1980, pp. 199-232.

**Peter von der Osten-Sacken**

1982    *Grundzüge einer Theologie im christlich-jüdischen Gespräch* (München: Kaiser).

**Cas J. A. Vos**

1995    *Die Blye Tyding: Homiletiek uit 'n hermeneuties-kommunikatiewe perspektief* (Pretoria: Raad vir Geesteswetenskaplike Navorsing).

1996a/b *Die Volheid daarvan* (I/II) (Pretoria: Raad vir Geesteswetenskaplike Navorsing).

2005    *Theopoetry of the Psalms* (Pretoria: Protea Book House).

**Theodoor C. Vriezen**

1948    *Oud-Israëlitische geschriften* (Katwijk aan Zee: Servire).

1978    "Prophetie und Eschatologie," in: Preuß 1978, pp. 88-128.

**Theodoor C. Vriezen/Adam S. van der Woude**

1976    *Literatuur van Oud-Israël* (Katwijk aan zee: Servire).

**J. Ross Wagner**

2002    *Heralds of the Good News: Isaiah and Paul "in Concert" in the Letter to the Romans* (Leiden: Brill).

**Peter Walbrunn**

1995    *Der Gerichtsgedanke in der Verkündigung* (Fankfurt am Main etc.: P. Lang).

**Francis Watson**

1997    *Text and Truth: Redefining Biblical Theology* (Edinburgh: T. & T. Clark).

**Francis Watson, ed.**

1993    *The Open Text: New Directions for Biblical Studies?* (London: SCM Press).

**Otto Weber**

1981    *Foundations of Dogmatics*, Vol. 1 (Grand Rapids: Eerdmans).

**Claus Westermann, ed.**

1963    *Essays on Old Testament Hermeneutics* (Richmond: John Knox Press).

1970    *The Old Testament and Jesus Christ* (Minneapolis: Augsburg).

1981    *Praise and Lament in the Psalms* (Atlanta: John Knox).

1982    *Elements of Old Testament Theology* (Atlanta: John Knox).

**Roger Norman Whybray**

1975    *Isaiah 40-66* (New Century Bible) (Grand Rapids: Eerdmans).

**Elie Wiesel**

1982    *Night* (New York: Bantam Books).

1995    *All Rivers Run to the Sea: Memoirs* (New York: Knopf).

**Florian Wilk**

1998    *Die Bedeutung des Jesajabuches für Paulus* (Göttingen: Vandenhoeck & Ruprecht).

1999    "Paulus als Interpret der prophetischen Schriften," in: *Kerygma und Dogma* 45: 284-306.

**Clark M. Williamson**

1989    *When Jews and Christians Meet: A Guide for Christian Preaching and Teaching* (St. Louis: Chalice).

1993    *A Guest in the House of Israel: Post Holocaust Church Theology* (Louisville: Westminster/John Knox Press).

**William H. Willimon**

1995    "Anti-Jewish Preaching," in: Willimon/Lischer 1995, pp. 11-13.

**William H. Willimon/Richard Lischer, eds.**

1995    *Concise Encyclopedia of Preaching* (Louisville: Westminster/John Knox Press).

**Paul S. Wilson**

1995    *The Practice of Preaching* (Nashville: Abingdon).

1999    *The Four Pages of the Sermon: A Guide to Biblical Preaching* (Nashville: Abingdon).

2001    *God Sense: Reading the Bible for Preaching* (Nashville: Abingdon).

**Marsha G. Witten**

1993    "Preaching About Sin in Contemporary Protestantism," in: *Theology Today* 50, no. 2: 243-53.

**Hans Walter Wolff**

1963    "The Hermeneutics of the Old Testament," in: Westermann 1963, pp. 172-81.

**George Ernest Wright**

1952    *God Who Acts: Biblical Theology as Recital* (London: SCM Press).

**Nicholas Thomas Wright**

1992    *The New Testament and the People of God* (Christian Origins and the Question of God: Volume 1) (Minneapolis: Fortress Press).

1996    *Jesus and the Victory of God* (Christian Origins and the Question of God: Volume 2) (Minneapolis: Fortress Press).

1997    *For All God's Worth: True Worship and the Calling of the Church* (Grand Rapids: Eerdmans).

1999    *Challenge of Jesus: Rediscovering Who Jesus Was and Is* (Downers Grove: Inter-Varsity Press).

**Frances Young**
1993    "Allegory and the Ethics of Reading," in: Watson 1993, pp. 103-20.
2003    "Alexandrian and Antiochene Exegesis," in: Hauser/Watson 2003, pp. 334-54.

**Jürgen Ziemer**
1990    "Der Text," in: Bieritz 1990, pp. 207-47.

**Walther Zimmerli**
1956    *Das Alte Testament als Anrede* (München: Kaiser).
1963    "Promise and Fulfillment," in: Westermann 1963, pp. 89-122.
1969    *Gottes Offenbarung: Gesammelte Aufsätze* (München: Kaiser).
1969a   "Der 'neue Exodus' in der Verkündigung der beiden großen Exilspropheten," in: Zimmerli 1969, pp. 192-205.
1978    *Old Testament Theology in Outline* (Atlanta: John Knox Press).
1984    "Biblische Theologie," in: *Berliner Theologische Zeitung* 1: 5-26.

**Walther Zimmerli/Joachim Jeremias**
1978    "Pais Theou," in: Gerhard Kittel et al., eds., *Theological Dictionary of the New Testament* (Vol. V) (Grand Rapids: Eerdmans), pp. 654-717.

**Meir Zlotowitz**
1977    *Koheles: A New Translation with a Commentary Anthologised from Talmudic, Midrashic, and Rabbinic Sources* (Brooklyn, NY: Mesorah Publications).
1986    *Ruth: A New Translation with a Commentary Anthologised from Talmudic, Midrashic, and Rabbinic Sources* (Brooklyn, NY: Mesorah Publications).
1989    *Lamentations: A New Translation with a Commentary Anthologised from Talmudic, Midrashic, and Rabbinic Sources* (Brooklyn, NY: Mesorah Publications).
2003    *Yonah: A New Translation with a Commentary Anthologised from Talmudic, Midrashic, and Rabbinic Sources* (Brooklyn, NY: Mesorah Publications).

# Sermons

## Printed Sermons

Ron J. Allen, ed., *Patterns of Preaching: A Sermon Sampler* (St. Louis: Chalice, 1998).

Thomas Aquinas, "The Twofold Temple," in: Fant Vol. I, pp. 196-99.

Aurelius Augustine, "The Lord's Prayer Explained to the Candidates for Baptism," in: Fant Vol. I, pp. 125-36.

Karl Barth, *Predigten 1913*, ed. Nelly Barth/Gerhard Sauter (Zürich: TVZ, 1994), Gesamtausgabe I/8.

————, *Predigten 1914*, ed. Ursula Fähler/Jochen Fähler (Zürich: TVZ, 1974), Gesamtausgabe I/5.

————, *Predigten 1921-1935*, ed. Holger Finze-Michaelsen (Zürich: TVZ, 1998), Gesamtausgabe I/31.

————, *Predigten 1935-1952*, ed. Hartmut Spieker/Hinrich Stoevesandt (Zürich: TVZ, 1996), Gesamtausgabe I/26.

————, *Predigten 1954-1967*, ed. Hinrich Stoevesandt (Zürich: TVZ, 1979), Gesamtausgabe I/12.

————, *Deliverance to the Captives* (New York: Harper & Row, 1961).

————, *Come Holy Spirit* (New York: Round Table Press, 1933).

————, *Call for God: New Sermons from Basel Prison* (London: SCM Press, 1967).

Karl Barth/Eduard Thurneysen, *Andachten für die Advents-, Weihnachts-, Passions und Osterzeit* (Berlin: Furche Verlag, 1936).

Walter Brueggemann, *The Threat of Life: Sermons on Pain, Power, and Weakness* (Minneapolis: Fortress Press, 1996).

————, *Inscribing the Text: Sermons and Prayers* (Minneapolis: Fortress Press, 2004).

George Arthur Buttrick, "Presence of God in an Alien World," in: Fant Vol. X, pp. 268-72.

William G. Carter, ed., *Speaking of Stewardship: Model Sermons on Money and Possessions* (Louisville: Westminster/John Knox, 1998).

Terry L. Chapman, "The Heart of the Matter," in: Carter 1998, pp. 49-52.

Bernard of Clairvaux, "On David and Goliath," in: Fant Vol. I, pp. 149-52.

James W. Cox, ed., *Best Sermons*, Vols. 1-7 (San Francisco: Harper & Row, 1988-94).

Charles E. Crain, "The Suffering Man and the Silent God," in: Cox Vol. 1, pp. 117-25.

Herbert O. Edwards Sr., "Things Are Not Always What They Seem," in: Long/Plantinga 1994, pp. 198-203.

Clyde E. Fant Jr./William M. Pinson Jr., *20 Centuries of Great Preaching: An Encyclopedia of Preaching*, Vols. I-XII (Waco: Word Books, 1971).

R. Benjamin Garrison, "On Being an Honorary Jew," in: Cox Vol. 1 (1988), pp. 171-80.

Stanley Hauerwas, *Cross-Shattered Christ: Meditations on the Seven Last Words* (Grand Rapids: Eerdmans, 2004).

Manfred Josuttis, *Offene Geheimnisse. Predigten* (Gütersloh: Gütersloher Verlagshaus, 1999).

Babydoll Kennedy, "Think about It! ACT ON IT!" in: *The African American Pulpit* (Spring 2001): 64-68.

Gary W. Klingsporn et al., eds., *The Library of Distinctive Sermons (Vols. 1-9)* (Sisters, Ore.: Multnomah, 1996-2001).

Thomas G. Long, "The Difference Between Brown and Green," in: Allen 1998, pp. 9-13.

———, "Bruised Reeds and Dimly Burning Wicks," in: Klingsporn Vol. V, pp. 19-26.

Thomas G. Long/Cornelius Plantinga Jr., eds., *A Chorus of Witnesses: Model Sermons for Today's Preacher* (Grand Rapids: Eerdmans, 1994).

James Earl Massey, "Songs in the Night," in: Cox Vol. 1, pp. 349-55.

Robert Murray McCheyne, "The Vision of Dry Bones," in: Fant Vol. IV, pp. 271-78.

Allec C. McSween, "The Darkness of Faith," in: Cox Vol. 7, pp. 96-101.

Nico M. A. ter Linden, *The Story Goes* (London: SCM Press, 1999).

William Powell Tuck, "Can I Sing When the Going Gets Tough?" in: Klingsporn III, pp. 117-24.

James R. Van Tholen, *Where All Hope Lies: Sermons for the Liturgical Year* (Grand Rapids: Eerdmans, 2003).

Steven P. Vitrano, "God's Promises Are for Believing," in: Cox Vol. 1, pp. 95-103.

J. Philip Wogaman, *Speaking the Truth in Love: Prophetic Preaching to a Broken World* (Louisville: Westminster/John Knox Press, 1998).

## Sermons from the Internet (retrieved February 2006)

Marjory Zoet Bankson, 2003, seekerschurch.org/sermons/away/20030330.htm.

Mike Bennett and Peter Eddington, "What Is the Church?" 2000, gnmagazine.org/bsc/10/lesson10.pdf.

Dennis Bratcher, "Letting Go of the Past," 1997, cresourcei.org/S-ps22.html.

P. Raniero Cantalamessa, "Good Friday," 1998, cantalamessa.org/en/1998venerdi.htm.

John Chrysostom, "Epiphany," catholicism.org/sermons/epiphany.htm.

———, "Adversus Judaeos (Homily I)," fordham.edu/halsall/source/chrysostom-jews6.html.

Andrew Clark, "Servants of God: Pattern for Living," 2001 sermoncetral.com/sermon.asp?SermonID=49622 &ContributorID=8307.

Jason Cole, "Why Did Jesus Die?" 2004, sermoncentral.com/sermon.asp?SermonID=67231&ContributorID=11028.

Adrian Dieleman, "My God Is Yahweh," 2003, trinitycrc.org/sermons/1ki17v01.html.

Daniel Dillard, "Praying for Forgiveness," March 6, 2005, gracerpc.com/sermons/2005/sermon03-06-05.htm.

Guy DuBarry, "The Meaning of Jesus' Baptism," 2003, bible-school.co.uk/baptism.htm (spelling slightly edited).

Gregory Fisher, "The Suffering Servant," 2004, sermoncentral.com/sermon.asp?SermonID=69883&ContributorID=11521.

Roy Fowler, "Funeral," 2004, sermoncentral.com/sermon.asp?SermonID=66421&ContributorID=2471.

Tammy Garrison, "Three Women & a Baby," 2001 sermoncentral.com/sermon.asp?SermonID=38509&ContributorID=4667.

Bruce Goettsche, "Abraham Meets Melchizedek," 1999, unionchurch.com/archive/032199.html.

John Hamby, "Prophecies of Christmas," 2003, sermoncentral.com/sermon.asp?SermonID=63982&ContributorID=2134.

C. Wayne Hilliker, "On Hearing the Gospel of God," 2000, chalmersunitedchurch.com/sermons/sep10s00.htm.

Eric Hollingsworth, "Friend of God," 2004, crechurch.org/CREC/sermons/genesis_18_1-8.htm.

Charles Holt, "Christ's Dove," 2003, sermoncentral.com/sermon.asp?SermonID=54430&ContributorID=1909.

Alan Jackson, "Their High Communion Find," 2000, westminsterpres.com/sermons/sermon_10-01-00.htm.

————, "Strong and Courageous," 2005, westminsterpres.com/sermons/sermon_01-09-05.htm.

Richard Jordan, "Sermon on Easter," 1998, mns.lcms.org/bethany-wabasso/CurrentSermon.htm.

A. Kirk, "That Which God Promised," no date, tlc3n1.org/sermon0428.htm.

William Klock, "Our Great Highpriest," 2005, homepage.mac.com/klock/ChristChurch/sermons/031305.htm.

Robin Langdon, "That's the Truth, Ruth," 2002, fpchawaii.org/sermons/fpcsermon 063002.pdf.

David Legge, "Communion and Reunion," 2002, preachtheword.co.uk/transcripts/sos01.html.

David E. Leininger, "Life Between Verse 4 and 5," 2002, presbyterianwarren.com/lament2.html#5r.

Paul Long, "Judah and Tamar," 2002, sermoncentral.com/sermon.asp?SermonID= 55390&ContributorID=9455.

Dow Marmur, "Jesus and the Jews — Today," 1998, jcrelations.net/en/?id=764.

Rex Marre, "It's Friday but Sunday's Comin'," 2004, stmarysbardon.org.au/040407%20Good%20Friday_Marre.htm.

Bruce McDowell, "The Promise Fulfilled," no date, tenth.org/tif/serpromise.html.

Lyle E. McKee, "Trying the Patience," 2004, stlconline.org/sermons/20041212.html.

Alan J. Meenan, "Can This Be the Christ? A Look at the Prophecies of Zechariah," 1999, fpch.org/hollywoodpulpit.org/sermon991219.html.

Maurice K. Mickles, "God Are You Still Here?" 2003, sermoncentral.com/ sermon.asp?SermonID=63295&ContributorID=8184.

Paul Mizzi, "Types of Christ," no date, tecmalta.org/tft155.htm.

Hedley Palmer, "Zion, City of Our God," 1996, iclnet.org/pub/resources/text/hpalmer/ psalms/ps-087.txt.

———, "Perennial Praises," no date, iclnet.org/pub/resources/text/hpalmer/psalms/ps-048.txt.

Jason Patrick, "Pretending Everything Is Okay," 2001, sermoncentral.com/ sermon.asp?SermonID=41172&ContributorID=6896.

Paul E. Penno, "A Peace Plan," 2002, tagnet.org/hayward/html/sermon_10.html.

Damian Phillips, "Who Has Believed Our Report?" 2001, sermoncentral.com/ sermon.asp?SermonID=41299&ContributorID=6779.

Wil Pounds, "Messiah ben David," 1999, abideinchrist.com/messages/2sam7v16.html.

Bruce D. Prewer, "The Jewish Thing," 2004, alphalink.com.au/~nigel/doc/20050904.htm.

Dale Rosenberger, "Easter 2003," 2003, firstcongregational.com/FCChurch/ sermon042003.shtml.

Kim Riddlebarger, "The Reign of Christ," 1998 christreformed.org/resources/ sermons_lectures/00000001. shtml?main.

Stephen Sizer, "Entering the Promised Land, 2000," christchurch-virginiawater.co.uk/ sermons/sermonjoshua119.htm.

Mark Stephenson, "How Can I Be Sure God's Promises Are Real?" 2001, westolivechurch.org/ld25.htm.

Wim van der Scheer, "Sermon on Genesis 2:4–3:24," 1996, xs4all.nl/~wvdschee/prk/ 01gen0204vv.html.

Tom Walker, "Some Things You'll Never Find Apart from Jesus," 1998, preacherscorner.org/july98-mini.htm.

Chris Ward, "The Long Road (God's Promises #5)," 2005, westminsterpres.com/sermons/ sermon_01-30-05.htm.

Kevin Weeks, "Defeating the Giants in Your Life," 2001, sermoncentral.com/ sermon.asp?SermonID=41952& ContributorID=7009.

## Unpublished Sermons

Rein Bos, "About Whom?" 1998.

———, "Story of Faith," 1999.

———, "Not with Our Ancestors," 2002.

———, "End and New Beginning," 2003.

# Index of Authors

# Index of Scripture References in the Sermon Illustrations